D1258228

History ⊹⊹⊹⊹ of ⊹⊹⊹⊹ World War I

Volume 2

Victory and Defeat
1917–1918

Marshall Cavendish
New York • London • Toronto • Sydney

Marshall Cavendish Corporation
99 White Plains Road
Tarrytown, New York 10591

Website: www.marshallcavendish.com

Library of Congress Cataloging-in-Publication Data
History of World War I
   p. cm.
   Includes bibliographical references and index.
   Contents: 1. War and response, 1914-1916 – 2. Victory and defeat, 1917-1918 – 3. Home fronts. Technologies of war.
   ISBN 0-7614-7231-2 (set) – ISBN 0-7614-7232-0 (v. 1) – ISBN 0-7614-7233-9 (v. 2) – ISBN 0-7614-7234-7 (v. 3)
   1. World War, 1914-1918.   I. Marshall Cavendish Corporation.

D521 .H48 2001
940.3–dc21
                                  2001017413

Printed in Malaysia

ISBN 0-7614-7233-9

Brown Partworks
Managing editor: Tim Cooke
Project editors: Ian Westwell, Dennis Cove
Designers: Duncan Brown, Paul Griffin
Picture manager: Susannah Jayes
Cartographers: Duncan Brown, Bob Garwood, Mark Walker
Indexer: Kay Ollerenshaw

Marshall Cavendish Corporation
Editor: Peter Mavrikis
Editorial director: Paul Bernabeo

Authors
Mike Sharpe, Steve Small, Donald Sommerville

Consultants
Oscar Lansen, University of North Carolina, Charlotte
Professor John H. Morrow Jr., University of Georgia
Professor William R. Keylor, Boston University

Volume 2
Victory and Defeat, 1917–1918

The Western Front, 1917   326

The cost of the western front • Planning the Allied attacks • The British attack at Arras • Nivelle's disastrous advance • British efforts in Flanders • The first tank offensive

Focus points: Field Marshal Douglas Haig • The Siegfried Line • Mine Warfare • F. R. J. Jefford • Allied Supreme War Council • Prime Minister Georges Clemenceau

The Eastern Front, 1917   348

Russia's last offensive • Russia's final collapse • War in the Balkans • Romania collapses

Focus points: Vladimir Ilyich Lenin • Dissent in the Ranks • Germany's Storm Troopers • Poland and Independence

The Wider War, 1917   366

The fight for Palestine • The advance on Jerusalem • The struggle for Mesopotamia • War in East Africa • The Italian front

Focus points: The Balfour Declaration • The Arab Revolt • Erwin Rommel

The War at Sea, 1917   384

The Allied convoy system • The battle against the submarine • German surface actions • The Mediterranean theater • Baltic operations • Japan's naval contribution

Focus points: Captain Adolf von Spiegel • Admiral William Sims • The Convoy System • Otranto Barrage • Vice Admiral Miklós Horthy

Germany's Last Attacks   402

Germany's great gamble • German forces and tactics • The Emperor's Battle • The Lys Offensive

Focus points: Bruchmüller's Timetable • Marshal Ferdinand Foch • Lieutenant Ernst Jünger • Field Marshal Herbert Plumer • The First Tank Battle

U.S. Baptism of Fire   418

Third Battle of the Aisne • The Battle of Belleau Wood

Focus points: Preparing the AEF for War • General Robert Lee Bullard • The Hello Girls • Equipping the AEF • Edwin L. James • U.S. War Artists

The Allies Fight Back   436

Second Battle of the Marne • U.S. troops defend the Marne • Aisne-Marne Offensive • Foch's dynamic leadership • Battle of Amiens • The Allies take control

Focus points: Captain Jesse Woolridge • *Stars and Stripes* • The Black Day of the German Army

The Final U.S. Offensives   452

The St. Mihiel attack • Meuse-Argonne Offensive • The AEF's final advance

Focus points: General Hunter Liggett • U.S. Women at War • The Lost Battalion • Sergeant Alvin York

Europe's Other Theaters   470

Turmoil on the eastern front • Germany and the Ukraine • Nationalism and the Baltic states • Allied victory in Italy • Final moves in the Balkans

Focus points: Leon Trotsky • Allied Interventions in Russia • U.S. Forces in Italy

The Wider War, 1918   487

Allied plans in Palestine • Final battles in the Middle East • The African campaign concludes • Central and South America • The Far East

Focus points: Field Marshal Edmund Allenby • T. E. Lawrence • Dunsterforce

continued

The War at Sea, 1918   502

The convoy battles • Transporting U.S. forces to Europe • War in the Mediterranean • The German Navy surrenders

Focus points: The Northern Barrage • The *Tuscania* Sinking • The Kiel Mutiny • Lieutenant Francis Hunter

The Collapse of Germany   514

Breaking the Hindenburg Line • Germany seeks an armistice • Ending the war

Focus points: Deneys Rietz • Liberating Belgium • Compiègne and the Armistice • Rosa Luxemburg • The Human Cost of War

Europe after the Armistice   530

The aims of the Allies • The peace terms • Problems with the peace

Focus points: The League to Enforce the Peace • Winston Churchill • John Maynard Keynes • The League of Nations

Peace and the Allies   550

France: reconstruction and recovery • The Third Republic • The French search for security • The French colonies • British economic and social problems • Britain and Ireland • Italy: the road to fascism • Japan becomes a world power

Focus points: Aristide Briand • The Locarno Treaty • The Maginot Line • Ireland: Partition and Independence

The Defeated Powers   570

Germany's political turmoil • Chaos in Bavaria • The "enemy within" • The Weimar Republic • German economic problems • Austria-Hungary: an empire shattered • Turkey: the end of the Ottoman Empire • Russia in turmoil • The Russian Civil War • Communism in Russia • The new Russian economy

Focus points: The Dawes Plan • Adolf Hitler • The Munich Putsch • The Battle of Warsaw

The U.S. Legacy   590

U.S. power in a global context • Wilson and the League of Nations • Immigration, patriotism, and xenophobia • Harding, Coolidge, and Hoover • Prosperity and the automobile • Hollywood and the Jazz Age

Focus points: Carrie Chapman Catt • The Red Scare • Carl Sandburg • Henry Cabot Lodge • The Nineteenth Amendment • The Eighteenth Amendment

The Wider Impact   612

India and Britain • The Middle East • Revolution in China

Focus points: Mohandas Gandhi • Zionism • Palestine • Mao Zedong

Bibliography   632
Index   633

SET CONTENTS

Volume 1: War and Response, 1914–1916

Map Key	1	The War at Sea, 1914–1916	170
Maps and Diagrams	2	The Wider War, 1914–1916	188
Introduction	4	The Western Front, 1916	206
The World before the War	8	America and the Growing	
The United States before the War	28	Conflict, 1914–1916	226
The Move to War	50	Neutrals and Supporters	248
The July Crisis, 1914	70	The United States Moves to War	260
The World Response	86	The U.S. Military Commitment	280
The Central Powers' Forces	100	The Search for Peace	300
The Allied Forces	116		
The Western Front, 1914–1915	132	Bibliography	312
The Eastern Front, 1914–1916	152	Index	313

Volume 2: Victory and Defeat, 1917–1918

The Western Front, 1917	326	The War at Sea, 1918	502
The Eastern Front, 1917	348	The Collapse of Germany	514
The Wider War, 1917	366	Europe after the Armistice	530
The War at Sea, 1917	384	Peace and the Allies	550
Germany's Last Attacks	402	The Defeated Powers	570
U.S. Baptism of Fire	418	The U.S. Legacy	590
The Allies Fight Back	436	The Wider Impact	612
The Final U.S. Offensives	452		
Europe's Other Theaters	470	Bibliography	632
The Wider War, 1918	487	Index	633

Volume 3: Home Fronts / Technologies of War

The German Home Front	646	Support Services	868
France at War	666	Naval Warfare	882
The British Home Front	686	War in the Air	902
Home Fronts Elsewhere	706		
The U.S. Home Front	718	Bibliography	922
Women and the War	738	Glossary	923
Wartime Arts and the Media	756	For Further Research	925
The New Peace	774	Time Line of World War I	928
Remembering the War	790	Index of Personalities	938
Tactics and Weapons on Land	808	Index of Places	943
Artillery at War	828	Index of Battles and Campaigns	948
Armor and Transport	848	General Index	950

The Western Front, 1917

Those areas in Belgium and northeastern France that Germany had taken in 1914 not only lay behind the trench lines of the western front but were also by far the most valuable of all its gains in the first weeks of the war. They provided coal and iron ore for several of Germany's major industries, which were being increasingly starved of raw materials thanks to the British naval blockade. In political terms, the two regions were a potentially useful

By 1917 Britain and France believed they could deliver a knockout blow to Germany on the western front. However, their hopes of victory were swept away by Germany's defensive strategy.

▶ *The western front in 1917 was dominated by French and British offensives, while the Germans were content to remain on the defensive, particularly along the newly created Siegfried Line. This long defensive barrier was known to the Allies as the Hindenburg Line.*

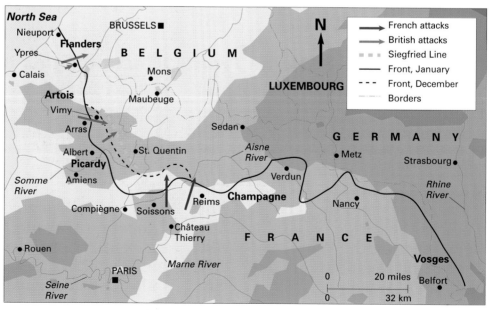

French attacks
British attacks
Siegfried Line
Front, January
Front, December
Borders

North Sea
Nieuport
Ypres
Calais
BRUSSELS
Flanders
BELGIUM
Mons
Maubeuge
Artois
Vimy
Arras
Sedan
LUXEMBOURG
N
GERMANY
Metz
Strasbourg
Albert
St. Quentin
Aisne River
Picardy
Somme River
Amiens
Verdun
Rhine River
Compiègne
Soissons
Reims
Champagne
Nancy
Château Thierry
FRANCE
Rouen
PARIS
Marne River
Vosges
Belfort
Seine River
0   20 miles
0   32 km

◄ *A German corpse on the battlefield, surrounded by the detritus of war. By 1917 there were 11 European nations at war, plus the Japanese and Turks, tens of millions of men under arms, and millions of dead, wounded, or captured.*

▼ *French troops shelter in the ruins of buildings at Verdun. After the bitter fighting of 1916, France had lost nearly half of its prewar military manpower. Worse followed in 1917, sparking a series of mutinies that were to halt French military operations for much of the year.*

bargaining chip in any peace talks with the Allies, although the likelihood of such talks was receding fast.

The effective German commander in chief, General Erich Ludendorff, saw the protection of these areas as paramount to a successful conclusion to the war. However, he was also able to recognize that Germany's manpower was being stretched increasingly thin because of its commitments elsewhere. Although Russia was being torn apart by political unrest and its armies appeared to be fatally weakened, Ludendorff could not afford to entirely denude the eastern front of German troops.

Equally, Austria-Hungary was showing some signs of war weariness, and its armies were becoming increasingly ineffective. It was likely that Germany would have to shoulder a greater burden of responsibility on both the Italian and Balkan fronts in 1917, as well as maintain its commitment in the western and eastern theaters. Ludendorff did hold out some hopes that a German-led Austro-Hungarian offensive against the Italians might lead to the collapse of the latter. Worrying for Ludendorff was the growing possibility of the United States siding with the Allies, a situation that

KEY FIGURES

FIELD MARSHAL DOUGLAS HAIG

Haig (1861–1928), the commander of the British forces in France from December 1915 until the war's end, remains a controversial figure. Some believe that his inflexible adherence to offensive action produced huge casualties for little gain. Others believe that he was more open-minded to new ideas and tactics and also had to adapt his thinking to an entirely new type of warfare.

Haig, originally a cavalry officer, served in India, in the Sudan in 1898, and in the Boer War from 1899 to 1902. In 1914 he was made lieutenant general and given the command of I Corps of the British Expeditionary Force (BEF) in France and Belgium. Praised for his leadership in the First Battle of Ypres in 1914, he was promoted to full general and was given control of the First Army of the BEF under the supreme command of General John French.

In December 1915 Haig was appointed commander of the BEF, which he led in the Battle of the Somme in 1916. After the British failure at the Third Battle of Ypres in 1917, Haig was criticized for continuing the offensive after any chance of a decisive victory had receded. However, he oversaw a series of British advances on the western front during 1918. After retiring in 1921, Haig devoted the rest of his life to the welfare of ex-servicemen.

would eventually mean a massive U.S. military buildup on the western front that Germany could not match.

The Allied leadership seemingly faced fewer strategic dilemmas at the beginning of 1917. In the latter part of 1916, a joint conference of the Allied nations that had been held at Chantilly, outside Paris, had agreed that the western front was the priority and that the British and French armies would undertake large-scale offensives along it in 1917. It was intended that these attacks would be supported by efforts from the Russians and Italians, who would attempt to tie down German forces or their allies in their respective theaters. However, it appears that the British and French were not fully aware of the extent of the growing political turmoil in Russia or the limited offensive capabilities of the Italian Army.

To make matters worse, the British and French did not have a unified command structure to integrate fully their own military efforts on the western front, and some of their most senior generals had little faith in their opposite numbers. Indeed, the decision that was made by David Lloyd George, the British prime minister, to place the whole of Field Marshal Douglas Haig's

British Expeditionary Force temporarily under French command in 1917 was bitterly opposed by its commander.

The cost of the western front

If there was general agreement on all sides that the western front was the decisive theater, the generals had yet to find a master plan to achieve a major breakthrough. The front remained the least fluid and also the most costly of all the World War I battlefields. By the beginning of 1917, the British had lost a total of nearly one million men. French casualties totaled nearly three million, while the German Army had lost nearly 2.5 million troops. The bloody battles of 1916, especially those at Verdun and the Somme, had been particularly costly, with no immediately obvious advantage gained by either side.

In terms of their total prewar military manpower, France had lost approximately 47 percent, Germany about 22 percent, and Britain about 15 percent by the beginning of 1917. These figures were very high, and for the strategists on both sides they caused serious concern, since it was generally accepted that casualty levels that rose above 25 percent were unsustainable in the successful conduct of military operations.

▲ **British Prime Minister David Lloyd George (right) pays a visit to the western front in 1917. He was cautious about the chance of success of any new offensives, fearing the casualty toll they might bring. Albert Thomas, the French minister of munitions, is to the left of Lloyd George.**

◄ **British troops take an opportunity to wash in the water available at Langemarck, Ypres, in October 1917. Frequently sodden and plagued by lice, the trench-bound troops led a life that was far from conducive to good health.**

Despite these losses, the sizes of the armies on the western front were still colossal. In trenches that stretched in an unbroken line from Switzerland to the North Sea, the Allies had some 3.9 million men—2.6 million French and 1.2 million British, together with 100,000 Belgians—divided into 169 divisions. On the other side of no man's land, there lay 129 German divisions, totaling about 2.5 million soldiers. Both sides were also engaged in the training of fresh troops, which during 1917 would swell the Allied armies by 15 divisions. The German Army, in part also helped by troops to be transferred from the eastern front beginning in December and continuing into 1918, increased by around twice the Allied number of divisions.

Any attempt at resolving the stalemate on the western front had to come through either a political or a radical military settlement. The least bloody solution would have been a negotiated peace—the many unsuccessful attempts to arrive at such a solution are examined elsewhere (see Volume 1, pages 301–311). In the event, by late January 1917 the rhetoric of peace had vanished and left only the military solution. The new military options were either attrition (inflicting more casualties on the enemy than suffering oneself) or a successful breakthrough of the trench system, followed by traditional outflanking

▲ *A French gun being towed to the front. As the war progressed, greater use was made of motor vehicles to move all manner of military items, although horses and mules remained vitally important in logistical support.*

maneuvers to end the trench deadlock. Attrition, as the Battle of Verdun had shown, was clearly costly in lives to both sides and was likely to have dangerous consequences politically. The politicians, not to mention the wider public, would not stomach growing losses for no obvious gain. Thus, achieving a decisive breakthrough, if possible with minimal casualties, was the preferred military option. It was argued that such a breakthrough would bring a clear-cut victory and a rapid end to the war. However, although many Allied commanders believed they had the "magic formula" with which to achieve the desired breakthrough, none had been tested to the limit.

As the new year dawned, France placed a new leader in command of its forces. Joseph Joffre was replaced on December 31, 1916, by General Robert Nivelle. Nivelle was a very different officer from his British counterpart, Field Marshal Douglas Haig. Outgoing, persuasive, and with the ability to charm many of his political masters, Nivelle had inherited the Verdun front in 1916 after the initial German attack had been repulsed, and his subsequent gains won

him international renown. Nivelle's innovative tactics, which involved huge artillery bombardments, seemed to represent a possible solution to the stalemate on the western front. His claims of total victory at little cost beguiled many politicians, both French and British.

However, the French Army that Nivelle inherited was in a parlous state. The huge manpower losses of the past two years, suffered without any significant recovery of French territory, had eaten away at the morale of the troops, as had the failure of the French Army's officer corps to understand the futility of all-out attack during a war that generally favored the defense.

There were strengths within the French Army's ranks, most notably its well-trained artillery. The French also had an excellent corps of engineers; it had adapted well to the western front despite having trained for a more fluid form of warfare. The engineers had constructed an elaborate road network behind the French line, allowing for the rapid redeployment of troops from one sector to another, and had learned to build effective trenches. Nevertheless, the infantry, numerically the greatest part of the French Army, was seriously weakened. Although it still possessed an experienced body of officers, the ordinary soldiers had suffered horrendous casualties and fought under appalling conditions in which their well-being was clearly of secondary concern.

The British armies on the western front were very different in character from the British Expeditionary Force that had been sent to France in August 1914. That volunteer army, small, highly professional, and experienced, had been all but wiped out by 1915, leaving only a thin sprinkling of professionals to teach new conscripts the ways of soldiering in 1916 and beyond. Prior to the war the British general staff had never even imagined that it might be forced to fight a war on such a scale or for such a duration, and its commanders were simply overwhelmed by the sheer volume of work. Throughout early 1916 the new, conscript British Army learned its craft, while the French bore the brunt of the fighting. By January 1917 the British Army had grown into a vast force that had learned its trade in the bloody Battle of the Somme. For the past year it had been led by Field Marshal Douglas Haig, who, like France's Nivelle, believed a decisive breakthrough could be achieved on the western front, although Haig was dismissive of the new French commander's grandiose claims of an easy victory.

The German commanders on the western front had failed to achieve their aim of a speedy victory, and their troops were now suffering. In the trenches the loss of experienced officers and men at Verdun and along the Somme River was beginning to be felt, and on the home front the pool of manpower available for military service was being drained rapidly. Forced to accept that his country was likely to be embroiled in a multifront war for the indefinite future and currently without the strength to win decisively, Ludendorff opted in fall 1916 to adopt a more flexible defensive stance on the western front, which he termed "defense in depth." Construction of this new defensive system, known as the Siegfried or Hindenburg Line, began in October 1916.

▼ **British soldiers eating their meal in the trenches at Arras in March 1917. One man maintains a lookout for signs of enemy forces. The year saw the Allies launch two large offensives on the western front.**

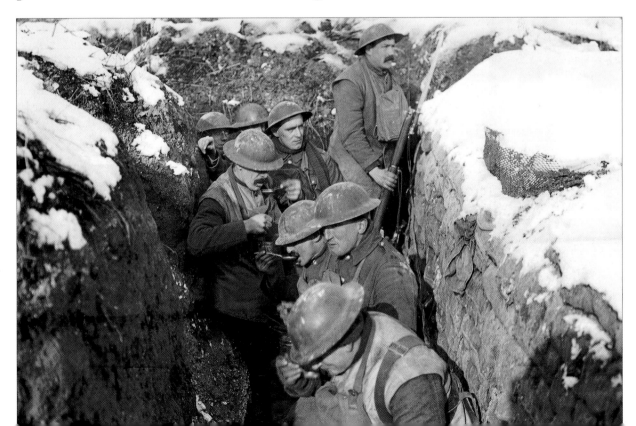

The Siegfried Line

By late 1916 Germany was facing acute manpower shortages on the long western front. Its planners opted to surrender territory to reduce the length of the line and retreat to a new, consolidated defensive position, a strategy known as "defense in depth."

On August 29, 1916, Field Marshal Paul von Hindenburg became chief of staff of the German Army and, together with his quartermaster general, Erich von Ludendorff, ordered the construction of a system of fortifications some 20 miles (32 km) behind the bulging northern and central sectors of the western front, stretching from Arras to Soissons. To the Germans, this new and straighter defensive system was the Siegfried Line, but the Allied soldiers called it after its supposed creator—Hindenburg—although Ludendorff was actually the driving force behind the plan.

Ludendorff aimed to shorten his front line; those troops no longer defending the trenches were to be used as a reserve, one that could be rushed to deal with any Allied break-through. With these troops out of the trenches, Germany's daily

◄ *A view of the barbed wire in front of the Siegfried Line near Heninel, May 1917. This area came under attack by the British during the Arras battles.*

▶ *As the Germans retreated to the Siegfried Line, they laid waste to the areas they abandoned. These trees have been felled to block a road and to deny any cover from air observation.*

casualty figures would also be reduced. The line also marked a departure in the tactics of fighting trench warfare, heralding the development of what became known as "defense in depth." Troops would not be expected to hold a continuous first line of trenches at all costs and suffer the horrors—and severe casualties—of a prolonged enemy preparatory bombardment. Ludendorff also increased the overall depth of the defensive zone to be held by his troops.

The first line comprised a series of lightly held outposts, which were designed to forewarn of an attack and delay the initial enemy advance, thereby allowing defensive lines farther

▼ *Wire strung out above the trenches hampered any entry into them for those attackers who had managed to overcome all the other obstacles above ground.*

back time to prepare. The second line, sited some way behind the outpost line, was known as the "battle zone." Around 1,500 yards (1,376 m) deep, this section comprised numerous strong points and concrete pillboxes. All were protected by dense thicknesses of barbed wire and liberally supplied with machine guns. Behind the battle zone was the "final line," where the artillery was positioned and where further nests of machine guns were built.

Between February 23 and April 5, the German Army carried out Operation Alberich, the withdrawal to the Siegfried Line, which was accomplished without any interference from the Allies. Behind the old front line, the Germans razed villages, cut down forests, and destroyed bridges and roads. The Siegfried Line proved a formidable barrier. Although the Allies captured some parts of it in 1917 at a high cost, much of it was held until the final days of the war.

Planning the Allied attacks

In early January 1917 Allied aircraft began to undertake detailed reconnaissance of the German positions, but over the next three months none was able to detect the Siegfried Line nearing completion, despite intelligence that the work was progressing apace. In contrast, during early February German intelligence officers scored a major coup when they intercepted Italian diplomatic messages going to Russia, which revealed that the French were planning a major offensive somewhere on the western front in April, one that would involve at its maximum 1.2 million men backed by some 7,000 artillery pieces. British support was expected.

The Allies emerged from their often acrimonious negotiations with a broad plan for an attack in the French sector of the western front along and north of the Aisne River, near Reims, supported by a preliminary British attack east of the French town of Arras to draw German reserves away from the Aisne.

▼ *A large howitzer in action from British positions among the ruins of Tilloy-les-Mofflaines during the Battle of Arras in April 1917. The battle saw the first use of the "creeping" barrage—artillery fire which advanced systematically ahead of infantry—devised by the British.*

▲ Canadian troops attempt to consolidate their muddy positions at Vimy Ridge in April 1917. More than one Canadian soldier died for every yard of the German line that was captured, but the attack was widely regarded as a great success.

Nivelle argued that a massive onslaught on the German lines along the Aisne, chiefly in the direction of the German-held Chemin des Dames ridges, would bring victory within a mere 48 hours. France's war minister, Hubert Lyautey, General Henri Philippe Pétain, the hero of the Battle of Verdun, and Britain's Field Marshal Douglas Haig were opposed to the plan. Nevertheless, Nivelle won approval for his scheme from the French and British prime ministers, Aristide Briand and David Lloyd George. Lyautey resigned in protest.

Nivelle was able to persuade the British to take over a large sector of the French line, freeing more French divisions for the main attack. The British offensive was scheduled for April 8, to be preceded by a massive five-day artillery barrage, which would itself be eclipsed by the barrage before the French attack on April 12. Preparations at Arras began in earnest at the beginning of January. In great secrecy the British stockpiled millions of artillery shells and built an extensive road network around the town, which consumed some 50,000 tons of timber and

206 trainloads of crushed rock. Various essential supplies flowed into the sector. Under the town of Arras itself, British and Canadian engineers completed an enormous system of interconnecting tunnels to complement the already extensive sewer system, thus allowing Allied troops to shelter in safety before moving up to the front.

From February 21 Allied officers began to detect signs that Germany's Operation Alberich was under way. This was the planned withdrawal by German forces to the newly constructed positions of the Siegfried Line, and it continued until April 5. Reconnaissance reported that the new front line was held by a network of bunkers and behind these were a series of widely separated trenches, heavily protected by dense rolls of barbed wire. Most of the German withdrawals seemed to be in the French sector, causing concerns among French officers that were worsened by the loss of an important map outlining their forthcoming offensive. However, the need to maintain pressure on Germany and thus ease the burden on Russia outweighed the French concerns, and Nivelle's plan remained intact. First, however, the British diversionary attack at Arras had to begin.

The British attack at Arras
The focus of the British offensive along a 15-mile (24 km) front at Arras was a narrow corridor to the south of the Scarpe River overlooked by the village of Monchy-le-Preux. An essential part of the attack was a diversionary advance on Vimy Ridge, which dominated the river terrain and was felt by some Allied observers to be nearly impregnable.

Responsibility for the overall attack was given to General Edmund Allenby, commander of the British Third Army, and the British First Army under General Henry Horne. Four Canadian divisions under General Julian Byng, part of Horne's command, were tasked with capturing Vimy Ridge, and the eight divisions of the Third Army with the assault on the central and southern sectors, where they faced the Siegfried Line. The British also had 40 tanks available, but the unreliability of these machines was well established and few officers expected them to last long. In support, the British and Canadians had amassed 2,817 artillery pieces, which began to destroy the German wire entanglements on April 4. Under the terrifying barrage of high-explosive and gas shells lay the men of General Ludwig von Falkenhausen's Sixth Army.

On the evening of April 8, some 30,000 members of the Canadian Corps began to move up to the front line. Early the next morning Allied guns began pounding the German trenches and artillery positions around Vimy Ridge, and the Canadian infantry went over the top. Following very closely behind a "creeping" barrage, the advancing Canadians captured the formidable *Zwolfer Graben* trench system within 30 minutes. An hour later the trench line southeast of the village of Thélus was also under Canadian control. Soon after, the 3rd Division took the huge Schwaben Tunnel complex, but several of its forward-lying machine-gun posts survived, and these caused heavy casualties. The Canadian 4th Division was especially badly hit. One of its units suffered casualties amounting to more than 50 percent within just a few minutes of advancing.

Immediately south of Vimy Ridge, part of Allenby's Third Army also attacked and managed to push forward some 3.5 miles (5.6 km)—the greatest depth of advance by the British Army on a single day since late 1914. Results elsewhere, chiefly south of the Scarpe, were negligible, however. The Germans were able to hold the village strongpoint of Monchy-le-Preux against repeated British attacks. In an attempt to stretch the German defenses, General Hubert Gough's British Fifth Army launched an attack farther south. Despite the use of some tanks, it was repulsed by the Germans at Bullecourt.

By April 12 the Canadians were firmly in control of Vimy Ridge. Forced to the bottom of the high ground, the Germans were unable to launch a successful counterattack, and that night, under the protection of darkness, they withdrew. On the 14th Haig called a halt to the British attacks to await news of Nivelle's offensive along the Aisne River. When it ended in failure (see below), the British First and Third Armies were ordered to move forward again on April 23. After two days of heavy fighting, little ground was gained, although the combat continued into

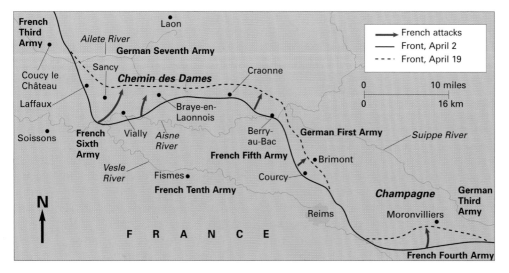

◄ *The Nivelle attack was supposed to rapidly cut through the German lines on the Chemin des Dames ridges and pave the way for total victory. Hopes of a swift French advance were dashed in a matter of days.*

▲ The opening of the Nivelle Offensive. The puffs of smoke mark the shell falls during the accompanying artillery bombardment. Stumps and branchless trees litter the desolate landscape.

May. British casualties totaled 150,000 men; the Germans recorded losses of 100,000. At the end of the Battle of Arras on May 16, the British were left in possession of the northernmost 6 miles (9.5 km) of the Siegfried Line.

In assessing the limited British success at Arras, Ludendorff laid the blame squarely on Falkenhausen, commander of the German Sixth Army, who had failed to implement Ludendorff's new defensive strategy by ordering the front line of trenches to be held at all costs. This failure had subjected many of Falkenhausen's troops to the full intensity of the British barrage and reduced their effectiveness as fighting men. Also, he had not deployed his troops close enough to the rear of the second main trench to allow for the rapid counterattacks that Ludendorff envisaged as part of his strategy for the Siegfried Line.

Nivelle's disastrous advance

The action of the Nivelle Offensive, a massive assault on German positions along the Aisne, involved more than one million French soldiers ranged along a broad front between Roye and Reims. The German soldiers of the First and Seventh Armies facing them, under the leadership of generals Fritz von Below and Maximilian von Boehn, were better prepared than the defenders of the Arras sector, due in no small part to intelligence gleaned from the captured French map. Four days later than scheduled, at 6:00 A.M. on the 16th, the French artillerymen switched from their protracted preparation barrage to a creeping barrage, and the French Fifth and Sixth Armies, under the command of generals Olivier Mazel and Charles Mangin, respectively, launched their attacks against the strongly defended German front line.

The assaulting troops were soon in some difficulty, as they ran into a hail of machine-gun fire from forward outposts. As French infantrymen were scythed down in droves, it was becoming brutally clear that the new defenses had survived the artillery preparations. Even if they managed to bypass the outposts of the forward slope of the defenses, on cresting the ridges the

French attackers found the barbed wire on the reverse slope still largely intact. All along the line the French met swift and powerful counterattacks, and by the end of the first day, neither of the two armies had made any real inroads, although some 40,000 casualties had been suffered. Almost 150 new French tanks had also been lost.

Nivelle refused to accept that his strategy was not working and ordered Mazel to attack northeast the next day, in the area where the greatest advances had been made. The attacks continued until April 20. Mangin made small gains west of Soissons, but the major breakthrough that Nivelle expected did not take place. By April 25, over 96,000 of his troops had been killed, wounded, or were missing. German losses totaled nearly 83,000 men. It was clear by this stage that the Nivelle Offensive had failed in its aim to produce a sudden, massive breach in the German line and

had instead degenerated into a bloody slogging match on a broad front. Further attacks were ordered, and by May 5 a small stretch of the Chemin des Dames ridges was secured. When the offensive ended on May 9, the French had suffered some 187,000 casualties. German casualties amounted to around 163,000 men. Nivelle was sacked a week later and replaced by Pétain.

By the time of Nivelle's departure, the French Army was on the point of collapse. The first cracks began to appear on April 21, when troops of the 1st Infantry Division were reported to be on the brink of open mutiny. As casualties mounted in the following weeks, indiscipline began to spread through the ranks until by early May French divisions were willing to defend their trenches but refusing to attack. This "collective indiscipline," as the French military leadership chose to term the mutiny, had engulfed some 68 of the French Army's 112 divisions by mid-June. The crisis was turned around only slowly by Pétain. Some mutineers were executed, but Pétain began to address

▼ Thoroughly smashed by artillery and mines, these are the remains of German trenches taken by the British in June 1917, during the Battle of Messines Ridge.

the day-to-day concerns of the soldiers, and their conditions were improved. Remarkably, the Germans never knew of the mutiny until it was over.

With the French Army in wholesale disarray, it was clear that British troops would have to bear the brunt of the fighting on the western front until the end of the year. The limited successes at Arras, although they were achieved largely against areas of the line where the new German defensive system had not been implemented, encouraged some people to believe that the British had found a way of breaking the impasse on the western front, despite the fact that the offensive had subsequently become bogged down. Haig, the British commander, believed that he had the opportunity to crash through the German defenses and end the war at a stroke. He devised an ambitious plan centered on the Belgian city of Ypres, already the site of two previous battles. The new Ypres offensive would also divert German attention from the French, who were still recovering from the recent mutinies.

British efforts in Flanders

By 1917 Britain's ability to wage war had vastly increased, both in terms of the number of men available for frontline service and the industrial output of war supplies. Haig had been planning an ambitious scheme to push the Germans back along the Belgian coast by breaking their line between the North Sea and the Lys River. Combined with an amphibious landing to the rear of the German lines that would be engineered by British naval forces, it would force the Germans to quit the lowlands of Flanders and would create a giant salient, or bulge, in their line, which could be exploited. An essential element of the land offensive would be the capture of Messines Ridge, a natural strongpoint just southeast of Ypres that overlooked the British positions and had long been a bastion of the German defenses since its capture in December 1914. If the ridge were taken, German positions in the lowlands might become untenable.

General Herbert Plumer, commander of the British Second Army, had begun making plans for a major British attack

Mine Warfare

When the trench lines became fixed on the western front in 1914, various methods were tried to break the stalemate and pave the way for a successful offensive. One of the most difficult and dangerous was the digging of mines under the enemy's trenches.

The basic mining technique was to dig a tunnel, known as a sap, under an enemy position and then pack it with huge amounts of explosives, which would be detonated moments before an attack was launched. Yet mining was far from a straightforward affair, not least because local geology greatly affected the feasibility of any tunneling operation. If mines were to be successful, the element of surprise was essential. Thus the huge volumes of spoil from a tunnel had to be removed with great care and hidden beyond the eyes of a prying enemy. Tunnelers had to work methodically over months and sometimes even years to minimize the noise created by their underground activities.

At the beginning of the war, only the Germans—and to a lesser extent the French— had

specialist tunneling companies, and it took the British, who became the chief tunnelers, some time to catch up. In January 1915 the British began to recruit their own tunneling companies, with many of the men being miners or the builders of sewer tunnels. By the end of 1915 the British, who occupied the terrain on the western front best suited to mining, had begun to wrest the initiative from the Germans.

The growing confidence of `the British miners was clearly demonstrated on the first day of

◀ *Inspecting a tunnel built by the 1st Australian Tunneling Company in September 1917. Water has entered, an eternal elemental enemy and the cause of much discomfort.*

Mining was a nerve-racking experience for both the tunnelers and for their intended targets. Tunnelers had to work in dark and often damp conditions, roofs were prone to collapse, the air was often foul (mice and small birds were taken underground to give early signs of bad air or poisonous gas), and an enemy might try to destroy a tunnel with their own explosive-filled countermine, known as a camouflet, or attempt to break into the tunnel and fight it out.

For those above ground, the threat of mines clearly played on the mind. As there was no specialist equipment to monitor any underground activity, mines could be detected only by placing an ear to the ground or sinking a water-filled barrel into the bottom of a trench—any vibrations would create movements on the surface of the water.

the Battle of the Somme, July 1, 1916, when several mines were blown under the German front line. However, the greatest use of mines occurred on the first day of the Battle of Messines Ridge, June 7, 1917. Nineteen mines, under construction since January, had been packed with 500 metric tons of explosives and were blown simultaneously. One mine created a depression that became known as Lone Tree Crater. It measured 250 feet (76 m) across and was 40 feet (12 m) deep. The detonations at Messines could be heard in southern England. Whole sections of the German trenches— and their human occupants— were completely obliterated, and many of the survivors were far too disoriented to fight back against the British.

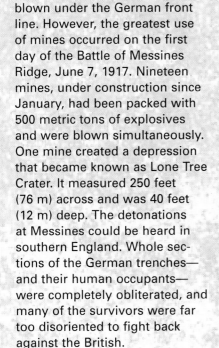

▲ *Former miners and underground engineers were in high demand on the western front as both sides sought to tunnel within the other's lines and detonate huge charges.*

▼ *Excavating a mine was difficult, dangerous, and labor-intensive work. There was also the constant threat of a cave-in or even discovery by an enemy in its own nearby tunnels.*

at Messines in the winter of 1916–1917. His plans aimed to minimize British casualties and centered on the use of 20 huge explosive mines placed under the German lines. Beginning in the summer of 1916, great lengths of tunnel snaked out beneath the German positions from the British lines. German countermining failed to discover 19 of the 20 tunnels, which were filled up with explosives in the following spring. Employing 2,300 guns and 300 heavy mortars, along with 300 aircraft to gain local air superiority, Plumer began a massive bombardment of the German lines on May 21, 1917. Simultaneous explosion of the mines took place at 3:10 A.M. on June 7. The blast killed an estimated 10,000 German soldiers and was clearly audible in London.

Under a devastating creeping barrage, Plumer next sent forward nine divisions, which took all of their preliminary objectives in the first three hours of the battle. General Hubert Gough, the commander of the British Fifth Army, also took advantage of the situation to make some significant territorial gains. German counterattacks the following day were repulsed. These actions continued until June 14, but by this time Messines Ridge had been completely occupied by the British. The Battle of Messines Ridge was the first on the western front since 1914 in which the defensive casualties (some 25,000 men) had exceeded the losses of the attacking force (17,000 men).

With Messines Ridge safely in British hands, Haig planned for a major offensive at Ypres. Encouraged by the gains made at Messines, he was convinced—mistakenly—that a major victory could now be won. At this time he was still unaware of the full extent of the crisis within the mutinous French Army. Haig also had a shortfall of nearly 100,000 infantrymen at the time because Lloyd George, the British war leader, was withholding replacements in the belief that Haig's plan had little chance of success. Nevertheless, Haig continued preparing for an offensive in the Ypres salient.

The German Fourth Army, under General Sixt von Arnim, Haig's opponent at Ypres, had held the high points

east of the town and overlooking the coastal lowlands since the end of May 1915. It had become obvious to both Arnim and his officers that this strategically important ground would again be attacked. Senior officers of Arnim's Fourth Army set about creating a three-tier system of defenses, with concrete pillboxes in the forward zone, backed by a secondary zone in which counterattack forces were entrenched and a third zone for the artillery. Extensive use was also made of barbed wire, and the infantry were trained in the tactics of counterattacking. By the end of July, these changes had largely been implemented, and the Germans were prepared for any British action.

The opening attack of what is now known as the Third Battle of Ypres, or Passchendaele, was made toward the high ground of Passchendaele Ridge. It was entrusted to General Hubert Gough's Fifth Army. It was flanked on the right by General Herbert Plumer's Second Army, and pivoting on the left was General François Anthoine's French First Army. At 3:50 A.M. on July

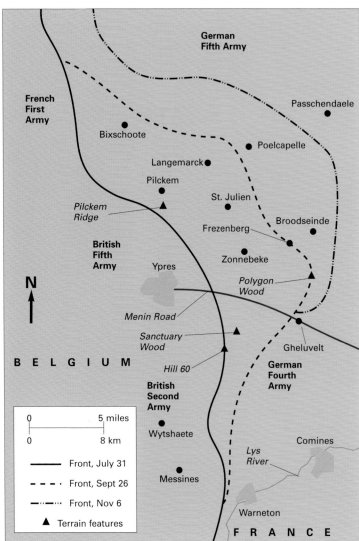

▲ **The Third Battle of Ypres was a British offensive to smash the German defenses in Flanders. It failed and cost the Allies 300,000 casualties.**

◄ **Amid the mud and water the British fire on German positions around Langemarck during the Third Battle of Ypres.**

31, after a 10-day preliminary bombardment during which time 3,000 Allied guns hurled around 4.25 million shells onto the German positions, the Allied infantry went over the top in what was the first stage of the offensive—the Battle of Pilckem.

In the center Gough's main attack ran into a stubborn defense and then began to encounter powerful counterattacks. By the evening, the German Fourth Army had held off the main advance and restricted the Allies to small gains on the left of the line. That night the rain began, but Allied attacks continued unabated the next day. Torrential rain

▲ German prisoners and the wounded intermingle behind British lines in September 1917 during the Battle of the Menin Road, part of the Third Battle of Ypres.

for four days turned the Ypres lowlands into a mud bath, a situation worsened by the British heavy bombardment having destroyed the drainage system in the area. The heavy, cloying mud immobilized infantry and tank crews alike. Haig brought the lowlands offensive to a temporary halt, having captured the first and second German defensive zones, but he had lost 23,000 British and French soldiers.

A renewed two-day offensive, the Battle of Langemarck, was begun on August 16 but again foundered in the mud without taking the critical high ground. On August 25 Haig switched the focus for the attack to Plumer's Second Army on the right and gave him a month or so to prepare. Plumer heralded his attack, known as the Battle of the Menin Road, with a devastating creeping barrage 1,000 yards (900 m) wide, which preceded a series of short punches into the German defenses. Once the limited objectives had been reached, the infantry was ordered to

organize a defense in order to repulse the expected counterattacks until the artillery, covering from the high ground at Messines, could be advanced.

The attacks resumed on September 20, and Plumer's tactic met with initial success. On September 27, following another British success at the Battle of Polygon Wood, the German leadership was forced to acknowledge that Plumer and Haig had devised a method of defeating Ludendorff's defensive system, and so the Germans revised their tactics by crowding more soldiers into the forward zone, although only a few of the concrete pillboxes had survived. Plumer, in turn, decided to dispense with the preliminary barrage and rely on the element of surprise. At 6:00 A.M. on October 4 British forces assaulted under cover of a creeping barrage, heralding the Battle of Broodseinde. The attack caught the Germans completely by surprise—they lost possession of the ridge east of Ypres and suffered more than 30,000 casualties.

Heavy rain again returned to the battlefield, but despite the reservations of Gough and Plumer, Haig ordered further attacks toward the Passchendaele Ridge—the last piece of high ground in the Ypres salient. Attacks on the 9th and 12th of October were unsuccessful, as the advancing British soldiers labored through soupy mud and mustard-gas attacks. After three more attacks in October and one on November 6, the village of Passchendaele was finally taken by British and Canadian infantry, thereby eradicating the salient.

These gains were limited, however, and the offensive had cost the Allies about 310,000 casualties, compared with 260,000 on the German side. In the aftermath Haig faced a barrage of abuse for continuing with the attacks long after the operation had lost any real strategic value. He had planned for a decisive battle with limited casualties, but what he presided over was a battle of attrition. The consequences of the final offensive at Passchendaele were immense. It embittered thousands of British troops against their leaders and also sapped their will to keep fighting; it caused politicians in Britain, chief among them Lloyd George, to question Haig's leadership; and it compelled the British military to look for an alternative type of offensive. However, Haig had powerful friends, including members of the British royal family. Lloyd George had little faith in Haig, but he was unlikely to be replaced.

The first tank offensive

The British were to make one more major attack on the western front in 1917. The plan was to launch a massed tank attack toward the town of Cambrai. So far the tanks had showed only limited promise, and in the thick mud at Passchendaele had failed dismally. Colonel John Fuller, chief of staff to the tank corps, had already suggested a massed raid on dry ground between the Canal du Nord and the St. Quentin Canal; this plan had the approval of General Julian Byng, commander of the Third Army, but was vetoed by Haig.

After the failure to break through at Ypres, Haig changed his mind and ordered a massive tank attack against that sector of the Siegfried Line at Cambrai supported by Byng's Third Army. Launched at dawn on November 20, it took the Germans completely by surprise. Employing 476 tanks and 6 infantry and 2 cavalry divisions, the Third Army gained 4 miles (6 km) in the first day. Progress toward Cambrai continued over the next few days, but with increasing numbers of the tanks falling casualty to mechanical failure, insufficient infantry reserves, and the rapid reinforcement of General Georg

---

EYEWITNESS

F. R. J. JEFFORD

Jefford was the commander of a British tank at the Battle of Cambrai on November 20, 1917. He later recorded the problems he faced:

"It took all one's wits to watch the course of the battle from the enclosed world inside the tank. First, we had to use the periscope to judge the effect of our firing. Secondly, by lifting the shutters of the peep holes, we could watch the fate of the other tanks next to us, which wasn't pleasant when they were hit. It was also important to watch the visual compass in order to know one's direction if it became necessary to get out of difficulties quickly. It was extremely difficult to concentrate the gunners on the required target when under shell or machine-gun fire. The gunners had vertical gaps through which to aim their telescopic sights but inside the tank, when machine guns sprayed our armored plating, it was like the sparks flying around in a blacksmith's forge. When I was using my forward machine gun, it was impossible to sustain firing for any length of time, as the hot sparks hit my hand and wrist. My skin was mottled for days afterward."

Extract taken from Tank Battles of World War I *by Bryan Cooper, first published in 1974.*

POLITICAL WORLD

ALLIED SUPREME WAR COUNCIL

In late 1917 a German-led offensive, the Battle of Caporetto, nearly knocked Italy out of the war. Britain, France, and the United States could not allow one of their Allies to be defeated and organized a conference to discuss plans to aid Italy.

The conference, held at Rapallo on the northeast coast of Italy, began on November 5. Although the immediate concern of sending military aid to Italy was quickly resolved, the talks soon became much more wide ranging. It had become increasingly clear that the Allies needed to coordinate their war plans much more closely, and the subsequent discussions centered around this issue. Britain's prime minister, David Lloyd George, suggested the creation of what became known as the Supreme War Council to oversee and coordinate the Allied war strategy.

The council, which was to meet regularly at Versailles, west of Paris, was to comprise the prime ministers of Britain, France, and Italy and the president of the United States or their representatives. Those meeting at Rapallo further agreed that the council was to be permitted to discuss overall military strategy and the allocation of troops to the various war theaters. The council did not have any immediate impact on the war, but in spring 1918 its value was revealed. General Ferdinand Foch was appointed commander over all the Allied forces on the western front. The Allies could now develop coordinated plans with which to defeat Germany's last great offensive of the war.

▶ British tanks pass captured enemy guns at Graincourt in November 1917 during the Battle of Cambrai on their way to the attack on Bourlon Wood.

▼ All of the nations fighting on the western front in 1917 suffered severe losses, although the British and French, who launched the major offensives, recorded the overall greater numbers of casualties.

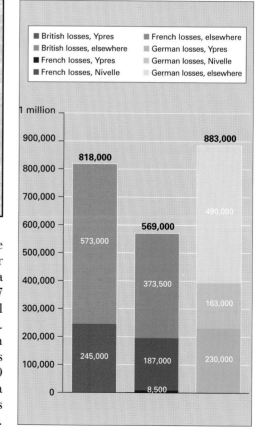

Legend:
- British losses, Ypres
- British losses, elsewhere
- French losses, Ypres
- French losses, Nivelle
- French losses, elsewhere
- German losses, Ypres
- German losses, Nivelle
- German losses, elsewhere

1 million

818,000
573,000
245,000

569,000
373,500
187,000
8,500

883,000
490,000
163,000
230,000

von der Marwitz's Second Army, the advance slowed down. On November 30, 29 German divisions launched a counteroffensive, and by December 7 German forces had regained almost all the ground they had lost at the start. During two weeks of fighting the British suffered 45,000 casualties. Although it is estimated that the Germans lost 50,000 men, Haig considered the offensive a failure, one that confirmed his doubts about the ability of tanks to win the war.

The failure at Cambrai ended the great Allied offensives of 1917, which had cost the lives of 500,000 Allied soldiers for no appreciable gain. The war was doomed to drag on into a fourth year. There was a clear lack of coordination between the Allies on the western front, although this latter issue was to be resolved by the provisions of the Rapallo Conference held in November. Britain and France also knew that American troops arriving in the western European theater offered the promise of victory in the new year. In addition, the French now had a leader in Georges Clemenceau who exercised firm control over their war effort.

Germany could look to the future with very little reason for optimism. If military matters on the western front were not resolved soon, before the arrival of the full might of the American Expeditionary Force, then the war was truly lost. Germany's military planners had little choice but to gamble everything on one final, all-out offensive in the spring of 1918.

KEY FIGURES

PRIME MINISTER GEORGES CLEMENCEAU

Clemenceau (1841–1929) became French prime minister in November 1917 and proved a superb war leader of a country that had been run for much of the war by ineffective and divided coalitions. He soon rooted out defeatists, took greater charge of military policy, and was instrumental in establishing a unified Allied command.

Clemenceau was an outspoken opponent of General Joseph Joffre, chief of the general staff, whom Clemenceau believed was not fully competent, and those who favored a negotiated peace. In November 1917 the French president, Raymond Poincaré, appointed Clemenceau prime minister. Clemenceau immediately clamped down on dissent, and senior politicians who were calling for peace or had seeming pro-German views were arrested.

Clemenceau played an important role in persuading the British to accept General Ferdinand Foch as supreme Allied commander. He also insisted that the exhausted French Army lead the offensive in the summer of 1918. At the Paris Peace Conference in 1919, which was established to define the war's peace terms, Clemenceau demanded that severe penalties be imposed on Germany. Failure to achieve all of his demands led to his resignation as prime minister in January 1920.

Clemenceau (left) greets Field Marshal Douglas Haig.

The Eastern Front, 1917

Allied efforts on the eastern front and in the Balkans were in difficulty. Russia was beset by revolution and the Central Powers were untroubled by a large Allied force in Greece.

Russia, the key Allied power in the east, gave most cause for concern to Britain and France in 1917, not least because the Russian military machine was very clearly disintegrating day by day in the first few months of the year. Discontent deep within the ranks of the ordinary soldiers of the Russian Army stemmed from a number of major grievances, including shortages of food—particularly after

▼ Bad news from the front appears in Petrograd, the Russian capital.

▲ *Russian prisoners of the Germans move to the rear after another defeat on the eastern front. By late 1916–early 1917, the Russian Army was on the point of collapse, with the ordinary soldiers increasingly losing faith in their commanders and believing that their suffering was of little concern to those who directed the war.*

the bread ration was cut during December 1916—irregular leave, concern for the welfare of families at home, hostility toward war profiteers and draft dodgers, and perhaps most ominously, a growing disenchantment with the war itself. Much of this growing unrest with the war was directed toward the Russian high command, which had been led by the ineffective Czar Nicholas II since 1915.

By January 1917 the Russian Army had suffered enormous losses, a million in 1916 alone. Aside from two imaginative generals, Alexey Brusilov and Nikolai Yudenich, the leadership had shown a rigid devotion to formal large-scale frontal attacks, which were enormously costly in lives. It was also staffed almost wholly by hard-line monarchists, arch supporters of the czar, whose unswerving

incompetence and sycophancy toward their ruler had contributed to many military failures. To compound the problem, many experienced officers had been killed or captured in the war's early campaigns.

On the home front the situation had also become increasingly critical as dissatisfaction among the urban working classes escalated—a feature found in all of the major warring powers during the third year of the war. Shortages of foodstuffs in Russia had become acute during the winters due to a general decline in agricultural output between 1914 and 1917 and the inability of the poor railroads to deliver such quantities of food as were needed in the cities.

Popular veneration of the czar among the country's citizens, one of the cornerstones on which his autocratic power

had been built, was replaced by growing discontent with his rule. Within his own government, corruption and inefficiency were rampant, and the czar's reactionary policies, including the occasional dissolution of the Duma (Russian parliament), spread dissatisfaction to those groups with traditionally more moderate political agendas. Additionally, the state's many ethnic minorities were growing more and more restive under Russian control. Ultimately, it was the government's inefficient prosecution of World War I and the shortages of basic goods that early in 1917 finally provided the challenge that the old regime could not meet.

In early January of that year a limited Russian offensive was launched into the German-held province of Kurland on the northern tip of the eastern front. Beginning on the 7th, the Russian attack was the only major offensive during the first six months of 1917. It was launched by the Russian Twelfth Army along a 30-mile (48 km) front to the west of Riga along the Aa River, manned by much smaller German forces. The early progress seemed to offer hopes of a victory, and the Russians were able to take several towns. Although the Germans launched counterattacks on January 22, they failed to regain the lost ground. The offensive was generally considered by the high command to be a victory for the Russians. However, events in the Russian capital, Petrograd (formerly St. Petersburg), were conspiring to ensure that it would be the last of the war launched by the Russian Army under the direction of the country's long-standing ruling elite and the czar.

Preceded by a series of strikes, riots over the scarcity of food broke out in Petrograd on March 9, when a 200,000-strong crowd confronted the police on the city's streets. The unrest was initially confined to civilians but within three days the greater part of the capital's military garrison had joined the revolt. The

his senior commanders could no longer support his retention of the throne of Russia. When his brother, Grand Duke Michael, subsequently refused the throne, more than 300 years of rule by the Romanov dynasty in Russia came to an end. A committee of the Duma appointed a provisional government under Prince George Lvov to succeed to the authority of the czar, but it faced a rival in the radical left-wing soviets, committees formed in factories, workshops, and military units that claimed to represent the masses of the people and so to be the rightful heirs to power. Strongest of these was the Petrograd Soviet of Workers and Soldiers Deputies, which had some 2,500 delegates, chosen from factories and from military units in and around the capital. Friction between the moderate Duma and the radical soviet grew steadily.

The Petrograd soviet soon proved that it had greater authority than the provisional government, although both sought for differing reasons to continue Russia's participation in the war for the

▼ As the fighting in Petrograd persisted between those loyal to the czar and those opposed to his regime and any government associated with "old" Russia, the fighting at the front continued. This Russian soldier was killed during the continuing battles against the German forces in the province of Kurland.

180,000-strong garrison was supposedly composed of some of the czar's most loyal soldiers and promonarchy officers (the greater part of the latter drawn from the upper class). However, many of these officers had been killed in battle and their places filled by the urban middle class, while the rank and file were raw recruits and bitter veterans, whose continuing loyalty was doubtful.

Nicholas II was at first unconcerned, despite the fact that his capital's garrison was in revolt and that the Duma had formed a provisional committee, which anticipated the creation of a new, more representative government. The czar's staff was more alive to the crisis and suggested that a force be sent from the front to quash the unrest. Nicholas refused, convinced by his chief of staff, General Mikhail Alexeyev, that such an action would provoke revolution.

Nicholas, increasingly powerless, had little room to maneuver and abdicated on March 15 after being informed that

KEY FIGURES

VLADIMIR ILYICH LENIN

Lenin (1870–1923), born Ulyanov, was the son of a civil servant. When Lenin was sixteen, his elder brother was executed for an alleged conspiracy to kill the czar, and Lenin became involved in radical political activity. He was exiled to Siberia until 1900. In 1901 he changed his name to Lenin.

By the 1905 revolution Lenin was prominent in Russian socialist circles, but his involvement in the failed coup forced him into exile, where he developed his view of Marxist philosophy. After 1914, he opposed the war, espousing the military defeat of Russia as a necessary precursor to revolution.

German attempts to destabilize Russia after the March Revolution in 1917 led to his transportation from Switzerland to Petrograd. On arrival at Petrograd, Lenin delivered the April Theses, which called for the transfer of power to the workers, redistribution of wealth, and an immediate cessation of hostilities. His views won support from the more extreme Bolsheviks, notably Leon Trotsky.

Bolshevik involvement in the July 1917 uprising forced Lenin back into exile, but enthusiasm for his pacifist doctrine grew and he returned to a rapturous welcome on October 23. With Trotsky, he set in train the revolutionary uprising that brought him to power in November, and he went on to initiate peace negotiations with the Germans.

moment. The Duma had only purely nationalist motives, while the soviet wished to defend the revolution, fearful that defeat by Germany would bring about its collapse and the re-creation of the old regime. The only revolutionary members of the Petrograd soviet that sought peace, the Bolsheviks, were in no place to demand an immediate end to the fighting as their leader, Vladimir Ilyich Lenin, was still in exile.

On March 14 the Petrograd soviet issued Order no. 1, which directed soldiers at the front to obey only the orders of the soviet and not those of the provisional government. It also called for committees of soldiers and sailors to take control of their units' arms and to ignore any opposition from their officers. The order served to subvert the remnants of the troops' discipline and unleashed a wave of violence. By mid-April some 50 percent of the officer corps had been executed or murdered. The provisional government was unable to countermand the order to any degree. All that now prevented the

◀ *Citizens of Petrograd flee for cover in March 1917 as sporadic fighting breaks out between those loyal to the czar's regime and supporters of the revolutionary movement.*

▼ *A popular demonstration against the czar prepares to march through the Russian capital. It includes those who have had firsthand experience of the horrors of war, including widows and men blinded in combat.*

the eastern front, as his increasingly powerful faction, the Bolsheviks, had already expressed their support for a peaceful settlement. In April Lenin was transported from exile in Switzerland across Germany to Petrograd with the full complicity of the German government, whose intelligence officers saw Lenin's arrival in Russia as an opportunity to undermine the authority of the provisional government.

When he reached the Russian capital, Lenin addressed a large crowd, spelling out his aims and intents. These so-called April Theses proved too radical, even for some Bolsheviks, who felt they were premature, and Lenin achieved little. His time would come later. However, the Germans further exploited the chaos in Russia by transferring some troops up to the western and Italian fronts. Offensive action on the eastern front was seriously considered, but German intelligence reports indicated that the March Revolution had increased the rate of deterioration of the Russian Army's morale. Any German military activity threatening the Russian heartland might, it was argued, reunite the armed

Petrograd soviet from openly declaring itself the real government of Russia was the fear of provoking an immediate reactionary conservative coup.

Russia's last offensive

While the soviets urged the soldiers to depose their officers, the leaders of the provisional government foresaw that a full German victory in the war would bode ill for Russia, as Germany was likely to demand huge swathes of Russian territory in any peace settlement, and its members also remained conscious of their nation's obligations toward the western Allies. Militarily, the March Revolution appeared a disaster for the western Allies. The Central Powers saw it as an excellent opportunity to focus attention on the western and Italian fronts. Throughout the war, agents in Russia had provided the German leadership with excellent intelligence, and in early 1917 they were sending reports of a nation in chaos. In Lenin, the Germans saw the opportunity for a rapid conclusion to the war on

DISSENT IN THE RANKS

By mid-1917 the Russian Army was on the point of collapse. Morale was low, and many soldiers were wavering in their support for the recently appointed provisional government headed by Aleksandr Kerensky, which was planning to launch a major offensive on the eastern front at the beginning of July. However, more radical political groups wanted to undermine Kerensky's authority by fomenting further unrest in the ranks. Among their weapons were leaflets distributed by their supporters. Many railed against the officer class and the futility of war:

"Brothers! We beg you not to obey an order that is meant to destroy us. An offensive is planned. Take no part in it. Our old leaders have no authority now. Our officers want to make an end of us. They are the traitors. They are the internal enemy. They would like everything to be as before. You know well that all our generals have been put on reduced pay, and they want this revenge.

"We shall be thrown back when we reach the enemy's wire. We cannot break through. I have reconnoitred in the enemy lines and I know that there are 10 rows of it, with machine guns every 15 yards. It is useless to advance. If we do we shall be dead men, with nothing left to hold our front.

"Pass this on, brothers, and promptly write other letters of the same sort."

▶ *A German howitzer pounds the retreating Russians in Galicia, August 1917. This photograph indicates that not all combat in World War I centered around trench warfare as it typically did on the western front.*

forces. It was better to allow the revolutionary turmoil sponsored by the soviets to continue. However, the provisional government was still in control, and its leadership believed it could harness the revolutionary fervor to launch one last offensive against the Germans.

The Socialist Revolutionary Alexander Kerensky, Russian minister of war from May 1917 and one of the few men of dynamism in the provisional government, recognized that a "liberty offensive" against the autocratic Central Powers would enhance the new government's authority both at home and abroad and unite popular sentiment, besides relieving pressure on the western front. One of his first actions as minister had been to purge the Russian high command, appointing Brusilov as the new chief of staff. Kerensky sent political commissars to the front, with instructions to rally the troops. These commissars were to become a key part of the new Red Army. At the front, enthusiasm for a renewed offensive was less easy to discern. The eighth point of Order no.1 had exempted those troops who had participated in the March Revolution from further service at the front, and unsurprisingly, it was these men who called loudest for no renewed action. Officers at the front were quick to point out this refusal to heed the provisional government's call to arms, but their warnings were unheeded.

Planning for the Kerensky Offensive, the last great Russian attack of the war, followed similar lines to those of the Brusilov campaign of 1916 in eastern Galicia, although the lack of reliable forces restricted it to two main thrusts. Brusilov took command of the Seventh and Eleventh Armies, which were to attack the Austro-German South Army under General Felix von Bothmer along a 40-mile (64 km) front around Brody. The offensive was launched on July 1, following a two-day bombardment. It made rapid gains, forcing the

▲ *In 1917 the eastern front saw the Russians launch their last attack of the war—the Kerensky Offensive.*

line. Desertion then became endemic throughout the ranks. To the southwest General Lavrenti Kornilov's Russian Eighth Army attacked along a 60-mile (96 km) front south of the Dniester River on July 6, and by the 12th some units had advanced 20 miles (32 km) and were within reach of some important oil fields. However, the strain was beginning to tell, and Kornilov began to suffer familiar problems. On July 16, with his armies in disarray, Brusilov halted the offensive. Russian troops were abandoning their positions and streaming to the rear in growing numbers. Brusilov was later sacked and replaced by Kornilov.

By this time fully reinforced, on July 19 Bothmer's South Army counterattacked the Russians. For seven hours prior to the assault, German artillery hammered away at Brusilov's right wing, and it was here that the advancing infantry overwhelmed the Russian troops. Attacks on the central and southern sectors of the Russian line followed in quick succession.

On the first day of the battle alone, Bothmer's forces advanced 10 miles (16 km), and soon no Russian forces existed south of the Pripet Marshes. In the next three weeks the Russian retreat turned into a rout. The front stabilized during early August, largely due to the fact that the Germans lacked

South Army back toward Lemberg. Low morale, poor supply lines, and the rapid arrival of German reserves soon slowed the advance. The leading units, feeling they had sacrificed enough, refused to persevere with the attacks, while those to the rear refused to come up to the

sufficient troop reserves, supplies, and adequate transport to allow them to continue their pursuit. Nevertheless, Austro-Hungarian and German forces had recrossed the Galician frontier on either side of the Dniester and reached Czernowitz by the 3rd.

At home in Russia things were even less encouraging. Between March and October 1917 the provisional government was reorganized four times. The first government was composed entirely of liberal ministers, with the exception of Kerensky, and subsequent governments were weak coalitions of rival political factions. None of them was able to cope adequately with the major problems then afflicting the country. Furthermore, the power of the government was increasingly threatened by the growing number of soviets. Based on the Petrograd model and in far closer contact with the sentiments of the people than the government, soviets had been organized in all of the country's cities and major towns and in the armed forces. In these soviets, antiwar sentiment favoring Russian withdrawal from the conflict on almost any terms was rife, partly because of the increasing domination of the soviets by radical socialist factions. Attending the First All-Russian Congress of Soviets, convened

on June 16, the Socialist Revolutionaries were the largest single bloc, followed by the Mensheviks and Bolsheviks.

Kerensky replaced Lvov as head of the provisional government in July. On the 16th, units of the Petrograd garrison rose up against the government in protest at an order to return to the front. Fomented by the antiwar Bolsheviks, the revolt spread to sailors at Kronstadt naval base and civilians in towns all over Russia, but Kerensky found sufficient loyal troops to regain order. In the aftermath key Bolshevik leaders were imprisoned and the movement temporarily suppressed, although Lenin was able to escape to Finland. However, the episode did much to improve the Bolsheviks' standing with the increasingly pacifist populace and further undermined the government.

Increasingly unable to halt Russia's slide into political, economic, and military chaos, Kerensky's party suffered a major split as the left wing broke from the Socialist Revolutionary Party. Yet while the provisional government's power waned, that of the soviets was increasing, as was the Bolsheviks' influence within them. By September the Bolsheviks and their allies, the Left Socialist Revolutionaries, had overtaken the Socialist Revolutionaries and Mensheviks and held majorities in both the Petrograd and Moscow soviets.

Russia's final collapse

Although these political events indicated that Russia was heading for a second revolution, it was the increasing unwillingness of the armed forces to continue the fight that was the chief cause of its outbreak. The failure of the Kerensky Offensive had sapped the will of even those Russian soldiers who had remained loyal to the cause and resisted the temptation to desert. Germany sought to exploit these circumstances to the full and launched an offensive in the northern sector of the front that aimed to clear the salient in the line

▼ *A lone soldier loyal to the Russian provisional government attempts to use force to return deserters to their positions. However, the initial trickle of deserters would soon turn into a torrent, signaling the collapse of the Russian Army and the effective end of the country's military role in the war.*

west of Riga forced by the Battle of the Aa River. Capturing territory around Riga would herald the prospect of a German attack on Petrograd itself and force the Russians to sue for peace. The final Russo-German engagement of the war on the eastern front could begin.

On the west bank of the Dvina River, General Oskar von Hutier's well-trained and fully equipped German Eighth Army was opposed by the Russian Twelfth Army under Kornilov, who, forewarned of the arrival of German reinforcements from Galicia, had already made arrangements to retreat. On September 1, along a short 5-mile (8 km) front south of Riga, the main body of the German force attacked. Hutier had devised a new set of tactics for the offensive. Surprise was achieved by dispensing with a long preliminary artillery bombardment in favor of a short barrage. As soon as the barrage ended, assault troops rushed forward and advanced behind the Russian front line. Russian strongpoints were to be mopped up by following waves of troops. The tactics, later named after Hutier, proved wholly successful, and would later be applied on the western and Italian fronts.

To the north three German divisions crossed the river on pontoons and rapidly gained a bridgehead. The Riga fortress was encircled and captured with minimal casualties on September 2, as the Russian defenders streamed eastward in disarray. In the Gulf of Riga, German assault forces took Osel and Dagö islands. The remnants of the Russian Twelfth Army were pursued along the Dvina River for three weeks, but the planned German march on Petrograd was abandoned as the imminent collapse of the provisional government effectively ended Russian military operations on the eastern front.

As Hutier's offensive continued, unrest was spreading across Russia. One after another the numerous non-Russian peoples of the former empire were demanding autonomy or independence from Russia, either spontaneously or at the prompting of the German authorities

▲ *German troops sheltering along a railroad prepare to advance against crumbling Russian positions on the eastern front toward the end of 1917.*

357

Germany's Storm Troopers

In September 1917, during the fighting outside Riga, German General Oskar von Hutier pioneered the use of infiltration tactics to break through entrenched Russian positions. The German victory suggested that he had discovered a "magic formula," which might herald the end of the stagnation of trench warfare.

The new tactic represented a radical departure from standard military doctrine at that time. Instead of a long preliminary bombardment (which often warned an enemy of a forthcoming offensive) followed by a massed infantry rush at the enemy's forward trenches, small infantry units whose ranks were filled with specially trained troops known as storm troopers infiltrated between enemy strong points after these had been hit by a short "hurricane"

▶ *German storm troopers move into position prior to the opening of their large-scale spring 1918 offensive on the western front.*

◀ *General Oskar von Hutier (left) was the architect of storm-trooper tactics, first put to the test on the eastern front in 1917. The operation was wholly successful.*

barrage of smoke and gas shells designed to mask the advance of the storm troopers. The strong points were not attacked directly by the storm troopers but left to follow-on forces. The storm troopers were tasked with driving deeper and deeper into the enemy-held territory, attacking artillery positions, command posts, and so on. The idea was to keep the enemy off balance and make it difficult for it to formulate a response.

Although storm troopers received special training to hone their new skills, much of their equipment was standard. However, they tended to carry more grenades than regular soldiers and advanced with light artillery and mortars. In the final months of the war, some men were equipped with the world's

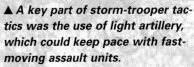

▲ *A key part of storm-trooper tactics was the use of light artillery, which could keep pace with fast-moving assault units.*

first practical submachine gun, the Bergmann 18/1, which greatly enhanced their firepower. However, the key assets of the storm troopers on the battlefield were speed of movement, flexibility, and initiative.

Nevertheless, infiltration tactics brought their own problems, not the least of these being the need to keep the swiftly advancing storm troopers supplied with ammunition and the like. This problem often overtaxed the means of the German supply services, and although the storm troopers could make use of captured supplies, this ploy was too chancy and unreliable. During the Battle of Caporetto, for example, storm troopers broke through the Italian front and advanced a distance of 60 miles (96 km), but problems of resupply prevented them from capitalizing on their initial gains. Equally problematic was the gradual exhaustion of the men who filled the ranks of the storm-trooper units.

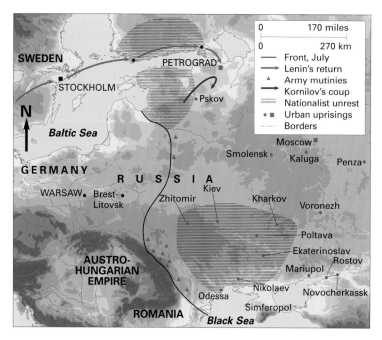

occupying their countries. Finns, Estonians, Latvians, Lithuanians, and Poles were, by the end of 1917, all in various stages of revolutionary activity. At the same time, Ukrainians, Georgians, Armenians, and Azerbaijanis were also actively promoting their own nationalist demands. If this was not bad enough, the provisional government's authority and influence were fading away in Russia proper during the late summer and fall of 1917. Kornilov, returning to Petrograd from Riga and removed from his post as commander in chief, launched a coup on September 9. This was defeated by pro-Bolshevik forces, who were requested to block Kornilov by Kerensky.

Through the summer and early fall the Bolshevik political program of "peace, land, and bread" had won the party considerable support among Russia's hungry urban workers and disillusioned soldiers. On November 6 and 7 the Bolsheviks and Left Socialist Revolutionaries staged a nearly bloodless coup, occupying government buildings, telegraph stations, and numerous other strategic positions within the city of Petrograd. Kerensky's attempt to

▲ *Russia is rent by revolutionary turmoil during 1917. Revolution ended Russia's part in the war.*

organize resistance proved futile, and he fled the country. The Second All-Russian Congress of Soviets, which convened in Petrograd simultaneously with the coup, approved the formation of a new government, which consisted mainly of Bolsheviks under the leadership of Lenin, who had returned from hiding in Finland on October 23.

The November Revolution effectively heralded the end of Russia's participation in the war. It was Lenin's decree of November 8 that undermined the eastern front by provoking a homeward rush of soldiers anxious to profit from the expropriation of land from their former landlords. Also on that same day, Lenin issued his decree on peace, offering negotiations to all belligerents but precluding annexations and stipulating a right of self-determination for all peoples concerned. On November 26, the new Bolshevik government unilaterally ordered a cessation of hostilities against the Central Powers.

An armistice between revolutionary Russia and the Central Powers was signed at Brest-Litovsk on December 15.

The peace negotiations were complicated and protracted. On the one hand, Germany wanted peace in the east in order to transfer troops to the western front, but it was at the same time concerned to exploit the principle of national self-determination in order to control as much territory as possible. On the other hand, the Bolshevik negotiating team wanted peace quickly in order to be free to consolidate their shaky new regime in Russia, which was beset by revolts and nationalist independence movements, but they were also aware of Germany's desire to foment nationalist uprisings against the Bolsheviks. The Bolshevik strategy was to drag discussions out for as long as they possibly could, thereby giving them the time to crush the nationalist risings in Russia. The Germans, who were very anxious to make peace quickly, became increasingly frustrated as the peace talks dragged on into 1918, and they moved toward the threat of renewed hostilities in order to try to force the Bolsheviks into signing a brutal peace treaty.

▼ *The German military delegation to the Brest-Litovsk armistice talks in December 1917 greets the Bolshevik party on its arrival. The new head of the Russian team, Leon Trotsky, stands in the center of the photograph. He replaced Adolf Ioffe, the previous leader, after the talks had bogged down.*

War in the Balkans

Although the war on the eastern front and the political turmoil in Russia dominated the thoughts of the Allied leadership throughout 1917, events in the Balkans were also giving some cause for concern. The French-led Army of the Orient under General Maurice Sarrail, who was given overall command of the Allied forces operating in Greece and the southern Balkans in January 1917, was faced with several problems—not least because the front was stalemated. Sarrail's polyglot army, a mixture of British, French, Russian, and Serbian troops, faced a combined Austro-Hungarian, Bulgarian, and German force that, although it was comparatively small, was still efficient. However, Sarrail faced greater problems. First, his own force—some 600,000 men on paper—was severely reduced by disease. Estimates suggest that just 100,000 were fit for service.

More important, Sarrail led an army that was based in Greece, yet Greece was not at war with the Central Powers. The country's ruler, King Constantine I, had married Princess Sophia of Prussia, making him Emperor Wilhelm II's brother-in-law, and he was decidedly pro-German in outlook. However, many prominent figures supported the Allies, not least the former prime minister Eleuthérios Venizélos. Venizélos had lost and regained his position on several previous occasions but became the focal point for those opposed to the king's support of the Central Powers. He had been exiled for his views though, first to Crete and then Salonika.

By mid-1916 Greece was in a state of virtual civil war, and Venizélos established a provisional government, one backed by the Allies. Over the following months the Allies used diplomatic pressure and military power, not least a naval blockade of the Greek mainland, to force Constantine's abdication. This feat was accomplished by June 12, 1917, when the king fled to Switzerland a day

Poland and Independence

Poland had ceased to be an independent state in the late eighteenth century, and in 1914 most of the country was a province of Russia, with the exception of Galicia, which was controlled by the Austro-Hungarian Empire, and Silesia, Posen, and West Russia, which were ruled by Germany.

At the outbreak of World War I, Polish nationalist movements, although strongly supported by ordinary Poles, were divided on the best way to achieve independence. The

◄ *Polish refugees flee the fighting in their country. Many hoped to gain independence from Russia, Austria-Hungary, and Germany.*

◀ *Members of the Polish Council of Regency depart the meeting that saw their appointment, October 15, 1917.*

Early in the war, Poland was devastated in a series of campaigns. By fall 1915 Russian Poland was occupied by Germany, and Dmowski was forced into exile. On November 5, 1916, Austria-Hungary and Germany announced the creation of a Polish state, governed by a council of state but firmly under their protection. They saw Poland (and its potential armed forces) as a useful ally in the ongoing war with Russia. This attitude far from satisfied the nationalists, who recognized that Poland would be little more than a puppet of its powerful neighbors. Relations between the Poles and the Central Powers deteriorated through 1917. Pilsudski, commander of the Polish Auxiliary Corps, refused to swear an oath of allegiance to Austria-Hungary and Germany in March and was arrested on July 30. The council of state resigned at the end of July, and a German governor was appointed.

In November 1918 Pilsudski was released and returned to Poland, which was ruled by a German-controlled and ineffective council of regency. On the 14th the council resigned, leaving Pilsudski in charge. Poland's independence was far from secure, although it was to be recognized by the Treaty of Versailles. The main threat, however, lay with Russia. Its leadership planned to export the revolution westward and to reincorporate Poland into Russia. The plan was a recipe for war.

war was seen as offering the possibility of a new Polish state, but Poland was likely to gain autonomy only by joining the Central Powers or by siding with their opponents, chiefly Russia.

Most prominent of the Polish nationalist leaders were Roman Dmowski, of the National Democratic Party in Galicia, who supported the Allies, and Józef Pilsudski, who built a private army in Galicia with the aim of liberating Poland from the Russians with the help of the Central Powers. Poles fought for both the Central Powers and the Allies. Pilsudski was one commander of a force known as the Polish Legions, which was ultimately subject to Austro-Hungarian military authority.

after the Allies had delivered a firm ultimatum demanding his removal. The king was replaced by his second son, Alexander, despite a last-ditch attempt to replace Constantine with the equally pro–Central Power Crown Prince Paul. All of this scheming came to nothing. On June 26, 1916, Venizélos returned to Athens, where he established a new pro-Allied government. Three days later, war was declared on the Central Powers, although the Greek forces were beset with factional infighting over the following months. The expansion of the country's armed forces was slow, not least because of mutinies, but by 1918 250,000 Greek troops were able to support the Allies in the Balkan campaign.

While civil unrest engulfed Greece in the second half of 1916, Sarrail began preparations for a new offensive all along the line for the spring of 1917, mirroring the previous fall's abortive drive into Serbia. He was backed by many Allied politicians, who saw it as a useful opportunity to divert German attention from the forthcoming Nivelle Offensive on the western front. Nivelle's attack was to begin early in April, and an attack in the Balkans prior to its opening might lead to German units being withdrawn from the western front to meet the threat.

However, the German, Bulgarian, and Turkish troops opposing Sarrail's force

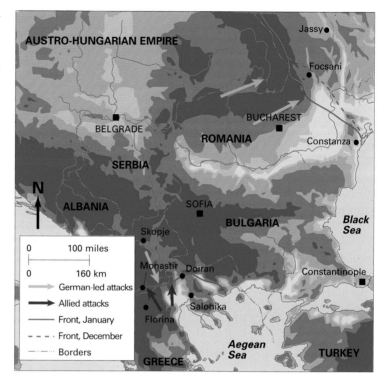

▲ *During 1917 the fighting in the Balkans was stalemated in the Salonika theater.*

▼ *Bulgarian troops in Macedonia enjoy a hot meal in their trench.*

in the southern Balkans still held positions that overlooked the narrow valleys along which the Allied forces would have to advance. Operations began on March 11, when French and Serbian forces began a drive north between Monastir and Lake Prespa. To the east, in the Lake Doiran sector, General George Milne's British force attacked the next day, but the various Allied units were still poorly coordinated, and the

planned attacks in the center of the line were delayed. German reconnaissance aircraft spotted the buildup, and the advances were checked within a week by rapid but scanty reinforcement. The Allies suffered 14,000 casualties, many of them lost to sickness.

German counterattacks in the west forced the French and Serbians back to the outskirts of Monastir by March 19, and Sarrail called off all of the attacks. Offensive action was resumed in the Doiran sector on April 24 and again in early May, coinciding with an inconclusive action on the Vardar River, but the failure of these actions forced the abandonment of the Allied offensive. Little had actually been gained. Throughout the botched campaign, the Allied forces had been harried by the aircraft of the German Army Air Service, which enjoyed almost complete domination of the skies. For the rest of 1917, the battlefront stagnated. The only other development of note, one that was to greatly improve the fortunes of the Allies in 1918, was the replacement of Sarrail by General Marie Guillaumat on December 10. Guillaumat, who had gained an excellent reputation on the western front, did a great deal to improve Allied relations in the Balkan theater and set about planning a major offensive for 1918.

Romania collapses

If the fighting had been inconclusive in the far south of the Balkans in 1917, matters were much more serious a little farther to the north. Romania had believed that by declaring war on the Central Powers in August 1916, it could exploit the recent Russian success on the eastern front to achieve national unification and capture coveted tracts of Austria-Hungary. It was a false hope. The country was invaded by the Central Powers in September 1916, and vast swathes of territory had been surrendered by early December, including the capital, Bucharest. The Romanian

government, led by King Ferdinand, was left in control of a small portion of the country, centered on the town of Jassy in the northeast. Russian troops moved into the region to bolster the Romanian defenses. Over the following few months Romania was stripped of raw materials, cereals, and over 250,000 head of livestock by the Central Powers. Romania's oil fields around Ploesti also helped to fuel their war effort.

During 1917 King Ferdinand tried to defend his country with the remnants of his army and the Russian forces that had come to his aid. Recruitment of new troops was very difficult, and Ferdinand had to promise extended suffrage and limited land reform as an incentive. By July Ferdinand had assembled sufficient strength to go on the offensive, but this planned operation was doomed by the unrest in Russia and the collapse of its armed forces.

This failure sealed Ferdinand's fate—he resigned as head of the armed forces and was replaced by General Constantine Prezan. The prime minister, Ion Bratianu, agreed to an armistice with Germany on the 9th and then resigned. A final peace treaty followed in May 1918.

▲ *A Turkish mounted unit patrols the country's border with Greece, which finally edged toward outright support for the Allies in 1917.*

The Wider War, 1917

During the second half of 1917 the French forces on the western front were ravaged by mutiny, Russia was raked by political unrest and seemed likely to desert the Allies, and the British forces were suffering horrendous losses at the Third Battle of Ypres, better known as Passchendaele. It seemed to some that outright victory was not going to be won in the European theater. A number of British politicians saw Turkey as the best source for some major morale-boosting news. The weakest of all the Central Powers, Turkey's forces were spread thinly across much of the Middle East. It had little support from its European allies, chiefly Germany, and the Turkish provinces of Palestine and Mesopotamia, where there were buildups of mostly British forces, offered the Allies some hope of significant progress.

The Allies were desperate to win victories overseas to convince their disenchanted civilian populations that the war could be won quickly and at little further cost in lives.

The fight for Palestine

General Archibald Murray's British command in Egypt, depleted during mid-1916 as troops were recalled to the western front to fight along the Somme River, successfully defended the Suez Canal in August and spent the remainder of the year preparing for a major advance across the Sinai Peninsula into Turkish-controlled Palestine. Later, in December, General Philip Chetwode's Desert Column occupied El Arish, some 60 miles (100 km) along the coast, and from there menaced Turkish positions in Palestine. In late December and into

▼ *A British howitzer opens fire on Turkish forces on the Sinai Peninsula in early 1917.*

the new year, pockets of Turkish resistance were eliminated. By January 9, 1917, the peninsula had been cleared.

With Sinai secured, Murray began to plan his move against Palestine. By early 1917 he had created a supply route right across the peninsula. Water was the key problem, and despite specially built pipelines, subsequent battles were centered on the capture of water sources and the towns and villages that surrounded them. Murray's valuable, if incomplete, supply route had been built by the Egyptian Labor Corps and included some 220 miles (350 km) of new roads, 360 miles (570 km) of railroad track, and 300 miles (480 km) of water-carrying pipelines. Established in January 1916, when the British hired 10,000 local workers to improve links between Cairo and Sinai, by mid-1917 the corps had grown to 185,000 men.

A further 28,000 Egyptians were employed as drivers and attendants by the Camel Transport Corps, which bore some of the resupply requirements of the advancing British forces beyond the railheads, roads, and pipelines. In addition to his vital supply network, among Murray's most important assets were the aircraft of the Royal Flying Corps' 5th Wing, based at Ismailia at the center of the Suez Canal, and the seaplanes aboard the carriers *Ben-My-Chree*, *Anne*, and *Raven*, which together formed his primary reconnaissance tool.

In the event demands for reinforcements delayed Murray's advance until the spring. By March reinforcements had swollen German General Kress von Kressenstein's Turkish Expeditionary Force to 18,000 men, which included artillery and air detachments. This force was ranged along a new defensive line stretching some 25 miles (40 km) inland from the coastal town of Gaza to Beersheba, thereby blocking the main route into Palestine—its commander had been ordered to hold at all costs. Murray gained permission for an attack on Gaza and concentrated his best forces under General Charles Dobell, whose Eastern Force outnumbered the defenders by nearly two to one. Dobell

▲ *Members of a Turkish cavalry detachment sharpen their weapons. Mounted troops played a much more important role in Palestine than elsewhere. However, their effectiveness depended on the availability of water.*

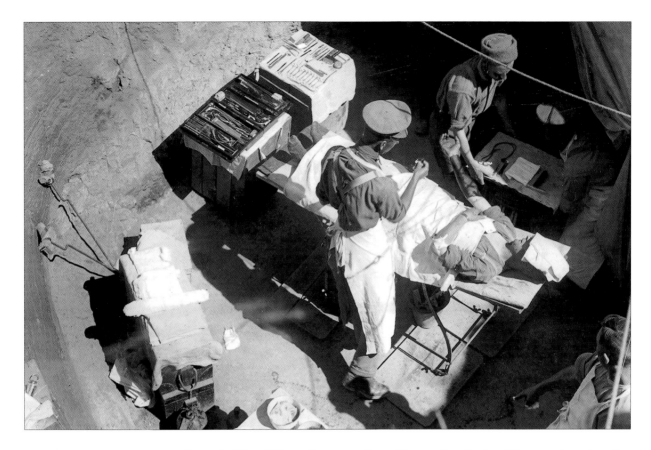

▲ British medical staff remove a bullet from the arm of a soldier wounded by Turkish fire during the fighting in Palestine. Although battle casualties could be heavy, many more men on all sides were incapacitated or killed by a variety of diseases.

massed the bulk of his units near the coast, some 5 miles (8 km) from the heavily defended town.

On March 26, undetected in a dense sea fog, Dobell's cavalry units were able to cut their way through to the rear of the town, but the supporting infantry attack on the southeastern approaches struggled in the difficult terrain. By dusk the infantry had taken control of most of the ridge to the east of the town, and Kressenstein, believing the position lost, prepared to order a retreat. However, during the night Murray, perhaps losing his nerve, recalled his cavalry. The next day a Turkish counterattack fell on the infantry divisions left on the ridge. This move, together with increasing water shortages, forced Dobell to order his men to retreat. The British lost 4,000 men against around 2,400 Turkish and German casualties. Estimating enemy losses at three times that number,

Murray implied to his superiors that the attack, the First Battle of Gaza, had been a success. He was therefore mistakenly encouraged to attack again.

Galvanized by the prospect of a victory in the Middle East and somewhat misled by Murray's unrealistic report, the British sent a company of eight Mark I tanks and 4,000 gas shells to Palestine in support of the next assault on Gaza. Reinforcements had brought Kressenstein's defending forces up to their previous strength, and guessing correctly that the forthcoming British attack would again fall on Gaza, he concentrated his troops and artillery in newly fortified positions that were dotted around the town.

On April 17 British land- and sea-based artillery began shelling the Turkish positions, heralding the Second Battle of Gaza, but the following infantry assault became bogged down in the Turkish defenses. By the end of the first day, no real gains had been made at a cost of 6,500 British casualties. In comparison, Turkish and German losses amounted to some 2,000 men. The next day, once again threatened by dwindling water supplies, Dobell ordered his troops to retreat and entrench along a new line facing the Turkish positions. Here the British forces remained immobile, racked by disease and baked by the sun, until the following fall.

The Second Battle of Gaza had not produced the decisive breakthrough that had been expected and came as a great disappointment to the British government. In June 1917 the British made changes in the theater. General Edmund Allenby, transferred from the command of the Third Army in France, replaced Murray at the head of the British forces in Palestine. General Harry Chauvel was given command of the Desert Mounted Corps, and the infantry divisions were allotted to Chetwode and General Edward Bulfin.

Under orders from the British war leader, David Lloyd George, to take Jerusalem by Christmas, Allenby built up his forces during the summer and early fall, boosting his total strength to more than 80,000 men. Kressenstein's Turkish Seventh and Eighth Armies, despite the arrival of German reinforcements, were outnumbered and reliant on a long and tenuous supply line running along the region's only railroad, which was increasingly being menaced by Arabs who supported the Allies and who sought to gain independence from the Ottoman Empire. Their guerrilla campaign against the Turks stemmed the flow of supplies to Palestine and tied up thousands of Turkish troops.

Although the wider Arab leadership expected to gain their independence thanks to their support for the Allies and create Arab homelands across the whole of the Middle East, they were unaware that the British were secretly agreeing to back the creation of a Jewish state in Palestine. Britain's foreign secretary, Arthur Balfour, revealed as much in November, when he penned a brief note to Baron Rothschild, a prominent supporter of the Zionist cause. The British and French had already secretly carved up much of the Middle East between themselves. In May 1916, they had agreed to the Sykes-Picot pact. Named after the principal negotiators, Britain's Mark Sykes and France's Georges Picot, the pact gave

▼ *This Turkish artillery piece in Palestine was photographed at the precise moment of firing. Many of Turkey's artillery units were equipped with weapons of German manufacture.*

▲ *Although the Allied campaign in Palestine was primarily a British operation, other countries did provide some troops. These men belong to the Italian Detachment in Palestine and are pictured on maneuvers in 1917.*

Britain control of Palestine and much of Mesopotamia, while France would take charge of Syria and Lebanon.

This pact was concealed from the Arabs, who only learned of it when the details were published by the Bolsheviks in Russia late in 1917. The Balfour Declaration and the Sykes-Picot Agreement soured relations between the Arabs and the Allies, yet the war in Palestine, backed by the Arabs, continued.

Turning his attention away from impregnable Gaza, Allenby decided instead to move against Beersheba. Leaving three divisions to hold the northern sector of the front, he planned to launch a surprise attack against Beersheba on October 31. Capture of the town's wells was crucial to the offensive's overall success—without water his troops, particularly the cavalry units, would not be able to push deeper into Palestine. Once they were established at Beersheba, the British forces were under orders to swing northward behind the Turkish defenses in the direction of Gaza.

On the night of October 30, 40,000 British troops moved into position for the attack on Beersheba. Others would make a diversionary attack on Gaza itself, which it was hoped would encourage the Turks to reinforce their right flank at the expense of their left, thereby easing the task for the main British attack. Gaza was also bombarded by French and British warships to strengthen the deception.

The opening phase of the assault on Beersheba began early on the 31st. By late afternoon the British forces had driven the Turks back into the town. At 4:40 P.M. two Australian cavalry units broke through Beersheba's eastern

THE BALFOUR DECLARATION

Arthur Balfour was the British foreign secretary between 1916 and 1919. Although increasingly marginalized in the government by Prime Minister David Lloyd George, he had close links with the Zionist movement, which was lobbying for the creation of a Jewish state in Palestine.

Pressured by two leading Zionists, Chaim Weizmann and Nahum Sokolow, Balfour wrote a note to Baron Lionel Rothschild, head of the British branch of the prominent banking family, on November 2, 1917. The note, popularly known as the Balfour Declaration, offered British support to Zionist efforts to establish a Jewish home in Palestine.

The concluding paragraph of the declaration revealed British intentions. It read: "His majesty's government view with favor the establishment in Palestine of a national home for the Jewish people, and will use its best endeavors to facilitate the achievement of this objective, it being clearly understood that nothing shall be done which may prejudice the civil and religious rights of existing non-Jewish communities in Palestine, or the rights and political status enjoyed by Jews in any other country."

Arthur Balfour (right), author of the declaration named after him, and Britain's prime minister, David Lloyd George.

defenses, from where they turned to attack the town. Although faced with Turkish machine guns, the cavalry was able to gallop through the defenses into Beersheba itself. The Turkish Seventh Army was overrun and forced to retreat before the wells could be destroyed.

On November 6 Allenby launched his main attack northward against the Turkish Eighth Army defending Gaza, and his troops took all of their objectives by midafternoon. That evening the Turks began to retreat, narrowly avoiding capture as the Desert Mounted Corps raced across the country to the sea. When British troops arrived on November 7, Gaza had been abandoned under the orders of General Eric von Falkenhayn, who had arrived as the new commander in the theater on the 5th. In the weeks that followed, the Turks retreated 75 miles (120 km)—the

The Arab Revolt

In June 1916 the native peoples of much of Arabia rose up against their Turkish masters, who had governed the region since the sixteenth century. Waging a hit-and-run guerrilla campaign against the Turks, the Arabs provided invaluable support to the regular Allied forces fighting in Palestine.

The Arab population of Arabia, some six million, was divided between settled and nomadic peoples, and most of them owed allegiance to local sheikhs. The only active Arab independence movement before 1916 was led by Sherif Husein Ibn Ali, controller of much of the Hejaz region along the shores of the Red Sea, an area including the holy cities of Mecca and Medina. His stature made him the focus for Arab nationalism.

The sherif's second son, Abdullah, built close links with the British, leading to the supply of rifles and other military equipment at the beginning of the uprising in spring 1916. On

◄ *T. E. Lawrence, better known as Lawrence of Arabia, was a noted supporter of Arab nationalism and a military adviser to Arab forces fighting the Turks in Arabia.*

June 5 Ali, Husein's eldest son, proclaimed the revolt outside Medina. There then followed successful attacks against local Turkish garrisons. Mecca and Jedda were quickly taken. The last Turkish bastion in Hejaz fell in September.

The Arabs were organized into three groups by late 1916. The Southern Army under Ali was mainly concerned with capturing Medina but also conducted operations farther south into Yemen. The Eastern Army under Abdullah kept a close watch on Ibn Rashid's Shammar tribe of central Arabia, who continued to support the Turks. The most important Arab force was the Northern Army, commanded by the sherif's youngest son, Feisal, and operating in Hejaz.

The British government sent a party to Jedda to review the situation. It included the noted Arab scholar Colonel T. E. Lawrence, later to be known as Lawrence of Arabia. He traveled inland to meet Feisal and returned in November as Feisal's British adviser.

With his encouragement Feisal went over to the offensive in January 1917, raiding Turkish supply lines all over northern Arabia. In July Feisal took the key Turkish-held port of Aqaba, making it his main base.

With the forces under Abdullah and Ali preoccupied elsewhere, Feisal's Northern Army was the revolt's main strike force; he coordinated its advance with the British push into Palestine. More and more Turkish troops had to be committed when Lawrence launched a series of raids in late 1917.

In the spring of 1918 British backing for the revolt was increased. However, relations

▲ *Arab guerrillas head back to their encampment following a raid on a Turkish position or railroad in the Hejaz region of Arabia.*

between Husein and the British cooled when the Arabs discovered details of the Balfour Declaration (see page 371).

As he advanced, Feisal appointed Arab governors in newly conquered territories to prevent the British from installing their own men, but he reluctantly had to accept mandate (that is, foreign controlled) status for Syria, Transjordan, and Lebanon in early October. At the Paris Peace Conference in 1919, Feisal was unable to secure full independence for the Arab nations. Consequently, Arab nationalism and the desire for independence from foreign rule continued to be a strong political force in the Middle East.

Eighth Army along the coastal railroad, and the Seventh by road toward Jerusalem. Allenby's victory at the Third Battle of Gaza wholly transformed the strategic situation in Palestine. The battle had forced the Turks to abandon their main defensive line. Allenby now had Jerusalem in his sights.

The advance on Jerusalem

Falkenhayn had brought with him reinforcements in the shape of the German-Turkish Yilderim (Thunderbolt) force. This had been assembled at Aleppo in Syria during the summer, originally for operations in Mesopotamia. The British successes in Palestine had forced a reappraisal of Germany's strategic priorities in the Middle East, and instead of using the force in Mesopotamia, it was sent to Palestine to reinforce the Turkish units retreating after the Third Battle of Gaza, which by November 10 had established a line 20 miles (32 km) south of the city of Jerusalem.

Falkenhayn launched an immediate counterattack against Allenby's right flank, held by the Australian Mounted Division. However, the Yilderim force, exhausted by its long march to the front, failed to achieve a breakthrough and withdrew toward Jerusalem.

On November 13 Allenby launched a renewed assault on the coastal positions held by Kressenstein's Turkish Eighth Army, sending his infantry to assault a ridge just to the northwest of Junction Station, where the Beersheba railroad joined the Haifa-to-Jerusalem line. The attack faltered in rocky terrain choked with cactus bushes around El Mughar, the highest village on the ridge, but an assault from the north by an 800-strong cavalry force overwhelmed the defenders, and as darkness fell the whole ridge was in British hands. The following morning British armored cars entered Junction Station, cutting communications between the two increasingly isolated Turkish armies and forcing Kressenstein to retreat to positions beyond Jaffa.

The arrival of the Yilderim force gave Allenby cause for concern, however. Fully expecting a major Turkish counterattack against his scattered units, he paused to plan for the advance on Jerusalem. Falkenhayn had established the Turkish defensive line from the coast of the Mediterranean Sea to Jerusalem, where the 15,000 troops of Fehzi Pasha's Seventh Army were guarding the approaches to the city at the end of a fragile supply line. Allenby launched his main attack on the Seventh Army's positions west of Jerusalem and a diversionary advance against Kressenstein's Eighth Army on November 18. Slowed only by heavy rain, the main force turned north on

◄ *A unit of the Desert Mounted Corps advances deep into Palestine as the British push the Turkish forces in the region back toward Jerusalem. The corps, which contained troops from both Australia and New Zealand, proved to be one of the most effective fighting forces in the whole Arabian campaign.*

▼ *British artillery in action on November 12, 1917, at a time when the Turkish forces opposing them in Palestine were being pushed back ever closer to Jerusalem, which was the ultimate objective of the Allied campaign.*

the 21st, aiming to cut the road to Falkenhayn's headquarters at Nablus and surround the city, but it met with strong Turkish resistance. Losses of nearly 50 percent were suffered by both sides in two days of fighting, with neither achieving a significant advantage. The second attack succeeded in preventing reinforcements from being transferred but otherwise failed.

Although he was still awaiting the arrival of much of the Yilderim force from Aleppo, Falkenhayn launched a major counterattack against the thinly guarded British supply lines during the early morning of November 27. However, his forces were unable to break through. To the west a supplementary attack by two Turkish divisions toward the lightly held area inland of the coast made little progress. Both battles quickly degenerated into stalemate over the next few days, allowing Allenby to rush reinforcements to the front.

In driving winter rains the British commander renewed his main attack against Jerusalem on the night of December 7–8. Infantry advanced to the east along the main road and pushed back the Turkish defenders some 5 miles (8 km) before first light. After fierce fighting during the day, the attackers were halted, and operations were suspended to allow a second advance to come up from the south

through Bethlehem. The pause gave the Turkish Eighth Army to the north of Jerusalem, now heavily outnumbered, ample opportunity to retreat toward Nablus and Jericho. That same day, December 9, Jerusalem formally surrendered. Allenby made his triumphant entry, on foot, two days later. As they fell back, the troops of the Turkish Seventh Army were subjected to frequent bombing raids by Royal Flying Corps aircraft. However, Allenby was prevented from consolidating the victory by the rapidly deteriorating weather, which turned the ground into a quagmire and delayed the pursuit north of Jerusalem. His forces moving along the coast, though, were able to send the Turkish Eighth Army into headlong retreat.

By late December the Yilderim force had reached almost full strength, and its troops had swelled the Turkish Seventh Army to nearly 20,000 men. Falkenhayn chose this moment to launch the final offensive of the year, sending his troops against the 33,000 defenders of the Khadase Ridge just north of Jerusalem on the night of December 26–27. They were repulsed,

with both sides suffering about 1,500 casualties, and turned back toward Jericho. Exhaustion and rain then halted operations for the rest of the winter.

The loss of Jerusalem was a huge blow to the prestige of the Ottoman Empire and effectively ended any hope of using the Yilderim force in an offensive role. It also brought to an end Falkenhayn's brief period of command in Palestine. In February 1918 he was sent to Lithuania and replaced by General Otto Liman von Sanders, who had been serving with the Turks in a variety of roles since 1913. Although the fall of Jerusalem was a clear victory for the British, it had been won at considerable cost. Between October and December, 1917, the British forces lost 19,702 men. Nevertheless, they had also advanced many miles, a feat that would not be matched by the Allies on the western front until the second half of 1918.

The struggle for Mesopotamia

By the end of 1916, the British forces in Mesopotamia, previously neglected and demoralized by the surrender of General Charles Townshend's besieged

▲ *Turkish prisoners are marched into captivity during the British advance from Gaza toward Jerusalem in the second half of 1917, a period that marked a total transformation in the fortunes of the Allied forces fighting in Palestine.*

▶ *British general Edmund Allenby and his staff enter Jerusalem on December 11, 1917, thereby marking an end to Turkish dominance of Palestine.*

forces at Kut-el-Amara in April 1916, had been transformed out of all recognition. General Frederick Maude had been promoted from a divisional command in Gallipoli to become commander in Mesopotamia in August 1916. Maude was a meticulous officer and held back from advancing immediately. It was far too hot, and he needed to await reinforcements and build fully functioning supply lines. These projects would take three months to complete.

Maude's staff, originally largely composed of Indian Army officers, was bolstered by the arrival of British Army officers, who were tasked with the wholesale reform of the force's previously chaotic supply system. Under their supervision the facilities at Basra, the vital port through which the British brought in supplies, were expanded. Specially designed supply ships were deployed, shallow in draft to cope with the waters of the Tigris and Euphrates Rivers, which ran northward to the front line. In addition, a light railroad was constructed from Basra, and a metalled road was also built. The British had determined that the logistical problems that had frustrated their campaigns from 1914 through 1916 would not dog any future operations in the theater.

Reinforcements brought the Anglo-Indian strength in Mesopotamia up to 150,000 men by the fall of 1916. The troops were better served by improved medical facilities, which had previously been overwhelmed by widespread outbreaks of sickness and disease. The supply of machine guns, artillery, armored cars, and aircraft was greatly increased. The Royal Flying Corps had provided 24 fighters, which were to prove invaluable for reconnaissance. In contrast the Turks, who employed no more than 2,500 doctors throughout the whole of their armed forces, suffered even worse losses through sickness than did the Allies. The 50,000 men of the Turkish Sixth Army, under Khalil Pasha, were no strangers to such hardships.

By December Maude considered that his forces were ready to march on Kut-el-Amara. Its recapture would be the first step toward the eventual objective—Baghdad. Maude sought and gained permission from his superiors to undertake a limited offensive before the winter rains set in but was warned that he must strive to keep his casualties as low as possible. After the loss of the town the previous April, both sides had reorganized their positions, which straddled the Tigris River outside Kut-el-Amara. The local Turkish commander, Karabekir Bey, was forewarned of the impending British attack and had set his men to work strengthening their trench lines, but his requests for reinforcements were refused.

The British began to bombard his positions from both sides of the river on the night of December 13–14 and followed with an infantry assault on the trenches at Sannayait on their right. Karabekir Bey hastily committed most of his reserves to deal with this threat,

and when the main British assault on the other bank moved forward, it met with little resistance. Spearheaded by cavalry units, the forces on the southern bank were in a position to cross the Tigris and get behind the Turkish trenches at Sannayait on the 15th.

▲ *Turkish troops advance to meet the British thrust along the Tigris and Euphrates Rivers in Mesopotamia. The British defeated them after hard fighting and entered Baghdad, the region's capital, on March 11, 1917.*

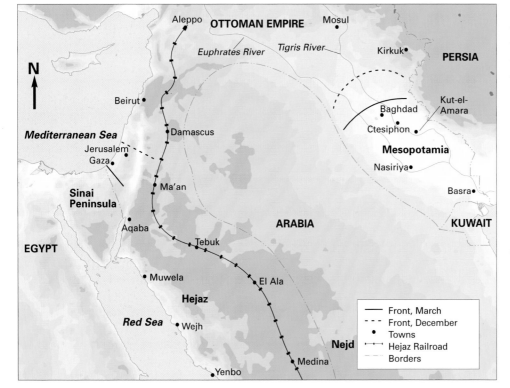

◄ *The fortunes of the British-led forces in the Middle East were transformed in 1917. The previous year had ended in failure and frustration, but 1917 saw a number of severe defeats inflicted on the Turks.*

News of Maude's early successes encouraged the British high command to remove the restraints it had initially placed on his advance, freeing him to assault the main Turkish fortifications defending the high ground of the Khadairi Bend, a tight loop in the Tigris immediately to the north of Kut-el-Amara. The Turkish defenses consisted of two concentric lines of deep trenches, located behind a thinly held line of machine-gun posts. After taking these on December 22, Maude's engineers began to dig short trenches directly toward the main Turkish positions. By January 7, 1917, they were within a few hundred yards of the eastern sector of the Turkish defenses.

Over the next two days, the British launched diversionary attacks at several points, while the Turkish trenches at the mouth of the Khadairi Bend suffered heavy artillery bombardment. On the 9th the British infantry finally went forward. The Turks mounted two strong counterattacks, which were ravaged by British artillery fire. The Turks were pushed back toward the river. By the end of the month, the position was in British hands, and Maude was able to look over the Turkish strongpoints on the opposite bank of the Tigris.

While the fighting at the Khadairi Bend was still raging, other units of Maude's command had attacked and taken the Turkish strongpoint south of Kut-el-Amara on January 15, at the only place were it was possible to ford the Shatt-al-Hai River, before flooding on January 16 prevented any further moves around Kut-el-Amara.

On February 17 Maude attacked again at Sannayait, to the north of the Tigris, forcing Khalil Pasha to abandon plans for an offensive drive through Persia to the Gulf, and began meticulous preparations for the final assault on Kut-el-Amara. Maude aimed to cross the river from the west bank behind the town and cut the Turkish line of retreat.

The final blow against Kut-el-Amara was delivered on the 23rd, when Anglo-Indian forces crossed the river via a pontoon bridge to deliver a frontal attack. The crossing achieved initial surprise but was held up by a skillfully managed Turkish rearguard action. The town fell two days later, but most of the

▼ *A British gunboat on the Tigris River outside Kut-el-Amara opens fire on Turkish positions in December 1917. These shallow-draft vessels were a valuable addition to the force's firepower.*

Turkish garrison was able to escape Maude's attempt at encirclement and retreat toward Baghdad. Pursuing the Turkish Sixth Army along the road to Baghdad, Anglo-Indian cavalry ran into several Turkish machine-gun emplacements. Armored cars had to be brought up, marking the successful operational debut of this weapon in Mesopotamia. The British advance resumed until Maude eventually called a halt some 45 miles (72 km) short of Baghdad.

The forces available to Khalil Pasha for the defense of Baghdad amounted to about 12,300 men—10,000 from the city's garrison and the 2,300 survivors of the retreat from Kut-el-Amara. Troops recalled from operations in Persia, where they were attempting to undermine British and Russian authority, were not yet available. Khalil was faced with the choice of either abandoning the city in the face of the far stronger British or attempting to hold the line at Ctesiphon, where the British had been halted in November 1915. He opted to hold Ctesiphon, but after beginning work on fortifications around the ancient ruins, decided to hold Baghdad itself, placing defenses along the Diyala River and on either side of the Tigris, some 20 miles (32 km) from the city.

These new positions were incomplete when the Anglo-Indian forces arrived at the Diyala River on March 8. Attempts to establish a bridgehead across the rain-swollen river failed, and Maude switched the main body of his attack to the southwest, sending his troops across the Tigris to attack the weaker Turkish positions there. Khalil sent the bulk of his force to meet them and so left just one understrength unit to hold the Diyala. These positions, the last before Baghdad, were overrun by the British on the 10th. The city was abandoned, and the British entered the next day.

Khalil's forces still represented a threat to Baghdad, particularly if they were allowed to link up with Ali Ishan Bey's 15,000 men retreating from

▲ *One of the highpoints of the campaign against the Turks in Mesopotamia in 1917 was the recapture of Kut-el-Amara in late February. Here, local residents look on as their town is reoccupied.*

Persia. Maude elected to launch a limited attack up the Tigris to seize the railhead at Samarrah, along with holding operations in the west, to prevent the Turks from flooding the Euphrates River, and northeast, to block Ali Ishan. Turkish and Anglo-Indian forces fought a series of battles up the Tigris. By April 21 the Turkish troops had retreated to a ridge less than 10 miles (16 km) from Samarra, but the arrival of strong British reinforcements convinced the local commander to abandon the town early on the 23rd.

Ali Ishan Bey's Turkish XIII Corps, which had defeated a British force sent to intercept him at Jebel Hamrin, was then harassed by two British infantry brigades and forced to retreat into the mountainous country. Pursued by British cavalry, he left a small force to occupy them and marched to Dahuba, where he fought a small engagement on April 30 and then disappeared into the mountains in order to regroup. Having lost 18,000 men in battle since mid-March and almost twice that number to sickness, Maude also took the opportunity to pause and consolidate. During the summer months the heat prevented any offensive actions by either side.

On September 27 and 28 another British offensive opened with attacks on all three fronts, prompted by fears that the Yilderim force was about to join the action. Maude turned northwest, along the Euphrates River, aiming at the oil fields of Mosul. The fall of Ramadi on the Euphrates about 60 miles (96 km) to the west of Baghdad effectively secured the city, and in November the main Turkish force in Mesopotamia was driven from Tikrit, on the Tigris midway between Baghdad and Mosul. However, Maude, having transformed the campaign from one of stalemate to one of victory, died on November 18 of cholera contracted from contaminated milk. His successor was General William Marshall, whose last offensive action of the year, an advance up the Diyala, failed in its objective of dealing with Ali Ishan's elusive forces. It was clear, though, that Turkish control of the region was virtually extinguished.

War in East Africa

In East Africa, despite growing supply and equipment problems, General von Lettow-Vorbeck's small German colonial force continued to evade the larger Allied force. After the recall of General Jan Christiaan Smuts, the overall director of operations in the theater, to London early in the year, General A. R. Hoskins took charge. The devastation wrought on his European and Indian troops by disease and sickness had to some extent been alleviated by the deployment of locally raised units and the arrival of West Indian troops, but Hoskins was unable to deliver the quick victory that Smuts had promised and was replaced by South African general Jacob van Deventer in May.

By this time the British forces, including the 35,000-strong King's African Rifles and several units of Rhodesian and South African volunteers, were being harassed by a breakaway group of German troops. The small force, which included 700 askaris (local forces), about 15 Germans, several hundred bearers, and three field guns, marched north into British-held territory, and for the next eight months the Germans remained at large, evading the 4,000 troops that were eventually deployed to try to catch them. After a 2,000-mile (3,200 km) pursuit the German forces were finally surrounded by the British and compelled to surrender.

Few actions were fought through the hot summer months, but during September Deventer sent strong British columns south and southwest from the coast with the intention of attacking the main German force. Although he temporarily halted the British some 50 miles (80 km) inland, Lettow-Vorbeck was finally forced to retreat into Portuguese East Africa (Mozambique) in late November. In this region he found plentiful supplies of food and then embarked on a grueling trek in

▼ *Further good news for the British in Mesopotamia came with the capture of Baghdad on March 11, 1917. A British infantry regiment parades down one of the city's main streets to complete the occupation, watched by a crowd of locals.*

the face of pursuing Allied forces, a trek that would not bring him and his small band of troops back into Allied-occupied East Africa until September 1918.

The Italian front

Repeated attempts to break through the strong Austro-Hungarian positions along the mountainous Isonzo River in northeast Italy during 1915 and 1916 had steadily weakened the Italian Army. Its commander in chief, General Luigi Cadorna, had relied on large-scale frontal attacks, which resulted in very few gains for the loss of large numbers of his trained officers and experienced soldiers. With morale low and a growing number of desertions, Cadorna authorized numerous executions of his soldiers to counter the growing problem of what he saw as cowardice. However, morale among the Austro-Hungarians was little better. Their casualties had been almost as high, and there was growing unrest among the various ethnic groups that filled the ranks of the armed forces. The commander in chief, General Conrad von Hötzendorf, was replaced by General Arthur Arz von Straussenberg on March 1, 1917, on the orders of the new Austro-Hungarian ruler, Emperor Charles I.

Another Italian assault along the Isonzo River in May and June, the 10th such by Cadorna, won very little ground. However, an offensive which lasted from August 17 to September 12 proved more successful. General Luigi Capello's Italian Second Army captured much of the Bainsizza Plateau, north of the border town of Gorizia. In reality it was a small gain, but the Italian success alarmed the Austro-Hungarians, who seemed closer than ever to total collapse. In order to avert such an event, Germany's military planners sent several divisions to reinforce the Isonzo position. They formed part of the joint Austro-German Fourteenth Army commanded by German General Otto von Below. The Fourteenth Army underwent

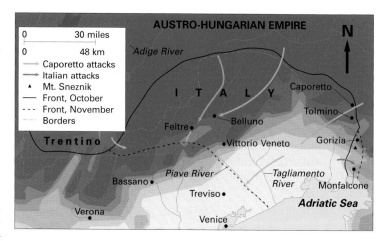

intensive training in the tactics of mountain warfare, and a battle plan was drawn up by a German expert in such specialist tactical methods—General Konrad Krafft von Delmensingen.

The German-led offensive, known as the Twelfth Battle of the Isonzo or the Battle of Caporetto, was boldly planned, very ably organized, and well executed. Although the Italians had more troops holding the Isonzo, their opponents had a numerical advantage at the focal point of their attack—the high ground around the town of Caporetto. On October 24 Below's Austro-German Fourteenth Army led the offensive. The Italian Second Army under Capello bore the brunt of the German-led onslaught and rapidly collapsed.

Under threat on both its northern and southern flanks, Capello's army fell back in confusion, leaving a huge gap in the Italian front, through which poured the advancing Fourteenth Army. Italian units elsewhere were likewise forced to withdraw to avoid being encircled. The pace of the Austro-German offensive was maintained. Below's force had reached Udine, the former site of the Italian general headquarters, by October 28 and was on the Tagliamento River by the 31st.

However, Below's great success had far exceeded the hopes of the planners of the offensive, and the Germans could not exploit their speedy advance as

▲ The stalemate on the Italian front was temporarily broken in October 1917 with the opening of the German-planned and superbly executed Battle of Caporetto.

▼ Italian prisoners hurry into captivity during the Battle of Caporetto, while behind them German troops maintain the momentum of their rapid advance.

EYEWITNESS

ERWIN ROMMEL

Although better known as one of Nazi Germany's most outstanding commanders during World War II, Rommel also took part in World War I as an officer in one of the German Army's units that specialized in mountain warfare. In October 1917 he took part in the Battle of Caporetto, in which he and his men seized a key Italian position:

"With the feeling of being forced to act before the adversary decided to do something, I left the edge of the forest and, walking steadily forward, demanded, by calling and waving my handkerchief, that the enemy surrender and lay down their weapons. The mass of men stared at me and did not move. I was about 100 yards [90 m] from the edge of the woods, and a retreat under enemy fire was impossible. I had the impression that I must not stand still or we were lost.

"I came to within 150 yards [125 m] of the enemy. Suddenly the mass began to move and, in the ensuing panic, swept its resisting officers along downhill. Most of the soldiers threw their weapons away and hundreds hurried to me. In an instant, I was surrounded and hoisted on Italian shoulders. 'Eviva Germania' [Long Live Germany] sounded from 1,000 throats. An Italian officer who hesitated to surrender was shot down by his own troops. For the Italians on Mrzli peak the war was over. They shouted with joy."

Extract taken from Rommel's book Infantry Tactics, *first published in 1937.*

effectively as they wished because it proved difficult for vital supplies and equipment to keep up with Below's lightning advance across the mountainous terrain. Cadorna was able to rally his remaining 300,000 troops behind the Piave River by November 12, but there was no way of hiding the scale of the defeat. The Italians had suffered some 40,000 men killed and wounded, with 275,000 troops taken prisoner. German and Austro-Hungarian casualties were about 20,000 men.

Caporetto sealed the fate of Cadorna. Although he had done well to form a new defensive line along the Piave River, he was replaced by General Armando Diaz on November 7, before the battle officially ended. Diaz managed to hold the Piave front against direct assaults and against attempts to turn its left flank by an advance from the Trentino region to the north. The Italians were strengthened by the arrival of British and French units that had been rushed south from the western front.

Although Caporetto was undoubtedly a disaster for Italy—and the Allies as a whole—it did have one beneficial consequence. It was clear that the Allies needed a powerful body to fully coordinate their actions against the Central Powers. A conference of the military and political leaders of the Allies was held at Rapallo in northern Italy in early November, chiefly to develop a response to Caporetto, but out of this conference came the joint Supreme War Council (see page 346).

As 1917 ended, the Allies were clearly in the ascendancy across the Middle East and in East Africa and had stabilized the situation in Italy. However, there were some senior military figures who argued strongly that these war theaters were merely sideshows, unimportant campaigns against small German forces or Germany's weaker allies, which were using troops that could be more profitably deployed elsewhere.

They stressed that the war could only be won by defeating the main German force on the western front and that any major diversion of troops away from this theater was a misuse of resources. They also argued that the U.S. forces flooding into Europe had to be concentrated along the western front. The German high command had also reached a similar conclusion. It planned to use troops freed from the eastern front following the collapse of Russia in an all-out offensive timed to win the war before U.S. forces could influence its outcome.

The War at Sea, 1917

By the beginning of 1917, the major naval engagement of the war, the Battle of Jutland in 1916, had already been fought, and it had confirmed that Germany's main fleet had to be kept intact by avoiding any such risky ventures in future. Although he had sunk more British warships than he had lost at Jutland, the commander of Germany's High Seas Fleet, Admiral Reinhard Scheer, recognized that his surface warships could not directly challenge Britain's Home Fleet. Consequently his battleships were largely withdrawn from operations in the North Sea. For the remainder of the conflict, activity in the North Sea chiefly focused on smaller forces—cruisers, destroyers, and torpedo boats. The order to avoid risking the battleships was given by Germany's emperor, Kaiser Wilhelm II, who feared the repercussions of a decisive Allied naval victory, and

By 1917, the naval war was delicately balanced. German submarines were inflicting heavy losses on the Allies, but they had bottled up the main German surface fleet.

▶ *Four oilskin-clad crewmen prepare a deck gun aboard a U-boat. Coming to the surface to use such a weapon left the submarine highly exposed to damaging enemy counterfire, but it was often the preferred method of attack—especially against unarmed merchant vessels.*

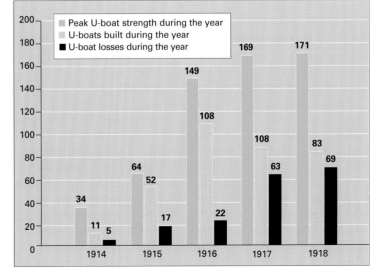

◀ *German torpedo boats confined to harbor in March 1917. Only Germany's largest fleet vessels remained totally confined to port in the face of the Allied blockade. Light forces like these were often used for raids in the English Channel and North Sea.*

▼ *This chart indicates the changes in strength of the German U-boat fleet between 1914 and 1918. The overall picture is of a rise in the yearly total available but also a gradual rise in losses, which grew following the introduction of convoys by the Allies in 1917.*

thereafter Germany's navy fell into decline and then into open mutiny during the final weeks of the war.

Although much of the surface fleet remained inactive, Germany's submarines posed a continuing threat, chiefly through their increasingly successful attacks on merchant ships supplying the Allies. By 1917 the German submarine arm, numbering only 111 boats, had achieved results out of all proportion to its size and was sinking about 300,000 tons of Allied shipping each month. However, submarine captains were operating under certain constraints that limited their actions. Admiral Henning von Holtzendorff, commander of the High Seas Fleet from 1909 and head of the naval general staff from spring 1915, was already a convert to the strategy of unrestricted submarine warfare, but he tended to exaggerate its effect on Britain's ability to wage war, despite evidence to the contrary. In December 1916 he had argued for a resumption of unrestricted submarine warfare by claiming that

Germany's U-boats could deliver total victory in a mere five months. He firmly believed that Britain—in particular its military machine and war industries—could be starved into submission. Kaiser Wilhelm II embraced the scheme enthusiastically, and on February 1, 1917, Germany declared unrestricted submarine warfare.

Chart legend:
- Peak U-boat strength during the year
- U-boats built during the year
- U-boat losses during the year

1914: 34, 11, 5
1915: 64, 52, 17
1916: 149, 108, 22
1917: 169, 108, 63
1918: 171, 83, 69

CAPTAIN ADOLF VON SPIEGEL

Captain Adolf von Spiegel commanded a German U-boat during World War I and was involved in the campaign to starve the British into surrender. Here he describes an attack on a cargo vessel.

"The steamer appeared to be close to us and looked colossal. I saw the captain walking on his bridge. I saw the crew cleaning the deck, and I saw, with surprise, long rows of partitions right along all decks, from which gleamed the black and brown backs of horses. 'Stand by for firing a torpedo!' I called down to the control room. 'Fire!' The death-bringing shot was a true one, and the torpedo ran toward the doomed ship at high speed. I could follow its course exactly by the light streak of bubbles which was left in its wake. Then a frightful explosion followed.

"All her decks were visible to me. From all the hatchways a despairing mass of men were fighting their way on deck, stokers, officers, soldiers, grooms, cooks. They all screamed for boats, tore and thrust one another from the ladders leading down to them, fought for the lifebelts and jostled one another on the sloping deck. All among them, rearing, slipping horses are wedged.

"Then—a second explosion, followed by the escape of white hissing steam from all hatchways and scuttles. The white steam drove the horses mad. I saw a beautiful long-tailed dapple-gray horse take a mighty leap over the berthing rails and land into a fully-laden boat. At that point I could not bear the sight any longer, and I lowered the periscope and dived deep."

Extract from Adolf von Spiegel's memoirs, 1919.

The submarines, now free of any restrictions, sank 181 ships in January, 230 in February, and 325 in March. Among the March losses were four U.S.-flagged ships, sunk over a period of two days commencing on March 15. The vessels were the passenger liner *Algonquin*, the *City of Memphis*, the *Vigilancia*, and the tanker *Illinois*. In the United States there was popular revulsion against the sinkings (more were to follow), and President Woodrow Wilson gradually moved closer to a declaration of war by the United States against Germany. When the declaration came on April 6, it removed any reason for Germany to pull back from the policy of unrestricted warfare. With U.S. shipping now wholly in the firing line, the U-boats took an increasingly heavy toll.

In April some 354 ships, or one in every four that sailed from British ports, were sunk, for the loss of two U-boats. This total represented some 834,549 tons of shipping, compared with the monthly average of 600,000 tons that was felt to be necessary to bring Britain to its knees within a few months. The Germans had calculated that if the world's merchant shipping could be sunk at the monthly rate of 600,000 tons, the Allies, being unable to build new merchant ships fast enough to replace those lost, could not carry on the war for long. At the same time, the

▶ *A merchant ship lists prior to sinking following an attack by a U-boat in the Atlantic, one of many that cost the lives of thousands of merchant seamen.*

Germans began an extensive building program that, weighed against their current losses of one or two U-boats per month, promised a substantial net increase in submarine numbers.

The Allied convoy system

Crisis loomed for Britain, and belatedly, on April 27, its naval leaders at last adopted the convoy system for the protection of merchant ships, a system not utilized since Napoleonic times (see page 388). There were some senior British naval commanders who argued the convoy system would be of doubtful value, chiefly because convoys could only sail as fast as the slowest ship and thus would delay many of the faster ships. Only the direct intervention of Britain's prime minister, David Lloyd George, finally ended the debate—convoys would be introduced. The British leader was supported by the U.S. Navy's Admiral William Sims, who had recently been placed in charge of all of the U.S. warships operating from British bases. The problem of fast and slower merchant ships was overcome by assigning vessels to fast or slow convoys.

A typical small convoy in World War I consisted of two long columns of merchant ships sailing in tight formation with a number of armed vessels surrounding them and sailing between the columns and a shield of destroyers farther out sailing a zigzag course to search for submarines. Larger convoys, usually of 30 ships, were arranged in five or six columns with 500 yards (460 m) between the ships and 800 yards (730 m) separating the columns. Destroyers were stationed in front and to the side of the convoy. The ratio of destroyers to merchant ships was usually around one to three. Typically, a convoy heading from the United States to Britain would cross most of the Atlantic without protection and only rendezvous with its escorts some 300 miles (480 km) from its destination, as this was the beginning of the area of the most intense U-boat activity.

KEY FIGURES

ADMIRAL WILLIAM SIMS

Admiral William Sims (1858–1936), who had a noted fondness for Britain, was sent to London in 1917, shortly before the United States entered the war, and became a strong advocate for the commitment of U.S. naval forces to the key campaign against Germany's submarines.

In 1910 Sims, who had been born in Canada to an American father and graduated from the U.S. Naval Academy in 1880, attracted criticism for unofficially promising military support for Britain. However, his close links with French and British naval officers led to an appointment as a liaison officer in March 1917. When the United States declared war in April, Sims took charge of the various U.S. warships operating from British bases and was soon promoted to vice admiral. In June he was made overall commander of all U.S. naval forces operating in European waters, a position he held until the end of the war.

Sims was a staunch supporter of the U.S. naval role during the war and had an excellent relationship with senior officers of other Allied nations. However, he was critical of Admiral William Benson, the U.S. chief of naval operations, and Secretary of the Navy Josephus Daniels. Sims felt that neither responded with vigor to the needs of the U.S. Navy once the United States had gone to war in 1917.

The Convoy System

By 1917 German submarines were taking a fearful toll of Allied shipping, particularly around the coast of Britain and in the Mediterranean Sea. In response the Allies turned to an age-old strategy to reduce their losses—the introduction of protected convoys of merchant vessels, a system out of favor for a century.

Gathering together merchant and transport vessels into convoys was neither a new nor an untried method of protecting shipping at the outbreak of World War I, but it was used only sporadically in the first two years of war, chiefly for Allied troop transports and important cargoes. A ship bound for one of the Allies' ports had to set sail by itself as soon as it was loaded and then run the gauntlet of the U-boats operating in the Atlantic and Mediterranean. The seas were thus dotted with sin-gle and unprotected merchant ships, and any scouting U-boat could rely on several targets coming into its range during the course of a cruise.

The convoy system remedied this problem by grouping merchant ships within a protective ring of destroyers and other naval escorts. It was logistically possible and economically worthwhile to provide this kind of escort for a group of ships. The combination of convoy and escort would force the U-boat to risk the possibility of a counter-attack in order to sink the merchant ships and thus give the Allies a chance to reduce the U-boats' numbers.

After the German declaration of unrestricted submarine warfare in February 1917, losses of Allied merchant shipping escalated, exposing the weakness of the half-hearted convoy system and the current antisubmarine tactics. Despite evidence showing that convoys could actually reduce losses drastically, in January 1917 the Operational Division of the British Admiralty produced a report that came down firmly in opposition to the system. It suggested that the sudden arrival of a mass of ships at a port would overwhelm the unloading facilities, leaving ships idle as they waited to be unloaded. Better, it reasoned, to stagger the arrival of ships so that a continuous stream would pass through a port.

Other objections included the belief that there were insufficient

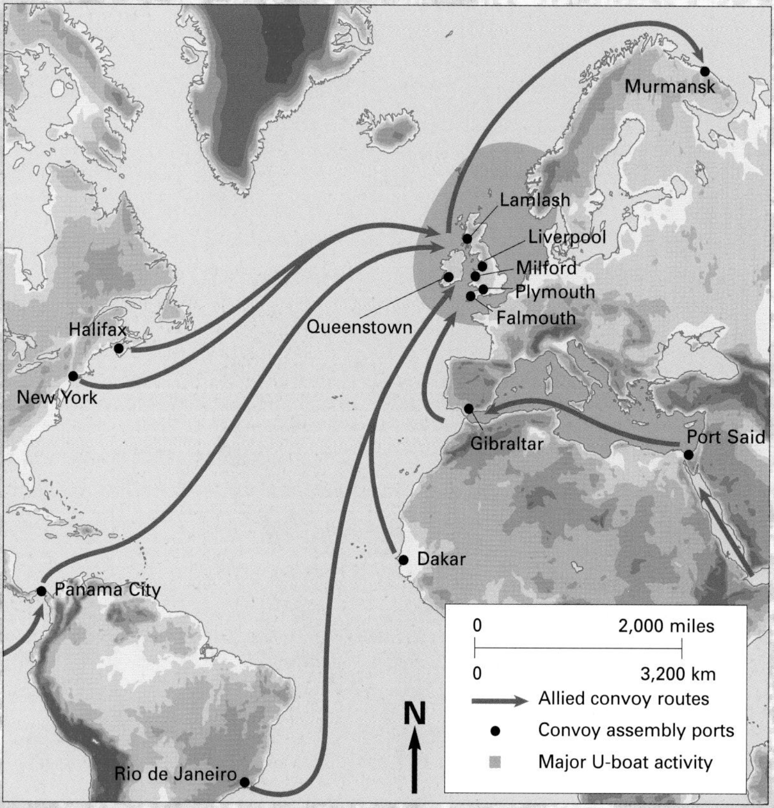

◄ *U-boat tactics concentrated on narrower stretches of ocean where shipping bound for Britain converged at choke points, often to the southwest of the country.*

Map labels: Murmansk, Lamlash, Liverpool, Milford, Plymouth, Falmouth, Queenstown, Halifax, New York, Gibraltar, Port Said, Dakar, Panama City, Rio de Janeiro

0	2,000 miles
0	3,200 km

→ Allied convoy routes
● Convoy assembly ports
▦ Major U-boat activity

N

ings, and losses to U-boat attack began to decline markedly.

The problem of unloading was solved by allocating prearranged berthing spaces at multiple ports and by instituting 24-hour shifts for the longshoremen. The greatest problem faced by the Allies was the shortage of ships to escort merchant vessels, as many as one for every three merchant ships. Destroyers were desperately needed in every Allied theater of operations, but the shortfall in these warships was eased as U.S. and Japanese ships became available. More than any other factor, the convoy system checked the U-boat campaign and was a major influence on the outcome of the war.

▲ *The adoption of convoy formations enabled the Allies to provide better protection for greater numbers of vital merchant ships.*

escort vessels and that a large formation of huddled ships would present a bigger target for U-boats. Also, among British Royal Navy officers there was a common disdain for the seamanship of merchant crews, which led them to question the merchant ships' ability to perform the complex maneuvers necessary to hold formation. Finally, any convoy would only be as fast as its slowest ship, thus increasing its vulnerability.

After a closer analysis of the facts by the new British minister for shipping, Norman Leslie, and a junior Royal Navy officer, Commander R. G. A. Henderson, a second report was put before the Admiralty. The enormous losses during April 1917 convinced them of the need to adopt convoying, more or

less as a last resort. The first transatlantic convoy sailed on April 28 and reached Britain without loss on May 10. Thereafter convoying was introduced for all oceanic sail-

▼ *Destroyers being constructed in a dockyard in 1917. The Allies had to make good the losses they had suffered at the hands of the U-boats and needed plenty of ships just for convoy escort duty.*

▲ *A destroyer flotilla under the command of Commodore Joseph K. Taussing, led by USS Davis, arrives at the British naval base at Queenstown, Ireland, on May 4, 1917. It marked the entry of the U.S. Navy into the war in Europe.*

The convoy system had a profound impact on the success of the U-boats. The first convoy from Gibraltar to Great Britain sailed on May 10, the first from the United States the previous month, and ships plying the South Atlantic traveled in convoy from July 22 onward. By the end of May, a month in which merchant shipping losses fell to 549,987 tons, the quantity of shipping available to carry the vital foodstuffs and munitions to Britain had been reduced to just six million tons in total. In June 631,895 tons, some 272 ships, went down, most of them in the southwestern approaches to Britain—but the tide was turning. By October 1917, 99 convoys had arrived in Britain, a total of 1,502 ships; just 10 had been sunk while sailing in convoy.

Toward the end of 1917 the use of convoys led to an abrupt fall in sinkings by U-boats—300,200 tons in September and about 200,600 in November. The system was so quickly vindicated that it was extended to shipping outward bound from Britain. One glaring problem was the shortage of escort vessels, a deficit exacerbated by the continued Allied shortage of destroyers, which were needed to undertake many other important operations. Germany had also developed the more powerful, long-range Deutschland class of submarines. Although clumsy and slow in the dive, these large vessels had a superior range to that of earlier boats, enabling them to reach Allied shipping lanes sited far from any protection. The first of them, *U-155*, sailed on its maiden cruise to the Azores in June 1917 and by September had sunk 19 Allied ships. Despite these losses, German commanders soon observed that the British had grasped the principles of antisubmarine warfare and that gathering ships in convoys considerably reduced the opportunities for attack.

The battle against the submarine

In the first years of the war, the Allies had few means to take the fight to Germany's submarines. Q-ships, seemingly innocent trawlers that actually carried guns, were being developed, but they had increasingly limited success as

U-boats became wary of approaching any suspicious vessels. By 1917 German submariners had learned to expect decoys, and torpedo rather than surface attacks became the norm. Q-ships, of which some 200 saw service, managed to sink 11 U-boats between July 1915 and late 1917, but 18 of their number were lost. These numbers suggest their impact was limited, and they were withdrawn from service in the fall of 1917.

Thus, between 1916 and 1917, the destruction of a U-boat was a matter of luck as much as judgment. Captains of antisubmarine warships had to patrol in waters where U-boats were known to operate and hope to catch a submarine on the surface, preferably in daylight. However, by late 1917 more than 50 percent of all ships lost to submarines were sunk at night. There were some successes, and from the early summer of 1917 onward, U.S. naval vessels were joining in the campaign against the U-boats operating off the waters of Britain. The first U.S. destroyers arrived in Ireland on May 4 and established their base at Queenstown on the south coast. Their first confirmed U-boat success came in November. On the 17th two U.S. destroyers, the *Fanning* and the *Nicholson*, intercepted and badly damaged the German U-boat *U-58* under Captain Gustav Amberger with depth charges and gunfire off southwest Ireland. The *U-58* was forced to the surface and was eventually scuttled by its crew. However, stalking enemy

▼ *U.S. Navy gun crews ready for action. The addition of the strength of the American fleet meant, effectively, that Britain's supply routes could be secured indefinitely.*

submarines was a dangerous task, as was confirmed on December 6 when the U.S. destroyer *Jacob Jones*, which had been present at the *U-58* sinking, was torpedoed by the *U-53* under Captain Hans Rose. The destroyer sank in eight minutes, taking 44 of its 108-strong crew to the bottom. Some of the *Jacob Jones*'s crew were rescued by Rose, who radioed the position of the remaining survivors to the British.

A more scientific approach was needed to antisubmarine warfare. In 1914 the only method of destroying submerged boats was by means of mines, anchored at various depths along busy sea routes or used to block hostile submarine bases. However, the most widely deployed device was the contact mine, which exploded when one of the stubby detonators dotted all over its outer shell was touched by a vessel's hull. During the war, an estimated 75 U-boats were destroyed by mines, making them by far the most successful of all antisubmarine

weapon. Most "kills" were achieved in shallow coastal waters but more aggressive techniques of finding and attacking submerged submarines were needed, particularly to deal with those U-boats stalking convoys in deeper waters.

Most prominent among these was the hydrophone, a crude device for identifying the noise produced by submarine engines operating underwater, thereby giving an indication of the boat's position. However, the version developed in World War I needed to be towed behind the antisubmarine warship, and it had insufficient power to penetrate deep water; it could thus be neutralized by submarines that ran beneath its effective operating depth. By 1917, though, its use had become more widespread— by August some 2,750 vessels were equipped with the device.

Equally, the detection of submarines was of little offensive value without the means to attack them underwater. From

▼ *Prisoners crowd the deck of the German raider* Möwe (Seagull) *at Kiel in March 1917, having been accumulated over the course of four months at sea, during which time the vessel sank or captured 27 ships.*

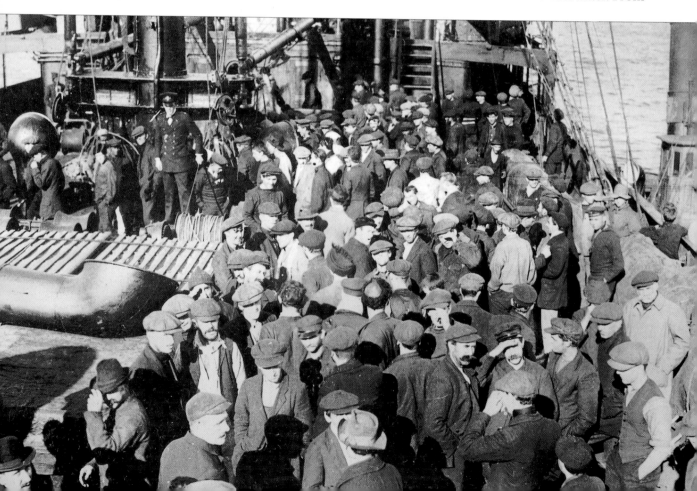

1915, however, the depth charge—basically a 200-pound (90 kg) drum of high explosive fitted with a pressure detonator that could be set to explode at a certain depth—was available. On locating a U-boat, the detonator was set to the supposedly correct depth and the charge rolled off the back of the vessel. An explosion in the vicinity of the U-boat was usually sufficient to crack its pressure hull. Depth charges were initially only marginally effective, and between 1915 and the end of 1917 they accounted for just nine U-boats. However, their use had risen steadily during 1917, with an average of between 100 and 300 launched per month.

Aircraft, both fixed-wing and lighter-than-air ships, were employed on convoy protection and antisubmarine patrol work, but they were effective more in a reconnaissance than in an offensive role. By the war's end Allied aircraft had sunk only one U-boat. Utilizing a U.S.-built flying boat, a British pilot bombed and sank the German *UB-32* in the North Sea on September 22, 1917. However, fixed-wing aircraft did undertake bombing raids against German submarine bases in occupied Belgium during 1917.

German submarines were not the only danger to Allied shipping in 1917. A number of surface raiders were still at large. Warning of their potential came on January 10 when the *Seeadler*, the only sail-powered commerce raider deployed by Germany during the war, claimed two victims while patrolling south of the Azores. The vessel's captain, Count Felix von Luckner, would go on to have other successes during the year. Patrolling in the Pacific and Atlantic, the *Seeadler* accounted for 16 Allied merchant ships before the raider was wrecked in the Society Islands on August 2. A second raider, *Wolf*, scored several successes, too. Although its main role was to lay mines in busy sea-lanes, this former merchant ship was also able to sink 12 cargo vessels and

returned home only in February 1918, having evaded Allied warships searching for it. The *Möwe*, Germany's most successful raider of the war, was also at large during the first months of 1917. The former cargo ship had already sunk 15 ships on its first cruise, and on its second, which began in November 1916 and lasted for four months, the *Möwe* accounted for 27. However, this was the vessel's last sortie—upon returning home it was converted into a minelayer.

German surface actions

During the first months of 1917, with his larger warships holed up in port and with the greater focus of the naval war

▲ **The British-built** Seeadler **(Sea Eagle)** *was a deadly German commerce raider that put to sea disguised as a harmless Norwegian cargo ship.*

firmly centered on the submarine, Scheer was prompted to launch a series of destroyer raids on British shipping out in the English Channel. Destroyers became perhaps the most important surface vessels in the final two years of the war, a view reflected in a rapid increase in their production. Their speed, range, and armaments gave them the flexibility to operate with the larger warships, in coastal operations, and also in minelaying and antisubmarine roles. Scheer's main aim was to show the German public and his own sailors, whose morale was beginning to suffer, that the German surface fleet was still active and was able to disrupt the flow of Allied troops and supplies to the western front.

Scheer's first attack, on February 25, achieved very little, but when the German destroyers ventured out again on March 17, two British destroyers and a small coaster were sunk. The third attack, on the night of April 20–21, involved 12 German destroyers from Zeebrugge in occupied Belgium operating against shipping in the Straits of Dover, the narrowest part of the English

Channel, and resulted in a bitterly fought action. Two British destroyers, *Broke* and *Swift*, intercepted the raiding ships and sank two German destroyers. The *Swift* dispatched one raider with a torpedo, and the *Broke* torpedoed and then rammed another, sending it to the bottom. The actions of the British destroyers proved a sharp jolt to the Germans, who kept their destroyers away from the English Channel until 1918, although they carried out a number of bombardments of towns along the English east coast. In response to these actions, the British mounted their own raids, chiefly with the intention of curtailing the activities of the U-boats operating from ports in Belgium. There were naval bombardments against Ostend and Zeebrugge, both ports being used as U-boat bases, during May and June, but the effects were negligible and the submarines continued to operate.

German destroyers were very active in the North Sea in the latter part of the year, where they were able to strike against convoys sailing between Scandinavia and Britain. The German naval

▼ **The British flotilla leader Broke**. *The destroyer was one of two British vessels that intercepted a larger German raiding force in the English Channel in April 1917. It sank an enemy destroyer, and the remainder of the flotilla fled.*

attacks in the area were in part prompted by the constraints placed on the U-boat offensive by the introduction of the convoy system and the closing of the English Channel to German surface warships. Initially the German raids had some success. For example, on October 17, 1917, two light cruisers, *Brummer* and *Bremse*, attacked a convoy of 12 merchant ships that were escorted by two British destroyers, *Mary Rose* and *Strongbow*. Nine of the cargo ships and both the destroyers were sunk. A further success followed on December 13, when a convoy of ships from northern Scotland bound for Norway was attacked by torpedo boats. However, the latter incident prompted the British to tighten their defensive measures in the northern theater, and successful attacks became less frequent before they eventually ended in April 1918.

In November 1917 the larger warships of the German High Seas Fleet made their last major foray into the North Sea. The island of Helgoland, off the Danish coast, was a major German naval base, and the waters outside the harbor had been heavily mined by the British. In mid-November Germany sent out a flotilla of minesweepers to clear a path through the minefield, a move that provoked an attack by British battlecruisers. With several German dreadnoughts giving support fire, the minesweepers were able to withdraw. Ultimately, German battleships had been rendered impotent by the numerical superiority of the British Home Fleet and its decision to mount a long-range but highly aggressive blockade of the North Sea. The strength of this blockade grew in 1917.

The Mediterranean theater

Prior to the war most naval strategists had predicted that a major battleship engagement would be fought in the Mediterranean, chiefly between the forces of Austria-Hungary, France, and Italy. Each was dependent on free passage through its waters, and it seemed inevitable that the Mediterranean would be bitterly contested. However, the predicted engagement did not materialize, with the belligerents fearful of losing their most powerful ships. As in the North Sea, the mighty battleships were held in readiness to oppose any sortie by an enemy's battleships. Most naval action was confined to encounters

▲ *Shells burst around a burning German minesweeper on December 8, 1917, during a naval engagement in the North Sea waters of the Helgoland Bight.*

between smaller warships, coastal bombardments, and submarine warfare. All sides particularly strove to defend their major naval bases.

For Austria-Hungary these were the maritime ports at the northern end of the Adriatic Sea, which to the south led into the Mediterranean. Its navy was heavily outnumbered by the French and Italian fleets permanently stationed at the mouth of the Adriatic and was thus confined to home waters. The presence of large numbers of French and Italian surface warships was a lesser obstacle to Austria-Hungary's submarines, which could slip out of the Adriatic and strike at Allied shipping in the Mediterranean Sea at will.

► British drifters, each armed with a 6-pounder gun, at anchor in the harbor of Taranto, Italy. These vessels were used to form part of the antisubmarine Otranto Barrage and were also fitted with hydrophones and depth charges.

OTRANTO BARRAGE

The battle in the Otranto Straits on May 15, 1917 was the largest surface action of the naval war in the Mediterranean and also the first involving submarines, surface vessels, and aircraft together.

The Austro-Hungarian Navy routinely sent destroyers to attack the British trawlers forming the Otranto Barrage at the southern end of the Adriatic Sea. The navy's future commander, Miklós Horthy, planned an enlarged attack on the barrage. On the night of May 14, the cruisers *Novara, Helgoland,* and *Saida* sailed from Cattaro. Two destroyers made a diversionary attack, flying boats served as spotters, and submarines lurked off the Italian bases at Valona and Brindisi ready to intercept any enemy forces.

The cruisers opened fire on the barrage ships at 3:30 A.M. on the 15th, and within two hours they had sunk 14 ships. The destroyers sank two others. By sunrise a British task group was steaming to intercept. At 7:45 A.M. they caught the Austrian destroyers, disabling one while the other escaped to safe waters. At 9:00 A.M. the Allied squadron met with Horthy's main force and engaged in a two-hour running fight. The *Novara* received a long-range hit. Horthy was severely wounded. *Saida* managed to tow the *Novara* away while the enemy remained inactive, fearing the arrival of Austrian reinforcements.

This threat led to the employment by the Allies, from fall 1915, of a standing line of trawlers and other small vessels equipped with antisubmarine nets. Stretching southeast from the port of Brindisi for some 60 miles (96 km), the Otranto Barrage, as it was called, was designed to block the passage of submarines into the Mediterranean Sea. Britain sent 60 trawlers to support the effort, but only 20 could be on station at any given time, and the barrage did not present any great obstacle to submarine movements. The trawlers were protected by patrols of Allied aircraft and warships but were the target of frequent nighttime raids by Austro-Hungarian vessels. In May 1917 a concerted attack led by Vice Admiral Miklós Horthy, who later became the commander of the navy of Austria-Hungary, forced the

VICE ADMIRAL MIKLÓS HORTHY

Hungarian naval officer Miklós Horthy de Nagybánya was appointed captain of the Austro-Hungarian fast cruiser *Novara* in late 1914 and took part in several surface actions that confirmed his talent for naval combat.

Horthy (1868–1957) first came to prominence in May 1915, when he led a squadron that sank 14 Italian merchant ships off the coast of Albania. He also played a part in planning the Otranto Barrage attack in May 1917 and emerged with great credit. Following the naval mutiny at Cattaro in March 1918 and the resignation of Admiral Maximilian Njegovan, he was promoted to command of the Austro-Hungarian Navy and set about improving the generally demoralized fleet.

His last major offensive action was an attack on the Otranto Barrage in June 1918, which was abandoned after the loss of the dreadnought *Szent István*, but Horthy showed great leadership in preserving the loyalty of the Austro-Hungarian fleet until the disintegration of the empire. Returning to his homeland, he organized and led a successful uprising against the new communist government in 1919. He was made regent in March 1920, a position he managed to hold until 1944.

Horthy at a ceremony proclaiming the heroes of Hungary.

trawlers to abandon night work altogether, but the barrage remained central to Allied antisubmarine policy in the Mediterranean until the end of the war.

Baltic operations

Offensive action in the Baltic Sea for much of the war was dominated by extensive minelaying operations by the Russian Baltic Fleet and elements of the German Navy, with both sides chiefly attempting to block the flow of supplies to the other. Russian surface vessels only rarely ventured out into the open sea from their bases, as their main role was to protect the Russian capital.

By early 1917 the Russian fleet had grown into a formidable force that included 558 combat ships, a number of launches, and over 500 auxiliary transport vessels. Under construction

▲ *Vice Admiral Eggard Schmidt (left) aboard a German torpedo boat near Osel during the 1917 operations to seize Russian-held islands in the eastern Baltic.*

were 15 battleships, 14 cruisers, and 269 naval planes. However, despite its undoubted strength, it had been rocked by a series of mutinies since 1915. In February 1917 elements of the Baltic Fleet had even supported the Bolshevik revolutionaries. At Helsinki and Kronstadt, the largest Baltic ports, sailors rioted and several unpopular officers were murdered, including the commander of the Baltic Fleet, Vice Admiral Adrian Nepenin, and also the chief officer of the port of Kronstadt, Admiral Robert Viren.

In the spring of 1917, after a particularly severe winter that had contributed to the paralysis of operations in the eastern Baltic, Germany took advantage of the political turmoil besetting Russia and embarked on a series of attacks aimed at the weakest link in Russia's fleet—its submarines. Within a short time six had been destroyed, including the *Bars*, *Lvitsa*, *Gepard*, and *Yedinorog*. To replace them Britain sent four small C-class submarines to the Baltic. In June these submarines mounted reconnaissance patrols off the Baltic coast and in the Gulf of Riga to forestall German moves toward Petrograd, while Russian boats continued to wage war against the

now well protected convoys of Swedish iron ore that was destined for Germany and its war industries.

The Kerensky Offensive in the first week of July, the last Russian attack of the war, saw the disintegration of the Russian Army. Taking advantage of this crisis, the Germans launched an offensive toward the Baltic port of Riga by the Eighth Army, which crossed the Dvina River virtually unopposed and captured Riga on September 3. The German high command asked its navy to aid in the conquest of the Russian-held islands at the entrance to the Gulf of Riga, whose capture would allow German ships to threaten Petrograd.

The commander of the Russian Baltic Fleet was Rear Admiral Alexander Razvozov. He could call on only two battleships, three cruisers, three gunboats, and 21 destroyers under Vice Admiral Mikhail Bakhirev to block the German amphibious operations in the eastern Baltic. The German commander, Vice Admiral Eggard Schmidt, had more than 300 vessels at his disposal and an assault force of some 25,000 troops. Arriving off Osel Island on the 12th, the German dreadnoughts bombarded the coastal batteries before putting troops ashore for an advance on Arensburg in the east. The only damage sustained by the Germans was to the dreadnoughts *Grosser Kurfürst* and *Bayern*, both of which struck mines. To the north, light forces clashed as the Germans tried to approach Moon Island through the passage separating Dagö and Osel Islands.

By the 14th German land forces had crossed Osel, cutting off the Russian batteries at Zerel in the south. Both sides now concentrated on the struggle for the more northerly Moon Island area, and the Germans brought up heavy warships to support their light naval forces. During the day the German dreadnought *Kaiser* hit the Russian destroyer *Grom*, which was further damaged by German destroyers before sinking. However, the Russians still controlled Moon Island and thereby one of the northern exits from the Gulf of Riga.

In the south German minesweepers cleared the Irben Straits to allow heavy units to break through to the Gulf of Riga, although operations were held up by Russian batteries resisting at Zerel until the 15th. With Osel Island in German hands and the minefields of the Irben Straits cleared, heavy German ships entered the Gulf of Riga on the 16th. As they headed north for Moon Island, the British submarine *C-27* torpedoed and badly damaged a support ship. On the 17th the German dreadnoughts *König* and *Kronprinz* battled the Russian pre-dreadnoughts *Slava* and *Grazdanin*. Both Russian warships were hit, *Slava* heavily. *Slava* was finally scuttled in shallow water and finished off by torpedoes from a Russian destroyer. Retreating north, the Russians continued to lay defensive minefields in the vicinity of Moon Island, one of which sank a German destroyer on the night of the 17–18th. The Russians evacuated Moon Island on the 18th as the Germans landed, and the next day Dagö Island was also occupied. By the 20th surviving Russian ships had slipped past Worms Island and made for bases in the Gulf of Finland.

The Battle of Moon Sound was the last fought by the Russian Baltic Fleet in World War I. In November 1917 it sided with the Bolsheviks, who were attempting to seize control of Russia. One of its vessels, the cruiser *Aurora*, which was anchored in the Neva River, heralded the Bolshevik revolution by firing a blank shell on the Winter Palace in Petrograd on the 7th. Vice Admiral Alexander Kolchak's Black Sea Fleet, Russia's only other operational naval force during World War I, continued to maintain its blockade of the Bosporus Strait and Constantinople until the summer of 1917, and as late as October 31 it was attacking Turkish ships. However, revolutionary events in the Russian capital took precedence. The Imperial Russian Navy took no further part in the

▼ *German troops en route to occupy Osel Island following its successful capture from the Russians in September 1917.*

▲ *Surrendered German submarines flying the flag of Japan. The Japanese made an important but little-known contribution to the Allied struggle at sea throughout World War I.*

war, and many of the Black Sea Fleet's warships were scuttled to prevent them from falling into the hands of the revolutionary forces.

Japan's naval contribution

On June 11, 1917, the Japanese destroyer *Sakaki* was lost while operating off the coast of Greece, sunk by the Austro-Hungarian submarine *U-27*. Although it might seem unusual that a Japanese warship should be operating so far from home, in fact Japan rendered vital worldwide naval support to the Allies during the war. Its warships patrolled the Pacific and Indian oceans searching for German commerce raiders, thereby freeing other Allied warships for service elsewhere. The Japanese were also asked by the British to send a force against Austro-Hungarian and German U-boats in the Mediterranean.

British requests for naval assistance in the European theater and the South Atlantic grew more insistent in late 1916 and early 1917 as the naval situation deteriorated. The Japanese government responded by pressuring the British for

recognition of Japanese claims to the Shantung Peninsula in China and the Pacific islands taken from the Germans. Japanese officials argued to their British counterparts that in their desire to retain their conquests they were asking no more than the Russians, whom the Allies were already permitting to occupy Constantinople. The British cabinet wrestled with the problem through

January and February of 1917, worrying about the potential response of the United States, which was edging closer to participation in the conflict.

In February 1917 the Japanese Navy agreed to expand the area of patrols already protecting commerce in the Dutch East Indies, Sulu Sea, South China Sea, and Indian Ocean as far south as the Cape of Good Hope. It also increased its involvement in safeguarding commercial shipping operating off Australia's east coast and New Zealand.

Japan also gave considerable help to the Allied cause by supplying arms and shipping. In 1914 they returned to Russia three cruisers captured in the Russo-Japanese War of 1904–1905, which were subsequently used by the Russian Baltic Fleet. Japanese factories supplied arms and munitions to both Russia and Great Britain. In 1917 Japanese shipyards hastily constructed (in five months) 12 destroyers for France, and Japanese sailors delivered the ships to the Mediterranean. Later in the war Japan and the United States agreed that Japanese shipyards would produce 371,000 tons of shipping for the U.S. Shipping Board. Although the war ended before the merchant vessels were complete, Japan willingly helped in this effort, according to an American

account. Moreover, the Japanese government agreed to charter an ever-growing portion of Japan's merchant fleet for Allied use.

In early 1917 Japan finally deployed forces to the European theater of operations. The lead Japanese warships departed Singapore, under the command of Admiral Sato Kozo, for the Mediterranean on March 11. The remainder of the Japanese squadron, totaling a cruiser and three destroyer groups, quickly followed and commenced operations against German and Austro-Hungarian submarines that were threatening Allied shipping in the Mediterranean. (Allied losses there in April 1917 totaled 218,000 tons, 7 percent of the total sinkings there during the entire war.) Desperately short of escorts, the Allies seriously considered the idea of reducing the number of ships transiting the Mediterranean by sending them on the safer passage around the Cape of Good Hope. By late summer British doubts about the competence and value of the Japanese warships had vanished. On August 21 Admiral George A. Ballard, senior naval officer at Malta, reported to his superiors that the Japanese had rendered invaluable service in escorting troop transports since their arrival at Malta.

▼ *The Japanese destroyer Shirakumo, photographed in 1914. From the outset of the war, Japan's ships had performed a valuable service in containing Germany and its allies.*

Germany's Last Attacks

In the spring of 1918 the German high command gambled all on a crushing victory on the western front, one that had to be won before U.S. troops gave the Allies overwhelming superiority.

As 1918 dawned, no one could tell which side was going to win the war. Both the Allies and Central Powers had cause to believe that they could triumph, but both also had potential weaknesses that could be exploited. The Germans had defeated Russia and left the Italian Army crippled by the end of 1917, and they knew that it would be several months before the United States was ready to fight in strength on the western front. All this was bad news for the British and French, but they could take heart from the fact that all of Germany's allies, particularly Austria-Hungary,

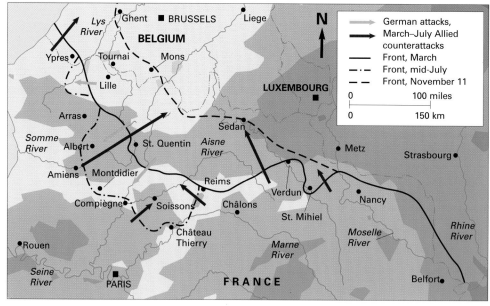

▶ *The western front in 1918 saw a return to the mobile warfare that had ended in late 1914. Germany's spring offensive gained much ground, but it was over by the summer. The Allies, vastly strengthened by U.S. forces, regained much of their territory and then punched through the German defenses.*

German attacks,
March–July Allied counterattacks
Front, March
Front, mid-July
Front, November 11

0   100 miles
0   150 km

concerned. Britain was now led by Prime Minister Lloyd George and France by Prime Minister Georges Clemenceau, who were both dedicated to defeating Germany and winning the war outright.

Some German politicians and many ordinary Germans did want to end the war. Over one million industrial workers went on strike in Berlin, the capital, and other cities in January 1918 to demand that their government make peace even if they had to give up any of the territory that had been conquered earlier in the war. However, Germany's military leaders saw their forces victorious in Russia and still occupying a huge piece of Belgian and French territory, and they insisted that any peace deal should allow Germany to hold on to a good proportion of these gains. The Allies could not accept this outcome. Therefore, the war would go on until one side could force the other to give up.

Germany's great gamble

By 1918 Germany's civilian government had virtually handed control of the country to the German Army's leaders. The head of the German Army was Field Marshal Paul von Hindenburg, but the real power lay with his principal assistant, General Erich Ludendorff. Together, they had made their reputations on the eastern front and had seen the campaign there culminate in the defeat of Russia in 1917. The German Army had new types of poison gas and had improved its attacking tactics. Above all, the Russian defeat allowed them to transfer huge numbers of troops from the eastern front to reinforce Germany's forces in France. Could they now bring the war on the western front to a similarly successful conclusion by aggressive action?

German strength on the western front rose from about 150 divisions in late 1917 to over 190 by March 1918, when the German attacks began. The Allied force remained at about 170 divisions, of which 6 were American (but none yet

▲ *German storm troopers train to attack high ground at Sedan, February 1918. Pioneered by General Oskar von Hutier in September 1917, the storm troopers' main tactic was to infiltrate between enemy strong points and then thrust deep into enemy territory.*

were close to collapse and that U.S. help was on the way, even if slowly at first. Also, although largely unknown to the Allies, their naval blockade was beginning to have an increasingly serious impact on the willingness of the German people to go on supporting their country's war effort.

Although there were various moves by politicians in all the major countries to find a means to make peace, they had little support. U.S. President Woodrow Wilson's Fourteen Points (see Volume 1, pages 310–311), first outlined on January 8, 1918, laid out an idealistic peace program for the future, but in early 1918 it was not a realistic basis for bringing the war to an end, at least as far as most leaders in other countries were

▲ *American troops disembark in France following the U.S. declaration of war against Germany on April 6, 1917. The American Expeditionary Force, later divided into three armies, totaled 1.3 million combat troops by the end of the conflict in 1918.*

in the front line). The U.S. strength would rise substantially as the year went on, but all the other armies on both sides were facing declining manpower resources. They would find it a struggle to keep their strength up or to find properly trained men to replace their casualties.

The western front in France and Belgium had always been the war's principal battleground, but by 1918, more than ever, it was clearly where the war would be lost or won. Germany now had the opportunity to take the initiative on the western front for almost the first time since the fall of 1914. Since then the British and French had been doing most of the attacking, choosing the times and places where the major battles would be fought out. In 1918 Ludendorff planned that it would be Germany's turn. However, he was a general in a hurry, because he knew his window of opportunity would not last long,

thanks to the increasing rate at which fresh U.S. troops were now arriving in the European theater.

The Allied leaders soon worked out that Germany would mount new and powerful offensives in France in the spring of 1918. The British and French generals knew that their own troops were tired and badly battered by the hard fighting of the previous years, but they also knew that more and more U.S. troops would soon arrive. The Allied generals thought they could hold out for the first difficult months. They remembered how hard they had found it to make decisive attacks on the western front and thought that the Germans would encounter similar problems. However, because they had spent so much of the war attacking, the British and French had gained little experience of fighting defensive battles, and they were not as well prepared for defense as they believed.

Ludendorff correctly assumed that the strongest Allied force at the start of 1918 was the British Expeditionary Force, which held the northern section of the western front. The chief aim of all the German attacks that he was planning was therefore to set the British up for a knockout blow. Ludendorff believed that if the British were decisively defeated, then Germany would be able to dictate favorable peace terms. He mistakenly thought that he could simply win the battle (something he thought he knew how to do) and the politics (which he did not understand) would look after themselves.

Ludendorff did not necessarily expect to be able to achieve all of his aims in one battle; the British and French had strong reserve forces, and he knew they would use them to help each other when they were attacked. He spotted an Allied weakness to help him overcome this obstacle. If the British were forced to retreat from their frontline positions, they would tend to move north and west to make sure that their supply lines to the ports on the English Channel coast were not cut, but if the French had to pull back they would tend to move south so that their capital, Paris, would not be vulnerable to German attack. Movements like these in different directions would split the British and French apart and make it more difficult for them to cooperate.

Ludendorff's plan of campaign therefore had various stages. His first attack would be in the Somme River region, just north of the boundary between the British-held and French-held sections of the Allied front. The Allies would have to commit their reserves to hold this attack, but even so they would be driven apart. The German forces would then swing northward and "roll up" the British from their right flank. Many of the roads and rail lines linking northern and central France also passed through nearby Amiens, and if the

▼ *A Schneider tank of the French Army returns from the front line, spring 1918. Although tanks remained unreliable, they were used in greater numbers than ever before, and they also spearheaded many major attacks.*

STRATEGY AND TACTICS

BRUCHMÜLLER'S TIMETABLE

The massive artillery bombardment that opened Germany's Operation Michael in March 1918 was the brainchild of Colonel Georg Bruchmüller. An artillery expert, he had created a complex timetable lasting several hours that targeted different British positions with a mixture of high-explosive and gas shells. The artillery barrage included the following stages:

4:40–5:30 A.M. A general barrage using phosgene, tear gas, and high-explosive shells against artillery and mortar positions, command and communication posts, and assembly areas in the rear of the British line.

5:30–5:40 A.M. A 10-minute break in the general barrage, during which the German artillery fires on the British frontline trenches.

5:40–7:10 A.M. The general bombardment ends, and there is sporadic shelling of the British front line for 30 minutes to pinpoint targets.

7:10–7:40 A.M. The British front line receives an intense bombardment, as do gun batteries and shell dumps in the rear.

7:40–8:20 A.M. The German artillery batteries adjust their range and direction slightly in an attempt to catch unaware any British units or positions close to the previous targets.

8:20–9:35 A.M. While the British frontline trenches are still being bombarded, long-range guns seek out targets in the rear.

9:35–9:40 A.M. The overwhelming majority of German guns, large and small, fire on the British first- and second-line trenches, while gas shells fall on batteries in the rear. Meanwhile, the storm trooper units prepare to advance.

9:40 A.M. The German guns begin a creeping barrage, a wall of shells that advances ever closer to the British front line at prearranged times. The storm troopers advance in its immediate wake.

▶ *German troops prepare an array of cylinders to project gas shells over enemy trenches on the western front in 1918. The German Army was the biggest user of gas during World War I, taking delivery of some 68,000 tons.*

▼ *Large-caliber German howitzers make ready for action on the western front in March 1918. These heavy artillery pieces were the cornerstone of the barrage that preceded the German offensive that month.*

achieve this end Ludendorff relied on the infantry and artillery tactics that had been so successful in Russia and Italy in 1917. In fact, as events would show, Ludendorff was so concerned with getting the details of his tactics right that he tended to lose sight of the larger objectives of his attacks.

The key to a successful attack was the artillery. The German Army had always been strong in artillery, and 1918 was no different. On the 50-mile (80 km) sector designated for the first of his offensives in March, Ludendorff assembled about 10,000 weapons of all types and calibers, roughly 50 percent of the artillery the Germans had on the whole 450-mile (720 km) western front. The artillery plan, developed by Colonel Georg Bruchmüller, featured a range of techniques designed to make possible the breakthrough and rapid advance that Ludendorff needed. The preparatory bombardment was to be short but punishingly intense; more than one million shells in five hours. However, even this stunning weight of firepower was not expected to smash through the British defenses; the aim was to confuse the British commanders and also to prevent their artillery from being able to respond effectively to the German fire.

The weapon that made this aim possible was poison gas. Only about half the German shells aimed at ordinary targets (and only 20 percent of those were aimed at artillery targets) were high-explosive shells that could smash and kill. The remainder contained various types of gas. Some shells were filled with the deadly phosgene compound, but many contained a nonlethal type of tear gas that the British gas masks did not keep out. Wearing gas masks was a tiring and unpleasant experience, and, Ludendorff and his team believed, a British soldier wearing his mask and suffering in addition from the painful effects of the tear gas would be virtually unable to take any part in combat.

Germans could advance far enough to capture this town, it would be even more difficult for the Allies to switch their forces between the different sectors of the front.

This first attack might even be successful enough to win the war on its own, but if not, the damage to the Allied forces and communications would be the edge that Ludendorff needed to make the second stage of his plan work. This would consist of further attacks on the British in the Arras sector and farther north in the area of the Lys River, near Ypres, in Belgium.

German forces and tactics

None of Ludendorff's plans could have worked, as he well knew, unless his forces were capable of quickly breaking through the Allied defense lines and forcing them to retreat rapidly. To

An effective artillery bombardment was worthless without an infantry attack to follow it up. Here Ludendorff's men also planned to develop the techniques that had been so effective in Russia and Italy the year before. The first wave of attacking units had almost all been specially trained and equipped for what were known as infiltration tactics. The first wave of attackers, sometimes called storm troopers, were to go forward in small groups, moving as quickly as possible. These storm troopers were to pass between any remaining centers of resistance in the British line that had survived the German bombardment and to keep going deeper into the British defenses. This advance would cut off and isolate the defenders, leaving them to be surrounded properly and destroyed by the follow-up forces.

The storm troopers' advance was to be covered by a "creeping" barrage, a bombardment fired in such a way that a line of exploding shells would advance slowly across the battlefield, if all went as planned keeping just ahead of the attacking soldiers. All attackers were ordered to advance as quickly as possible, remaining as close as they could to the creeping barrage—the safest place for an attacker to be because the defenders' fire would be most effectively suppressed there. They had pre-

arranged signals by which they could tell the artillery to move the creeping barrage forward more quickly than originally decided, but it was not possible for them to tell it to slow down. This was a strong incentive for the infantry to keep moving forward according to plan.

By 1918 properly prepared attacking forces would stand a reasonably good chance of capturing an enemy front line, but doing so was only the start of their problems. In order to reach open country, where they would be able to maneuver quickly, they would have to fight their way through trenches probably several miles deep, and the farther they went, the harder it was for their artillery to support them.

At the same time as the attackers were penetrating the defenses, the defenders would be bringing up reserves to make the defenses even deeper and stronger. The attackers would be advancing on foot through mud and shell holes, fighting as they went, while the defenders' reserves would be coming into battle by train and by road outside the range of artillery fire. It is not hard to see how the defenders could therefore quickly recover from any damage done by the initial attack.

Ludendorff's tactics were designed to short-circuit this whole raft of problems. The powerful artillery bombardment

▼ Rail-mounted German artillery on the western front in 1918. This system combined mobility and speed in deploying guns in the field.

However, Ludendorff was becoming increasingly worried about a weakness in the German Army. Some of his divisions were no longer capable of fighting a full-scale battle. In the preparations for the offensive, only about one-quarter of the German divisions in France received the special training and mobile artillery and machine guns needed for the planned attacks. Many of the other German units were now regarded as fit only for holding defense lines in quiet sectors of the front. These units were also given poorer rations and equipment, a situation that did not make the soldiers happy or any more ready to fight. The attack divisions, on the other hand, naturally suffered the most casualties, and there were few reserves of well-trained and motivated soldiers available to refill their ranks. The efficiency and fighting power of the German Army faced a steady decline.

Up to this stage in the war, there was no single leader in command of the Allied armies in France. The arriving American Expeditionary Force (AEF), under General John Pershing, did not yet have any troops in the front line, so the generals who mattered most were the French and British commanders in chief, Marshal Henri Philippe Pétain and Field Marshal Douglas Haig. Unfortunately for the Allied side, they had different plans for the coming year.

Pétain was gloomy. He had taken over command of the French Army at the worst moment in 1917, when three years of dreadful casualties and little success caused thousands of French troops to mutiny. Pétain's leadership had rebuilt his soldiers' confidence and willingness to fight, but he did not think they would be capable of mounting any large attacks for the rest of the war. Pétain wanted to wait for the Americans to arrive in strength before trying to attack the Germans, and in the meantime he would defend to the best of his capabilities and endeavor to keep casualties down to a minimum.

would so confuse the defenders that the storm troopers would be able to fight right through the whole British defensive zone in the first day of the battle. They would be out in the open and ready to take on the Allied reserves before the latter had a chance to get into position—or at least that was the theory.

One of the factors that had helped defenders get their reserves into position in earlier battles was that the preparatory artillery barrage often lasted for several days, giving plenty of warning of where an attack would take place. By 1918 improved artillery techniques allowed guns to be shot accurately "off the map" without a long process of firing ranging shots to correct their aim. With this improvement bombardments could still be effective even if they were comparatively short. This development in field practice was a vital factor in helping Ludendorff to preserve a degree of surprise and to plan a rapidly moving attack.

▲ **German infantry rest behind the lines on the western front in 1918. Germany's military leaders gambled all on these troops. If they were defeated by the Allies, there were no reserves to plug any gaps in the line.**

MARSHAL FERDINAND FOCH

Foch (1851–1929) was one of France's top generals during World War I. His calm and diplomatic manner allowed him to overcome the self-interest of the various Allies and create a united and workable strategy that would defeat Germany on the western front.

Before World War I, Foch saw service in the Franco-Prussian War (1870–1871) and then taught military theory that stressed the role of morale and will in battle, views that became somewhat discredited in the first weeks of World War I. In 1914 he was praised for his actions during the Battle of the Marne, and he gradually rose in rank and importance. In May 1917 he was made chief of the general staff, and he later served on the Supreme War Council, which was responsible for coordinating Allied strategy against the Central Powers.

Foch was made the Allied supreme commander on March 26, 1918, and coordinated the British and French response to Germany's Operation Michael. Thereafter, he successfully organized resistance to subsequent German attacks and was made a marshal on August 6 for his efforts. In the final months of the war, Foch coordinated the succession of Allied offensives on the western front that led to the defeat of Germany and oversaw the drafting of the armistice terms that ended the fighting.

Haig, however, was more optimistic. He overestimated how far the British offensives of 1916 and 1917 had weakened the German Army, and he hoped to attack again in 1918 once the early German attacks had been beaten off. He did not think that Pétain was determined enough and thought that, if worse came to worst, the British Army might have to look after itself. The most important thing was to make sure that the British supply lines to the English Channel were secure, and therefore Haig built up his defenses in such a way that the northern part of his lines was the strongest.

Haig and Pétain did not completely trust each other, and to make matters more complicated for the Allies, neither commander in chief was fully trusted by his own government. The French leader, Georges Clemenceau thought Marshal Pétain was a defeatist; he preferred a more aggressive type of commander, like Marshal Ferdinand Foch. Britain's premier, Lloyd George, thought that Haig had lost many lives in ineffective attacks in earlier years. He would have fired Haig, but the general had a number of powerful friends. Instead, Lloyd George looked for ways in which to limit Haig's authority. In the meantime the prime minister kept many trained troops at home in Britain, thinking that if Haig was kept short of men he would not be able to plan new and costly attacks.

In any war fought by a group of allies, it makes sense for the various countries to work together as closely as possible. However, for most of World War I, neither side was able to put this elementary idea into practice. On their side the Germans did much as they wanted and regarded their allies as more a nuisance to be ordered about than as genuine partners. On the Allied side it took until late 1917 for some degree of united planning and command cohesion to begin to emerge. The Supreme War Council that was formed in November 1917 had U.S., British, French, and

Italian representatives and was meant to coordinate operations on the western front and in Italy. The Supreme War Council did not have any real power—it did not fight any battles or control any troops. Even so, Lloyd George and Clemenceau hoped to use it as a way to reassert their authority over their top generals.

The Emperor's Battle

The German attack started on March 21 along a lightly defended 50-mile (80 km) front to the north and south of St. Quentin, between Arras and La Fère, and was heralded by a surprise artillery bombardment lasting precisely five hours. Ludendorff committed 63 divisions to the attack, divided up, from north to south, among General Otto von Below's Seventeenth Army, the Second Army under General Georg von der Marwitz, and the Eighth Army headed by General Oskar von Hutier. None of these frontline generals was given overall charge because Ludendorff wanted to keep the final say in all important decisions for himself. The

strongest part of the attack at first was at the northern end near Arras because this was the area where there were the most worthwhile objectives for the Germans. The offensive was code-named Operation Michael but is also sometimes known as the *Kaiserschlacht* (Emperor's Battle), so named in honor of the German emperor, Wilhelm I. It is sometimes also known as the Second Battle of the Somme.

In the *Kaiserschlacht* the Germans were helped by other weaknesses on the Allied side apart from their troubles at the top. The German attack happened to be aimed at a section of the western front that had previously been defended by French troops but had recently been transferred to British control. The new British defenders found that the defenses in the area had been neglected and there was not enough time to build these up again before the German offensive hit. Changes in the way the British organized their infantry forces and Haig's decision to keep his strongest units at the northern end of his line also helped to make this more southerly sector comparatively weak.

▼ *German storm troopers breach a barricade left by the British in a northern French town in spring 1918. Speed of forward movement was the mainstay of German tactics during the final part of the war.*

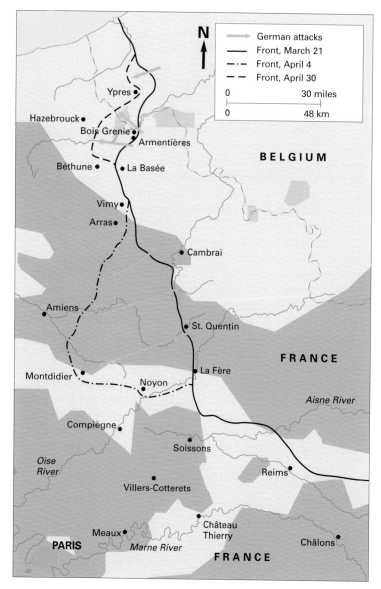

The map legend reads:

→ German attacks
— Front, March 21
—·— Front, April 4
––– Front, April 30

0   30 miles
0   48 km

▲ The two German offensives against the British in spring 1918 began with Operation Michael on March 21, which was directed against the British Third and Fifth Armies. The second attack, known as the Lys Offensive, began on April 9.

places there were too many troops in the front line and not enough in the main positions. There were many other detailed mistakes in the defenses. The defending forces were 14 divisions of the British Third Army under General Julian Byng in the northern part of the battle and 12 divisions of General Hubert Gough's Fifth Army to the south. The last was spread thinly along a front of some 40 miles (64 km) and had only recently taken over this particular sector from the French. The Germans had massive local superiority in troops and artillery.

At first the battle seemed to go completely the Germans' way. The artillery cut the communication links between the British commanders and their forward troops as the German storm troops advanced under the cover of a fortuitous fog. British frontline units were isolated and forced to surrender or were simply annihilated. Others were so bewildered by the crushing German firepower that they simply retreated when they did not really have to. Soon the German storm troopers were breaking into and then through some of the main British defenses. The British Fifth Army was smashed and a gap of roughly 40 miles (64 km) opened up in front of the Germans. By the 27th, Montdidier, 40 miles (64 km) away from the German start line, had fallen, and Amiens, a few miles distant, was threatened.

Part of Haig's reaction to the crisis was to seek for a means of coordinating the British and French strategic response to Operation Michael. He contacted General Henry Wilson, the recently appointed British chief of staff, and the British war minister, Lord Milner, demanding the appointment of "Foch or some other French general who will fight" to take supreme command.

The main German successes, however, were at the south end of their line. Ludendorff had to make a decision. Should he commit his reserves to exploiting that success or try to revive

Many British officers at every level did not really understand how to fight a defensive battle effectively and had not trained their troops properly in defensive tactics. The theory was that the frontline positions were not to be held too strongly—they were too vulnerable to enemy artillery fire. Instead, they were to hold out long enough to disrupt any German advance, which would be brought to a halt and then defeated by the troops in the main defense line a little farther back. This theory turned out to be easier to plan than to do. In some

his original plan and send them to reinforce what was meant to be his main advance toward the Channel ports? Instead of doing one thing or the other, he tried to do a bit of both over the next few days, changing his mind more than once and sending various units in different directions. Before the battle, Ludendorff had organized his forces brilliantly to make their success possible, but he was not nearly so effective as a commander once the battle had begun.

The German troops were also becoming as exhausted as their opponents from the heavy fighting. The German soldiers had ample supplies of weapons, but for many months past their rations had been meager and unappetizing. Discipline in some units now collapsed as they captured British supply depots and found them filled with the sort of food and drink that they had not seen for a very long time. Instead of carrying on with the battle, they stopped to eat and to get drunk. The German advance also took them across the ground that had been the Somme battlefield in 1916. This was still a devastated wasteland and helped to slow down their progress even further. All the time the British and French reserves were arriving to rebuild their line.

At the end of March, Ludendorff tried to renew his attack toward Arras but got nowhere. On April 4 a last attempt to push forward toward Amiens was also defeated, and on the following day Ludendorff gave orders for these operations to be halted in favor of a new offensive in the Lys River sector to the north. The Germans had advanced more than 40 miles (64 km) in some places, an astonishing feat compared with some earlier battles on the western front, but it had not been the decisive victory that Ludendorff needed. The vital railroad junction at Amiens, for example, remained in Allied hands, with the most forward German troops some 10 miles (16 km) away. Equally, Byng's Third Army had retreated but

was far from defeated and still blocked the way to the Channel ports. However, Gough was sacked for his Fifth Army's poor performance and replaced by General Henry Rawlinson. The Allies had suffered around 260,000 casualties, an enormous figure but still slightly less than Germany's total losses.

The near success of Operation Michael had also brought about developments on the Allied side that would stand them in good stead for the coming battles. In the first few days of the attack, both Haig and Pétain panicked. Pétain thought the war might be lost. He told Clemenceau: "The Germans will beat the English in open battle; then they will beat us as well." Haig

---

EYEWITNESS

LIEUTENANT ERNST JÜNGER

Jünger was a company commander in the 73rd Hanoverian Fusilier Regiment's 2nd Battalion during Operation Michael. A much-decorated and five-times wounded officer, he later recounted a brief fight for a series of British-held trenches on March 21, the beginning of the offensive:

"I jumped into the first trench. Stumbling around the first traverse, I collided with an English officer with an open tunic and his tie hanging loose. I did without my revolver and, seizing him by the throat, flung him against the sandbags, where he collapsed. Behind me, the head of an old major appeared. He was shouting to me: 'Shoot the hound dead.' I left this to those behind me and turned to the lower trench.

"It seethed with English. I fired off my cartridges so fiercely that I pressed the trigger 10 times at least after the last shot. A man next to me threw bombs [grenades] among them as they scrambled to get away. A dish-shaped helmet was spinning high in the air. A minute saw the battle ended. The English jumped out of their trenches and fled by battalions across the open."

Extract taken from Ernst Jünger's Storm of Steel, *first published in 1929.*

thought, incorrectly, that Pétain was delaying sending French reserves to join in the battle, and Pétain believed that the British were running off to the north, leaving the French to do all the fighting. In the hope of improving the situation, both were therefore happy to accept the appointment of Foch as coordinator of their forces' operations when this recourse was suggested by the political leaders at a crisis meeting on March 26. On April 3 Foch was formally named the Allied commander in chief, and he played a vital role throughout the rest of the year in keeping the various Allies working together effectively.

The Lys Offensive

It was clear that Operation Michael was bogged down, and Ludendorff opted to change the focus of his great attack. In another brilliant feat of organization, he had his force of heavy guns rapidly moved from the Operation Michael zone in preparation for a new attack farther north, in Flanders. This offensive, Operation Georgette, began on April 9 in the Lys River sector, south of Ypres. The British had two forces in the region, General Herbert Plumer's Second Army and the First Army under General Henry Horne. However, these armies were separated by the Lys. The

Germans committed two armies of 14 divisions to the attack: General Sixt von Arnim's Fourth Army in the north was to drive through Plumer's men and then strike for the coast by way of Hazebrouck, while to the south supporting attacks were to be launched by General Ferdinand von Quast's Sixth Army against a 12-mile (19 km) long front that stretched from La Bassée to Armentières.

The attack, which was preceded by a ferocious 4-hour artillery bombardment, began on April 9. The Portuguese 2nd and 40th Divisions, part of Horne's command, were the target for the first German attack by the Sixth Army. They were immediately pushed back nearly 5 miles (8 km) and collapsed. Troops of the British First and Second Armies were also forced to retreat on both flanks with heavy casualties. For a time it looked as if the Germans might capture the important rail junction at Hazebrouck. By April 12 they were just 5 miles (8 km) from the town, having opened up a breach in the British line some 30 miles (48 km) wide.

Haig was very worried once again, chiefly because he lacked reserves to halt the German advance. On April 11 he issued an order to his troops that read: "There must be no retirement. With our backs to the wall and believing

▼ *A French armored car, one of many that were utilized in support of British troops in April 1918 during the Lys Offensive. Armored cars were used from 1914 and were the precursors of the tank.*

KEY FIGURES

FIELD MARSHAL HERBERT PLUMER

Plumer (1857–1932) was one of the few British generals during World War I who fully understood the nature of trench fighting. A methodical commander, he won fame during the Battle of Messines Ridge in 1917 and also during Operation Michael in 1918.

In December 1914 Plumer was made commander of a corps of the British Expeditionary Force in France and became head of the Second Army in April 1915. Between 1915 and 1917, he was in charge of the defense of the Ypres salient in Flanders, which was considered a "quiet" sector from his appointment until the British offensive in June and July 1917. In June Plumer launched the Battle of Messines Ridge, one of the most successful attacks of the war.

From November, Plumer next spent some time in Italy organizing the British and French forces that had been sent south to aid the Italians after their disastrous defeat during the Battle of Caporetto. He returned to the western front in early 1918, just in time to face the German spring offensive. He was able to blunt the German attack against the Ypres salient and later took part in the final Allied offensives that defeated the German forces on the western front. In 1919 he was made a field marshal for his wartime services.

the Channel ports. The most important of these was Dunkirk, which lay some 25 miles (40 km) beyond the point of the greatest German advance. In reality, Georgette was a simply a cut-down version of an earlier plan called George that by April, the Germans lacked the resources to carry out. Therefore, by the end of April Ludendorff's victory plan had not worked. The Germans had captured a great deal of territory—far more, in fact, than the Allies had taken in any of their offensives over the previous years—but in reality the Germans found that they were worse off than they had been before. Casualties on the two sides since March 21 were about even, roughly 350,000 men each, but since mid-March around 180,000 U.S. troops had arrived in France, and three of the U.S. divisions that were already present had now joined in the fighting. It was clear which side was going to end up the stronger if this rate of attrition continued to be the case. Nevertheless, Ludendorff still intended to launch more attacks, but this time they would be against the French, who were supported by U.S. units.

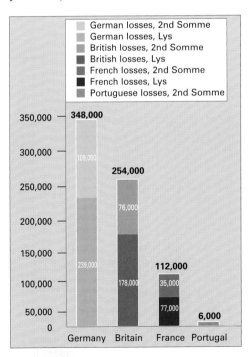

in the justice of our cause, each one must fight on to the end." Around April 18, chiefly due to Plumer's withdrawing his combat forces to more easily defended positions around Ypres, the German advance came to a standstill. Ludendorff, whose control of the great offensive was generally poor, ordered a number of new attacks in the following week, but they made little progress as French reserves bolstered the British line. On 29 April he therefore called off the advance for good.

Ludendorff's forces had advanced up to 10 miles (16 km), but he had not gained the most important objectives,

▶ *The losses suffered by the main forces taking part in Operation Michael and the Lys Offensive, March–April 1918. Although Allied casualties were high, including many prisoners, Germany's manpower was so stretched that it could not afford its own losses.*

The First Tank Battle

World War I saw the first encounter between rival tanks on the battlefield. It took place on April 24, 1918, outside the village of Villers-Bretonneux on the western front. It involved British and German tanks and lasted just 60 minutes.

Battles in which one group of tanks fights against another are a common feature of all modern wars, but they were very rare during World War I, mainly because of the fact that, while the British, French, and later the U.S. Armies deployed many tanks in their battles from the fall of 1916 on, there were very few tanks on the German side for them to fight against.

Germany made only one type of tank, the A7V, during the war and these only came into service in early 1918. In the end only about 20 A7Vs were ever built, compared with the many hundreds of Allied machines that would fight in all the major battles later in 1918. Generally, the Germans made use of captured Allied, usually British, tanks. There were probably only two occasions in the war when tank fought against tank. The action at Villers-Bretonneux took place during the series of great German offensives on the western front in the spring of the final year of the conflict.

Villers-Bretonneux lies about 10 miles (16 km) west of the vital road and rail communications center of Amiens. By mid-April the main German attacks were taking place farther to the

north, but the German generals decided to make a secondary attack at Amiens. They had only a relatively small infantry force of four divisions available but also deployed 13 A7Vs to strengthen the attack.

Throughout the spring of 1918 the British commanders operated their tanks in small groups hidden in their defensive zones. These tanks were tasked to appear "like savage rabbits from their holes" to defeat the German advances. The British

had three Mark IV heavy tanks and seven of the lighter Whippet type within the Villers-Bretonneux sector.

The German bombardment began at 3:45 A.M. on April 24, and their tanks and troops started forward at 6:00 A.M. The defending soldiers were taken aback by the huge A7Vs looming out of the morning mist and were soon retreating or surrendering. The Germans took about 400 prisoners at Villers-Bretonneux itself and in three

▶ *A German tank captured by the 26th Australian Battalion at Monument Wood near Villers-Bretonneux in April 1918.*

hours gained about 1,500 yards (1,360 m) of ground all along the five-mile (8 km) battlefront. By then, however, the British "savage rabbits" were on their way to counterattack.

The three British Mark IVs, commanded by Captain J. C. Brown, were from A Company of the 1st Tank Battalion. Two were the "Female" type, armed only with machine guns, which were of limited effectiveness against another tank, but one was a "Male" fitted with the more useful artillery weapons.

The tank battle began at about 9:30 A.M. The Germans had the upper hand at first. Brown's own tank and the other Female were both forced to retreat after being holed by shells from one of the A7Vs. Then the Male tank moved into range. Although the

▲ *A British Whippet tank as used at Villers-Bretonneux. Although not heavily armed, the Whippet was capable of high speeds.*

gunner had been half-blinded by German poison gas, he hit the leading German tank three times with his shells, resulting in its getting stuck in a sandpit. The crew jumped out and ran for their lives. The Mark IV then moved on and forced two more German tanks to retreat, bringing the German attack to a halt.

As this part of the battle was ending, the seven British Whippets caught troops of the German 77th Reserve Division forming up for a new advance a little to the south. The Whippets machine-gunned many of them, putting an end to any more German plans to attack, even though one of the Whippets was knocked out by an A7V. That night and the next day Allied troops recaptured Villers-Bretonneux. The first-ever tank-versus-tank battle was over.

U.S. Baptism of Fire

When General Erich Ludendorff was considering Germany's military plans for the western front in 1918, he had looked at various options both for where to attack and when. As far as timing was concerned, he had quickly come to the conclusion that he had to make his move in the early spring—even May would be far too late and his chance would have gone. However, after it had become plain that his first two attacks in March and April were not going to achieve the results he had hoped for and even though many of his best troops had been killed or wounded, he changed his mind. More attacks would do the trick, despite the fact that the preparations could not be completed until the end of May.

One result of the German offensives of March and April had been to draw French reserves into the fighting in the mainly British-held sector in Flanders in the north. Ludendorff still wanted to make his main attack there, because he still believed that the British were his toughest opponents and the ones he had to beat to win the war, but the French support made the northern sector just too difficult a target. He therefore decided to attack in the French sector much farther south. The objective of this attack was, not to make a decisive advance, but simply to do enough to force the Allies to move their

In May 1918 units of the American Expeditionary Force were thrown into battle for the first time to help block the series of German offensives that were designed to crash through the Allied lines on the western front.

▶ *Troops of the 369th Infantry Regiment, 93rd Division, are seen here in their trenches in France in May 1918. Known as the Harlem Hellfighters, the 93rd was the first African American unit to land on French soil, on January 1, 1918.*

reserves south to defend against it. Then, in his next attack after that, Ludendorff would strike in the north once more. This was a strategy of desperation, with the hoped-for German victory disappearing into an ever more doubtful future. Ludendorff was also having to acknowledge a steadily growing U.S. presence on the western front.

As U.S. Army units arrived in France, completed their combat training, and received equipment, they were gradually introduced to the realities of trench warfare. Divisions were usually given a brief tour of duty in the trenches in an area where no significant fighting was expected. The first U.S. units deployed in the front line were from the 1st Division. They were sent into a quiet sector of this sort, near Nancy, in October 1917. The first American battle deaths were suffered by that division's 16th Infantry Regiment on November 3.

It took every soldier some time to learn the skills that veterans took for granted. One novice infantryman wrote of his problems on sentry duty in the trenches: "I shot six Germans sneaking up on me one night, and when daylight came they were all the same [tree] stump." Matters were not made easier for the U.S. troops when Ludendorff ordered that whenever Americans were identified in the front line by German intelligence, they were to be shelled and raided fiercely in the hope of discouraging them before they had gotten used to trench warfare. The 26th Division suffered more than 600 casualties in one such attack near St. Mihiel on April 20–21, although for propaganda purposes the local French commander actually awarded the troops numerous medals and publicized the engagement as a victory.

General John Pershing, commander of the American Expeditionary Force (AEF), stuck to one great principle in deciding how to organize his forces in France. The United States would form its own force separate from those of the

Preparing the AEF for War

During 1917 and 1918 the United States had to build the American Expeditionary Force (AEF) virtually from scratch and then, with the aid of its Allies, prepare it for the realities of war in the trenches.

On April 1, 1917, the U.S. Army had fewer than 130,000 regular soldiers plus some 170,000 in various National Guard units. By the war's end there were roughly two million troops in France with more still training at home. Getting the few regulars and the huge body of recruits trained and organized to fight was a formidable task for an army that had just 19 general staff officers on duty in Washington, D.C., at the start of the war.

Every army in World War I measured its strength in divisions. Each division contained infantry, artillery, engineering, and other units and was theoretically capable of fighting any type of battle independently. The U.S. Army's divisions were large, about 28,000 men at full strength, compared with about half that in the European armies. They were probably too big, as large organizations tended to be clumsy in battle and difficult to command.

▼ *The Vosges Baccarat sector of the western front was a relatively quiet theater and was, therefore, ideal for introducing inexperienced U.S. troops to life in the trenches.*

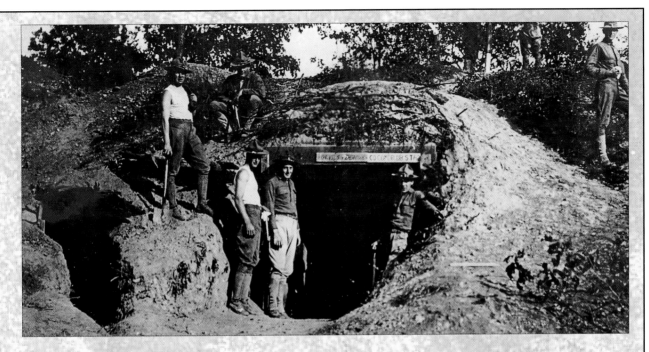

Divisions were supposedly in three different categories: Regular, National Guard, and National Army. In fact, despite their names, all three types ended up being manned principally by men who had been drafted. Men in the Regular divisions were therefore just as much in need of training as those in the National Army.

The training system that was established was meant to give men four months of basic training at home before their divisions were shipped to France. This covered drill, discipline, marksmanship, field craft, and the like. Once in France the plan was for three further stages of training before the division was considered to be combat ready. The division would be paired up with a veteran British or French unit. First, individuals and small groups would join their allies in the line to gain experience, then companies or battalions under foreign command would take over their own small sectors but

still under foreign command. Finally, the whole division would serve a tour of duty in some specially chosen quiet sector, often in the Vosges Mountains, north of the Swiss border with France. In addition to the foregoing there were numerous special military schools and training camps to teach particular skills.

Often events did not work out as hoped. As 1918 went on, some men were sent overseas having scarcely fired their rifles and ended up in the trenches within days of their arrival. Men sent to the special schools in France were often summoned back to their units before they had completed their courses, and few divisions actually went through the full three-stage program.

French instructors worked with most of the divisions in France, though Pershing unwisely sent most of them back to their own army in August 1918. Six divisions were trained by the British, using British equipment, methods, and instructors.

▲ *Although they were unprepared for the fighting on the western front, U.S. troops revitalized the Allied war effort. Here, soldiers pose by a dugout.*

Despite such exceptions, General Pershing vehemently insisted that, as far as possible, American troops should be trained in American tactics, which differed in important respects from those practiced by other armies. Pershing wrongly believed that success in battle was based on accurate rifle fire and maneuver from the infantry. He thought that the French and British had become too defensive minded in the course of the war and relied too heavily on their machine guns and artillery.

Pershing may have been right about the British and French losing some of their drive in the long years of war, but the "open warfare" training programs he ordered did not prepare his men for the grim reality of living and fighting in the trenches.

KEY FIGURES

GENERAL ROBERT LEE BULLARD

Bullard (1861–1947) graduated from West Point in 1885 and rose steadily through the ranks of the U.S. Army to become one of the top commanders of the American Expeditionary Force throughout the fighting on the western front in 1918.

Bullard's service as a junior officer included combat experience in the Philippines during the Spanish-American War of 1898. When the United States entered World War I, he was appointed a brigade commander in the 1st Division and took over the whole division in December 1917. He then led it during the successful action at Cantigny, the first independent U.S. attack of the war, in May 1918.

Bullard was again promoted in July 1918, this time to head III Corps, which he led successfully in the first stages of the Allied Aisne-Marne counteroffensive in July and August. He could speak French well, a skill that helped greatly in these Franco-American operations. The general led III Corps in the Meuse-Argonne battles in October and then was promoted again to command the newly forming U.S. Second Army. This unit saw little action before the armistice in November. Bullard retired in January 1925.

British and French, even though they were much larger and more experienced. U.S. troops would not be sent as individual reinforcements for the Allied forces, nor would units be divided up and sent here and there to various sectors of the front.

Pershing thought that it was essential to his country's honor and prestige that U.S. troops should fight in a single united body. He also believed that the ordinary soldiers would fight better in this way under their own commanders and alongside their own countrymen. British and French leaders pointed out that Pershing's method would deny his men the chance to learn from the hard-won experience that the other Allies had built up over more than three years of war. They also pointed out that, in the time it took to organize the AEF, Germany might even win the war while hundreds of thousands of U.S. troops in France were doing very little of the fighting.

Both sides in this argument had a point, but Pershing stuck to his guns and the other Allies had to accept his decision, although they tried again and again to make him change his mind. The French and British even tried to get President Woodrow Wilson to overrule his general, but Wilson flatly refused. Ultimately, Pershing was probably right. In the short term there were disadvantages in his scheme, but in the coming months the U.S. people would expect to hear of their own forces in action, and this sort of political necessity was one with which no general could really argue.

In response to the emergency created by the German March and April attacks, on April 2 Pershing did allow some of his units to be deployed separately to parts of the Allied line. A force of engineers was caught up in the battle near Amiens at the end of March and found itself fighting as infantry, not laying railroad track, its original mission. In mid-April Major General Robert Bullard's U.S. 1st Division was sent to the assistance of the French First Army in the

Amiens–Montdidier sector. This assignment led to the AEF's first attack of the war. In mid-May, after the division had gained more experience, French commanders planned to use it in an advance to straighten out a bulge in the defense lines near the village of Cantigny. The 28th Infantry Regiment was chosen to fight the battle, and May 28 was scheduled for the attack. As was now usual, the regiment rehearsed the operation behind the lines over ground that had been mocked up to resemble the actual battlefield. Supporting units were also assembled, including a large French artillery contingent to supplement the 1st Division's own guns and a detachment of 12 French tanks.

Early on the 28th the guns fired a two-hour preparatory bombardment and then switched to a rolling barrage as the infantry attack began. The German lines were quickly and easily captured, but consolidating the gains and holding on to them were different matters. General Oskar von Hutier, commanding the German Eighteenth Army, wanted to make sure that the Allied advance did not reach any nearer to Montdidier and therefore ordered fierce counterattacks. Through the 28th and 29th these were beaten off, but the 28th Infantry lost many casualties to German artillery fire. Hutier gave up his counterattacks when he decided that Montdidier was not the Allied objective and at the same time the French artillery and tanks were moved away to the south to help meet the main German offensive that had now started on the Aisne. This move brought the battle to an end. The 28th Infantry had suffered almost 1,000 casualties, more than 25 percent of its strength, typical

▲ *The 28th Infantry Regiment advances during the battle at Cantigny on May 28, 1918, which was the first attack by AEF forces. Two French Schneider tanks support the advance.*

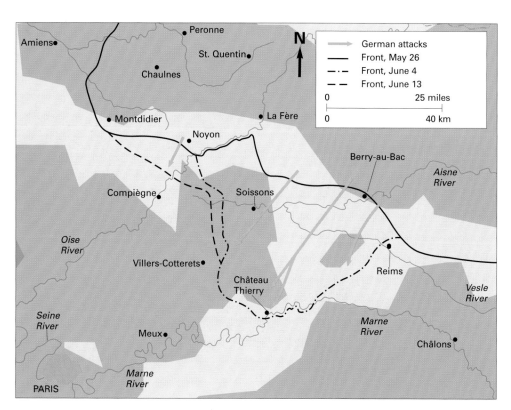

The second phase of the German onslaught on the western front in 1918 consisted of two offensives, one launched in late May and the other in early June. It was during these two attacks that U.S. troops were thrown into battle for the first time in small but significant numbers.

of the high price that attacking troops would have to pay to reach and hold their objectives against a tough enemy.

Third Battle of the Aisne

Shortly before the Battle of Cantigny, General Ludendorff launched the third of his major attacks on the western front. It was code-named Blücher, but it is often referred to as the Third Battle of the Aisne. At 1:00 A.M. on May 27 a thunderous German bombardment from more than 4,500 artillery pieces signaled its opening. The target was a 24-mile (40 km) sector of the Allied line along the Chemin des Dames ridges just north of the Aisne River. The German forces were from the First Army and General Max von Boehn's Seventh Army and had a total of 30 attack divisions and 11 of the poorer-quality trench divisions. Half of the attack divisions had fought in the earlier battles of the year and had not been rebuilt to full strength. The attack was therefore significantly weaker than the March offensive.

▶ *British and French troops await the advance of German storm troopers on May 29, 1918, during the Third Battle of the Aisne.*

▼ *German artillery at the Third Battle of the Aisne. This major offensive was a last attempt by the Germans to win the war before the United States became more heavily involved.*

Fortunately for the Germans, so were their enemies. This region had seen much fierce fighting earlier in the war but had been quiet for over a year. The Allied generals did not expect to be attacked there and so had only seven divisions in the front line, three of them British units that had been sent there to recover after being heavily defeated in the March battles. Even though seven Allied divisions were nearby, the Germans had a convincing superiority in numbers to start with.

The defending troops (including the British units) were part of General Denis Duchêne's French Sixth Army. Duchêne and his army group commander, General Louis Franchet d'Espérey, had decided to put too large a part of their defending force in the front line, disregarding the more sensible plans for defense in depth. Duchêne did not want to let the Germans capture any ground at all, but his method exposed too many of his frontline troops to the full power of the German artillery.

The Sixth Army's front line was smashed in the first hours of the battle, and the Germans' advance went on at an astonishing pace. On the first day they advanced more than 12 miles (19 km) and on the next day punched a gap 40 miles (64 km) wide and 15 miles (24 km) deep through the Allied front. The German commanders had expected that their whole offensive would only get as far as the Aisne and Vesle. However, the leading troops had crossed both of these rivers by the end of the first day—the advance had been so quick that several bridges across them were not blown up.

Ludendorff had a problem. Allied reserves would undoubtedly be on their way to the attack sector, so should he settle for his gains, close down the attack, and stick to his original plan? Or was this an opportunity too good to miss, and could the limited battle he had planned be converted into a decisive victory? Ludendorff's judgment and nerves were becoming increasingly frayed by the strain of his huge workload, yet he was less able to step back from the details of his work, which should have been left to his juniors, and see the big picture. It was no contest. Ludendorff would grab at the chance to fully exploit the breakthrough for all it was worth.

By May 30 the German troops had advanced 40 miles (64 km) to the Marne River near Château-Thierry, only 50 miles (80 km) from the center of Paris, the French capital. On the way they had crushed Allied reserve divisions as easily as they had destroyed Duchêne's front line. They had captured almost 60,000 prisoners, along with 650 artillery pieces and 2,000 machine guns. The road to Paris—and subsequent German victory—seemed open. The Allied commanders were worried but not as badly panicked as earlier in the year. Although the German attack had made a huge bulge in their front, it had not been able to capture the city of Reims at its eastern end. The Marne River was a barrier to the Germans' progress to the south, and the thickly forested area around Villers-Cotterets stood in their path to the west. Other Allied reserves, including U.S. forces, were on their way to hold these vital positions.

Three divisions of the AEF were already in the front line elsewhere—the 1st at Cantigny and the 26th and 42nd in other sectors—while Major General Omar Bundy's 2nd Division and the 3rd Division under Major General Joseph

Dickman were available. Once again there was a fierce argument among the Allied commanders. Pershing agreed to deploy these two divisions, but even with France's capital in danger, he refused to send other U.S. troops to join British and French formations to strengthen other parts of the defense.

The first U.S. troops to reach the threatened front were from the 7th Motorized Machine Gun Battalion of the 3rd Division. These arrived on the afternoon of May 31 and took up positions in Château-Thierry and on the north side of the Marne nearby, guarding the approaches to bridges over the river. They were just in time. They fought all the next day to cover the retreat of a French colonial division usually based in Senegal in Africa, only to be cut off when French engineers blew up the bridge with the machine gunners still on the wrong side of it early that night. They managed to find their way to another bridge and get across that before it, too, was blown. The remainder of the 3rd Division soon arrived and deployed along the Marne to the east of the town. On June 3 they defeated a daring German attempt to cross the river there using long ladders

▼ *German forces made considerable advances through the Allied lines in May 1918, and a decisive overall victory looked possible. Here, artillery is shown moving forward during the German attack.*

as temporary bridges. This defeat ended German attempts to cross the Marne for the moment. The main attack would now be made to the west.

The 2nd Division was sent into the line north and west of Château-Thierry, where the German drive was now aimed. The troops were transported to the front in a fleet of French trucks driven by Vietnamese drivers (Vietnam was a French colony at that time). The U.S. troops found the ride difficult and were also worried by meeting demoralized French troops doing their best to get away from the fighting. Some of the villages had been looted by the retreating French, and other Allied soldiers had simply got drunk.

Despite their problems on the way, the 2nd Division was deployed between June 1 and 3 on an 8-mile (12 km) front to the southeast and southwest of the small town of Belleau, about 5 miles (8 km) west of Château-Thierry. Up until

▲ *Trucks of the U.S. motor transport service leaving with troops of the 7th Infantry for rest and recuperation in 1918.*

PEOPLE AND WAR

THE HELLO GIRLS

In 1917 General John Pershing, commander of the American Expeditionary Force, had an advertisement placed in newspapers across the United States. It requested female volunteers to serve with the U.S. Signal Corps in France, which at the time relied on French operators with an often poor command of English.

Pershing added that the women had to be single, in excellent physical condition, speak fluent French, and be college educated. Some 7,000 applicants came forward, but just 450 were sent for training with the American Telephone and Telegraph Company. Subsequent training took place in military signaling procedures, and the first 33 telephonists sailed for Europe in spring 1918.

The women usually answered the telephone with "hello" and became widely known as the Hello Girls. Life near the front was very tough—48-hour shifts were common, and accommodation was often of poor quality. Despite their efforts, the women were considered to be civilians working for the U.S. Army and were denied veteran status after the war, even though they had been sworn in, wore military uniforms, and had to obey U.S. Army regulations. It was not until 1978 that a bill that gave the telephonists veteran status was signed by President Jimmy Carter.

Equipping the AEF

The United States had the world's biggest economy and largest industrial base at the time of World War I, but despite this fact the American Expeditionary Force (AEF) was not supplied with either U.S.-made or U.S.-designed weapons and equipment.

U.S. industries did not have enough factories equipped to make weapons or ammunition, and many of those that did exist were working at full capacity to complete orders that the British or French had already made. Making weapons requires special machinery and a highly skilled workforce. Putting these together to make new factories took time—and only then could manufacture even start.

The U.S. Army's rifle is a good example of this. When the war broke out, the standard rifle was the Spring-field M1903, but there were only 600,000 in stock, not enough for the number of troops the U.S. Army was about to field, and production was slow. However, the Remington and Winchester companies had been bought by the British earlier in the war and were making rifles for the British Army. The British sold the factories back, the British rifles were redesigned as the Rifle M1917 (Enfield) to fire the slightly different U.S. bullets, and over two million of these were made for the U.S. forces, more than 80 percent of U.S. wartime rifle production.

Machine guns were a slightly different story. The U.S.-manufactured Browning machine gun and automatic rifle were selected in 1917, but its production was slow to come on line. The first Browning machine gun was only used in France as late as the end of September 1918. The French Hotchkiss was an effective yet inferior substitute. However, as a result of delays in supplying the Browning automatic rifle, the AEF mainly had to use the French Chauchat as a light machine gun, a weapon experts describe as the worst design ever.

In some cases, though, it was correct to "buy foreign." The AEF generally used the British design for steel helmets, although U.S. units serving with the French used the latter's standard Adrian helmets, as well as French rifles. It made no sense to produce a specifically U.S. version of something as simple as a helmet when getting them to the troops in a hurry was all that mattered. However, the artillery was different. French artillery pieces were chosen as the basic equipment of U.S.

▲ *Elements of the U.S. 301st Tank Battalion going into action on the morning of October 17, 1918. The tanks were provided for the unit by the British.*

gunners. These were very effective weapons by the standards of the time, but the decision forced the AEF to rely on French factories for its ammunition supply when they were already at full capacity making shells for their own forces.

Another consideration was that items made or bought in Europe did not have to be shipped across the Atlantic. As a result, more men could be sent to France instead. Partly for this reason, a joint British and U.S. factory was set up in France to make heavy tanks. Making

used in France were therefore French- or British-made, although a number of them did have U.S. engines. Fighters included Nieuport, SPAD, and Sopwith types, and typical bombers were Breguets and De Havillands. The only U.S.-built aircraft to see combat were Airco DH4s, based on one of the British De Havilland designs. Of the 740 aircraft in frontline service in France at the end of the war, only 12 were U.S.-made. However, U.S. industries did develop and manufacture an aircraft engine. It was known as the Liberty engine, and some 18,000 were produced by the end of 1918, of which some 6,000 were sent to Europe.

▼ *Edward Rickenbacker, the American ace pilot, in a SPAD XIII. He scored the highest number of kills of all the U.S. pilots with a total of 26. He took part in the first U.S. air patrol of the war.*

use of a U.S. engine within a British-designed vehicle, they were commonly known as Liberty tanks. However, here again there was disappointment—few Liberty tanks were actually built before the war ended. Most tanks that saw service with the AEF were French Renaults, and only about 20 of these were actually built in the United States.

In 1917 the Army's Air Service, then a division of the Signal Corps, was probably the section of the U.S. military least prepared for war. The demands of war had seen the British, French, and Germans produce more advanced and powerful aircraft every few months, and U.S. industry had simply not kept up. Almost all the Allied aircraft

the 5th they met and defeated a number of German attacks around Belleau at the same time as German advances elsewhere were grinding to a halt in the face of other Allied reserves. Subsequently, the Germans called off Operation Blücher on June 4.

Ludendorff's decision to gamble and drop his original plan by prolonging the Blücher attack had gotten his men into trouble. The salient they had created was vulnerable to Allied counterattacks on its flanks. As a result Ludendorff decided to postpone the Flanders attack he longed to make in favor of first one and then another new offensive. Ludendorff was losing control, and his war-winning Flanders battle was looking less and less likely to be fought.

The first of these new attacks was designed to unite the salient in the Allied line made by Operations Michael and Blücher. It began on June 9, to the west of Soissons and toward Compiègne, a little to the north and west of the most recent battles, in an attempt to straighten out the German lines there. The defenders,

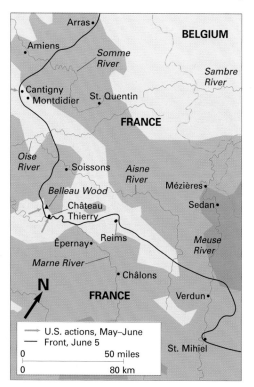

▲ **German troops at Soissons in June 1918. The offensive eventually became bogged down in the face of Allied resistance and German weariness.**

◄ **The first battles fought by U.S. troops on the western front, those at Cantigny, Château-Thierry, and Belleau Wood, took place during May and June 1918.**

drawn from General Georges Humbert's French Third Army, were warned by their intelligence service that the attack was coming and were able to fire a disruptive bombardment of their own just before the Germans started their own preliminary barrage. However, the French commanders repeated the mistake of having too many of their troops in the forward trenches, which lost them part of their advantage. Despite this problem, and even though the attacks were mounted by Hutier's veteran German Eighteenth Army, the Germans gained less than 10 miles (16 km) before they were fought to a standstill. A supporting attack in the general direction of Soissons by Boehn's Seventh Army on June 10 made even less progress.

Map labels:
Arras
Amiens
BELGIUM
Somme River
Sambre River
Cantigny
Montdidier
St. Quentin
FRANCE
Oise River
Soissons
Aisne River
Mézières
Belleau Wood
Château Thierry
Sedan
Épernay
Reims
Meuse River
Marne River
Châlons
N
FRANCE
Verdun
St. Mihiel

— U.S. actions, May–June
— Front, June 5
0   50 miles
0   80 km

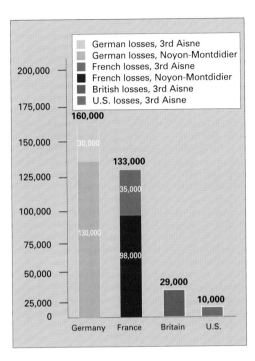

German losses, 3rd Aisne
German losses, Noyon-Montdidier
French losses, 3rd Aisne
French losses, Noyon-Montdidier
British losses, 3rd Aisne
U.S. losses, 3rd Aisne

160,000
30,000
130,000

133,000
35,000
98,000

29,000

10,000

Germany   France   Britain   U.S.

◄ *The second stage of the ongoing German offensive on the western front in May and June 1918 produced huge casualty lists for both Germany and the Allies alike.*

▼ *French troops, seen here awaiting train transport on the western front, combined effectively with U.S. forces to beat back the German offensive of June 1918.*

The French response to the crisis was swift. On the 11th, three French and two U.S. divisions, which had been hurriedly organized by General Charles Mangin, counterattacked Hutier's force and stopped it in its tracks. Ludendorff bowed to the inevitable and halted the Noyon-Montdidier Offensive on the 13th. The second German offensive was to be on the eastern flank of the Château-Thierry salient, but this would not take place until mid-July. This battle would eventually become known as the Second Battle of the Marne and will be covered in the next chapter. In the meantime the growing Allied strength was reflected in various small-scale counterattacks. One of the most significant of all of these was by U.S. forces in the Belleau area.

The Battle of Belleau Wood

After the troops of the U.S. 2nd Division had beaten off the German attacks on their positions during the first days of June, they decided that they were ready to advance themselves. This battle, which began on June 6 and lasted in its various phases until the 25th, is now known as the Battle of Belleau Wood, although it actually took place in a larger area than that covered by the forest itself.

The 2nd Division was unusual in that it was a U.S. Army formation that included two regiments of the Marine Corps. One Marine first sergeant, Dan Daly, became famous for urging his men to make a difficult charge with the cry: "Come on you sons-of-bitches, do you want to live forever?" Daly later denied having used these words, but earlier in his Marine career he had twice won the Medal of Honor and fought with great bravery at Belleau Wood before being wounded.

The Battle of Belleau Wood was on the front page of every newspaper at home in the United States. Journalists in France were not normally allowed to identify which units were involved in particular operations, but in this case the censors allowed a report on the Marines' part in the battle to be sent

▲ The Battle of Belleau Wood, *as painted by Frank Schoonover. U.S. Marines are shown in close combat with the German defending forces.*

EYEWITNESS

EDWIN L. JAMES

James was a correspondent for the *New York Times* on the western front during 1918 and was on hand to record the Battle of Belleau Wood in June. The battle was significant, both for the American Expeditionary Force (AEF) and the wider U.S. and Allied publics, for several reasons. It was the first time during the war that the enthusiastic but inexperienced U.S. troops had suffered large losses; the fighting showed the U.S. public that their country's military power was destined to have a significant impact on the outcome of the war; and the eventual U.S. victory at Belleau Wood greatly boosted Allied morale, with a corresponding drop in German hopes. The much-read report recorded the fighting around the wood on the 9th and 10th.

"I believe that when the history of the war is written, the Americans' capture of the Bois de Belleau will be ranked among the neatest pieces of military work of the conflict. At about three o'clock Monday morning [June 10] the Marines started, as soon as the artillery fire was stopped, to go through those woods. At the nearer edge of the woods, devastated by our shellfire, they encountered little opposition. A little farther on, the Germans made a small stand, but were completely routed; that is, those who were not killed. By this time, the Marines were fairly started on their way. They swept forward, clearing out machine-gun nests with rifle fire, bayonets, and hand grenades. The Germans started in headlong flight when the Americans seized two machine guns and turned them on the Germans with terrific effect. The Germans soon tired of this, and those nearest the Americans began surrendering. In the meantime, the Marines kept up the chase."

Extract taken from *Current History*, first published on June 20, 1918.

overnight and so there was not enough time to organize a proper supporting artillery barrage before the attack began at 4:00 A.M. the next morning. Belleau Wood was a rugged tract of land with huge boulders, steep ravines, and dense underbrush making forward movement difficult and at the same time providing good defensive positions for the German machine gunners. It was a recipe for heavy casualties.

Some U.S. Marines were shot down as they advanced across wheatfields toward the wood. Others broke into the wood and fought fierce close-range battles with the defenders, causing many casualties on both sides. By the end of the day, the Marines had gained some ground on either side of the wood, especially at the village of Bouresches a little to the south and east, but the Germans still held most of the wood itself. A little farther still to the south the division's 3rd Brigade, consisting of U.S. Army infantry units, also lost heavily around Hill 192.

However, the battle was far from over. The Marines sent in another series of full-scale attacks between the 10th and 12th. They managed to seize control of a little more of the wood, but only after taking yet more casualties. By now the Marines were exhausted. They had been fighting hard for almost two weeks without a rest, first in defense and then in attack, and had hardly had a proper meal during that time. They were relieved by units of the 7th Brigade from the 3rd Division, who made their own attacks on the 19th and 20th. The Marines were back in the line again in a few days' time, attacking once more on the 23rd. Two days later, after more bitter fighting, a battalion commander in the 5th Marines was at last able to signal to his headquarters: "Woods now U.S. Marine Corps entirely." The victory around Belleau was completed by a well-prepared and successful attack by the 3rd Brigade against Vaux, at the south end of the sector, on July 1.

off. This angered the 2nd Division's U.S. Army units, who felt their bravery in the action had been overlooked.

The 2nd Division was in the sector commanded by French general Jean Degoutte, who only made the decision to attack on June 5. Detailed orders therefore reached the frontline troops

U.S. WAR ARTISTS

In July 1917 the Committee on Public Information (CPI), the U.S. government's propaganda arm, suggested that artists be sent to Europe under the control of the U.S. Army's Signal Corps to record the American Expeditionary Force. The plan fell through, and it was not until the following December that the idea was revived, with the eight artists chosen being officially part of the Corps of Engineers. They began arriving in Europe during March 1918.

The artists sent to France were William Aylward, Walter Duncan, Harvey Dunn, George Harding, Wallace Morgan, Ernest Peixotto, J. Andre Smith, and Harry Townsend. Six were magazine illustrators, one was an architectural etcher, and one was a "real pure artist." Provided with two automobiles and official travel passes, they ranged along the western front. Each month suitable work passed through official military channels back to the CPI for morale and propaganda purposes in the United States.

There were initial complaints concerning the quality and quantity of the artists' early works, chiefly that they were short on human interest and action, but matters improved as the men became more accustomed to the war. During their period in Europe, the artists completed more than 500 pieces of art, many of which now reside in the Smithsonian Institution's Museum of American History.

Out of the Wire by Harvey Dunn, 1918.

Some 4,500 Marines were killed or wounded in this series of engagements, which was about 50 percent of the Marine force, along with a slightly smaller number of U.S. Army troops. The Germans lost 8,624 men. These figures still made it a rather minor battle by western front standards, but it had great effect on the Allies. Many people in France and at home in the United States believed that the Marines had saved Paris from the Germans. Though hardly true, this belief helped boost morale at a time when prospects were looking bleak for the Allies. Correspondingly, on the German side, the troops and their generals began to realize that the new U.S. forces were evolving into a tough opponent, even though they might still have a bit to learn about tactics.

The second half of June and the first half of July 1918 were actually rather quiet and uneventful on the western front as a whole. The Allied commanders were rebuilding their forces after the damage done by Ludendorff's four offensives and were not yet ready to launch their own counterattack. In June many of the German soldiers fell victim to the influenza epidemic that would sweep across the world in the coming months—it happened to reach them before it reached the Allies and did more damage because they were already weak from lack of food. Equally so, more U.S. soldiers would be killed by the epidemic than by the Germans. For the moment, however, this wave of illness was another cause for concern for the German high command, even as it was preparing for the fifth of Ludendorff's great battles.

Privately, even Ludendorff was beginning to recognize that the German Army might not have the strength to win the war, but he and Field Marshal Paul von Hindenburg were outraged when the German foreign minister, Richard von Kühlmann, spoke of the prospect of a compromise peace in the German parliament on June 24. They made sure that he was dismissed, replacing him with the more pliable Paul von Hintze, and went on with their plans for one more attack. It was destined to be the final German offensive of the war and it was to take place in July. It would be met with an Allied counterattack that would mark the failure of Ludendorff's attempt to bring the war to a successful conclusion. Within three short months Ludendorff would be forced to resign and flee to Sweden.

▼ *American soldiers passing through Meaux on their way to the front in 1918.*

The Allies Fight Back

For the first six months of 1918 the German Army had been doing the major part of the attacking along the western front. Because of the reinforcements he had received from the eastern front, the overall German commander, General Erich Ludendorff, had held the initiative. He had been able to choose where and when major battles were fought, and

By June 1918 the Allies had weathered a succession of German offensives on the western front. Nevertheless, they faced further attacks before they could launch their own large-scale offensives on the weakening German forces.

Allied commanders and their overstretched forces had had to defend with all their resources to keep from being overwhelmed.

From March through June both sides had lost some 100,000 men each month, who were killed, wounded, or taken prisoner. The British, French, and German armies had all been hit hard, but significant numbers of U.S. troops were at last joining the frontline Allied forces and proving themselves in battle. Even worse for the Germans was the fact that U.S. soldiers were arriving in France at the rate of up to 300,000 a month.

The Germans still had about as many divisions in service on the western front in June as were available in March, and they had been able to keep these up to nearly full strength. However, this feat had only been made possible by removing troops from other theaters of war where they were supporting Germany's allies, Austria-Hungary, Bulgaria, and Turkey, and by hurrying young men born

in 1900 through initial training into service at the front. These men would normally not have been considered for service until 1919, and the only other possible source of new manpower now that they were in uniform was the still younger "class of 1920," which could not be called or trained for some months yet.

Despite this somewhat depressing prospect, Ludendorff still clung on to the tattered remains of the strategy he had laid down earlier in the year, even if the timetable he had planned for it had long since been abandoned, albeit reluctantly. He eventually decided to launch another diversionary attack around Reims in the Champagne region of France, which would improve the German positions there and, more important, draw in Allied reserves from elsewhere. Then, finally, a decisive attack against the British in Flanders in the north would decimate the Allied forces and convince the latter to make peace on German terms.

▲ *Two British casualties of the Battle of Hazebrouck in April 1918, part of the German spring offensive that initially seemed likely to achieve a decisive breakthrough.*

◀ *The spring offensive cost Germany dear in terms of casualties. The final advance, as shown here, was turned back at the Marne in mid-June, leaving German forces unable to mount further offensive actions. From this point the Allies were in control.*

Privately, Ludendorff admitted that the plan might fail, but he fooled himself into believing that he had no other choice. He explained his reasoning in his memoirs: "There were hopes that if the offensive at Reims succeeded, there would be a very decisive weakening of the enemy in Flanders. I gave serious thought to the question, whether, in view of the spirit of the Army and the condition of our reserves, it would not be advisable to adopt the defensive. I finally decided against this policy, because quite apart from the bad influence it would have on our allies, I was afraid that the Army would find defensive battles an even greater strain than an offensive, as such a policy would make it easy for the enemy to concentrate."

The truth was that Ludendorff was burying himself in more work, concentrating on the details and trying to ignore the dreadful overall situation. He was not the only one to be over-optimistic. At home in Germany the chancellor, Georg von Hertling, the head of the government, also believed that the Allies would soon be desperate to make peace. At the front many of the ordinary German soldiers spoke of the attack as the *Friedensturm*, the "Peace Offensive"—which only made their disappointment when it failed all the more severe and damaging.

What Ludendorff did not know at the time was that the initiative had already partly slipped away from him to the Allies. By breaking the codes that were used for German radio messages, the French intelligence services were giving General Ferdinand Foch, the Allied supreme commander, accurate information about German plans. Foch knew where they planned to attack and was improving his defenses accordingly, and, more important than this, he was also preparing a counteroffensive that would strike into the west flank of the

great salient north of Château-Thierry. The Allied commanders would benefit greatly from good top-level intelligence such as this in all of their planning for the remainder of the year.

Second Battle of the Marne

The First Battle of the Marne in 1914 had been a turning point in the war, for in that battle the German advance on Paris had been stopped and thrown back. During the First Battle of the Marne it had become certain that the war would not be a short one, which Germany might have won, but a long one, which Germany would probably lose. The Second Battle in 1918 would be the catalyst for German defeat. The German Army would use up the last of its attacking power with little effect, and allow the Allies to take over once and for all.

▼ *The high level of casualties in the spring offensive of 1918 saw many German reserve troops, such as these, called into action. Despite early successes, the tide turned against the Germans in July, when Ludendorff finally abandoned any idea of a renewed assault in Flanders.*

The German plan for the Second Battle was a two-pronged attack to the west and east of the city of Reims. To the east lay General Karl von Einem's Third Army and the bulk of the First Army under General Bruno von Mudra. To the west of Reims stood the remainder of Mudra's command and General Max von Boehn's Seventh Army. Reims had held out against German attacks during Ludendorff's third offensive of the year at the end of May, but this new attack, Ludendorff believed, would surround and capture the city, while at the same time making the German lines throughout the region easier to defend if necessary. If it went according to plan, the advance would gain some 30 miles (48 km) along an 80-mile (128 km) front toward Châlons-sur-Marne and Fère-en-Champenoise. The planned attack was to be mounted by almost 50 divisions, supported by the usual massive artillery force, this time of some 5,000 guns and other weapons.

The east and west wings of the attack had very different results. To the east of Reims, the Allied defending forces were from General Henri Gouraud's French Fourth Army, 14 divisions strong. The earlier intelligence warnings of the attack were confirmed by information from German deserters and other sources. Late on July 14 the French artillery units were able to begin their own spoiling bombardment of the German lines, which were packed with the storm troopers ready to attack, a full 30 minutes before the Germans' bombardment started.

Even so, Gouraud knew that the Germans would have artillery superiority, and he accordingly made sure to employ defense-in-depth tactics to the fullest extent. He thinned out the defenses of his front line and kept his reserves a little way back, out of range of most of the German guns but ready to move into battle at the right moment. Many of the German shells fell on empty trenches. When the German

infantry moved forward, they took heavy casualties from carefully positioned machine guns without being able to do any corresponding damage to the Allied units in return.

The U.S. 42nd (Rainbow) Division was among the defending units in this sector. Colonel Douglas MacArthur, the division's chief of staff, later described how the Allied artillery bombardment had disrupted the attack. Nonetheless, the German storm troopers broke into the defenses of the U.S. 167th Infantry and were only pushed back after a vicious

▲ Colonel Douglas MacArthur of the U.S. 42nd Division in World War I went on to become one of the most colorful and controversial figures of World War II. It was he who masterminded the U.S. victory over Japan in the Pacific.

hand-to-hand battle. By the end of the first day of the German offensive, the attack was completely stalled. Ludendorff had to agree when Einem gave orders for the advance to be abandoned. Half of Ludendorff's plan had failed within hours of its having begun.

U.S. troops defend the Marne
West of Reims, where the German Seventh Army attacked, it was a slightly different story. Most of the defending forces were from the French Fifth Army under the command of General Henri Berthelot, who failed to benefit properly from the warnings provided by the French intelligence service. Berthelot deployed too many of his troops in forward positions, because they were well sited to stop the German attacking forces even before they got across the Marne River—or so Berthelot thought.

The defending troops included significant U.S. forces and also two divisions of Italians (sent to the Marne in exchange for British and French troops deployed in Italy). All forces suffered badly from the German bombardment; there were more than 1,000 U.S. gas casualties on this day alone. With a variety of small boats and then improvised bridges, the Germans swarmed across the Marne for several miles on either side of Dormans, and between there and Reims the Italian troops were forced to retreat.

General Henri Philippe Pétain began to consider redeploying to the sector some of the troops on their way to join the Tenth Army for the counteroffensive. He was overruled by Foch, who judged that the Germans had in fact made a mistake and would not go very much farther. To support Pétain, Foch arranged with Field Marshal Douglas Haig, the commander of the British Expeditionary Force, for some British reserves to be sent to the Marne, but, meantime, preparations for the counterattack would go on. One of the factors that gave Foch confidence to do

▼ **American troops in action during the Second Battle of the Marne, 1918, as painted by Mal Thompson. Several artists were sent with the AEF in 1917 to record the story of the war.**

this was the effective defense put up by the U.S. troops in the front line. A small part of the 28th Division, which was operating as part of a French unit, was badly cut up by the initial German advance, but the 3rd Division, in action with General Jean Degoutte's French Sixth Army to the east of Berthelot's force, did a great deal better.

General Joseph Dickman's U.S. 3rd Division was holding the Allied line near Château-Thierry, at the western end of the German attack. The German advance fell on its 30th and 38th Infantry Regiments. The 30th Regiment fought off a German assault but then pulled back, with its inexperienced troops losing their nerve under the hail

EYEWITNESS

CAPTAIN JESSE WOOLRIDGE

Woolridge served as a company commander in Major Guy Row's 2nd Battalion of the 38th Infantry Regiment during the Second Battle of the Marne in July 1918. His men, who successfully beat off attacks by much stronger German forces, were dug in along the line of the Marne River. He later recorded the fighting on the 15th:

"The enemy had to battle their way through the first platoon on the river bank—then they took on the second platoon on the forward edge of the railroad, where we had a thousand times the best of it—but the [Germans] gradually wiped it out. My third platoon [took] their place in desperate hand-to-hand fighting, in which some got through only to be picked up by the fourth platoon, which was deployed simultaneously with the third... By the time they struck the fourth platoon they were all in and easy prey.

"It's God's truth that one company of American soldiers beat and routed a full regiment of picked shock troops of the German Army. The Germans were carrying back wounded and dead [from] the river bank, and we in our exhaustion let them do it—they carried back all but 600, which we counted later, and 52 machine guns... We had started with 251 men and 5 lieutenants...I had left 51 men and 2 second lieutenants."

Extract taken from the Jesse Woolridge Archive held by the Hoover Institution.

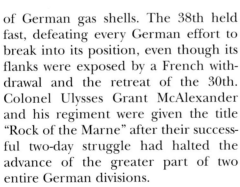

of German gas shells. The 38th held fast, defeating every German effort to break into its position, even though its flanks were exposed by a French withdrawal and the retreat of the 30th. Colonel Ulysses Grant McAlexander and his regiment were given the title "Rock of the Marne" after their successful two-day struggle had halted the advance of the greater part of two entire German divisions.

At the end of the first day of the offensive, the Germans had gained no more than 3 miles (5 km) of ground along a 10-mile (16 km) front. This advance was an abject failure compared with their advances in earlier battles. On the 16th they continued to make a little ground, but casualties were mounting at an alarming rate. On July 17, even though they now had 14 divisions across the Marne, the German forces could drive

forward no farther and came to a halt. The second half of Ludendorff's plan had also failed.

An important element in the Allied success in the Marne battle—indeed in all the fighting for the rest of 1918—was that the Allies now held and retained the upper hand in the new battlefield of the air. Quentin Roosevelt, son of former president Teddy Roosevelt, was killed in air combat nearby on July 14, but other Allied pilots had better fortune. More than 200 French bombers attacked the bridges and crossing points over the Marne on the 15th, though without putting them out of action. Other pilots were deployed over enemy lines to report on the Germans' movements, to find targets for the Allied artillery, and to continually harass the German ground troops with machine-gun attacks. U.S. fighter pilots like Billy

Mitchell and Eddie Rickenbacker, the top-scoring U.S. ace of the war, were also in action above the battlefields.

Ludendorff had been dismayed by the lack of progress made by his latest offensive. On the 15th and 16th his staff officers could see that he had no real idea what to do next. The troops that had managed to get across the Marne were hopelessly exposed. They could not be properly supplied while the bridges over the river were being destroyed or regularly damaged by Allied air attacks. Worse still, they could not even pull back safely without serviceable bridges they could use in their retreat.

By the 17th Ludendorff thought he had worked out a plan. The Seventh Army would stop its attacks and would be sent orders to retreat on the 20th. In the meantime the artillery reserve would start its move north to Flanders for the long-awaited battle there. However, on the morning of the 18th, Ludendorff was at a planning conference for this attack when he heard that the Allies had beaten him to the punch. The French Tenth Army was counterattacking from Villers-Cotterets. Chancellor Hertling of Germany later summed up just how important this turning point in the war was to the Allies: "We expected grave

events in Paris for the end of July. That was on the 15th. On the 18th even the most optimistic of us knew that all was lost. The history of the world was played out in three days."

Aisne-Marne Offensive

The Allied counteroffensive on July 18–19 hit the right flank of the great salient that had been captured by the German attacks in late May and early June. The assembly area for the advance was in the heavily wooded country that lay around Villers-Cotterets, which helped to conceal the preparations from the Germans. A total of 24 Allied divisions took part in the attack, with others joining in later. Most of these were part of General Charles Mangin's Tenth Army. The principal target was the system of rail lines passing near Soissons. If the Allied advance could capture this, a whole section of the German front would be compelled to give way because troops in the sector depended heavily on supplies brought by this route.

Mangin's men were mainly French, with some British and Italian support, but the advance was to be spearheaded by the U.S. 1st and 2nd Divisions. Of the one million U.S. troops in France by mid-July, approximately 33 percent

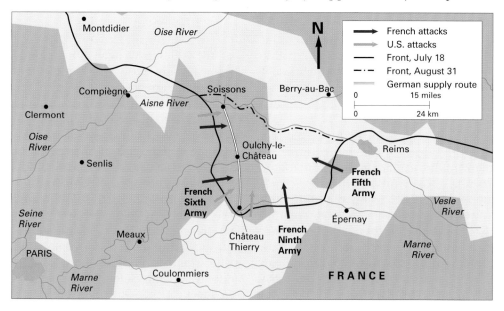

◀ The Second Battle of the Marne was fought during July and August 1918 and began with the Germans punching a small salient in the Allied line. However, an Allied counter-offensive from July 18 regained the ground.

▲ *U.S. infantry soldiers were a major factor in the Allied counterattack on the Marne salient. It was during this action that U.S. troops began to prove their worth to the Allied cause.*

would take part in the fighting in the Marne or Aisne sectors. For the first time U.S. troops were beginning to make their strength felt in the war.

Although the attack had been in preparation for several weeks, it was not the case that the troops to carry it out were already in position. Some of the U.S. troops only rushed up to the start line literally minutes before the attack was due to begin. The advance was led by over 500 tanks, with some being deployed with every division in the first wave of the advance. This time along most of the front there was no preliminary bombardment. The guns instead started with a rolling barrage and the infantry moved forward immediately. This tactic, too, helped to surprise the

defenders. By the end of July 18 the advance had gained 5 miles (8 km) of ground and had captured around 12,000 prisoners and 250 guns.

The U.S. 1st and 2nd Divisions both managed to advance beyond their initial objectives on that first day, despite being held up by the slower progress of a French Moroccan division in line between them. Both the French and Germans involved in the battle were deeply impressed by the aggression and commitment shown by the U.S. troops that made these advances possible, but they also commented on how their inexperience led to their suffering very high losses. When the 1st Division was finally relieved four days later, it had lost over 7,000 men killed, wounded, or captured,

PEOPLE AND WAR

STARS AND STRIPES

Stars and Stripes was the name of a newspaper that was produced and published in France for the soldiers of the American Expeditionary Force. The first issue was published on February 8, 1918, and it continued to appear for 71 weeks, every Friday, until June 13, 1919, well after the war had ended.

The first print run of *Stars and Stripes* was fewer than 30,000 copies, but the circulation later topped 500,000. The paper was not given away free; soldiers had to buy it if they wanted to read it, and at 50 centimes, roughly 10 cents, it was quite expensive compared with newspapers at home. A single copy was likely to be read out to small groups or passed between individuals. The paper included serious news about the war, advice to soldiers about how they should behave in a foreign country, and so on. Some content was more fun, however, including sports reports, stories, and cartoons.

Among the reasons the paper was so popular were that most of the staff were enlisted men and that the letters page published complaints and gripes from ordinary frontline soldiers. The doughboys did not think that *Stars and Stripes* was simply another example of senior U.S. Army officers telling them what to do. After the war ended, several journalists who had been associated with *Stars and Stripes*, including Harold Ross and Alexander Wolcott, founded the *New Yorker* magazine.

about 25 percent of its strength. The 2nd Division was pulled out on the 20th with 5,000 casualties.

These casualties were only one sign of toughening German resistance. Fewer than 200 Allied tanks were available for battle on the 19th, although many of the remainder had broken down rather than been knocked out. By the 20th more American, French, and British units joined in the attack. These included the U.S. 4th and 26th Divisions; a number of other U.S. units were also involved over the next few days.

The Germans were still pulling back, but it was a controlled withdrawal rather than a headlong retreat. In response to the Allied advance the Germans had pulled back in stages as they were attacked, starting from around Château-Thierry and eventually finishing on a new defense line along the Vesle River. The Germans did not go willingly, and there was fierce fighting throughout the sector until the first days of August. On the 6th the front began to stabilize for the moment on the line of the Vesle. It had been a great Allied victory for which Foch was promoted to the rank of marshal. All the same, the two sides' casualties were about even, at 150,000 men. On the Allied side these included about 100,000 French, with the rest split evenly among the Americans, British, and Italians.

One consequence of the attack was that Ludendorff had to abandon his plans to attack in Flanders once and for all. Instead, the German reserves in Flanders had to be sent south to bolster the Marne front and the sectors on its northern flank. For a time Ludendorff spoke of a new defensive policy that would have at its center the occasional small-scale attack designed to wear away

▶ *The scale of the losses suffered by Germany and the Allies during the Second Battle of the Marne and at the Battle of Amiens, July–August 1918. The German losses could not be replaced.*

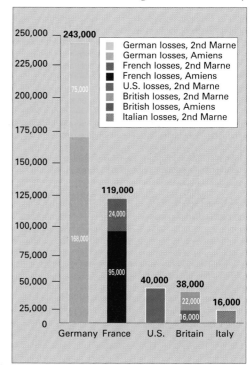

gradually at Allied superiority. However, he did very little to make this plan become a reality, and it would soon prove to be as much a case of wishful thinking as his earlier strategy had been.

Foch's dynamic leadership

From the time of his appointment as co-ordinator of the Allied armies in March (and as supreme commander from mid-April), Foch had a transforming effect on the conduct of the war. Previously, the British and French had tended to cooperate reluctantly and as little as possible.

From March 1918 on, this situation changed, and both Allied defensive and offensive operations increasingly became multinational, with French, British, U.S., Italian, and other troops fighting side by side. It is hard to imagine that this would have taken place to the same extent without Foch's continual urging. He had seemed to lose confidence briefly at the start of the third German offensive in May, but apart from that lapse he had held firm to his plans to go over to the offensive when he could see that the German attacks had been blunted.

▼ *German troops taken prisoner by the French in mid-1918 await transport to the rear. What began as a trickle turned into a torrent as the morale of many ordinary frontline soldiers collapsed.*

▲ By August 1918 German troops were becoming increasingly demoralized owing to the obvious strength of the Allies, their own war weariness, and growing political strife at home. Some of them began surrendering after offering only token resistance. Here, an Australian howitzer is seen in action, as the Allies begin to press home their advantage.

However, Foch and the other Allied generals did not truly realize in the summer months of 1918 how serious a defeat they had just inflicted on the Germans. In July and August they had fairly limited objectives for their attacks, and Foch had to work hard to convince Haig that even these were possible at first. Foch's plans at this stage then envisioned a gradual dying down of operations in the fall, followed by a winter mainly devoted to preparations for truly decisive advances in 1919, when U.S. forces would at last be strong enough to play a leading role.

Throughout World War I railroads were the key factor in any large troop maneuvers and also in fighting battles. Although armies used more and more trucks and other motor vehicles as the war went on and had many horses to move artillery weapons and in other transport roles, they relied on railroads for longer-distance journeys and for the movement of large numbers of men and supplies. Men marched when they

were close to the front line, but they got to the sector by train. Both sides quickly built narrow-gauge lines near the front, but the presence or absence of excellent normal-gauge rail lines in a sector was a deciding factor governing how many troops could fight there.

Equally, it was essential to an effective defense or to a powerful attack concentration to be able to switch divisions from side to side along a front without having to detour many miles to the rear. For the Allies, therefore, a priority in the early summer would be to free various routes radiating out from Paris from any possible threat of German attack. Routes to the east via Château-Thierry and Châlons were cleared by the Aisne-Marne fighting, with Amiens being the next priority. For the Germans, however, the lateral routes between their forces in central France and those in Flanders were just as important as those leading back from each of those groups of armies to Germany. This necessity ensured that rail centers like Lille, Cambrai, St. Quentin, and later on Hirson and Mézières would be among the prime targets of the coming Allied attacks.

Battle of Amiens

The possibility of an Allied attack in the Somme region had been discussed by the Allied generals for several months. By the summer of 1918 Haig, the British commander, still tended to be rather cautious. He was only too well aware that his armies had lost as many men in little more than five weeks of fighting in March and April as they had in five months during the horrendous Third Battle of Ypres in 1917. The British divisions had been sent plenty of replacements for their casualties, but many of the newcomers were very young and lacked experience of battle. In any case, in July Haig was still worried that the Germans might make a powerful attack in Flanders, as of course Ludendorff wanted to do, and did not want to be caught off balance with too many of his troops committed farther south in the Somme sector.

In a series of conferences during July, Foch persuaded Haig first to attack east of Amiens and then to increase the size of the offensive from the very limited scale that Haig had initially planned. As well as encouraging Haig to use more of his own resources, Foch also committed General Eugène Debeney's French First Army to join the right flank of the battle. Haig, though, kept the objectives of the attack limited ones—he did not want his men to push on too far ahead of any reserves and be exposed to a German counterattack.

A preliminary operation on July 4 gave a strong indication of what the outcome might be. This attack near Hamel was mounted by the Australian 4th Division, along with a strong force of tanks and a small group of infantry from the U.S. 33rd Division. The 33rd

▼ *Australian forces, such as these troops coming out of the line after several hard days' fighting, provided the cutting edge for the Allied offensive to the east of Amiens in August 1918.*

Division was one of six that had been trained and largely equipped by the British, but only two, the 27th and 30th, would stay committed to the British sectors throughout the fighting to come. At Hamel the attack went like clockwork. There was no preliminary bombardment to alert the Germans, only a creeping barrage to accompany the tank and infantry attack. The objectives were achieved within two hours and 1,500 German prisoners taken. To make sure that the new positions could be held, supply tanks brought forward rolls of barbed wire, and British aircraft dropped ammunition for the infantry's machine gunners, probably the first time in warfare that a significant air-supply operation had been attempted.

The Allied force assembled for the main Amiens attack totaled 25 infantry divisions. Ten of these were from the French First Army on the right flank. The troops that were in General Henry Rawlinson's British Fourth Army sector were actually of four nationalities: British, Australian, Canadian, and American. The four Canadian and five Australian divisions provided the real cutting edge. They were probably the most effective troops in any of the Allied armies in 1918 and would spearhead many important attacks between this point and the end of the war. The U.S. 33rd Division was part of the British III Corps on the left flank. In support were some 3,000 artillery pieces, over 400 tanks, and about 1,800 aircraft, all adding up to a six-to-one superiority over General von der Marwitz's German Second Army.

The Allied planners tried hard to ensure that their attack was kept secret. Troops moved into the area at night and kept under cover by day; aircraft flew low over the German lines so they would not hear the noise of the tanks getting into position; and the artillery

▼ The Allied counteroffensive of August 1918 around Amiens saw Australian soldiers occupying enemy trenches, as shown here. The ferocity and skill with which their attack was delivered helped provoke thousands of German troops into surrender.

THE BLACK DAY OF THE GERMAN ARMY

In his memoirs, written shortly after the war, German General Erich Ludendorff described August 8, 1918, as: "the black day of the German Army in the history of this war... It put the decline of our fighting power beyond doubt."

In fact, the Allied attack east from Amiens that prompted this comment was probably not nearly as dangerous or successful as Ludendorff's comments suggested. The Allied forces had gained up to a maximum of 12 miles (19 km), but this advance was not the most worrying factor. What had really shocked Ludendorff was morale. There were reports he received about German soldiers giving up without a fight and letting themselves be taken prisoner. Indeed, the Allies captured 30,000 German troops on August 8. He also heard of reserve units going forward into the battle being taunted by retreating frontline troops that they were unnecessarily prolonging a war that was undoubtedly lost.

France's Marshal Ferdinand Foch had always believed that battles were lost and won in the minds of their commanders. The Black Day was probably the point in the war when, in his own mind, Ludendorff accepted that he had lost. However, if given firm leadership, the German Army probably had the resources to support an effective defensive strategy on the western front well into 1919. Instead, for the remainder of the war Ludendorff hesitated between holding his current positions, retreating to better ones, and trying to make peace with the Allies. In the face of the relentless Allied offensives, this indecision was a recipe for total defeat.

Some of the 30,000 German prisoners captured by Allied forces at the Battle of Amiens, August 8, 1918.

prepared for a creeping barrage fired "off the map," without any preliminary shooting to register on its targets.

Early on the morning of August 8, the offensive began. The Germans may have been expecting the attack, but they were surprised by its speed and power. Many German soldiers were terrified by the great mass of tanks lumbering toward them out of the morning mist. By late morning most of the Allied troops had reached their objectives, and thousands of German soldiers had been taken prisoner. Six German divisions had been completely shattered. A small group of armored cars even moved through into the German rear areas and drove about for the rest of the day machine-gunning any troops they met until they ran out of fuel and ammunition.

On the right flank of the attack, the French advanced rather more slowly than did the British forces, partly because they did not have any tanks to lead their attack. The only setback was on the left where a British attack near Chipilly was unsuccessful. The U.S. 131st Regiment was brought forward to head a new attack in this sector on the 9th, which was completely successful by the end of the day. Elsewhere on the second day progress

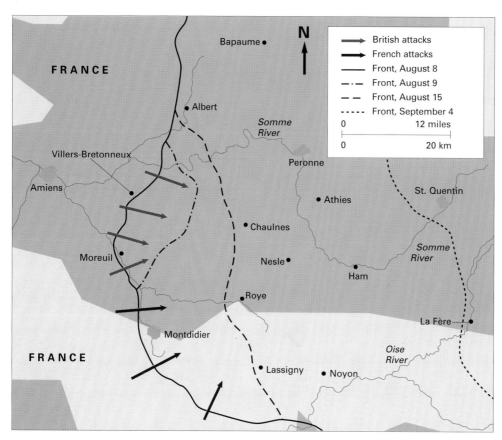

◀ *The decisive Battle of Amiens was a major boost to Allied morale as British and French forces halted the German advance and slowly began to recapture territory.*

was slower. The advance only gained some 3 miles (5 km), compared with 8 miles (12 km) the previous day, in part because only just over 100 tanks were still fit for action. By August 12 only six tanks were left in the fight, and the offensive was effectively over. The Germans had lost about 70,000 men, including 30,000 taken prisoner. Allied losses were less than half as heavy.

As the figures for the number of tanks available on the second and later days of the battle would show, armored vehicles had great limitations in 1918. They were easily knocked out by artillery fire, and even rifle and machine-gun rounds could sometimes penetrate their armor. They were very slow, and the crews had to operate in hot, noisy, and exhausting conditions. Above all, they tended to break down after only a few hours of operation. However, they could flatten any barbed wire not blasted away by the artillery and give attacking infantry a vital extra element of fire support when they were in among the enemy positions and unable to call in artillery fire.

Simply using tanks did not in itself make the difference between a successful attack and a failure. By 1918 the British and French had used their hard-won experience to develop infantry and artillery tactics into attacking systems at least as sophisticated as those of the German storm troops. The British had better equipment for locating enemy artillery batteries than did the Germans, and their infantry now generally operated in small squads centered on their machine guns, just as the Germans had learned to do.

The Allies take control

On August 10 General Ludendorff briefed the Emperor Wilhelm II on just how serious the situation was. The

450

emperor agreed that the war would have to be brought to an end. Even though Germany still had some 2.5 million soldiers in France and Belgium, it was doubtful if they could hold out even until the end of the year. A few days later a meeting of the German Crown Council formally agreed that Germany should ask the Allies for a peace deal, though this would have to wait for a "suitable moment" when the situation at the front was a little more stabilized. Charles, the Austro-Hungarian emperor, also visited the German headquarters the same day, and he and his team openly stated that they did not expect to be able to continue fighting for much longer either.

▼ *The Battle of Amiens was a decisive victory for the Allies. This photograph, taken afterward, shows tanks advancing through a nearby village, passing a wrecked Canadian ammunition wagon. German prisoners can also be seen being brought in.*

Following the success at Amiens, the Allied leaders prepared for still more attacks, although they did not yet know how badly beaten the Germans were. To keep the Germans off balance, Foch and Haig decided to make a series of attacks in succession all along the front, keeping each one going only as long as it was making good progress and then switching the effort to another sector. These attacks, however, were not seen as steps on the way to victory in 1918. They would undoubtedly weaken the Germans and regain French territory, but the decisive battles would have to wait until 1919.

For the rest of August and into early September, Allied forces advanced practically all along the line. To the north and south of the Amiens sector, French and British troops all attacked. Most of the U.S. troops were redeploying to take over their own section of the front at long last. Within days the British and French recaptured more or less all the territory that the Germans had taken earlier in the year. Reluctantly, the German commanders decided to retreat to the defensive positions they had held in 1917, the Hindenburg Line. These were well fortified, so they hoped that perhaps they could hold out there while something came of negotiations with the Allies.

At the same time as the Germans were retreating the Allies were gaining confidence. By the end of August, Foch was beginning to see a chance of winning the war within the year. As a sign of what was to come, a stunningly successful Canadian attack on an outlying section of the Hindenburg Line near Drocourt on September 2 showed that the German defenses were not as tough as the Germans had hoped. The first large-scale U.S. attacks of the war, the breaking of the Hindenburg Line, and a growing number of ever more desperate German peace attempts would be the major themes in the 10 weeks or so of war that now remained.

The Final U.S. Offensives

Before September 1918 the U.S. forces on the western front had been increasingly useful additions in what were mainly French and British operations, but from now until the end of the war in November, they would fight their own battles. They would go on to win notable victories and gain the respect of the German troops, even though, in the course of this process, mistakes were made and some U.S. lives were needlessly lost.

By late summer 1918 the American Expeditionary Force was able to undertake large-scale and wholly independent attacks on the western front, thereby contributing to the final Allied victory.

Strictly speaking, the United States was not one of the Allies but was what was known as an Associated Power. In accordance with this slightly detached status, General John Pershing, commander of the American Expeditionary Force (AEF), had been instructed from the first that he was to keep independent control of the U.S. forces on the western front at all times. He was not to permit his command simply to become divided between the British and French or placed under their direct command.

Although the Allies had seemingly agreed with Pershing on this point earlier in 1918, the British and French tried numerous times to make him change his mind. Faced by the great German offensives in the first half of the year, Pershing did compromise to some extent and allowed many of his troops to be used in British or French battles. Earlier chapters have highlighted some of the resulting actions in which U.S. troops fought alongside the Allies in the spring and summer of 1918. Many of these units were consolidated into the U.S. First Army when it was formed in August, but in the months that followed, roughly 25 percent of the combat troops of the AEF remained assigned to field operations with French

► *U.S. and French ammunition transports are moved to the front during the preparations for the U.S. offensive against the St. Mihiel salient, September 1918. The offensive was the first large-scale operation by General John Pershing's forces during the war and reflected the growing strength of the U.S. forces on the western front.*

or British forces. The operations through the fall of 1918 are described in more depth between pages 455 and 469.

The First Army was formally activated on August 10 and took over its own section of the western front in eastern France. Pershing himself took command of the force, while retaining his more senior position as commander in chief of the AEF. He initially assigned 14 divisions to the First Army, out of the 35 that he had in France at that stage (many of the others were not yet trained or ready for frontline service). Because infantry and machine gunners had been given priority for shipment to France in the spring and early summer,

► General John Pershing, as commander of the American Expeditionary Force (AEF), faced several problems in 1918. He had to turn a mass U.S. force into an effective fighting army, prevent it from being controlled by the other Allies, and also launch a number of major offensives.

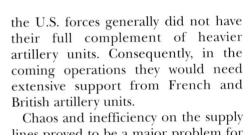

the U.S. forces generally did not have their full complement of heavier artillery units. Consequently, in the coming operations they would need extensive support from French and British artillery units.

Chaos and inefficiency on the supply lines proved to be a major problem for Pershing throughout the summer and into the fall. Mountains of supplies of every kind were sent over the Atlantic, only to pile up in French ports while the frontline troops went short of necessities. Some of the problems originated with poor planning and management by the War Department at home; some of it was down to Pershing and his staff changing their minds about what they needed and not communicating their requirements clearly to the suppliers at home; but by far most of the difficulties were caused by the poor performance of the Services of Supply (SOS) in France. Toward the end of July, Pershing appointed one of his leading combat commanders, General James Harbord, to take charge of the SOS. Harbord gradually improved the situation, although it took a little time.

▲ *An American supply train is seen resting in a shattered town in the eastern half of the St. Mihiel salient, September 18, 1918. This zone of the western front was selected to be the scene of the AEF's first major engagement with the enemy.*

As well as needing food, ammunition, and all other kinds of supplies when they began to fight bigger battles, the combat divisions suffered an increasing casualty rate, which brought with it an increasing requirement for replacements to keep the combat units up to strength. There were many problems and inefficiencies in this area also. As in the case of the SOS, some of the difficulties were the fault of the staff at home and some were due to Pershing.

Whoever was to blame for the problems the U.S. Army faced, the result was that some men were shipped to France within weeks of having joined the U.S.

Army, and they ended up in the front line only a few days later, untrained and poorly equipped for combat. A short time prior to the Meuse-Argonne Offensive in October, the 77th Division, previously made up mainly of New Yorkers, was sent 4,000 draftees who were from the western states. These men had been in the U.S. Army since July but had spent almost all the time since then traveling from camp to camp before finally being shipped across the Atlantic. Some experienced soldiers in the 305th Infantry supposedly charged these rookies five francs each to show them how to load their rifles.

The St. Mihiel attack

Since the early part of the war, the Germans had held a salient, or bulge, jutting into the Allied lines for 15 miles (24 km) on each side of the French town of St. Mihiel, some 20 miles (32 km) to the south of Verdun in eastern France. The area had seen considerable fighting in the first two years of the war but had been relatively quiet since then. In 1918 the salient still posed a potential threat to Allied operations throughout a wide area of eastern France.

From the time of the U.S. troops' first arrival in France, the salient was clearly earmarked as the region where the main force would be deployed, and in the summer of 1918, Pershing decided that St. Mihiel would be the target for the First Army's first great battle in mid-September. Not only was the salient a worthwhile objective but its defenses were run-down. It made sense to make this first battle a relatively easy one so that the morale of the troops and the support of the U.S. people at home were not weakened.

The decision to attack at St. Mihiel brought about another quarrel with Marshal Ferdinand Foch, the Allied supreme commander. As the other Allied forces met with more and more

▼ *U.S. infantry move toward the front line during September 1918, as part of the preparations for the assault on the St. Mihiel salient. In the first great U.S.-led offensive of the war, a total of 500,000 U.S. troops were assembled for the battle.*

▲ *The U.S. 167th Infantry Regiment holds positions in the St. Mihiel salient, September 15, 1918. Almost 20 divisions of the American First Army faced their first major test of the war here.*

success in the battles of July and August, Foch realized that the Allies had a real chance to win the war in 1918, but if they were to do so, they needed more from Pershing than the capture of a salient that the Germans might well withdraw from anyway. Foch wanted St. Mihiel canceled or scaled down and the U.S. troops committed to a larger offensive in the Argonne region to the northwest. When he proposed that some of the U.S. units there should be part of a French force, Pershing flatly refused. In the end a compromise was reached: the St. Mihiel offensive would go ahead and then Pershing would move most of his troops to the Argonne and fight that battle as an all-American one as well.

In an attempt to make the St. Mihiel operation easier, U.S. military planners developed a sophisticated operation to fool the Germans into thinking their first attack would take place in a different area. The place selected was the town of Belfort, far to the south, where there were numerous German-speaking people and where German spies were known to collect information. A radio network was set up to send coded messages that appeared to come from a large force assembling near Belfort. A general was sent from training duties to inspect the area and make a detailed plan for an attack, and a part of a copy of his work was "accidentally" left in the hotel room of a staff officer. He was delighted when, on returning to his room, he found it had disappeared. The Germans did move some additional troops into the Belfort area, but in view of other decisions they also made, it is doubtful if this U.S. deception made much difference at St. Mihiel.

Preparing for any big battle was a massive operation in World War I. A total of 500,000 U.S. and 100,000 French troops were moved into position, along with huge quantities of ammunition. Over 300 miles (480 km) of new rail lines and roads were built. Every day each division needed a trainload of food and many other items. The attack was to be supported by 3,000 guns, 260 tanks, and almost 1,500 aircraft. The greater part in each of these categories were French-manned, but a U.S. armored force, the 304th Tank Brigade under Colonel George Patton, and some 600 U.S. pilots under Colonel William Mitchell were also on hand to support the effort.

Despite the deception already described—and many efforts were made to hide the real preparations from the enemy—the Germans were not really fooled. They had only nine divisions, roughly 100,000 men, to defend the salient. Their positions were exposed, and it would not be very easy to reinforce them. In any case, even if an attack had not been planned, with problems in every other section of the front, it made sense for the Germans to shorten their front line and pull back in vulnerable sectors. Thus, as part of their general retreat all along the western front, some of the German artillery began to withdraw from the salient on September 11, the day before the battle started. This pullback could only make the attack easier.

The main U.S. attack was mounted by General Hunter Liggett's I Corps and the IV Corps under General Joseph Dickman along the southern face of the salient, with subsidiary operations by General George Cameron's U.S. V Corps against the west face and by the French against the southern tip. Nine

KEY FIGURES

GENERAL HUNTER LIGGETT

Liggett (1857–1935) was a high-ranking U.S. officer throughout the fighting on the western front in 1918. After graduating from West Point in 1879, Liggett saw little active service but was an influential figure in the U.S. military establishment, chiefly as the head of the War College Division.

In early 1918 Liggett was given command of the U.S. I Corps, the senior field command in General John Pershing's American Expeditionary Force. Liggett opposed the emphasis on "open warfare" training in Pershing's plans. The more realistic tactics he ordered his men to be instructed in stood them in good stead in the trench-dominated battles later in 1918. Liggett's corps led the attack on the St. Mihiel salient in September, and he commanded the corps through the first stages of the Meuse-Argonne Offensive. He was promoted to take charge of the First Army on October 16 for the final part of the advance.

Liggett was a little older than most of the other top U.S. generals. He had problems with arthritis and he was overweight, a situation that did not please Pershing. Liggett did not look like an effective soldier, but as he himself claimed: "Fat doesn't matter if it does not extend above the neck." He proved to be one of the clearest-thinking and most efficient U.S. military leaders of the war.

U.S. divisions were involved in the first stages of the offensive, but only five of them had a significant amount of battle experience. The main attack began with a four-hour preliminary bombardment, starting at 1:00 A.M. on the 12th. The subsidiary bombardments started at the same time, but the infantry in these sectors held back from attacking until later in the morning. The main attack was very successful due to the weak German defense. The U.S. 2nd Division successfully captured the town of Thiaucourt, some 5 miles (8 km) behind the German front, before midday, and other units reached their objectives for the second day of the battle before the first day's fighting had ended. Some

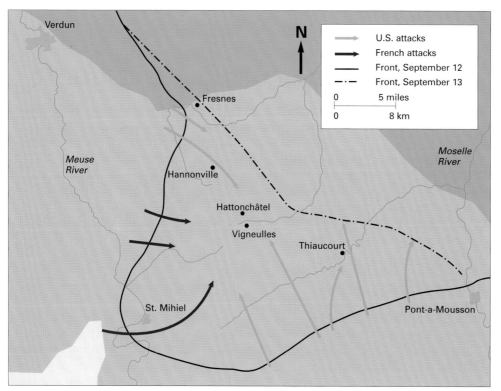

◄ *The Battle of St. Mihiel was the first truly independent offensive by U.S. troops on the western front. Fought in mid-September 1918, the battle retook a bulge in the front the Germans had been occupying since 1914.*

German troops gave up without a fight. One sergeant of the 89th Division captured around 300 prisoners using only an empty pistol.

The attacks on the west face of the salient made slower progress. The terrain in this region was more wooded, the German defenses stronger, and the pouring rain did not help either. By the end of the day, though, Allied aircraft could see that the roads out of the salient were packed with retreating German troops. At first, the Germans had hoped to continue with their planned, orderly evacuation, but the heavy U.S. attacks had made them decide to get out as fast as they possibly could.

On the 13th the two wings of the advance linked up around the town of Vigneulles, and further small advances had completely eliminated the salient three days later. U.S. casualties were around 7,000 men, plus some French losses, but U.S. forces captured over 13,000 Germans and killed or wounded probably 2,000 more, as well as liberating

French territory held by the Germans since 1914. The figures seemed to add up to a big success, and newspapers in every Allied country reported just that. Pershing received congratulatory messages from President Woodrow Wilson and other Allied leaders. However, this public praise was only part of the picture. Because of poor organization and staff work, a complete gridlock emerged in places behind the lines as soon as the troops began their advance. Some men ran short of food, and tanks ran out of fuel. Without these foul-ups the attack could have resulted in the capture of many more of the retreating German troops. The French prime minister, Georges Clemenceau, visited the battlefield and was shocked by what he saw. He would soon try to get Pershing fired for incompetence. Despite all these teething problems, Pershing was right in one respect. His First Army needed to start out with a victory, which St. Mihiel certainly was. The boost this gave to morale at home, in the other

Allied countries, and throughout the U.S. forces in France was invaluable for the much tougher battles to come.

Meuse-Argonne Offensive

When the plan for the Meuse-Argonne Offensive had been agreed upon by Pershing and Foch in early September, Pershing had summed up his resulting problem very neatly: "We had undertaken to launch within the next 24 days two great attacks on battlefields 60 miles [96 km] apart with practically the same army." This difficult move was achieved on time—as it had to be—because the U.S. attack was scheduled to begin simultaneously with French and British attacks on the German Hindenburg

▶ *U.S. light tanks move up to the front. A total of 189 of these French-built tanks were deployed for the Meuse-Argonne Offensive.*

▼ *An American soldier in combat during the St. Mihiel Offensive, as painted by Harvey Dunn, an official war artist of the American Expeditionary Force.*

Line defenses throughout northern France. Much of the credit for this achievement went to Colonel George Marshall, Pershing's chief of operations, who would be chief of staff of the U.S. Army in World War II and one of the architects of victory in that conflict.

The move involved sending 600,000 U.S. troops into the attack sector, while at the same time moving aside some 200,000 French who had been stationed there previously. There were only three minor rail lines and three poor roads leading into the battle area. To complicate matters even more, the First Army and its supporting troops were very short of motor vehicles and transport horses, and to make the situation more difficult still, all troop movements had to be made at night in an effort to preserve secrecy. The final complication, which no plan could ever prevent, was that it rained on almost every day of the battle, turning the roads and tracks into a sea of sticky, delaying mud.

Even without any rain the terrain over which the battle was to be fought was very rugged and difficult. Much of the ground was also densely wooded—the Argonne Forest covered most of the western side of the battlefield. There were numerous jagged hills and ridges,

U.S. Women at War

When the war broke out, many people thought that it was wrong for women to join the military in noncombat roles. Most men and many women still believed that some jobs were strictly "man's work" and that a woman's place was in the home.

The demands of wartime would see these ideas change substantially. In civilian life at home many women would take over "men's jobs" and do them well. Around 16,000 women put on uniforms and went overseas with the American Expeditionary Force (AEF), and many more worked in various positions with the military services at home. Women in uniform almost invariably did jobs that were normally done by women in civilian life—nursing, clerical and typing work, catering, and similar tasks.

All women in uniform were volunteers. None were drafted; and none assigned to combat units. Women were only brought into the military slowly, and the number serving did not reach its peak until after the armistice in November 1918. The largest number of women serving overseas were members of the Army Nurse Corps, which had been established as an all-female body in 1901. About 10,000 of the Nurse Corps's 21,000 personnel were with the AEF by the end of the war.

▲ *These U.S. nurses are just some of the 10,000 who served with the AEF during World War I, but they had no military rank.*

The U.S. Army remained grudging about giving them full military status. It refused to provide their uniforms, which instead were supplied by the American Red Cross. It also refused to fit them into the military hierarchy. Nurses were officially "officers without rank," and thus they had no actual authority over men sent to work in hospitals.

There were also some 200 so-called Hello Girls. These were French-speaking American women who were recruited to operate many of the U.S. Army's telephone switchboards. They wore uniforms and were paid by the Army and assumed that they therefore were effectively female soldiers. However, when they returned home after the war, they found out that the military authorities thought they were civilian employees and not entitled to veterans' benefits. They fought a long campaign for the recognition they deserved and were finally successful in 1978.

Several thousand more women went to France to work in canteens and other recreational and welfare facilities set up behind the lines and run by bodies like the Salvation Army, Red Cross, YMCA, and YWCA. These women wore uniforms in styles approved by the military authorities, but there was no doubt of their civilian status. Nor was there any doubt about the vital part they played in keeping the soldiers as happy and well cared for as possible.

▼ *This field hospital, set up in a church in Braisne, France, shows the conditions under which U.S. nurses worked.*

The welfare organizations included vaudeville-type shows in their program of entertainments for the troops. A few of the performers in these shows were women, some of them noted professionals from the showbiz world back home. The most popular was the singer and dancer Elsie Janis, who became known as the "sweetheart of the AEF."

Naval regulations did allow women to serve, and 11,575 were recruited by the U.S.Navy or U.S. Marine Corps as Yeomen (F). ("Yeoman" is a naval name for signaler.) All of these women served in clerical jobs, as typists, bookkeepers, and suchlike. Most served at home, but a handful were sent to France and a small number to places like Panama and Guam. None served at sea. The (F) designation was to ensure that no mistakes were made in this respect. Yeoman Smith could be assigned to a ship; Yeoman (F) Brown could not. However, in other respects they were full members of the U.S. Navy and were paid the same amount as men serving in the same job and grade.

and the riverbanks often merged into steep bluffs. The Germans had held this area since the early part of the war and had gradually built up a formidable network of defenses many miles deep. The toughest part of their defenses was known as the Kriemhilde Line, but the attackers would have to advance 10 miles (16 km) just to get into position to attack this defense line. The First Army's chief of staff, Colonel Hugh Drum, called the Argonne "the most ideal defensive terrain I have ever seen or read about." The U.S. commanders also failed to make use of the local knowledge accumulated by the French troops they were relieving in the sector to offset some of these difficulties. A further problem for the U.S. generals was

that the influenza epidemic that was raging around the world at that time hit their troops in France hardest during October. Thousands of troops died from its effects, and thousands more were incapacitated and unable to fight.

Nine American divisions, from three army corps, were in line for the first advance, with three more in reserve behind them. They were supported by 2,700 artillery weapons, 189 light tanks, and over 800 aircraft. The battlefront was roughly 20 miles (32 km) wide, stretching west from the Meuse River, just north of Verdun. The French Fourth Army under the command of General Henri Gouraud to the west was also to attack with additional tank, infantry, and artillery forces. Gouraud's eventual

▼ *Road and railroad links in the Argonne Forest were very poor and this problem, combined with tough terrain, made the U.S. offensive more difficult than the preceding assault on St. Mihiel. Here, U.S. tanks are seen moving up to the front line, September 26, 1918.*

objective was the complex of rail lines passing through Sedan, 40 miles (64 km) to the north, but the aim for the first stage of the assault was to break through so quickly that the Germans would not be able to reinforce their troops there.

Altogether the attackers had an eight-to-one superiority in infantry and artillery over the five understrength divisions of General Max von Gallwitz's German Fifth Army opposing them, though these units would soon be reinforced. Many of the German formations were regarded as weak and unreliable, but this description also applied in a different sense to some U.S. units. Two of the U.S. divisions had not even been given the usual introductory spell in a quiet sector of the front, and three others had little more fighting experience.

The attack enjoyed good progress at first, or so it seemed. In fact, it only lasted while the troops drove through the lightly defended German forward positions. As they did so, they lost communication with their supporting artillery and came within range of more and more German machine-gun posts. Many inexperienced soldiers were at first pinned down and then gradually picked off; neither they nor their commanding officers had the necessary training to work out what to do when they came under fire. German artillery sent high-explosive and poison-gas shells raining down to raise casualties even higher.

By the end of the second day, most of the U.S. divisions had pushed on 5 miles (8 km). In the center, the novice 79th Division had captured a very important

▶ *Meuse-Argonne was the final U.S. offensive of the war and lasted from September 26 until the armistice on November 11. U.S. forces suffered some 117,000 losses during the attack, chiefly during attempts to penetrate a series of fortified lines held by the Germans in late September and the first half of October.*

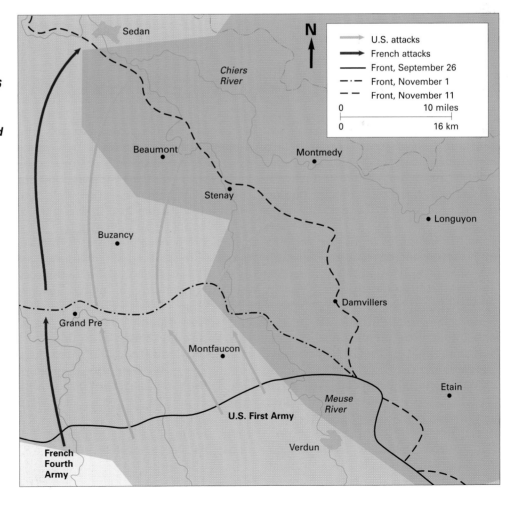

position known as Montfaucon Ridge, but units everywhere were becoming increasingly tangled together. In the 35th Division, for example, the divisional headquarters lost touch with one of its regiments, and one of the regimental commanders got lost and was unable to locate any of his men for over a day. As a result, orders were delivered late or not at all, and a German counterattack on the 29th took the last of the fight out of the troops. They saw no more action for the remainder of the war. Other divisions did much better, but by the end of the 28th the whole offensive had clearly ground to a halt.

Confusion and inexperience on the battlefield was matched by a shambles behind the line. All three roads leading to the front were completely jammed. The artillery needed to move forward to support the frontline troops in their new positions but simply could not do

so because of the mass of supply and communications vehicles already on the few roads available. Some troops in the front line ended up without food for several days, and wounded men suffered and died because they could not be got through to the hospitals.

Inexperienced administrative officers had tried to send much too large a mass of supplies on the limited road network and had not known how to make proper allowance for the effects of bad weather and German shellfire. The attack might well have gone better if Pershing had committed fewer troops and given them room to move and fight. Engineer units, reserve infantry, and anyone else who could be found were immediately set to work to improve the roads and get the traffic moving again, but this was work that really should have been done well in advance of the battle, not during it. Gradually, the worst of the mess was

▲ *A rail-mounted 14-inch (356 mm) gun seen in action during the Meuse-Argonne Offensive. Some 5,000 artillery pieces were deployed.*

▶ *The U.S. First Army paid a high price for the ground it took in the Meuse-Argonne battle, as shown by these casualties.*

sorted out and the guns and supplies moved forward once again. In addition, new troops also arrived in the first days of October, including some of the more experienced divisions that had been involved at St. Mihiel. The attack would have to be restarted.

The orders for the new attack showed that the U.S. commanders were beginning to learn their craft. Now that they were approaching the main German defense lines, they were usually spotted by German observation posts on the hills and ridges. The new plans emphasized neutralizing these posts with smoke and gas shells and also instructed the artillery to step up their counterbattery work against the German guns. Even with better artillery support, the infantry still struggled to advance under ferocious German fire. The veteran 1st Division took very heavy casualties, and it and the other attackers were reduced to the slowest rate of progress along the front. The so-called Lost Battalion of the 77th Division was cut off for almost a week in the Argonne Forest as other units struggled to come to its assistance.

There were many instances of personal bravery during the ongoing offensive. For example, in one action, on

PEOPLE AND WAR

THE LOST BATTALION

The Lost Battalion was the name that was given to some 550 U.S. troops, most from the 308th Infantry Regiment, commanded by Major Charles W. Whittlesey, who were cut off and surrounded by German troops in the Argonne Forest in October 1918, during the Meuse-Argonne Offensive.

On October 2, after already having been involved in attacks for several days, Whittlesey made an advance toward a rugged hillside known as the Ravine de Charlevaux. Flanking units did not keep up with his force and the battalion was surrounded by the Germans. The battalion faced intense fire from machine guns and trench mortars and was inadvertently attacked by U.S. aircraft.

For the next six days they fought off repeated German attacks, despite taking high casualties and running out of food early on. Medics even had to take bandages off the dead to use on the wounded. Eventually, on the 8th, attacks by the 82nd Division pushed the Germans back. More than 100 men of the battalion had been killed and some 200 wounded. For his leadership in the face of the enemy Whittlesey was awarded the Medal of Honor. However, he was deeply traumatized by his experiences in the Argonne and committed suicide after the war was over.

October 8, Corporal (later Sergeant) Alvin York of the 82nd Division's 328th Infantry Regiment was awarded the Medal of Honor for a brave individual exploit that led to the surrender of more than 130 German soldiers (see page 466).

By the middle of the month, the increasingly tired U.S. troops were ready to strike at the heart of the German Kriemhilde defenses, which lay along a ridge called Côte Dame Marie and to the east of there at Romagne and Cunel. On the 14th the 32nd Division gained a foothold on Côte Dame Marie, and the 5th Division and other units also broke into the defenses over the next two days. However, these forces were unable to achieve a breakthrough. Even the veteran units failed. The 42nd Division, for example, came into the front line on the 12th and kept up its attacks for the rest of the month. During that time, however, it only managed to advance about 1,000 yards (900 m).

All along the front, advance was a painfully slow process, capturing a pill-box here, a machine-gun post there, and all the time suffering a steady drain of casualties. The terrain was so broken and the conditions so difficult that there were few big attacks, just many desperate small-scale struggles. Many fit and unwounded men lost contact with their units and ended up some distance away from where they should have been. Pershing thought that his officers should shoot any soldier who tried to run away, but the truth was that most of these men had simply become disoriented and were not deserters or anything of the sort. Many of the men who were absent from their own unit ended up fighting bravely with another they had happened to meet. It was the sort of terrain where a soldier might easily get lost even when there was nobody trying to kill him.

By mid-October the AEF had become too big to be organized as a single army. On the 11th Pershing set up a Second Army, making General Robert Bullard commander. Pershing retained personal control of the First Army for

---

EYEWITNESS

SERGEANT ALVIN YORK

Tennessee-born Sergeant Alvin York became one of the most decorated soldiers of World War I because of his role in the U.S.-led Meuse-Argonne Offensive in October 1918. Highly religious, York had initially struggled during his basic training to come to terms with killing other human beings. Nevertheless, he was a superb marksman and on October 8, he singlehandedly stormed a machine-gun position, killing 25 and capturing 132 German troops. His own diary recorded the fight:

"There were over 30 of them [Germans] in continuous action, and all I could do was touch the Germans off [kill them] just as fast as I could. I was sharpshooting. I don't think I missed a shot. It was no time to miss.

"In order to sight me or to swing their machine guns on me, the Germans had to show their heads above the trench, and every time I saw a head, I just touched it off. All the time I kept yelling at them to come down. I didn't want to kill any more than I had to. But it was they or I. And I was giving them the best I had.

"Suddenly a German officer and five men jumped out of the trench and charged me with fixed bayonets. I changed to the old automatic and just touched them off too. I touched off the sixth man first, then the fifth, then the fourth, then the third and so on. I wanted them to keep coming. I didn't want the rear ones to see me touching off the front ones. I was afraid they would drop down and pump a volley into me."

Extract taken from York's personal diary.

another few days before handing it over to Liggett. Both Bullard and Liggett were good officers. Around the same time, Pershing also fired Cameron from V Corps, along with three divisional commanders and other senior officers, for poor performance in the attack, replacing them with officers who had proved themselves in combat. Pershing was criticized for some of these decisions, but overall he made good choices when selecting subordinates—a crucial skill for a top general.

Whether Pershing was up to the mark in other respects was a very different matter. Many British and French leaders thought that he was not. At this juncture in the war, when Pershing's advances were measured in yards, the other Allied troops were recapturing huge swathes of territory and fighting far larger German forces. They blamed Pershing for this discrepancy, not his men. Clemenceau wrote of this as follows: "Our worthy American allies, who thirst to get into action and who are unanimously acknowledged to be great soldiers, have been marking time ever since their forward jump in the first day. Nobody can maintain that these fine troops are unusable; they are merely unused."

Pershing had certainly made mistakes and was struggling to come up with a proper plan of operations. In his diary on October 14 he confessed his total lack of ideas: "I hope for better results tomorrow. There is no particular reason for this hope except that if we keep on pounding, the Germans will be obliged to give way." Many of his mistakes and problems were identical to those that his British and French critics had struggled to overcome in their own battles years earlier in the war, and he was working hard to fix them. Pershing himself could have learned more from his Allies and could have made sure that their knowledge was widely shared in the AEF, but even so, matters would only have improved to a degree. Some lessons in war can probably only be learned the hard way. They had been learned by the U.S. commanders in the Argonne.

▲ *German prisoners of war are seen here being escorted away from the front line by British cavalry troops. In the 47 days of the Meuse-Argonne campaign, the Allies captured 16,000 German prisoners.*

▲ Captured German field guns now in U.S. hands are turned on their former owners, October 9, 1918. The Meuse-Argonne Offensive had restarted five days earlier, but forward movement was slow and remained so for the rest of the month.

The other Allied leaders who wanted Pershing fired and his men taken under French or British command no doubt also had a political objective. With the end of the war approaching, the United States would have much less of a say in the upcoming peace negotiations if the AEF and its commander had been judged to have contributed little of value to the Allied victory. Clemenceau was the one who argued most forcibly for Pershing's removal, but Foch believed that Pershing was equal to the task. After all, it was true that the U.S. offensive was drawing German troops from the north, where the British and French forces were undertaking large-scale offensives of their own.

The AEF's final advance

General Liggett insisted on a pause in operations in the last days of October to allow the men of his First Army some opportunity to rest and reorganize. The First Army was to continue to push northward, and the Second Army was to extend the attack front with an eastward drive in a few days' time. On November 1, a powerful artillery barrage blasted the German positions and laid down a cloud of poison gas. This time the infantry and artillery worked well together, and the German front was broken. By the 4th the advance had gained up to 20 miles (32 km), and the German forces had decided they would have to withdraw north of the Meuse River. By the 6th some units had reached the Meuse near Sedan and were able to cut the rail route that had been the original objective. The Second Army began its attack on November 9, and both forces were planning new advances when the war ended two days later.

French officers noted how much better conducted the whole operation was than before. General Henri Philippe Pétain wrote: "a very remarkable improvement has taken place [compared with] the advance of September 26, road movements occur in order, orders are given well and in good time." In the very last days there was a brief confusion when various divisions tried to rush forward and gain the honor of freeing the city of Sedan. A number of U.S. troops may even have died in "friendly fire" incidents as a result, but this was an isolated problem in what was now a very much more professional AEF.

By the time the armistice came into effect on November 11, the Meuse-Argonne campaign had lasted for 47 days. It had cost the AEF some 117,000 casualties. The Germans may have lost as many as 100,000 killed and wounded, plus at least 16,000 taken prisoner. No one can really say how big a part the offensive played in the final defeat of Germany, although it has been estimated that the AEF's contribution to the Allied cause on the western front may have shortened the war by six months. What is certain is that the weeks in the woods of the Argonne, were a wet, muddy, hungry, and cold, terrifying and bloody experience for all who fought there.

▼ *Montfaucon Ridge, a strategically important position, was captured by these rookie U.S. 79th Division infantrymen on October 18, 1918, during the Meuse-Argonne Offensive.*

Europe's Other Theaters

As far as U.S. involvement was concerned, most troops who served overseas were sent to France, but others ended up in Italy and in northern or eastern Russia.

Although the western front was the most important theater of the war throughout 1918, it was by no means the only one in which significant fighting took place. Other major campaigns in Europe continued in Russia, Italy, and the Balkans.

Although the various events that are discussed in this chapter took place hundreds and sometimes even thousands of miles apart, it should not be thought that they were not linked together in the overall history of the war. This linkage was evident on both the Allied and Central Powers' sides.

Germany decided in 1918 to concentrate almost all of its military resources on the western front in a desperate gamble to achieve a decisive breakthrough. This decision was only made possible by the collapse of the Russian war effort and the beginning of the revolution there in 1917, both of which events effectively ended Russia's ability to take part in the wider war. Most of the German reinforcements sent to France in early 1918 came from Russia, but others also came from Italy and from the Balkans. These troop movements left Germany's European allies, Austria-Hungary and Bulgaria, to continue the fight in these theaters mostly on their own, although the Austro-Hungarians had the advantage of no longer having to fight Russia.

On the Allied side, significant British and French forces fought both in Italy and in the Balkans, instead of benefiting operations in France. The Allies were also worried that large quantities of supplies that they had sent to Russia might even fall into German hands and end up being used against them. Some Allied politicians still hoped that, whatever form the new Russian government took, it could be persuaded to continue the fight against Germany. On the other hand, at the start of 1918, leaders in all countries also worried that their troops and peoples might follow the Russian example and rise up in revolt, goaded by the suffering of what was already history's most devastating war.

Understanding what happened in eastern Europe during this period is made more difficult by the fact that a whole range of countries that now exist did not do so before World War I. Instead they were parts of the Russian

or the Austro-Hungarian Empire. In fact, independence movements existed throughout the entire region and were encouraged by the Allies or the Central Powers at various times throughout the war, whenever unrest might help to weaken their main enemies. These independence movements and the disturbances that they inspired would prove to be an increasingly important phenomenon during 1918.

In Russia itself the situation was also made a great deal more complicated by the fact that the Bolsheviks who had led the 1917 revolution were very far from being universally recognized as the country's legitimate government. Numerous left- and right-wing factions fought each other for power, and at the start of the year Czar Nicholas II and his family were still alive in communist captivity. They were being held by the Bolsheviks under close guard in the town of Ekaterinburg, and they were potentially

▲ This armored train is manned by troops of the Czech Legion, a pro-Allied 100,000-strong force stationed in Ukraine. Some Allied leaders hoped it could be used to defeat the Bolsheviks after the revolution.

▶ The Russian czarina Alexandra holding her son Alexei, the heir to the throne. The entire Russian imperial family was murdered by the Bolsheviks in July 1918 in the town of Ekaterinburg.

the focus for right-wing anti-Bolshevik groups. The oddest situation of all was that the single strongest military force in Russia in 1918 was actually a pro-Allied army, the 100,000-strong Czech Legion, which was stuck in the middle of the country and desperate to return home one way or another.

Turmoil on the eastern front

At the outbreak of World War I, the Germans had been a good deal more frightened by the prospect of fighting against Russia than against France and Britain. They worried that Russia's huge population and growing industries would soon begin to overtake Germany's military power, but it had not worked out that way. Russia's armies were defeated time and again, the country's economy and government became a shambles, and serious resistance to the Germans fell apart in 1917. The new government brought into power by the Bolshevik Revolution immediately asked the Germans for a peace deal. An armistice between the two was agreed upon in early December, and peace talks began on December 3 at Brest-Litovsk.

By that time, as a result of their victories in the years from 1914 to 1917, the

German and Austro-Hungarian forces had already occupied large areas of pre-war Russia, including present-day Poland, much of Belarus and Ukraine, and most of the Baltic states of Lithuania and Latvia. Although some German and Austro-Hungarian politicians supported relatively mild peace terms, the German supreme command, Field Marshal Paul von Hindenburg and General Erich Ludendorff, insisted on retaining control of these areas. The leaders of the Central Powers' delegation at Brest-Litovsk, Prince Leopold of Bavaria and General Maximilian Hoffmann, were ordered to impose harsh terms on the Bolsheviks. The Russians, whose delegation was headed by Leon Trotsky from January 9, 1918, did not want to accept the German

terms and tried to stall the negotiations. They hoped that in the meantime their revolution would grow stronger at home and would spread into Austria-Hungary and Germany. It did not.

Toward the end of January 1918, the Bolshevik government proclaimed the establishment of the Union of Soviet Socialist Republics (USSR), the official name for the country they would successfully establish in place of the old Russia at the end of the coming civil war. This war had in effect already begun in early 1918 with a Bolshevik invasion of the Ukraine, fighting in the Don River area between Bolshevik forces and cossacks led by General Lavrenti Kornilov, and other actions in the Baltic countries.

The prospect of Bolshevik success in these campaigns also worried the Germans and was another reason why the Brest-Litovsk negotiations broke down in mid-February. The Germans canceled the armistice on the eastern front and immediately sent their troops advancing even deeper into Russia. The operation, code-named *Faustschlag* (Punch), began on February 17 with 52 divisions and had more in common with a peacetime maneuver than a genuine military campaign. There were still very large German forces in Russia, even though many troops had been transferred to the western front, and some 50 divisions took part in the operation. There was very little organized Russian resistance. Some German troops simply boarded trains with their machine guns and artillery and moved east along the lines, stopping to occupy towns and villages as they reached them. In only two days, the German forces had advanced up to 150 miles (240 km). They also captured thousands of prisoners, along with many artillery weapons and machine guns, which were sent west to help in the fighting in France.

The Russians then knew they had no option but to accept the terms the Germans were offering, and they sent a telegram agreeing to them on February

---

KEY FIGURES

LEON TROTSKY

Trotsky (1879–1940) was one of the most important communist leaders of the Russian Revolution. He was born Lev Bronstein, but like several other communist leaders, he is better known under the new name he adopted in later life.

Trotsky was Lenin's principal assistant during the October Revolution of 1917 and became Commissar for Foreign Affairs in the first communist government. He headed the Soviet delegation in the peace negotiations with the Germans and their allies at Brest-Litovsk, trying to prolong talks in the hope that Germany, too, would succumb to revolution. After this strategy failed and the treaty was signed, Trotsky became Commissar for War. In this job he transformed the rather ineffective communist troops into the formidable Red Army and is credited as the mastermind who ensured that the communists won the civil war in Russia that soon followed.

After the death of Lenin in 1924, Trotsky quarreled with Josef Stalin, who took over at the head of the communist government. Trotsky was expelled from the Communist Party and thrown out of the country. He was murdered by the Soviet secret service in Mexico in 1940.

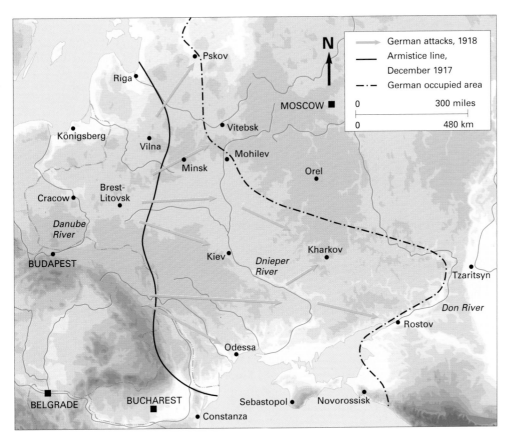

◄ **The final German offensive on the eastern front, which began in February 1918 and was met with little opposition from Russian troops, swiftly captured huge swathes of territory. One of the prime motives behind the attack was the capture of the Ukraine, which produced vast quantities of grain. Germany needed the grain to feed its increasingly hungry soldiers and civilians.**

19, two days after the advance began. The German generals were happy to have been given the chance for new victories and wanted to make as much of it as they could. So to delay things, they said that a telegram was not good enough and that they needed an acceptance in writing. Then, when the Russians complied, the Germans decided on even harsher terms, and while the Russians were deciding whether to accept these, the German troops kept grabbing even more of their country.

Vladimir Lenin, the head of the Bolshevik government, and Leon Trotsky only just succeeded in getting the other Bolshevik leaders to agree to the new terms, and the delegation went back to Brest-Litovsk at the end of February. However, the Germans refused to halt their troops until the treaty was actually signed, as it finally was on March 3. During this brief campaign the Germans were successful in capturing important cities like Minsk and Kiev and also gained huge tracts of territory in the Ukraine, Belorussia, and along the Baltic coast.

The terms of the treaty were brutal. Russia lost over 30 percent of its prewar population and a similar proportion of its general industries and best farming land. More than 90 percent of Russia's iron and steel and coal-mining facilities, the foundations of all heavy industries, were also taken away. Most of the Russian naval bases in the Baltic and Black Seas were to be given up. A total of 630,000 Austro-Hungarian prisoners of war were to be returned home immediately, and the Armenian parts of Turkey that had been occupied by the Russian Army earlier in the war were also to be returned.

Germany and the Ukraine

Before World War I many of the people of what was then the Kiev Province of the Russian Empire thought of themselves as rightfully part of a Ukrainian

Allied Interventions in Russia

During 1918 U.S. and other Allied troops were sent to various parts of Russia and ended up fighting a confused series of minor battles against a number of Russian groups with little obvious purpose and with disappointing and inconclusive results.

The intervention had a variety of motives. Especially in the first months of 1918, some Allied leaders hoped that they could persuade the new communist government in Russia to keep up some sort of military resistance to the Germans. On the other hand, many Allied leaders feared the spread of communism to their own countries and wished to see the communists in Russia defeated by their opponents in the developing civil war. Huge stocks of Allied supplies had already been delivered to the Russian Pacific and Arctic ports. Keeping these supplies from falling into communist or German hands was another aim. Finally, there was the aim of helping the Czech Legion.

The Czech Legion was a pro-Allied force of up to 100,000 men in 1918. It had been recruited from Czechs who lived in the prewar Russian Empire, along with many Czech soldiers who had deserted from the Austro-Hungarian Army or been taken prisoner. The Czech Legion fought effectively alongside the Russians in 1917, and at the start of 1918 it was stationed in Ukraine. It was the strongest single body of troops left of the Russian Army. With help from an Allied intervention, it might be transported from Russia to join in the war against Germany in other theaters or could stay in Russia and perhaps help to overthrow the communists.

All the above added up to a very vague combination of reasons for intervention, with various Allied leaders having changing priorities at different times. Some British and French leaders openly wanted to create a communist defeat, but no one had any clear idea of how their troops were to help achieve this end. U.S. president Woodrow Wilson rejected the idea of intervening in Russian internal affairs, but his orders were very vague, and in effect U.S. troops ended up intervening.

The first stage of the intervention began at Archangel and Murmansk, on Russia's Arctic

▲ *U.S. troops attend a parade on Russian Island, Siberia. These men are part of the expedition led by General William Graves that arrived in August 1918.*

coast. Small British and French forces arrived at Murmansk in June 1918 and at Archangel the next month, when 54 U.S. Navy personnel also landed. The main U.S. contingent, which was the 4,500-strong 339th Infantry Regiment, reached Archangel on September 11.

Under British command, there were vague hopes that the force could strike into Russia and link up with anti-Bolshevik forces, known as Whites, and win the

civil war. How such a tiny army was to achieve this goal from a position 700 forested and swampy miles (1,120 km) north of Moscow, the new Russian capital, was never made clear. The U.S. and other troops did, in fact, advance 100 or more miles (160 km) to the south on a broad front, fighting various skirmishes with communist troops. By early 1919 the futility of the campaign of intervention was clear. Wilson ordered U.S. troops to leave; the last had departed by the end of July.

An even larger U.S. contingent was sent to Vladivostok, on Russia's Pacific coast. Vladivostok was the terminus of the Trans-Siberian Railroad, which ran from Moscow to the port. Large quantities of supplies had been sent there for the Russians, and it was also a potential exit point for the Czech Legion. By the summer of 1918, the Czechs controlled about 3,000 miles (4,800 km) of the railroad, although most Czech soldiers were still deep inside Russia. In mid-July, as part of their operations, the Czech forces moved toward the town of Ekaterinburg, where the communists were holding Czar Nicholas II and his family prisoner. In order to prevent any of the royal family from being freed, the communists shot them all on the 16th.

About 9,000 U.S. troops, commanded by General William Graves, arrived in Vladivostok in August 1918, but the biggest Allied contingent was Japanese, eventually totaling 72,000 men. The Japanese had an eye to making gains of their own in the region, and one part of American policy was to keep this aim in check. Various military factions contended for power in eastern Siberia over the next 20 months, but Graves successfully limited the involvement of his men in the chaotic sporadic fighting. By the beginning of 1920, the communists had clearly won Russia's civil war. The Czechs finally left from Vladivostok, and the last U.S. troops followed them in April 1920.

Fewer than 200 U.S. soldiers were killed in action in the two sections of the intervention, a small number when compared with losses in the war as a whole, but even this price was seen as too high for a completely futile operation. The Red Army, organized with ruthless efficiency by Trotsky, had retaken most of Siberia by early 1920.

◀ *U.S. troops, seen here in northern Russia in 1919, were unable to influence the progress of the Russian civil war and were withdrawn by President Woodrow Wilson in April 1920.*

▼ *German and Russian troops fraternize on the eastern front, 1918. The Russian Revolution offered Germany an opportunity for expansion into large tracts of undefended territory, which they subsequently held on to as part of the Brest-Litovsk peace settlement.*

nation. In 1917, as the Russian government's authority fell apart, Ukrainian nationalists established themselves in Kiev and formed a government known as the Central Rada. In December 1918 the Bolsheviks created a rival authority in another Ukrainian city, Kharkov. On January 22, 1918, the Rada formally declared Ukraine's independence from Bolshevik Russia. Bolshevik troops attacked the Ukrainian nationalists the same month, and the Ukrainians looked to the Germans for help. The nationalists were invited to join the talks at Brest-Litovsk, and in early February they quickly made their own treaty with the Germans. The German advance

during February and March 1918 forced the Bolsheviks to retreat in Ukraine as elsewhere. Ukraine was one of Russia's main food-producing areas, and in return for recognizing and supporting the new Ukraine republic, the Germans and the Austro-Hungarians received huge shipments of Ukrainian grain to help alleviate the starvation being caused by the Allied naval blockade and the other effects of the war. Indeed, the treaty signed between the Ukraine and the Central Powers on February 9 was known by the latter as the *Brotfrieden* ("bread peace").

German policy throughout the territories they occupied in the east was to

take whatever they wanted, without considering the impact this policy would have on the people who lived there. Food and other raw materials were taken from the supposedly independent country of Poland that the Germans had set up in 1916, and Polish people were forced to go to work in Germany. Although Ukraine was also supposedly an independent state, a German military government was set up, first under the leadership of Field Marshal Hermann von Eichhorn, who was assassinated by Ukrainian nationalists in Kiev on July 30, 1918, and then under General Wilhelm Groener, to force the Ukrainians to grow more grain for Germany. Despite the Treaty of Brest-Litovsk, German troops still kept pushing deeper into Russian territory. In April they reached the Black Sea coast and the Crimea Peninsula, and farther inland they occupied important cities like Kharkov and Rostov.

Although Germany gained a great deal from the process of exploiting the occupied territories, the policy had its costs. A total of at least one million German troops remained in various parts of what had been the eastern front in the summer and fall of 1918, at a time when the German forces in France were desperately in need of more men. A milder policy might well have gotten the Germans almost as much food from the east and allowed them to move far more troops to the front line in France.

Nationalism and the Baltic states

The present-day countries of Estonia, Latvia, Lithuania, and Finland were all parts of the Russian Empire before World War I. All four would establish their independence in the turmoil at the end of the conflict, although Estonia, Latvia, and Lithuania were annexed by the Soviet Union during the World War II period and did not regain their independence until the fall of communism in the early 1990s.

Lithuania and also much of Latvia had been occupied by the Germans since

▲ *A great deal of Russian weaponry was taken and sent for use by German forces on the western front. Here, German troops examine a Russian armored car captured from the Bolsheviks in 1918.*

1915, with the rest of Latvia falling into German hands in February 1918. The Germans attempted to establish a puppet regime in Lithuania with a German prince, Wilhelm of Urach, at its head. Wilhelm was crowned King Mindove II on July 11, but his reign was brief. He was deposed by Lithuanian nationalists on November 2, and an independent republic led by President Antanas Smetona was proclaimed. Latvia had been granted a measure of autonomy by the Russian provisional government in July 1917, but the Latvian National Council declared full independence and the creation of a republic under President Karlis Ulmanis on November 11, 1918. Bolshevik forces immediately invaded the new republic, and the clash continued until 1920, when Latvian independence was recognized by Russia. Estonia declared independence on November 28, 1917, and resisted

▲ *German forces came to the aid of the anticommunist faction of General Karl Mannerheim but were unable to extend their control over the whole country. Armored trains, such as this one, were used by the Germans to cover long distances in relative safety.*

Bolshevik attempts to take over. Many of the Estonian aristocracy were of German descent, and they appealed for German help, which, in February 1918, the Germans were only too pleased to supply. They moved in and occupied the territory, only leaving after the general armistice in November. Following the German withdrawal, Bolsheviks invaded from Russia. The fighting continued until a local armistice was declared in late 1919, and full Estonian independence was secured by the Treaty of Dorpat on February 2, 1920.

What is now independent Finland had been a part of the Russian Empire at the start of the war in 1914, but it had a degree of home rule. Some 2,000 Finns joined the Russian Army, whereas another 2,000 left to join the German Army. The Finnish national assembly declared the country's independence on December 6, 1917, after elections had established a pro-German government. Finnish communists, known as the Red Guard, mounted an uprising on January 28, 1918, and loyalist forces,

known as the White Guard, under General Karl Mannerheim, a former senior officer in the Russian Army, called for German help to combat the coup. The Germans dispatched the Baltic Division under General Rüdiger von der Goltz to Finland, where it arrived on April 3. With this German assistance Mannerheim defeated the communists at the Battle of Viborg in April, after which the Germans tried unsuccessfully to extend their authority over the whole country. The German troops returned home when the world war ended and a provisional government was formed on December 12 with Mannerheim at its head. Finland finally established its independence at the end of 1920.

Most of Romania had been occupied by German, Austro-Hungarian, and Bulgarian troops by mid-1917, but a small eastern part of the country had remained free with the support of the Russians. The Romanian government established a new capital at Jassy in the province of Moldavia. The still occupied sections of the country contained grain, oil, and many other resources, which were stolen by the Germans and Austro-Hungarians, leaving hundreds of thousands of Romanians to die of starvation. The Russian collapse in late 1917 as a result of the October Revolution left the surviving Romanian government no option but to make a peace deal with the Central Powers, and an armistice was agreed on December 9. The Treaty of Bucharest of May 8, 1918, confirmed Romania's subservient position. The Romanians, however, repudiated the treaty, arguing that it was not strictly legal as it had not been signed by the country's monarch, King Ferdinand I, and they declared war again just before the armistice in November 1918. Romania therefore joined the peace negotiations in 1919 as one of the victorious Allied powers.

Allied victory in Italy

Following the German and Austro-Hungarian victory in the Battle of Caporetto in October and November 1917, the Allied position in Italy looked bleak at the start of 1918. The Italian Army was shattered by the defeat and the many unsuccessful battles it had fought on the Isonzo Front earlier in the war. The new commander in chief, General Armando Diaz, who replaced his predecessor, General Luigi Cadorna, in November 1917, would need many months to rebuild his forces and make them truly fit for battle again. Allied industries were ensuring that weapons at least would be plentiful. Also on the plus side for the Allies, the German forces that had made the victory at Caporetto possible were withdrawn from Italy and moved to the western front. On the other hand, in the early months of the year, the Allies withdrew about half of the British and French divisions that had helped stabilize the Italian front along the Piave River in December 1917.

After the collapse of Russia, the Austro-Hungarian high command was able to switch many troops from the eastern front to Italy in the spring of 1918, but despite this apparent boost

▼ *Allied gunners take a break on the Italian front. More than four months of fierce fighting between July and October 1918 saw the Austro-Hungarians retreat and seek a peace settlement.*

▲ Fighting in the Italian theater sometimes involved manning trenches at 10,000 feet (3,000 m). However, the decisive battles of 1918 were fought in the fertile plains of northern Italy.

the Austro-Hungarian Army was deteriorating fast. The empire was growing ever more short of food, and the various nationalities that made up the Austro-Hungarian Army were becoming less and less willing to cooperate effectively. Minor mutinies were breaking out across the country. Bands of former prisoners of war who had returned from Russia were wreaking havoc; and frontline troops were short of weapons and ammunition as production at home went into decline. On May 11 the country's ruler, Emperor Charles, met with Germany's Wilhelm II and was forced to accept German military control of his forces, although this development was destined to have little impact on the course of the war.

Austria-Hungary's generals did not appreciate what was happening, nor did they realize just how well the Italians had recovered from the disasters of 1917. The country's chief of staff, General Artur Arz von Staussenberg, and his generals decided to attack but they could not agree on the best plan. Two of the frontline commanders, Field Marshal Franz Conrad von Hötzendorf, the former

Austro-Hungarian chief of staff, and Field Marshal Svetozar von Boroevic von Bojna, who had been promoted from general for his role in the Caporetto victory, each wanted the offensive to be mounted in his sector of the Italian front.

Neither field marshal was given priority, and a two-pronged attack was eventually planned. Boroevic's Fifth and Sixth Armies were to advance toward the city of Padua in the coastal sector, and Conrad von Hötzendorf's Tenth and Eleventh Armies toward Verona in the Trentino district on the inland front west of Monte Grappa. Because of the mountains between the two sectors, they were not able to support each other effectively, while the Allies, operating on the plains on the other side of the Piave River, were able to maneuver their forces more freely.

By mid-June the Austro-Hungarians had gathered over 60 divisions for the two wings of the attack, the largest number they had fielded against Italy in the course of the war. The attack finally began on June 10 on the coastal sector. Despite the hindering of their artillery bombardment by a shortage of shells, the Austro-Hungarian Fifth and Sixth Armies seemed to do well at first. They soon got across the Piave and pushed forward up to 5 miles (8 km) through the Duke of Aosta's Italian Third Army on a 15-mile (24 km) front but this was as far as they could get. Fierce Italian counterattacks began and Boroevic had to retreat from June 19. His men were back where they started by the 22nd, having suffered more than 100,000 casualties. Air superiority was one factor in the Italian success. The Italian air arm, backed by British and French contingents, sent some 600 aircraft into this battle, shooting down more than 100 of their opponents. The temporary bridges the Austro-Hungarians had built over the Piave were attacked relentlessly, cutting off supplies and reinforcements to the front line and helping to force the retreat.

On the inland Trentino front the offensive began on the 15th and was stopped in its tracks even more efficiently by the Allied units. Allied intelligence had warned the attack was coming, and the Austro-Hungarian lines were heavily bombarded by Italian artillery even before the battle commenced. British and French forces were included in the defending Italian armies in this sector, and their attacks quickly retook the very minor gains the offensive had made at first. Austro-Hungarian casualties totaled 40,000 men in a week of fighting, and Conrad von Hötzendorf was fired for the failure and was replaced by Archduke Joseph. To make matters even worse, in the period between the beginning of July and the end of August, the strength of the Austro-Hungarian forces on the Italian front had fallen by 50 percent, a reduction that included a high proportion of desertions.

Although the Battle of the Piave was a clear Italian victory, Diaz remained cautious throughout the summer months, despite the signs of weakness among his own enemies and the Allied successes on other fronts. By the fall, though, he was under pressure from his political masters, chiefly Prime Minister Vittorio Orlando, to conquer as much territory as he could and help Italy claim a larger share of whatever spoils might turn out to be available at the peace conference that was likely to end the war. The result was the Battle of Vittorio Veneto, which began on the night of October 23.

By this stage of the war, the Italian forces were 52 divisions strong, plus three British and two French divisions and one U.S. unit, the 322nd Infantry Regiment. On paper the Austro-Hungarians had more divisions, but many of these were at little more than half strength. They were

▼ *These Italian troops are gathered for protection in woods along the Italian front in 1918. U.S., British, and French forces were all deployed in the Allied campaign here, but the majority of troops came from Italy.*

KEY EVENTS

U.S. FORCES IN ITALY

The U.S. commitment to the Italian front during the war was on a minor scale, but it showed that the United States was willing to aid its Allies in any theater of operations. The 332nd Infantry Regiment, as well as attached medical and supply units, arrived in Italy during July 1918. Its commander was Colonel William Wallace.

After a period of training in mountain warfare around Lake Garda, the regiment moved to Treviso, where it was made part of the Italian 31st Division. The regiment took part in the Battle of Vittorio Veneto in October and November, suffering its only casualties of the campaign (one man killed and six wounded) on November 4, the day that the armistice with Austria-Hungary began. Subsequently, the regiment made up part of the Allied forces stationed in Austria-Hungary and along the coast of the Adriatic Sea. In February and March 1919 the regiment moved to the Italian port of Genoa prior to repatriation, with its last elements leaving Europe on April 4.

Other U.S. personnel did serve on the Italian front. A base hospital was provided, as well as some ambulance units, and around 50 U.S. pilots served with the Italian Air Force.

short of artillery, and many troops had little will to carry on fighting. Diaz's plan was to launch an attack toward Vittorio Veneto on October 24 that would split the Austro-Hungarian forces in the Trentino region and along the Piave. Despite their problems, the Austro-Hungarians held out against the initial Allied advances. On the 26th, however, a French division, part of the Italian Twelfth Army under French General Jean Graziani, made a major crossing over the Piave River, and over the next two days British forces, part of the Italian Tenth Army under Britain's Earl of Cavan, spearheaded another significant advance, which finally managed to break through the Austro-Hungarian defenses. On the 28th the Austro-Hungarian commanders ordered a general retreat all along the front. On the same day Emperor Charles of Austria-Hungary asked the Allies for an armistice. By the time it was negotiated and went into effect on November 4, the Allied forces had advanced more than 60 miles (96 km) and had captured more than 400,000 prisoners.

The war in Italy was over, and the Austro-Hungarian Empire had disintegrated. Various nationalist movements, partly inspired by Allied support for their cause, were demanding that they get the right to self-determination. U.S. president Woodrow Wilson's Fourteen Points (see Volume 1, pages 310–311) of the previous January had specifically included a clause on the right of self-determination. Similar sentiments had been expressed during the Rome Congress of Oppressed Nationalities,

▶ *The Austro-Hungarian Army launched a final, failed offensive at the Piave River in June 1918, but internal divisions caused its collapse. The remnants were mopped up by Italian-led forces at Vittorio Veneto. Many Austro-Hungarians were captured, like these prisoners who are being guarded by British sentries.*

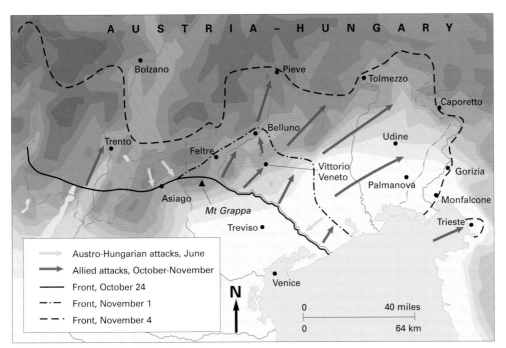

◄ **The Italian front in 1918 saw the Allies halt the last Austro-Hungarian offensive of the war, the Battle of the Piave, in June and then gain a decisive victory at the Battle of Vittorio Veneto during October and November.**

which took place in April. Sponsored by the Italian government, although that fact was not publicized, the congress was attended by exiled leaders of various nationalist groups within the Austro-Hungarian Empire. Although primarily concerned with the national aspirations of the Czech and South Slav (Yugoslavian) members, the congress's deliberations had a wider impact among Austria-Hungary's many peoples when they were made public.

Final moves in the Balkans

The final war front of the European theater of World War I was in the Balkans. There was no direct U.S. involvement in the fighting there because the United States was not at war with Bulgaria, although the other major Allied countries, including Britain and France, were. Bulgaria had joined the war on the Central Powers' side in 1915, aiming to make territorial gains at the expense of Serbia and Romania. By 1918 most of Romania and all of Serbia had been conquered, but fighting continued on the Salonika front, centered around the port of the same name in northern Greece.

Bulgaria's war effort had been supported by Germany up to 1918, but financial help was cut off in January, and other military assistance was mostly withdrawn in the early spring as Germany concentrated its efforts on the western front. Relations with Germany deteriorated even more when the Treaty of Bucharest between the Central Powers and defeated Romania was signed in May. The Bulgarians did not gain what they wanted by its terms. Instead, Germany took most of the spoils.

The Bulgarian people were also beginning to suffer from the effects of war. Some business leaders and industrialists prospered, but most of the ordinary 4.5 million Bulgarians struggled to get by, often having too little to eat. In June 1918 the monarch, Czar Ferdinand I, fired Prime Minister Vasil Radoslavov, and appointed a new government in July 1918 under the leadership of Alexander Malinov. Malinov managed to distribute the available food more fairly but could not get the military leaders to agree to support his attempts to leave the war. The Bulgarian Army shared in the problems; some troops on the Salonika front had already mutinied briefly in the spring of that year.

Although various Allied nations sent large forces to Salonika, they had, in fact, achieved very little by the start of 1918, primarily because hundreds of thousands of troops had fallen ill, mainly with malaria, a very serious and sometimes crippling disease. Without German assistance the Bulgarians certainly did not have the resources to defeat the Allied force, but for their part the Allies had failed to break through the mountainous terrain and well-fortified Bulgarian defenses.

The Allies, who included French, British, Italian, Serbian, and Greek troops, all under the overall command of a French officer, General Marie Guillaumat, had planned an attack in the spring of 1918. This was canceled when some French and British troops were withdrawn to meet the series of offensives being made by Germany in France. Guillaumat, too, went back to France in June and was replaced by General Louis Franchet d'Esperey. Franchet d'Esperey's troops were reinforced by large numbers of Greek soldiers during the summer, as Greece began to fight effectively on the Allied side now that the country's political troubles between 1915 and 1917 had ended. The strengthened Allied forces, some 200,000 troops, attacked on September 15 in the region of the Vardar River on the border between Greece and Serbia.

The Bulgarians still had around 200,000 troops commanded by General Nikola Zhekov in their order of battle, stretched thinly between the Aegean Sea in the east and the Albanian border in the west. However, they were badly outgunned by the far superior Allied artillery, and Zhekov was ill at the time of the Allied attack. Even so, they fought well at first, with machine-gun teams cutting down many of the attacking Serbian and French soldiers. British

▼ *Bulgarian troops, like these in action near Monastir in southern Serbia, had fought well during the war, but rapidly advancing Allied forces caused the collapse of their front in September 1918. Toward the end of the month, the Bulgarian government sued for peace.*

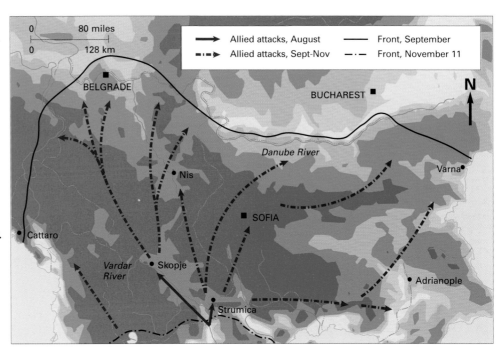

► *The final battles in the Balkans saw Bulgarian forces succumb to poor morale and overwhelming Allied superiority. Bulgaria asked for an armistice in late September, thereby allowing the Allies to complete their occupation of the Balkans.*

and Greek troops made further attacks near Lake Doiran a little to the east on the 18th, and they had captured important mountain defenses by the 20th.

By this time the Bulgarian front was collapsing. Allied troops were advancing rapidly in all sectors. Franchet d'Esperey refused a cease-fire offer on the 25th, the same day that British troops under the command of General George Milne entered Bulgarian territory. General von Scholtz, who was commanding the few German soldiers left in the theater, sent a message asking for help but was told that the only German troops who could be sent would have to come from the Crimea in southern Russia and would take more than a week to arrive. This disappointing news meant that he had no alternative but to retreat.

Troops in Sofia, the Bulgarian capital, mutinied on the 23rd, and there were risings in other areas. On the 28th the Bulgarian government asked the Allies for an armistice. British and Greek troops were still advancing into the country from the south, and French and Serbian forces were busy recapturing Serbia from the small number of

Austro-Hungarian troops in the region. Bulgaria agreed to an armistice with the Allies on September 30, the first of the Central Powers to do so, and Ferdinand fled into exile in Germany on October 4.

During October, in addition to disarming the Bulgarian forces, the Allied armies pushed all German and Austro-Hungarian troops back out of Serbia and Bulgaria. With Turkey now cut off from contact with its remaining allies, British troops under Milne also moved east toward Constantinople (Istanbul), the Turkish capital. Italian troops were sent in to occupy most of Albania. This move was in accordance with their government's announcement in June 1917 that it supported Albanian independence with the proviso that Albania should become an Italian protectorate. By the start of November, Allied troops were beginning to assemble in position along the Danube River, ready with plans to cross over to invade Austria-Hungary and Germany from the south. However, by this point the war as a whole was virtually over. In a matter of just seven weeks the Allies had advanced a distance of some 400 miles (560 km).

Valley. The Turkish Fourth Army on the inland flank also had to contend with Arab attacks on the rail lines that linked the whole Turkish force with their bases to the north.

As in his successful offensive in 1917, Allenby planned to fool the enemy commanders about where he would attack. He intended to advance on the plain near the coast and charge ahead with his cavalry once the Turkish front line had been broken, and so when the cavalry redeployed from the Jordan Valley to its attack positions, this maneuver was concealed. Fake camps were built, complete with dummy horses good enough to fool the few German reconnaissance aircraft. Also, new bridges were built over the Jordan River. A fictitious horse race meet was even advertised to take place behind the lines on the day the battle was to begin. To complete the picture, in the 36-hour period before the attack, Arab forces attacked Dera'a and other locations on the inland flank to distract the Turks even more. The deception worked, with the result that Liman von Sanders kept one-third of his troops in the secondary sector.

The attack was launched at dawn on 19 September behind a highly accurate creeping artillery barrage. The infantry broke through the Turkish trenches immediately, and the cavalry began to follow up the advance by 7:00 A.M. To increase the confusion behind the Turkish lines, British aircraft bombed headquarters, road junctions, and telephone exchanges. By midafternoon the Turkish Eighth Army's command post at Tulkarm had been captured, 15 miles (24 km) behind the front. The cavalry and armored cars kept going, capturing Turkish reserve units as they went. The next morning Liman von Sanders had to escape wearing his pajamas when the advance unexpectedly reached his headquarters in Nazareth.

By this stage the British forces were moving forward all along the front. They had already captured over 20,000

prisoners, with the total increasing by the hour. The remaining Turkish troops were retreating as fast as they could, being mercilessly bombed and machine-gunned as they went by the British aircraft. At the same time, the Arab force was keeping Dera'a under siege and inflicting heavy losses on the Turkish forces that were trying to retreat from the main front by that route.

Liman von Sanders tried to set up a new defense line near the Sea of Galilee, but this was brushed aside on September 25. The Arabs captured Dera'a two days

▲ *A damaged gun lies amid the wreckage of a Turkish transport convoy bombed by Allied planes as it retreated along the Nablus–Tulkarm Road, September 19, 1918.*

T. E. LAWRENCE

The British officer T. E. Lawrence, better known as Lawrence of Arabia, operated with Arab guerrilla forces to drive the Turks out of Palestine and Syria. Here, he describes how he and his men were joined by local people to take revenge after finding the women and children of a village called Tafas murdered by retreating Turkish troops in September 1918:

"The Arabs were fighting like devils, the sweat blurring their eyes, dust parching their throats; while the flame of cruelty and revenge which was burning in their bodies so twisted them, that their hands could hardly shoot. By my order we took no prisoners, for the only time in our war.

"Parties of peasants flowed in on our advance. At first there were five or six to a weapon; then one would win a bayonet, another a sword, a third a pistol. An hour later those who had been on foot would be on donkeys. Afterward every man had a rifle, and a captured horse. By nightfall the horses were laden, and the rich plain was scattered over with dead men and animals. In a madness born of the horrors of Tafas, we killed and killed, even blowing in the heads of the fallen and of the animals; as though their death and running blood could slake our agony."

Extract from Lawrence's *Seven Pillars of Wisdom*, 1935.

It was one of the most decisive victories of the war. On October 26 Turkish representatives came to meet the British on an island in the Aegean Sea to ask for an armistice. The Turks finally signed their surrender on the 30th, and it came into effect the following day.

Final battles in the Middle East

General Frederick Maude, who commanded the successful British operations in Mesopotamia in 1917, died late in the year, and he was replaced for 1918 by General William Marshall. In January 1918 Marshall set up the Dunsterforce expedition for operations in the Caucasus (see pages 494–495), and in the early months of the year, he also undertook some minor advances in Mesopotamia. His forces captured Hit in the Euphrates River valley in March and took Kirkuk, farther to the north, in May, but then they halted their attacks through the very hot summer period.

The British-Indian attack restarted in earnest in October 1918 with an advance up the line of the Tigris River toward the town of Mosul. The attack broke through the Turkish defenses at Al-Fathah on October 18, and the British won another victory at Ash Sharqat near the end of the month. The Turkish army in Mesopotamia surrendered on October 30, and the British forces moved on to capture Mosul on November 3.

Although the Mesopotamian campaign had ended with a British success, it had nevertheless cost over 30,000 dead on the Allied side. Up to 250,000 Allied troops were involved in the campaign at any one time. Many Allied generals thought that most of these resources and those that had been devoted to the Palestine campaign would have been better used against the main enemy on the western front in France.

The defeat of the Turks left the question of who would rule the territories they had lost during the war. The Arab armies thought that they had been fighting for their independence, from

later and massacred hundreds of captured Turks in revenge for a Turkish atrocity against an Arab village the day before. The Turkish armies had now fallen apart completely; only the few remaining German troops still fought effectively as they retreated. The Allied cavalry and Arab forces hurried north to Damascus, both entering the city in triumph on 1 October.

By later in October the advance had captured Aleppo in northern Syria, 350 miles (560 km) from where the battle had begun. No one knows how many thousands of casualties the Turks had suffered in the battle, but 75,000 were taken prisoner at a cost of fewer than 6,000 Allied soldiers killed or wounded.

Turkey or anyone else, and the Allies had promised to support this principle when it came to the peace conference after the war. These promises were restated during 1918 and at the end of the war, but this was not the only commitment the Allies had made.

In 1916 the British and French had made a secret deal called the Sykes-Picot Agreement (named after the British and French representatives who had negotiated it) that said that France would rule Greater Syria (roughly present-day Syria and Lebanon) after the war and that Britain would take control of Palestine and Transjordan (including modern Israel, Palestine, and Jordan).

In addition, there was the secret Balfour Declaration of November 1917, in which British foreign minister Arthur Balfour had told Jewish leaders that Britain would support the creation of a Jewish "national home" in Palestine. Balfour did not indicate how big this national home might be, or whether an independent country or something shared in some way with the Arabs was meant, but he had set down an important marker for the future, even though Jews made up less than 10 percent of the population of Palestine in 1918.

When the communists took over in Russia at the end of 1917, they made public all the secret treaties that the Allied governments had made, saying it was wrong to conduct diplomacy in this way—and in fact "no secret treaties" was also the first of President Wilson's Fourteen Points, (see Volume 1, pages 310–311). In the Middle East this action led to the Arabs finding out about the Sykes-Picot deal, which worried them

▼ *A combination of artillery barrage and aerial bombing was very effective in cutting through Turkish lines and disrupting their communications links. This British 6-inch (152-mm) field gun was photographed in action at Samarra in Mesopotamia in 1918.*

Dunsterforce

Dunsterforce was the name given to a force of roughly 1,000 British Empire troops sent into the Caucasus region in 1918. The force was named after its commander, General L. C. Dunsterville. Dunsterville was a school friend of the writer Rudyard Kipling, and he appears in some of Kipling's best-known work, fictionalized as the character Stalky.

In 1918 the situation in the Caucasus region was very confused, with numerous contending forces all striving for a variety of objectives. Before the Russian revolutions in 1917, most of the region was part of Russia, and Russian forces had pushed southward into Persia (now Iran) to make contact with the British earlier in the war. The Russians had also gained the upper hand in their battles with Turkey in 1916

and occupied large areas of northeastern Turkey. All changed after the revolutions.

In September 1917, the Georgian, Azerbaijani, and Armenian people had declared independence and founded a federation, known as Transcaucasia. Realizing the Russian weakness, the Turks attacked into Transcaucasia during the spring of 1918 and recaptured much of the territory they had

lost earlier in the war but withdrew many troops from Palestine to do so. Threatened by this advance, the Armenians made their own separate peace with the Turks in May 1918, effectively breaking up the Transcaucasia federation.

By this stage, the Georgians were worried by the Turkish offensive and possible attacks from Russian communists. They asked for German help, and German troops arrived to garrison the Georgian capital, Tbilisi, in the early summer. The real prize in the region was the oilfields of Baku on the Caspian Sea in Azerbaijan. Baku was briefly occupied by communist forces early in the year, but by the summer the Turks and British were heading in that direction, too.

Dunsterforce had begun its advance into northern Persia as far back as January 1918, only to

◀ *British and Armenian artillery-men defend Baku using a 6-inch (152 mm) Russian howitzer, August 1918. Dunsterforce was forced to retreat two weeks later.*

▲ *Dunsterforce troops advance under Turkish machine-gun fire toward the Binagarby oil wells, which had previously been under Armenian control.*

be forced to retreat when confronted by Russian revolutionary troops after an initial move of some 200 miles (320 km). The British force advanced again in June and successfully occupied the port of Rasht on the Caspian Sea. Dunsterville then decided to move on to Baku to help defend it against the coming Turkish attack. Dunsterforce reached Baku in late August but was forced to retreat in the middle of the next month when superior Turkish forces drew near. This was the final campaign of World War I in this region.

Dunsterville did return to Baku after the armistice at the end of World War I, as the area gradually became caught up in the Russian civil war that developed out of the revolution. By the end of 1920, most of Transcaucasia had been absorbed into the Soviet Union.

Although Lettow-Vorbeck had won one of the biggest battles of the East African campaign at Mahiwa in October 1917, he knew that he could not afford any more major engagements when he was so completely outnumbered. The Germans had fewer than 4,000 men left, and any significant casualties would leave their force too weak to continue.

Lettow-Vorbeck knew that he could not win the war in Africa, but his continued resistance cost the main German war effort absolutely nothing—there was no way to send him supplies from

▲ *Using guerrilla warfare tactics, such as the destruction of the Central Line railroad in East Africa seen here, the Schutztruppe (German colonial army) kept the British tied up for four years, forcing them to expend precious resources for no strategic gain.*

and also the implications of the Balfour Declaration. They continued to fight bravely and effectively through 1918, as has been described, thinking that doing so and setting up efficient governments in the areas they had captured would ensure that the promises made to them would be kept at the peace conference to come. This would prove to be a false hope.

The African campaign concludes
Through 1918 the major campaign of the war in Africa continued to feature unavailing attempts by the Allied forces to hunt down and destroy the *Schutztruppe* (colonial army) of German East Africa under its brilliant commander General Paul von Lettow-Vorbeck.

home or even communicate with him. With a force of 100,000 or more enemy troops occupied in chasing him or protecting locations he might attack, he was effective in keeping significant Allied resources from more important battles in the Middle East or Europe.

In late 1917 Lettow-Vorbeck decided to take this reasoning to its final conclusion; he would abandon his home territory of German East Africa and move south into Portuguese East Africa (now Mozambique). Without any base facilities at all, his troops would have to live off the land and whatever they could capture from the enemy. On November 25, 1917, Lettow-Vorbeck's men began crossing the Rovuma River into Portuguese territory. By this stage the German force consisted of about 200 Europeans, 1,700 askaris (local East African troops), 3,000 porters to carry supplies, and in addition, numerous wives and children of the African soldiers and porters.

Lettow-Vorbeck hoped that his men would be able to replenish their supplies quickly from the rich farmland of

▼ *From late 1917 until September 1918, the 4,000-strong* Schutztruppe *trekked over 1,250 miles (2,000 km), dodging their British pursuers and attacking vulnerable targets in Portuguese East Africa.*

the Portuguese territory, and he also thought that the Portuguese soldiers defending it would be weak and badly trained. He was right on both counts. The German force soon defeated various small Portuguese garrisons and captured food, ammunition, weapons, medical supplies, and much more. Another advantage the Germans had was that the Portuguese authorities had ruled their colony rather oppressively, and the native people often helped the German forces with food, supplies, and information.

Lettow-Vorbeck's move into Portuguese East Africa not only made things easier for the Germans in these ways, but it also made matters more difficult for their Allied opponents. General Jacob van Deventer, who now commanded the British Empire forces in East Africa, had to make a new plan to catch Lettow-Vorbeck. Deventer's much larger forces needed proper bases and supply lines, and they did not exist in Portuguese East Africa.

Deventer sent troops by sea to Porto Amelia on the Portuguese East African coast, only to find that the road into the interior of the country that was shown on his maps scarcely existed. It would take until April to make Porto Amelia a worthwhile base and begin operations from there in earnest. In the meantime Deventer sent some units to guard the Rovuma River in case Lettow-Vorbeck turned north again, and he established other forces on the shores of Lake Nyasa to block a move to the west. Finally, too, the British commanders began to recognize an important fact that the Germans had known all along: under African conditions, well-trained African troops were the most effective fighters and the best able to resist local diseases. Consequently, Deventer sent home most of his remaining white South African troops and began to put a lot more effort into building up his African regiments.

▲ *The German* **Schutztruppe,** *in common with the rest of the standing colonial armies in Africa, relied on local soldiers known as askaris for their manpower base. Askaris were by far the most effective troops for African conditions, as they could cope with local diseases and knew the terrain in which they fought.*

Even though African troops fought and survived best in the East African bush, they were far from immune to diseases like malaria or the insect parasites that brought crippling sores and infections. Other diseases, such as sleeping sickness (carried by the tsetse fly), were lethal to draft animals like horses and inescapable over much of East Africa. Consequently, away from the few roads and railroads, all supplies had to be carried by human porters. Over one million Africans were conscripted to work for the British forces in the course of the whole East African campaign, and about 100,000 died of disease, probably about one-quarter of these in the course of 1918. At the start of 1918, the death rate among the African porters was roughly 2 percent each month, and this was the case among men who were not expected to engage in combat.

Through the first half of 1918, Lettow-Vorbeck and his men headed mostly south, fighting and usually winning occasional skirmishes with Portuguese and other Allied forces on the way. At the beginning of July, they captured a Portuguese depot at Nhamacurra, in the south of the country, with more food, ammunition, and medical supplies than they could carry. However, the Allies were now beginning to close in from their new bases on the coast to the east and from Nyasaland (now Malawi) to the west. Lettow-Vorbeck decided to turn north, managing to slip between the Allied columns and escape once again.

By late September the German force had crossed practically the whole length of the country once more without being cornered or seriously engaged. On the 28th they crossed over the Rovuma into German East Africa, having traveled over 1,000 miles (1,600 km) in Portuguese territory. Despite some casualties Lettow-Vorbeck's force was virtually as strong as at the start of the year, even though the world influenza epidemic had even begun to reach into the African bush, claiming some victims among his men.

The British thought that Lettow-Vorbeck would head even further north, and so they hurried their forces out of Portuguese East Africa and into the central parts of German East Africa, but Lettow-Vorbeck outmaneuvered them yet again. He turned west and headed for the British territory of Northern Rhodesia (now Zambia).

In early November a German attack on a supply depot at Fife in Northern Rhodesia was beaten off, but Lettow-Vorbeck moved farther into the country and captured the town of Kasama on November 9. The Germans were still in this area on November 13 when the news reached Lettow-Vorbeck of the armistice in Europe. He did not believe the messages the British sent about this at first—he had no radio and no other means of contacting Germany—but the news was true. He finally surrendered to the British on November 25, 1918, still undefeated after four years of campaigning against Allied units 10 or more times as strong as his army. At the surrender Lettow-Vorbeck had 155 Europeans, 1,168 askaris, and 1,522 porters in his force.

▼ *The Indian Army was a valuable source of manpower to the Allies in a number of war theaters from the western front to Mesopotamia and Gallipoli. These units of the British-Indian 61st Pioneers are preparing to embark for East Africa to take part in the campaign against the German Schutztruppe. More than 1.3 million Indians served during wartime, of whom about 72,000 were killed.*

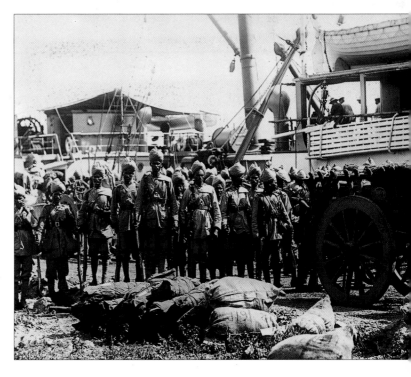

In January 1919 Lettow-Vorbeck and his German soldiers sailed home to a heroes' welcome in Germany, one more symbol of the might of the German Army for those who wrongly believed that their country had not lost the war but been betrayed by cowardly politicians.

Central and South America

A number of countries throughout the region declared war on the Allied side in the later stages of the conflict, and some made minor contributions to the fighting. Cuba had declared war under American influence in 1917, and its navy participated in antisubmarine work in the Caribbean, as did the four small warships of Panama from April 1917. Costa Rica and Nicaragua declared war on Germany in May 1918, and Honduras in July, but they had only tiny military forces. Haiti declared war on Germany in July, 1918 but, far from making an active contribution, was the scene of riots against the U.S. military occupation of the country later in the year.

After various Brazilian ships had been sunk by German submarines in 1917, Brazil declared war in October that year. Because there had been a prewar naval arms race between Brazil and other South American countries, Brazil had a comparatively strong navy. The smaller ships mounted antisubmarine patrols in the South Atlantic, and a detachment also arrived in the Mediterranean for operations there just before the end of the war. The two powerful Brazilian battleships were sent to the U.S. for updating so that they could join the main Allied fleets in Britain, but the modification work was not completed in time for them to see service. A number of Brazilian Army personnel served behind the lines on the western front, but no combat units were sent.

▼ *White South African troops, such as these seen on patrol, were at first used in German East Africa, but General Jacob van Deventer, commander of the British Empire forces, eventually sent them home, replacing them with askari troops, who were better suited to local conditions.*

The Far East

China was in turmoil throughout the years of World War I. The central government existed only in name, with various parts of the country instead being controlled in reality by provincial governors and local warlords. The central government declared war on Germany in August 1917, but it had no effective army or navy that it could spare from China's internal troubles, and therefore Chinese troops played no part in the fighting outside China.

However, despite this state of affairs, more than 300,000 Chinese did go overseas to work as laborers for the Allied armies along the western front and elsewhere. Most of these people were originally recruited from the parts of China near to the British colony of Hong Kong or the other areas of the country where Europeans had territory. During 1918 the French and British Armies each employed about 100,000 Chinese laborers in France on road and railroad building and similar tasks. A small number worked for the American Expeditionary Force. Others were drafted to assist in the Allied campaigns in East Africa and the Middle East.

The Japanese Army had played the major part in taking over Germany's small colonies in China in the early part of the war but did not serve outside Asia in the course of the conflict. However, by 1918, Japanese warships had been deployed to replace many British ships on patrol and escort duties in the Indian Ocean, and 12 destroyers were doing similar work in the Mediterranean. Japan also built a number of destroyers and smaller warships for the French and Italian Navies.

In other respects the final stages of World War I saw Japan already set on the course of expansionism that would become the matter underlying the Pacific half of World War II. Japanese troops were by far the largest contingent taking part in the Vladivostok operations from the summer of 1918 (see

▲ These German ships were sunk by Japanese warships in Tsingtao harbor, China, in 1914. Tsingtao was the main German military installation in the Far East, a naval base garrisoned by 4,000 troops. Japanese units, under the command of General Kamio, forced its surrender on November 7, 1914, after a brief siege. Japan held it until 1922.

pages 474–475), and other Japanese forces joined with the Chinese in anticommunist operations in Manchuria during 1918. These military actions were all designed to extend Japan's "sphere of influence" on the Asian mainland, exploiting the fact that the major European colonial powers and the United States were completely preoccupied with fighting the war. The final months of World War I also saw increasing tension between the United States and Japan, mostly reflected in plans by both countries to design and build new and ever more powerful battleships.

Siam (as Thailand was usually known in the World War I period) was one of the few other Asian countries that was independent. Siam declared war on Germany in 1917, and a medical unit went to France in 1918. The Philippines also had a degree of self-government before World War I but was still effectively an American colony. Several thousand Filipinos volunteered to serve with U.S. forces in the course of the war.

The War at Sea, 1918

The crucial struggle in the war at sea in 1918 was the battle between the German submarines and the Allied convoy system. Could the Germans finally sink enough of the Allied supply vessels and transports by using torpedoes and submarine-laid mines to starve Britain into surrender or drown the thousands of U.S. troops in the North Atlantic before they ever reached France? Or would the trends that had begun in the later months of 1917 continue and the Germans gradually achieve less and less success while losing more and more of their submarines?

As in the earlier years of the war, there was one aspect of Allied naval strategy that remained unchallenged by the Germans. There was no way they could breach the Allied blockade of the North Sea to receive significant supplies from abroad. Although the German economy did not depend as heavily as the British one on foreign food and raw materials, the effects of the blockade had built up gradually and were really biting by 1918.

At the beginning of the year, German civilians were getting only 1,000 calories of food a day, about half of their needs. Due to malnutrition, child mortality rates were up by 50 percent from prewar levels. On the production front, the Germans could not match the Allied output of guns, tanks, aircraft, or anything else. The Allied blockade was not the only factor in bringing about this disintegration of the German home front and economy, but it was a vital though brutal weapon in the Allied armory.

During the final year of the war in 1918, the Allies finally overcame the threat posed by the German submarine fleet and they also effectively neutralized the surface warships of the Central Powers.

German civilians were not the only ones to feel the war's impact. Shortages had caused long lines to grow outside Britain's food shops in late 1917. The government responded to this situation by introducing a rationing system from February 1918. People were no longer permitted to buy as much food as they could afford. Instead, the supplies were to be organized so that everyone got a fair but limited share.

The convoy battles

As in 1917, the focus of the struggle between the German U-boats and the Allied navies and merchant fleets was in the ocean approaches to Britain and in British coastal waters. The system of convoys for oceangoing shipping that the Allies had introduced during 1917 had proved to be so successful that the German submarines had been forced to change their tactics at the start of 1918. At the height of the U-boats' operations in mid-1917, more than half of their successes took place at least 50 miles (80 km) out to sea, and most during daylight. From early in 1918 more than half

▲ *By 1916 the Royal Naval Air Service had established around 50 coastal stations, from which planes, such as this Short 184 seaplane, could provide air support and reconnaissance for convoys entering the ocean approaches to Britain.*

◄ *The success of long-range merchant convoys from the United States in spring 1917 encouraged the expansion of the convoy system. Losses were drastically reduced in the Atlantic, but U-boats continued to pose a major threat in the Mediterranean.*

of the sinkings were within 10 miles (16 km) of land, and half of them were also undertaken at night.

Until the end of 1917, the British had kept to the old tactic of antisubmarine patrols in their coastal waters. However, in December they began to introduce escorted coastal convoys, but as this system was not fully in place until the summer of 1918, many unescorted ships continued to be lost in the meantime.

Air support was also more practical in coastal waters than in the distant ocean, and during the year the British greatly increased their maritime aviation forces. However, most of the airships or aircraft used were obsolete types, no longer useful in combat operations over France. Aircraft could force a sighted submarine to submerge, but they had no weapons likely to damage a submerged submarine—although some planes did carry depth charges in the final year of the war—and no equipment to detect or follow one. They were also mainly used on patrol rather than convoy escort work, even though a convoy with an air escort almost never lost a ship.

Despite such Allied shortcomings, the German U-boats found life more and more difficult as 1918 went on. Allied shipping losses gradually declined during the year, and in the period from

▲ *A view of the ocean as seen from the deck of a surfaced U-boat. Derived from the German word* **Unterseeboot,** *meaning "submarine," the term* **U-boat** *was commonly used by the Allies to signify all German submarines, even though it was more properly applied only to large, long-range craft.*

April to June, more new merchant ships were built in the United States and Britain than the German submarines were able to sink for the first time since the full-scale German submarine campaign began. This trend continued to the end of the war.

The U-boat force began 1918 with a total of 132 boats in service, of which 33 were at sea on operations. Construction of new boats was slow, and losses were gradually increasing. By the end of April, 24 boats had been lost, and the force was now 125 strong with 55 at sea. May was the worst month of the war for the U-boat fleet, with 15 lost. By the time of the armistice in November, the total number of submarines lost in the whole war reached 178 vessels.

The German U-boat force could be sunk by gunfire, depth charges, ramming by surface ships, by Allied submarines, or by aircraft (probably only one instance in the whole war). A significant number of vessels were also lost in accidents, but the largest single cause of submarine sinkings was mines. This particular area of

naval warfare was one in which the Allies increased their success rate in 1918, the final year of the war.

The main mine barrier in existence at the start of 1918 was the one that had been laid across the Dover Straits between southern England and northern France at the eastern end of the English Channel. The British had set up minefields and warship patrols across the Dover Straits from early on in the war, but they only realized at the end of 1917 that these were almost completely ineffective in blocking the U-boats' passage. However, the introduction of new types of mines and other changes in tactics made the blockade much more effective through 1918. In the whole war before 1918, only 5 U-boats were sunk there; 14 were lost in 1918.

By the end of May, the Germans had given up trying to use the Channel route, and instead they sent all their U-boats into the Atlantic, around the north of Scotland. A U.S.-led project, the Northern Barrage, was meant to block this route, but this project did not, in reality, noticeably curtail German submarine operations.

Many of the German submarines were based at Bruges, an inland port in occupied Belgium. On the night of April 22–23, the British launched an amphibious attack on Zeebrugge, one of the exit ports for the Bruges base. Some 75 vessels were involved, all under the command of Rear Admiral Roger Keyes. While British shore parties attacked the German batteries that were guarding the entrance to the Bruges Canal, three old cruisers, the *Intrepid*, *Iphigenia*, and *Thetis*, sailed for the entrance to the canal, where they were to be scuttled. However, the German batteries were not silenced, and the three British blockade ships came under intense fire and were scuttled in the wrong position. Although the ships blocked the exit to sea, the Germans dredged a channel around the vessels. A parallel raid on Ostend, another exit port to the Channel, also failed. A further raid against Zeebrugge was made on May 9, although with limited impact.

German submarines continued to operate from Bruges until the area was over-run by Allied ground forces in the final days of the war. Nevertheless, the overall Allied campaign against Germany's submarines was ultimately successful, with the submariners paying a high price. A total of 5,364 submarine crewmen were killed between 1914 and 1918 out of an estimated total of 13,000 who served.

Transporting U.S. forces to Europe
Whatever their problems in fighting the U-boats in general, the Allied forces were very successful in transporting U.S.

▼ *The British raid on the Belgian port of Zeebrugge in April 1918 failed to halt the German U-boat patrols in the Atlantic. This aerial view of the entrance to the Bruges Canal shows the scuttled hulks of* Intrepid, Iphigenia, *and* Thetis.

The Northern Barrage

Throughout 1918 the Allies attempted to prevent the German submarine fleet from attacking convoys sailing across the Atlantic to Europe. Part of their strategy involved the creation of a vast minefield across the North Sea, from Britain to Scandinavia. It was the most important operation carried out by the U.S. Navy.

German U-boats had their main bases in Belgium and also at home in their own country. A quick look at a map of Europe makes it clear that if they were to be able to strike at Britain's trade with North America and the rest of the world, they would have to pass through the English Channel between Britain and France or around the north of the British Isles in order to reach the Atlantic shipping routes. The Northern Barrage was the name given to

the Allies' ambitious plan to block this northern passage with a huge array of minefields.

For the U.S. and British forces, blocking the North Sea was a mammoth task. What was needed was a series of minefields covering an area of about 250 miles (400 km) by 20 miles (32 km), with the mines being moored in stormy seas. Initial estimates suggested some 400,000 mines would be needed, but a newer design allowed this

enormous figure to be revised downward to "only" 100,000.

Despite the potential problems, the plan was strongly backed by U.S. naval commanders, especially Admiral Henry Mayo, commander of the U.S. Navy's Atlantic Fleet. It was agreed to go ahead at a meeting with the British in September 1917. However, because of the huge number of mines required, the minelaying could not begin until March 1918. In overall command

◀ A U.S. destroyer on patrol for German submarines in the North Sea during an operation to extend the minefields of the Northern Barrage, late 1918.

explode, the ship had to bump into them, and thus many more would have been needed to make a minefield effective. Unfortunately, the new mechanism did not work very well, and in the event some 5 percent of the mines exploded accidentally, soon after they were laid, sometimes damaging the mine-laying ships. Another problem was that the mines were not powerful enough to crush the tough hull of a submarine if they exploded at the full length of their wires' range.

More than 56,571 U.S. and 13,596 British mines were eventually laid, beginning on March 3, 1918. However, it is doubtful that the results that were achieved justified the huge effort involved in laying them. The minefields probably sank four, possibly six, German submarines, but they never came close to stopping them from reaching the Atlantic. The number of U-boats passing through the area actually increased during the final months of the war.

of the U.S. force was Rear Admiral Joseph Strauss, although the day-to-day work of U.S. Mine Squadron One, the chief unit involved in minelaying, was overseen by Captain Reginald Belknap.

Most of the mines to be used in the barrage were made in the United States and shipped from a special depot in Virginia to Scotland. These mines were of a new type that trailed wires through the water; any ship touching one of these wires would make the mine explode. For older types of mines to

▶ The various barrages laid by the Allies to prevent German U-boats from attacking vessels in the English Channel and the waters off the British Isles.

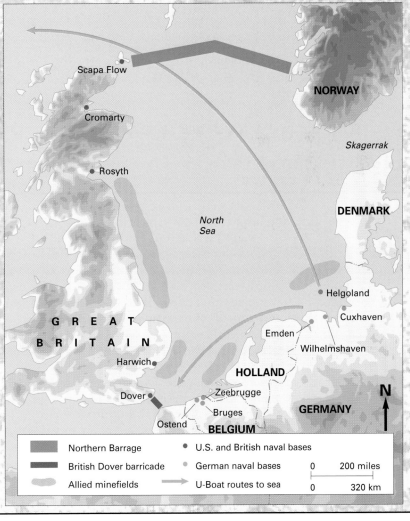

Scapa Flow
NORWAY
Cromarty
Skagerrak
Rosyth
DENMARK
North Sea
Helgoland
Cuxhaven
GREAT BRITAIN
Emden
Wilhelmshaven
Harwich
HOLLAND
Dover
Zeebrugge
Bruges
GERMANY
Ostend
BELGIUM

N

▬ Northern Barrage	● U.S. and British naval bases
▬ British Dover barricade	● German naval bases
Allied minefields	→ U-Boat routes to sea

0   200 miles
0   320 km

KEY EVENTS

THE *TUSCANIA* SINKING

Of the roughly two million U.S. troops who crossed to Europe by November 1918, fewer than 650 were killed in attacks by German submarines. Almost all of the ships that were hit were actually on the return leg of their voyages, steaming back to the United States from Britain or France. However, some transports, including the British liner *Tuscania*, were hit when full of troops while heading for Europe.

The troopship sailed from Hoboken, New Jersey, on January 24, 1918, bound for Le Havre, France, by way of Halifax, Nova Scotia, where it was to join Convoy HX-20 for the onward journey. The liner carried 2,013 U.S. troops and a crew of 384. On February 5, the *Tuscania* was spotted by Lieutenant Commander Wilhelm Meyer of the German submarine *U-77*. Two torpedoes were fired at 5:40 P.M. The first missed, but the second scored a direct hit.

Of the just under 2,400 people aboard, most were able to take to lifeboats and were rescued by other ships of the convoy before the *Tuscania* slid beneath the waves at 10:00 P.M. An estimated 230 people perished—166 U.S. troops, most of them from the 32nd Division, together with 44 members of the British crew.

troops safely to the theater of war. Roughly 200,000 sailed to France in 1917 and 1.8 million in 1918 with negligible losses from submarine attack. Just under half of them were carried in U.S. ships, and just over half of the escorts were provided by the U.S. Navy. Most of the rest of the transports and escorts were British. Approximately 75 percent of all the U.S. troops transported to Europe sailed from New York. Five other ports in the United States and four in Canada were also used.

The troops often found their voyages crowded and uncomfortable, but most at least arrived safely. Seasickness was a big problem. One soldier remembered that he got six meals a day, "three down and three up." Other soldiers traveling in calmer weather on British ships found the British-style food served to them so bad that they could not eat it. There was the constant fear of U-boat attack. The first vessel carrying U.S. troops to be sunk was the liner *Tuscania*, which fell victim to a German submarine on February 5, 1918. However, the troopships were sometimes able to strike back for themselves. On May 12, for example, the British liner *Olympic* (sister ship of the *Titanic*), packed with U.S. troops, rammed and sank the German submarine *U-103*.

Roughly 50 percent of the U.S. troops were shipped to French Atlantic ports such as St. Nazaire and Brest, while the remainder disembarked at British ports. Liverpool received the most, some 884,000 men, with Brest in second place (791,000). Brest also became one of the largest U.S. Navy bases for the convoy protection forces. The other major U.S. base was at Queenstown (Cobh) in Ireland. Between these two locations, Admiral Henry Wilson commanded a naval combat force of up to 40 destroyers. Other bases included Gibraltar and St. Nazaire. Three battleships were also based at Berehaven, southern Ireland, for much of the year.

Although no U.S. warships involved in convoy protection and antisubmarine activities were sunk in 1918, some suffered combat damage. For example, on August 15 a New York–Brest convoy was attacked. The USS *Montana* suffered torpedo damage, as did the USS *West Bridge*. The latter, already reporting mechanical failure, was abandoned by its crew, four of whom died in the attack. The *West Bridge* did not sink immediately but was towed back to Brest, where the warship finally sank.

As in the earlier years of the war, Allied naval supremacy depended on the Grand Fleet of more than 30 British battleships and numerous supporting vessels based in northern and eastern Scotland. From December 1917 this fleet was further strengthened by a U.S.

Navy squadron made up of five battle-ships (with four of them usually on duty at any one time) commanded by Admiral Hugh Rodman.

These ships operated as part of the main British fleet, not as an independent force. They were designated the Grand Fleet's 6th Battle Squadron and used British tactics, signals, formations, gunnery control systems, and much more. Like the British ships in 1918, they saw very little action—the main German force, the High Seas Fleet, left port only once in the course of the year, in April, but managed to dodge British attempts to intercept it and returned to base. German submarines fired torpedoes at U.S. battleships on several occasions. The battleship *New York* probably collided with a German submarine and may have sunk it in one of these encounters in October.

By the end of the war, the U.S. Navy had roughly 370 ships of all sizes and types and over 500 aircraft operating in the European theater. These were under the overall command of Admiral William Sims, who was based in London. Sims had gotten himself in trouble before the war for being too pro-British, but during the war this inclination turned out to be greatly beneficial. The close cooperation between the British and U.S. naval commanders that Sims encouraged was to prove an important factor in bringing about the eventual defeat of the U-boats.

Most U.S. Navy ships, however, were not sent to Europe but remained on service in home waters as part of Admiral Henry Mayo's Atlantic Fleet. These units saw very little actual action. Nevertheless, the Germans sent three long-range U-boats to operate off the

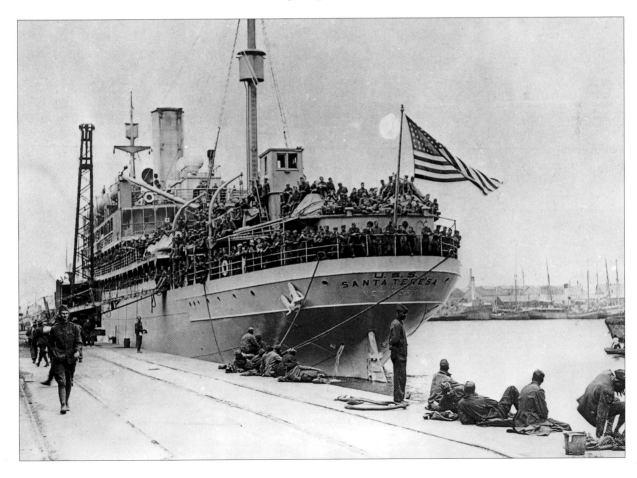

▼ *U.S. troops on the USS* Santa Teresa *waiting to disembark in Brest, France. In 1917 a total of 200,000 U.S. troops were transported across the Atlantic. The following year the figure rose to 1.8 million.*

▲ *An Italian dread-
nought enters
Taranto inner
harbor. Taranto
was the base for
the main Italian
battle fleet
throughout the
war. The Italian
Navy helped to
negate the threat
of the Austro-
Hungarian fleet in
the Mediterranean
and emerged from
the war essentially
intact, losing only
one major battle-
ship to sabotage.*

east coast between June and August.
They sank about 60 mainly very small
merchant ships, and mines laid by one
of them also sank the only large U.S.
warship lost during the war, the old
cruiser *San Diego*. The incident took
place on July 19, and the ship went
down in around 20 minutes, although
all but six men of the crew of 1,100 survived. The battleship *Minnesota* was
damaged by a German mine off the
eastern seaboard on September 29.

War in the Mediterranean

U.S. ships made a significant contribution to the development of the naval
war in the Mediterranean. The Allied
force in this sea was a genuinely multinational one, with British, French,
Italian, and even Japanese ships all taking part. Allied shipping losses in this
theater were proportionately high for

much of the war, including 1918, when
they amounted to between 25 and 33
percent of the total.

The German and Austro-Hungarian
submarines that were operating in the
Mediterranean were based in the
Adriatic Sea, chiefly at Cattaro and Pola,
and from there they needed to pass
through the narrow Straits of Otranto
at the southern end of Italy to reach the
open sea. The Allies tried to block this
route with the Otranto Barrage, a
defensive barrier of mines, nets, and
warship patrols. Some 35 U.S. Navy sub-
chasers were employed in this operation in 1918, but this mammoth Allied
effort was generally ineffective.

One dramatic aspect of the war in the
Adriatic was captured on movie film
and is believed to be the only live-action
sequence of a World War I ship sinking.
On June 10 an Italian torpedo boat,

M.A.S.15, scored a hit on the Austro-Hungarian battleship *Szent István*. A few hours later the battleship's damage-control measures failed, and the vessel simply rolled over and sank. Commander Luigi Rizzo of *M.A.S.15* became a national hero. He had already been lauded for a daring raid on the Austro-Hungarian naval base at Trieste in December 1917. Again using a fast torpedo boat, he entered the harbor and sank the old battleship *Wien*.

During the second half of 1918 morale among the Austro-Hungarian sailors had slowly declined. Warning signs had been evident earlier in the year, when there was a mutiny at the Cattaro naval base. Beginning on February 1, it lasted just 48 hours, and five ringleaders were subsequently executed. However, the incident led to the dismissal of the fleet's commander in chief, Admiral Maximilian Njegovan, on March 1. His replacement, Admiral Miklós Horthy, was able to maintain the fleet's loyalty until the end of October,

when he was ordered by Austria-Hungary's emperor, Charles I, to surrender his warships to the recently established South Slav (Yugoslavian) National Council on the 30th. However, there was one last act. During the early hours of November 1, the Italians, unaware of the effective surrender of the Austro-Hungarian fleet, were able to infiltrate Pola harbor, place an explosive charge on the hull of the battleship *Viribus Unitis*, and send it to the bottom.

The final year of the war also saw the collapse of the Turkish Navy. In fact, it had been of little importance for some time, apart from two warships. These were the *Breslau* and *Goeben*, both gifts from Germany in 1914 that had encouraged Turkey to declare war on the Allies. By January 1918 both were operating in the Mediterranean and undertook a raid on the Allied naval base at Mudros on the Greek island of Lemnos. *Breslau* was sunk in a minefield, and *Goeben*, coming to its aid, was damaged by a mine and ran aground. It

▼ *The Austro-Hungarian battleship* Szent István *was sunk in the Adriatic on June 10, 1918, by a much smaller vessel—an Italian torpedo boat,* M.A.S. 15.

THE KIEL MUTINY

The Kiel Mutiny was a rebellion by sailors of Germany's High Seas Fleet in late October 1918. It took place at the main naval bases of Wilhelmshaven and Kiel and heralded the collapse of the German government.

Admiral Franz von Hipper, commander of the High Seas Fleet, planned to take his ships out into the North Sea on October 30 to provoke an all-out battle with greatly superior British and U.S. forces. The hope was that, somehow, in going down fighting, the action would help Germany make peace on better terms. Ordinary German sailors heard of the plan, and most had no wish to go down fighting for what was clearly an already lost cause. They refused to obey orders, and on some warships they disabled the engines or locked up the officers.

The disturbances spread ashore from the ships at Kiel, where the base commander, Crown Prince Heinrich, fled in disguise from the mutineers. The sailors made contact with equally disgruntled industrial workers, and they formed committees demanding the creation of a German republic and insisting that the government make peace. By November 6 a moderate socialist local leader, Gustav Norske, stated that the mutiny was beyond control and that any attempt to halt the unrest by military force would provoke outright and widespread rebellion right across Germany. Three days later the government collapsed, and socialists in the German parliament proclaimed a republic.

was subjected to heavy but inaccurate bombing from British aircraft, and it was eventually towed back to the port at Constantinople (Istanbul), where it stayed under repair until the end of the war. The failed sortie by the two warships effectively ended the Turkish Navy's involvement in World War I.

The German Navy surrenders

By the fall of 1918, Germany had clearly lost the war both on land and at sea. Civilian politicians were back in control of their country and knew that the only sensible thing to do was to make peace as soon as possible. As part of the peace negotiations, they promised the Allies on October 20 that German submarines would cease their attacks on passenger-carrying ships. In effect, this made naval operations impossible. The next day the

▼ *Admirals Sims and Rodman of the U.S. Navy watch the surrender of the German High Seas Fleet from the deck of USS* Texas, *November 21, 1918. This picture was painted by Bernard F. Gribble.*

German Navy's overall commander, Admiral Reinhard Scheer, signaled all the U-boats to return home, though this order took some days to take effect and Allied ships were still being sunk up to the armistice in November.

Nevertheless, Scheer and a number of other German admirals, chiefly Franz von Hipper and Adolf von Trotka, were ashamed that their surface fleet had done so little to further Germany's war effort since the Battle of Jutland in 1916—it was still the second largest in the world but had done next to nothing to present a challenge to the British. They decided to send their battleships to sea for one last attempt to cut off and destroy a part of the British fleet. They hoped that this exploit would somehow win Germany better peace terms, but the ordinary German sailors were more realistic. They knew it was a suicide mission, and refusing to obey orders, they took control of their ships on October 30, 1918. This collective outbreak of disobedience became known as the Kiel Mutiny, and it immediately signaled the end of the German High Seas Fleet as a potential fighting force.

On November 11, 1918, Germany agreed to an armistice with the Allies. Its terms included the surrender of the High Seas Fleet, which was to leave its home bases on the 19th, sail across the North Sea, and arrive off Rosyth, Scotland, where it would surrender to the British and U.S. warships based there. The mission was given the codename Operation ZZ. The major part of the German surface fleet (10 battleships, 6 battlecruisers, 8 light cruisers, and 50 destroyers) arrived on the 21st after being met by around 350 Allied warships that were placed at battle stations. When the German vessels finally anchored, Admiral David Beatty, the British commander in chief, sent out a brief but momentous signal: "The German flag will be hauled down at sunset and will not be hoisted again without permission."

EYEWITNESS

LIEUTENANT FRANCIS HUNTER

When the German High Seas Fleet surrendered in November 1918, it was accompanied into Scottish waters by both British and U.S. naval units, more than 350 vessels in total. Included in this vast Allied armada was the U.S. Navy's 6th Battle Squadron under the temporary command of Rear Admiral William Sims. Hunter watched the arrival of the German warships from the squadron's flagship, the battleship *New York*:

"It was a most disappointing day. It was a pitiful day, to see those great ships coming in like sheep being herded by dogs to their fold, without an effort on anybody's part. They were as helpless as sheep. About two hours' vigil satisfied our commanders that such was the case, and we secured battle stations. Later investigation showed that all our precautions [to fight the Germans if need be] were quite unnecessary. Not only had the powder and ammunition been removed from the German ships, but [also] their range-finders, gun sights, fire control, and [the] very breech blocks as well. They came as mere skeletons of their former fighting selves in a miserable state as to equipment, upkeep, and repair."

Extract taken from Hunter's *Beatty, Jellicoe, Sims, and Rodman—Yankee Gobs and British Tars, As Seen by an "Anglomaniac,"* first published in 1919.

Between November 22 and 26, the German fleet made its way to its final resting place, the anchorage at Scapa Flow in the Orkney Islands, off the north of Scotland. All of the German warships had arrived by the 27th. By the middle of December, most of their 20,000 crewmen had departed, leaving just skeleton crews on the vessels totaling some 5,000 officers and men. However, as events in 1919 would prove, the Allies would be denied the great prize of Germany's High Seas Fleet.

The Collapse of Germany

The main theme of the war from late August until the armistice was agreed to on November 11 was the collapse of Germany's war effort. For the German people as a whole, soldiers and civilians alike, it had been a long and difficult four years. A great number of German people were starving, and over 1.5 million soldiers had been killed in action since 1914. All of these enormous sacrifices had been made in the hope of victory, but now every report emanating from every

By the late summer of 1918, the Allies were poised to launch a series of offensives on the western front that forced the German military and political leadership to seek an end to hostilities within a matter of weeks.

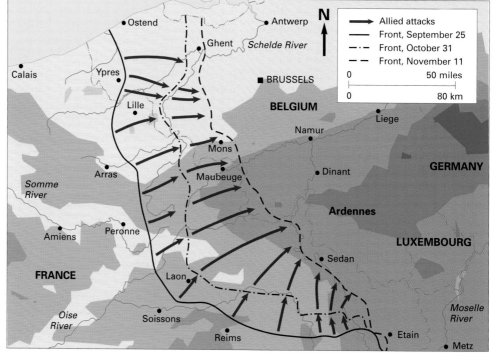

▶ *The final weeks of the war on the western front in 1918 saw a gradual retreat of the German Army in the faced of various Allied attacks. Although many German soldiers offered only token resistance, others fought back stubbornly to stave off total defeat.*

In mid-August Germany's military leaders had finally agreed in meetings with Emperor Wilhelm II that they could no longer win the war, but they were far from sure what to do next. Germany's diplomats would have to make the first approach to the Allies, but the soldiers and politicians could not agree on how the approach should be made. Although they had been realistic enough to recognize the need to make peace, the German leaders still believed that they could keep many of the conquests they had made.

Accordingly, Ludendorff decided that the German forces in France had to hold on to as much captured territory as possible—this would be a valuable bargaining chip at any peace negotiations, he thought. He also did not want to retreat too far or too quickly in case it further damaged morale and increased opposition to the war at home. For these reasons Ludendorff rejected suggestions that the German Army might be better off making a substantial planned retreat to new positions, even though a slow and limited withdrawal on the western front made sense militarily.

At the start of September, the Allied generals implemented a change to their strategy. Previously, they had not really expected to win the war before 1919, when the American Expeditionary Force (AEF) would have been big enough to ensure total victory. However, the Allies' supreme commander, Marshal Ferdinand Foch, began to appreciate that they had a chance to win the war before the year was out, provided that the Allied forces could keep up enough pressure on the Germans. Strongly supported by the British commander in chief, Field Marshal Douglas Haig, Foch decided that the next big Allied move would be a series of offensives against Germany's Hindenburg Line fortifications. One component of this proposed advance was to be the U.S. First Army's full-scale attack in the Meuse-Argonne sector, which is described on pages 459-469.

▲ *Morale was low among these battle-weary German troops on the western front in 1918, as retreat followed retreat. Continual withdrawals, coupled with news of upheaval at home, caused many soldiers to lose the will to fight.*

front brought only the bitter reality of defeats. The war would have to end—but how and when?

As these months proceeded, German defeats in battle were rapidly followed by retreats all along the western front, with the ordinary soldiers increasingly unwilling to keep on fighting. At home in Germany, there was constitutional upheaval. Civilian politicians gradually were able to regain control over their country's government and military machine from Third Supreme Command—the virtual military dictatorship headed by Field Marshal Paul von Hindenburg and General Erich Ludendorff—only for this new democracy to be threatened by bouts of public disorder and near revolution. The whole process of disintegration was hurried on by the surrender, one by one, of Germany's key allies—Austria-Hungary, Bulgaria, and Turkey.

▲ French cavalry-men examine a German trench, with a mortar, shells, and other trophies, taken during the September assaults on the Hindenburg Line. These carefully planned operations were designed to minimize Allied casualties and maximize the pressure on the German defenses.

Earlier in the war the British and French generals had been criticized for putting too much effort into individual, uncoordinated offensives and persisting with them long after they had run out of momentum, thereby producing enormous casualties for little gain. They were determined not to make the same mistake again. They would shift the focus of their attack from sector to sector, beginning a new advance in a different location whenever the Germans stabilized the front in another. To keep up the pressure on the enemy leaders even more, long-planned Allied offensives would also start during September on the Salonika front (see page 484) and in Palestine (see pages 488-492). To any observer it was clear that Germany's

already threadbare reserves of troops would not be able to deal with all of these concurrent offensives.

Breaking the Hindenburg Line

The Hindenburg Line was the name given to the series of defensive positions along much of the western front that the Germans had held during 1917 and early 1918. The Germans had advanced from these positions during their attacks in the first half of 1918, but by the end of September they were just about back where they had started thanks to Allied counterattacks. The Allies prepared to break through these defenses along most of the front in northern and central France, although the Germans had improved the fortifications of the Hindenburg Line since they were first built. They were formidable defenses, but they might have been stronger still if the German leaders had decided to retreat to them as soon as they had realized that their 1918 offensives were going wrong rather than be pushed back to them fighting losing battles on the way. The British and French had battered these defenses with little success during 1917, and the Germans hoped that they and their new U.S. allies would have as tough a time in 1918.

The U.S. First Army's attacks in the Meuse-Argonne sector from September 26 gradually pushed the Germans back in that area of eastern France. The U.S. troops found progress hard going and costly in casualties, but eventually they ground their way through. This push, however, was only one component of the overall Allied strategy—the first of several offensives all along the key sectors of the western front. On September 27, British, French, and some U.S. forces began another big attack in the Cambrai and St. Quentin areas to the northwest, and on the following day British and Belgian troops advanced farther north, to the east of the Belgian town of Ypres. Each of these attacks was carefully prepared so that the ordinary soldiers knew exactly what they were meant to do and had the weapons and training to make it possible. The Allied artillery was now far stronger and better organized than ever before, capable of finding and neutralizing German artillery positions and infantry strong points with a precision previously unknown. There were now hundreds of Allied aircraft available, along with numerous tanks in every important sector—although they were still as slow as they had been in earlier battles and broke down just as regularly.

In effect, the various Allied armies now had devised their own versions of the storm-trooper and infiltration tactics that had made possible the great German advances earlier in the year. The artillery, backed by machine guns, tanks, and aircraft, crushed or at least subdued the enemy defenses. The infantry then occupied them with comparatively few losses and therefore was well placed to hold them against any German countermoves. The Australian troops fighting alongside the British gave the new tactics the name "peaceful penetration," which described exactly what would be achieved when they worked properly. In earlier battles in the war, too many Allied soldiers had died going "over the top" against tough German defenses; now careful planning and coordination of the full range of weapons and technology reduced casualties and ensured steady progress.

The German positions in the Cambrai and St. Quentin areas were made even stronger by being based along various canals in the area. The canals themselves could not be crossed by infantry or tanks without first being filled in or bridged, but doing so was the least of the problems. In some places the canal banks had been cut steeply down as much as 150 feet (45 m) below the countryside, and in other places where the banks were low, the canals were surrounded by marshy land overlooked by the main German defenses, which were

---

EYEWITNESS

DENEYS RIETZ

Rietz, a South African, had fought against the British during the Second Anglo-Boer War (1899–1902) yet served with the British Army during World War I. As an officer of the 1st Battalion of the Royal Scots Fusiliers, he was involved in the attack on the Canal du Nord sector of the German-held Hindenburg Line in late 1918. The advance began at 5:20 A.M. on September 27, and Rietz later recorded the speed at which the German defenses were captured:

"The barrage moved forward and the moment had come. Bissett dropped his arm as a signal, and the men swarmed over the parapet straight for the German lines. I have a confused memory of shells spurting and flashing, of men going down in great numbers, and, almost before there was time to think, I saw German soldiers rise from behind their breastworks to meet the attackers, and then the Scots Fusiliers were clubbing and bayoneting among them.

"Seeing that our men were on their objective, I rushed quickly across no man's land and dropped down into the great Hindenburg trench. Flushed with victory, the men were rounding up prisoners and shouting down the dugout staircases for others to come up, a process they expedited in places by flinging Mills grenades into the shaft openings."

Extract taken from Rietz's autobiography, *Trekking On*.

---

held by units drawn from General Otto von Below's Seventeenth and General Georg von der Marwitz's Second Armies.

British and Canadian troops of General Henry Horne's British First Army began their attack across the Canal du Nord in the Cambrai area on September 27. By this stage of the war, the Canadians and the Australians were probably the most effective fighting troops on the western front, and they spearheaded many important and successful attacks in the following weeks. In the Cambrai attack the Canadian Corps, commanded by General Arthur Currie,

---

KEY EVENTS

LIBERATING BELGIUM

Belgium bore the initial brunt of Germany's invasion of western Europe in 1914, and most of the country was under occupation by the end of the year. However, the Belgian Army under King Albert I clung to a small strip of land in the southwestern part of the country, and it was from here in October 1918 that he led the Allies' Flanders Army Group to liberate his realm.

The decisive advance began with a breakout from the Ypres salient in late September and early October and was followed by the Battle of Courtrai, which began on October 14. Initial progress was slow, partly because of supply problems, but the advance was ultimately successful, and the pursuit of the retreating Germans continued over the following weeks. By the time of the armistice on November 11, however, more than 50 percent of Belgium was still nominally under German control, including Brussels.

It was not until the 22nd that Albert was able to return to his capital, which had been abandoned in the face of overwhelming odds on August 20, 1914. In the intervening period, some 14,000 Belgian troops had been killed, and many more civilians had died or suffered various illnesses under German occupation.

---

managed to fight its way through the whole German defensive position, gaining about 10 miles (16 km) of ground and capturing many German prisoners over the next five days, at which point the focal point of the Allied operations was switched elsewhere.

Preliminary Allied attacks on the St. Quentin Canal sector that lay a little to the south also began on the 27th, with the main assault scheduled for the 29th. This was probably the toughest section of all the German defenses—if the Hindenburg Line could be broken here, then the German plan to hold out long enough to make a favorable peace had no chance of working. The attacking troops were drawn from General Henry Rawlinson's British Fourth Army and from the French First Army under General Eugène Debeney, with the crucial parts of the front allocated to the Fourth Army's Australian Corps under General John Monash, which included two U.S. Army divisions.

The U.S. 27th Division took heavy casualties in the preliminary operations on the 27th and 28th, but both it and the 30th Division were able to play a full part in the main operation beginning on the 30th. The heart of the German defenses in this sector was an underground section of the canal near the village of Bellicourt. The Germans used the canal tunnel and other underground workings as a base and a secure refuge from the Allied bombardment. The attacking Australian and U.S. troops therefore did not make as much progress as they had hoped at first. Then a flanking attack by British units managed to cross an open section of the canal a little to the south, forcing the Germans to retreat. The most formidable section of the Hindenburg Line had fallen.

Even this was not the end of the bad news for the German generals. In the northern sector, the British Second and Fifth Armies and Belgian forces under

King Albert had begun attacks east from Ypres on September 28. These, too, were soon very successful. In 1917 it had taken the British weeks of the most horrible fighting to gain even a few hundred yards of territory in this sector. This time the Passchendaele Ridge was captured during the first day of the battle. Altogether, in the last few days of September, the various Allied attacks captured some 50,000 German prisoners, a clear sign that the German Army's fighting power was truly on the decline.

Austria-Hungary's leaders had told the Germans at the end of August that they intended to sue for peace, and

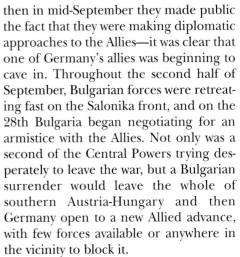

▼ British infantry, artillery, and cavalry prepare for the assault on the Hindenburg Line in late September 1918. The defenses were breached with ease and many prisoners were taken, indications that the German Army had lost the will to continue fighting.

then in mid-September they made public the fact that they were making diplomatic approaches to the Allies—it was clear that one of Germany's allies was beginning to cave in. Throughout the second half of September, Bulgarian forces were retreating fast on the Salonika front, and on the 28th Bulgaria began negotiating for an armistice with the Allies. Not only was a second of the Central Powers trying desperately to leave the war, but a Bulgarian surrender would leave the whole of southern Austria-Hungary and then Germany open to a new Allied advance, with few forces available or anywhere in the vicinity to block it.

The news of the imminent Bulgarian surrender reached the German military headquarters behind the western front at the same time as the generals were trying and failing to cope with the new Allied offensives. The effect was crushing. Ludendorff may have just managed to recover from his panicked reaction to the disaster of the first day of the Battle of Amiens in August, but he was now dithering about what Germany might have to give up in peace negotiations and which gains might be kept. The new crisis swept away the possibility of keeping any territory, and Ludendorff, the driving force behind the Third Supreme Command, became convinced that peace had to be made as soon as possible.

Ludendorff and Hindenburg met, and they both agreed that they would advise Wilhelm II that Germany, too, must begin negotiating for an immediate armistice. On September 29 they reported their views to the emperor and also advised him that the Allies were unlikely to negotiate with Germany's existing leaders. A new government would have to be appointed, one that, for the first time, would be fully responsible to the German parliament and through that to the democratic will of the people. For the old German leadership this step was nothing less than a political revolution, one that most of it was loath to accept. Instead of the German Army dictating the whole of national

policy, the military would come under government authority, and Wilhelm would become a constitutional monarch, a figurehead with as little real power as his British cousin, King George V. For the time being, Hindenburg and Ludendorff remained at the head of the German Army, but their power was declining day by day. The generals hoped that bringing civilians into the government would have two effects. First, it might reduce the growing unrest in Germany that was hitting war production and damaging the morale of the armed forces, and second, it would switch some of the blame for the nation's problems away from the military to the politicians.

Germany seeks an armistice

The new German government took office on October 3, 1918. Prince Max of Baden, a relative of the emperor but a liberal who had opposed Germany's submarine campaign, was appointed chancellor, replacing Georg von Hertling. The new chancellor included leading left-wing Social Democrats Matthias Erzberger and Gustav Stresemann in his cabinet, men that the military leadership and right-wing politicians did not trust. The next day Prince Max sent a message to the U.S. president Woodrow Wilson asking him to arrange an armistice on the basis of the president's famous Fourteen Points of January 1918 (see Volume 1, pages 310–311) but without making clear Germany's position. This request was too vague for the Allies to accept. In previous wars an armistice had normally been regarded as simply some sort of temporary cease-fire while other negotiations went ahead that might or might not lead to a peace deal. Wilson and the other Allies certainly did not want a break in the fighting that would only allow the Germans to rebuild their forces. They wanted to be sure that Germany accepted the most important point—that its forces would withdraw from all foreign territory they had occupied during the war.

Various messages passed back and forth between Wilson and the German leaders over the next three weeks. President Wilson wanted to make sure that Prince Max's government really spoke for Germany and that it would be obeyed by the German military. The president was aware as well that any deal he made would also have to be accepted by Britain and France. This first stage of negotiations with Germany came to an end on October 20, when the German government agreed to accept the Fourteen Points fully and as part of this promised they would immediately call off their unrestricted submarine campaign against Allied ships.

While all this negotiating was taking place, Allied forces were continuing to advance all along the front in northern France. The British forces on the left flank were capturing the largest numbers of prisoners and liberating the greatest amount of territory, but the French and U.S. armies were also gaining ground and wearing the Germans down. Each week thousands of German soldiers decided that they had done enough, and they allowed themselves to be captured by their enemies without

▲ *These German prisoners, seen here in a clearing depot in Abbeville, were taken at the Battle of St. Quentin Canal. The canal sector was regarded as the strongest part of the Hindenburg Line, but it fell to the Allies with relative ease.*

◄ *A German machine gunner killed at his post on the Hindenburg Line, 1918.*

gunner who was prepared to sacrifice his own life could cause heavy casualties and could hold up the advance of large Allied units. Many German soldiers did just that.

The speed of the Allied advance created its own set of problems. As they retreated, the Germans destroyed railroad lines, road bridges, and so on. These installations took time to rebuild, and it became harder and harder for the Allies to keep their forward units supplied with food and ammunition. The retreat also had the effect of shortening the German front line and concentrating German troops in a smaller area, making defense much easier. The Germans would also soon be gaining some reinforcements as the young men back home were rushed through their basic training. In addition, the worsening weather as winter approached would make Allied attacks more difficult.

Even with all its losses, the German Army still had the physical resources to go on fighting for some time, but its aims were no longer to win outright victory, only to delay total defeat. Every ordinary German soldier could see that the Allies had more men, more guns, more tanks, and more aircraft and knew how to use them effectively. The German people were losing every battle against their existing enemies, and their newspapers told them (accurately) that up to 10,000 more U.S. soldiers were arriving in France every day.

Although the German government had accepted the demands President Wilson had made, the details of the armistice terms had still to be worked out, and this whole package needed to be agreed to by the other Allies, especially Britain and France. There were aspects of the Fourteen Points that Britain and France did not like. In a future war Britain's survival might well depend on the Royal Navy's ability to blockade its enemies, so Britain could not accept the "freedom of the seas" clause. The French government also

putting up much of a fight. From August through October, more than 300,000 Germans were taken prisoner on the western front, and 4,000 artillery pieces were captured with them.

British and Canadian forces captured the town of Cambrai and the last sections of the Hindenburg Line in that area on October 9. French units freed Laon on the 13th, and on the 17th British forces took Lille. By then the Germans were also evacuating their submarine bases along the Belgian coast, making their defeat at sea as on land even more certain. This sort of progress did not mean that the Allied offensives had become simple and straightforward. Some units of the German Army continued to fight very effectively, and a determined and well-positioned machine

▲ A German soldier, wounded in the head, waits to be moved by stretcher bearers, August 1918. Although the final phase of the war saw many German troops allow themselves to be captured, many others fought on, even knowing that eventual defeat was inevitable.

terms must make it impossible for the Germans to restart the fighting at some future date. The Germans would have to agree to evacuate occupied territory very quickly and to surrender many of their artillery weapons, machine guns, railroad engines, and much of their other military equipment.

Foch thought that the Germans had been so badly beaten that they would give in and that it was not worth a single Allied soldier's life to prolong the war worrying about the details. Haig was not so sure the Germans were ready to surrender at all. He pointed out how difficult it was to keep advancing, and he thought that the war might well go on into 1919. Pershing had a slightly different view, one that turned out to be justified by later events. He thought that the Allies should keep fighting a little longer to make it even clearer to the Germans that they had lost the war. He thought that if the war ended with the German Army still occupying parts of France and Belgium and huge territories in eastern Europe (as eventually it did), then the German Army and the German people might come to believe that they had not in fact been defeated.

Ending the war

By late October Ludendorff had again changed his mind about ending the war. He thought that Prince Max had gone too far toward offering total surrender to the Allies, and he sent out a message to the troops saying that the proposed armistice terms were unacceptable to the German Army. He said that this sort of surrender was dishonorable and that the troops should fight to the finish. The German parliament and government were extremely angry with Ludendorff for this intervention. The emperor was equally furious that the general had intruded on his ultimate authority as commander in chief. Faced with this stiff opposition, Ludendorff was forced to resign his post on October 26, 1918, seemingly still blind to the part

insisted on making Germany pay compensation (called reparations) for the damage caused to its country by the war, and France also wanted to occupy part of Germany to ensure that the Germans would not attack them again and to ensure that the required reparations were paid in full. By November 4 Wilson had agreed to these modifications to his plan, and he asked the Germans to send their nominated representatives to make the final deal.

The president and the other Allied political leaders delegated responsibility for working out the military terms of the armistice to their commanders in France: Foch, Haig, and the commander of the AEF, General John Pershing. The generals insisted that the armistice

he had played in bringing about the final defeat of Germany. His replacement was quickly named as General Wilhelm Gröner.

By this stage Germany's home front was disintegrating at least as fast as its armies were being beaten on the western front. By late 1918 war and civil production generally was down to almost half of its 1913 level. The owners of big businesses had prospered, but many ordinary Germans were much worse off financially than before, and many had too little to eat. Soldiers at home on leave or recovering from wounds could see these problems for themselves. Many did not want to go back into battle or, if they did go back, told their comrades at the front just how bad things were at home.

Political change of some sort had become inevitable. Many thought that the only way to change things was to force the emperor to abdicate and to set up a republic. More extreme left-wingers wanted a revolution like the Russian one of 1917. When the fleet was ordered to make a last sacrificial attack on the Allied navies, the sailors at Kiel mutinied. They refused to take their ships to sea and instead went ashore to join workers' groups demanding an immediate end to the war. Revolutionary and protest movements now spread from city to city across Germany. No one could tell how this chaos might end, but one thing was clear: the war had to stop straightaway.

Germany's allies were also hurrying toward their final defeats as their empires fell apart. In mid-October the semi-independent puppet Polish government that the Germans had established in the former Russian province earlier in the war declared its full independence. At the same time the Allies recognized the rightful existence of an independent Czechoslovakia; they had already committed themselves to supporting an enlarged Serbia, which was to be known as Yugoslavia. All of these nations were to be formed out of the old Austro-Hungarian and Russian Empires. Even the central components of Austria-Hungary split apart. The recently appointed Hungarian prime minister, Alexander Werkele, announced his country's separation from Austria on October 19, and his successor from the 31st, Mihály Károlyi von Nagkároly, successfully negotiated a separate armistice with the Allies.

Under the pressure of new defeats in Italy, Austria's armistice was signed on November 3. Germany's ally Turkey had already left the war, signing its armistice on October 30. Germany's emperor, Wilhelm, bowed to the inevitable on November 9th and did not try to protest in public when the politicians announced his abdication. He slipped across the border into the neutral Netherlands, where he remained until his death in 1941. The last obstacle to the ending of the war had gone, although the fighting continued right up to the armistice.

The final negotiations between the German delegation headed by Matthias

▼ The French city of Lille had been occupied since the German invasion in 1914, but in October 1918 the British 57th Division marched in to secure its liberation.

Compiègne and the Armistice

By the beginning of November 1918, Germany was seeking an end to hostilities as quickly as possible, but the Allies were determined to exact harsh terms from their defeated foe before they would sign any armistice documents.

The final negotiations and the signing of the armistice that ended World War I took place in a railroad carriage that was parked in the forest of Compiègne, near Paris. The Allies chose this location rather than risk the security of their military headquarters by allowing the discussions to be conducted there. The talks began on the morning of November 8, and the agreement was signed at 5:30 A.M. on the 11th, coming into effect at 11:00 A.M. the same day.

France's Marshal Ferdinand Foch and a British admiral, Rosslyn Wemyss, headed the Allied delegation at the peace conference. The head of the German team was Secretary of State Matthias Erzberger, who was leader of the moderate Center Party in the German parliament. Erzberger had been very reluctant to take part in the talks, rightly guessing that he was signing his own death warrant by doing so—he was eventually assassinated by right-wing extremists in 1921. Significantly,

▶ *In November 1918 military leaders of the principal warring nations met in a railway carriage at Compiègne, near Paris. Marshal Foch is second from the right.*

of their trenches and set out to march home, often to be welcomed as returning heroes, but neither the soldiers nor ordinary German civilians had yet properly come to terms with what all these events meant.

In the years after the war, many Germans came to believe that their country, and especially their army, had not really lost World War I. They blamed weak civilian politicians for betraying the whole nation by agreeing to the punishing and humiliating Allied peace terms. They said that the German Army had not been defeated in battle but had been "stabbed in the back" by these traitors. This claim was not true. Germany's war effort was falling apart on the war fronts as completely as it was at home, and it was the Army's leaders above all who bore the responsibility, although they had stepped aside at the last minute to let others take the blame.

there were no senior representatives of the German Army or Navy at the talks.

The Germans were more or less told what they had to sign. The Allies demanded that the German Army hand over one-third of its artillery weapons and about half of its machine guns and withdraw from all occupied territory on the western front within one month. The Allies demanded to occupy areas of Germany on the east bank of the Rhine River. Until the Germans had signed a final peace agreement, the Allied naval blockade would continue. The Germans pleaded for more lenient terms, telling Foch that otherwise they would not be able to control the Bolshevik-style revolution that was developing in their country and warned that this could then

▲ *The people of Paris celebrate Armistice Day, November 11, 1918, in the Place de la Concorde. However, the settlement sowed the seeds for World War II.*

spread to Britain and France. Foch agreed to extend slightly the time the Germans would be given to evacuate occupied territory, and he made some other minor concessions. As for revolution, he said, the various Allied powers could look after themselves.

In truth, it was a slightly inconclusive and messy end to the war. Civilians in all the Allied countries celebrated wildly with parades and holidays. Allied soldiers were glad to have survived, but otherwise most were just too tired to bother partying. The German troops climbed out

One German soldier who believed in the "stab in the back" was a 29-year-old corporal who was temporarily blinded by poison gas during the British attacks in October. He later wrote that Germany would have won the war if only a few thousand Jews had been executed in 1918. This view was unsustainable, like all his racist theories, but many Germans would come to believe in his ideas and support the corporal in his political career in later years. His name was Adolf Hitler, and his Nazi regime would drag Germany into another world war just two decades later. Undoubtedly, he got his start on his rise to national power from the untidy way that World War I was brought to an end.

▼ The chancellor of Germany, Prince Max of Baden. He was forced to resign on November 9, 1918.

Erzberger, a political moderate, and the Allies commenced on November 8 in a railroad carriage in the forest of Compiègne, some 40 miles (64 km) northeast of Paris. Foch, heading the Allied delegation, made some minor concessions to the Germans, and they signed the agreement in the early hours of the 11th. The cease-fire came into effect at 11:00 A.M. the same day. The war was over at last, yet parts of France and Belgium remained temporarily in enemy hands as German forces withdrew in reasonably good order back to their homeland. They were followed by the Allies, who steadily advanced from Belgium and France, without fighting, to occupy parts of Germany east of the Rhine River.

In the various Allied capitals around the world, huge crowds gathered to celebrate the armistice, but the mood elsewhere was far from joyous. The end of the hostilities did not bring peace and stability to the governments and peoples of the defeated powers. Even as the armistice was coming into force, Germany itself was undergoing further political upheaval. The chancellor, Prince Max of Baden, had hoped to establish a constitutional monarchy headed by the deposed emperor's eldest grandson but was thwarted by members of his own government. The move was so unpopular that Prince Max lost all credibility, and he had to resign on November 9, when he handed power to the leader of the Social Democratic Party, Friedrich Ebert. Ebert's deputy, Philipp Scheidemann, announced the creation of a German republic on the same day, although without informing his superior. This move was an attempt to satisfy those of the German people who wanted moderate reform. However, as the Kiel Mutiny and subsequent uprisings in various German cities demonstrated, some Germans wanted greater political change—the creation of a Bolshevik-style state.

Ebert's position in Germany was far from secure because of these political tensions. He attempted to reach an accommodation with the more radical elements in the country's political life, not least the leaders of the radical Spartacus League, Karl Liebknecht and Rosa Luxemburg. Liebknecht had been

KEY FIGURES

ROSA LUXEMBURG

Luxemburg (1871–1919) was one of the leaders of the left-wing *Spartakusbund* (Spartacus League) political party in Germany at the end of the war. In conjunction with Karl Liebknecht, she was one of the leaders of an unsuccessful coup in 1919.

Luxemburg was born in what is now Poland, and as a young woman was one of the founders of the Polish Communist Party. She later moved to Germany and joined the Social Democratic Party (SDP), but when war came in August 1914 she broke with the SDP because it supported the military effort. Luxemburg opposed the war and wanted to bring about a socialist style of government through a workers' revolution. With another revolutionary, Karl Liebknecht, she founded the Spartacus League in the second half of 1915 to advocate these views but was imprisoned by the German government for her antiwar stance in 1917.

Set free in October 1918, she tried to exploit the turmoil in Germany to create the revolution she had long wanted. In the first two weeks of January 1919, there were two weeks of violent political unrest in the German capital, Berlin, led by Liebknecht and Luxemburg and known as the Spartacist Revolt. The attempted coup collapsed due to the intervention of right-wing militia (Freikorps) and German Army units. Both Luxemburg and Liebknecht were taken prisoner by members of the Freikorps on the night of January 15 and immediately executed. Their bodies were dumped in a Berlin canal, and the revolt they had fomented soon collapsed.

imprisoned for antiwar activities in 1917 and was only released in October 1918, but he was a popular figure among the more radical groups. Ebert was able to reach some temporary accommodation with the more left-wing groups, but their long-term support for the new republic could not be guaranteed.

Fearing further civil unrest, Ebert, as cochairman (with Hugo Hasse) of the provisional Council of People's Commissars, had already turned to a German general, Wilhelm Gröner, for military support on November 10. Gröner, who had effectively replaced Ludendorff after the latter's dismissal on October 26, agreed but on the condition that the new government did not pursue any major reforms of the German Army's officer corps. Gröner's scheme, as expressed in his memoirs, was "to win some strength in the new state for the [German] Army and officer corps by our activity; if that succeeded then the best and strongest elements of old Prussia were saved for the new Germany despite the revolution." As will be seen, Ebert's reliance on the German Army to maintain order against a backdrop of growing turmoil was revealed within a matter of weeks. Events at the end of 1918 and beginning of 1919 clearly demonstrated that the armed forces continued to play a central role in German politics. Ebert, a moderate, was elected first chancellor of the new German republic on February 11, 1919, and he remained in power until his death in 1925. Throughout this period he remained preoccupied with the economic crisis facing Germany and also with the constant threat of revolution from both political extremes.

World War I had finally ended, but the outcome had been costly and was far from clear cut, as the situation in Germany showed. For the Allies, particularly the French and British, there had been no great and final victories on German territory. The British effectively ended the conflict where for them it had begun in August 1914—at the Belgian town of Mons. Between the end of 1914 and November 1918, when Mons was recaptured, they had advanced less than 100 miles (160 km)—most in the last weeks of the fighting—at a cost of 2.7 million casualties among troops from both Britain and its empire. Britain's long list of casualties was echoed by many other nations. Had the sacrifice of so many brought about a fair and lasting peace or merely been the prelude to further rounds of bloodletting?

527

The Human Cost of War

When World War I ended in 1918, it had been the costliest conflict ever fought, with millions of men being killed and wounded. Civilians were also victims of a war in which the destructive power of modern weapons was seen for the first time.

❚❚ To my son. Since your eyes were closed, mine have never ceased to cry." This is the inscription on a plaque placed by a soldier's mother on the site of the 1916 Battle of Verdun. The bereaved parents of Verdun were French and German, but the same inscription could equally have been found on millions of British, Russian, or U.S. graves or those of many others.

A notable aspect of the war was that hundreds of thousands of the dead were never found or could not be identified. In British war cemeteries all across northern France there is no name on tombstone after tombstone, only the simple dedication, "A Soldier of the Great War, Known unto God." The Menin Gate memorial at Ypres carries the names of 54,896 British soldiers who have no known grave but were killed in the fighting nearby, a similar number of names to that inscribed on the Vietnam Veterans' Memorial in Washington, D.C. As that

comparison between only one of many major British monuments and America's whole loss from a later traumatic war shows, the human cost of World War I was vast. The killing was on a scale never seen before and only equaled since during World War II.

▼ *The number of service personnel of the various Allied powers who were killed outright or who later died of wounds received during World War I.*

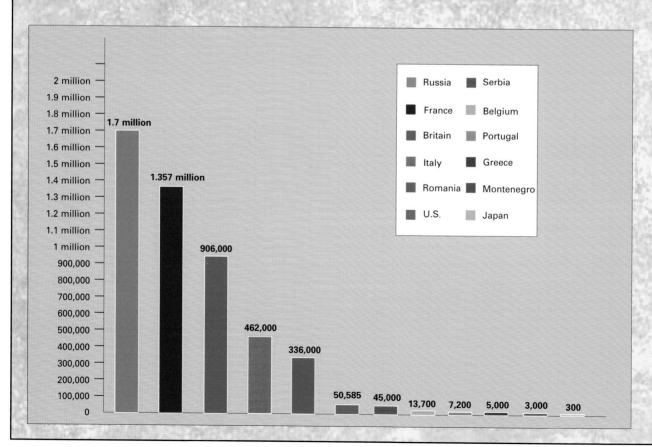

No one knows exactly how many soldiers were killed or wounded in the war, and reckoning the total of civilian casualties is even more difficult. Some countries did not keep reliable records of casualties, and eastern Europe, the Middle East, and other areas were so disrupted by revolutions and political changes after the war that any records there may have been were lost. It is also hard to be sure how many civilian deaths were caused by the war. The worldwide influenza pandemic during 1918 and 1919, for example, probably killed more than 50 million people. Some of these deaths may have occurred because the people concerned had already been weakened by the war—such as through wounds, or stress, or poor food or in some other way—but there is no way to put a figure on this.

Other civilian losses that are directly attributable to the war include about 500,000 Germans who starved because of the Allied naval blockade, many of them after the armistice in 1918. Comparable numbers of civilians probably died from starvation in Serbia and Romania, and several times more in Russia. More than 500,000 Armenians were murdered in genocidal attacks by the Turks—Adolf Hitler later cited these approvingly in discussions of his own plans for murdering Europe's Jews. The Turkish government continues to this day to argue that the deaths were not a deliberate policy.

The lowest estimate of the number of military deaths in World War I is about 10 million, but some figures are as high as 20 million. Germany and Russia each lost at least 1.7 million service personnel (though the true Russian figure may very well be much higher), France lost 1.4 million men, Britain and the countries of the British Empire one million, and so on down a very long and dreadful list.

For the United States the war was less costly than World War II (290,000 dead) or the Civil War (620,000 dead). About 120,000 U.S. servicemen died, roughly 50,000 of them in battle. As in all previous wars in history, more soldiers died of disease than in the fighting, even in the U.S. forces, which had among the best medical services. About 204,000 Americans were wounded. For many of these, as for the 25 million or more wounded in other countries, and the countless millions of widows, orphans, and mourning parents, the pain and suffering caused by the war would continue for many years.

In addition to conventional war injuries, a new psychological form of damage was identified. Known as shell shock, this condition could vary from frayed nerves to a complete mental collapse. It probably came about from the unremitting nature of trench warfare, in which men would be subjected to the constant fear of death for weeks at a time. Although outwardly unscarred, these men also were the victims of war.

▼ *The number of Central Powers' service personnel who were killed outright or died of their wounds reflects their respective military efforts in World War I.*

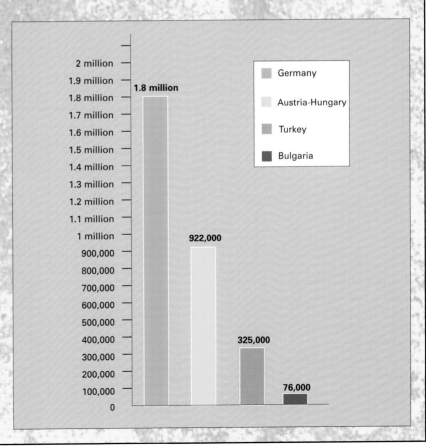

Europe after the Armistice

The cost of the war in human and financial terms was immense. Over 10 million people had died, 20 million had been wounded or disabled, and well over 100 billion U.S.

The most destructive conflict the world had ever witnessed finally came to an end on November 11, 1918. The search for an equitable peace, though, proved almost impossible.

dollars had been spent. Large areas of Belgium and northern France lay in ruins; chaos reigned in much of eastern and central Europe; starvation wracked both Austria and Germany; and Russia was in the grip of civil war and famine.

In political and dynastic terms, the upheaval had been just as dramatic. Four empires were in ruins and four ancient ruling houses would be toppled. In the Middle East, the great Turkish Empire that had once reached from Budapest to the Persian Gulf had crumbled, with its sultan, Mehmed VI, soon to be deposed by nationalist Turks. The Austro-Hungarian Empire was disintegrating into several squabbling successor states as its emperor, Charles I, fled into Swiss exile. Germany was plunged into turmoil by the Emperor Wilhelm II's abdication, and its fledgling republican government had to grapple with both socialist revolutionaries and right-wing reactionaries. In Russia, meanwhile, the civil war intensified, as "Red" Bolshevik revolutionaries fought three separate "White" antirevolutionary forces in a vicious conflict.

Conditions in France, Britain, and Italy were better, and the domestic consequences of the war for the United

▶ *The scene in the church quarter of Loos, northeast France, November 1915. At the war's end, great tracts of Belgium and northern France lay in ruins after four years of fighting.*

States were relatively minor. However, even the victors could not escape a terrible influenza pandemic that swept around the world in 1918 and 1919, killing more people than the war itself. It has been estimated that 20 million people died of "Spanish flu." For most of Europe's exhausted peoples, there was no real lull after the storm: hunger, war, and revolution shaped the postwar landscape until the early 1920s. Perhaps even more important than the destruction and death was the legacy of hatred and mistrust that the war left behind. The fervent nationalism that unleashed the war was in no way diminished by the end of it. Indeed, the war had merely inflamed long-standing rivalries and confirmed old hatreds. It had also sparked a Bolshevik revolution that threatened the capitalist world system and promised a new era of class struggle and civil war. The fact that all the major Allies intervened in the Russian Civil War (see pages 586–587) shows how concerned they were to overthrow communism before it spread.

It was against this bleak backdrop that the world's statesmen gathered in Paris in January 1919 to negotiate the treaties that would bring a formal end to the hostilities. As we shall see, some delegates came to the table with worthy aims and high hopes that a new, peaceful, and democratic Europe could be constructed from the ruins of the old order. Nevertheless, the treaties that ensued were also the result of revenge, mistrust, and old-fashioned secret diplomacy; they merely planted the seeds of an even more destructive world war in the poisoned soils of postwar Europe.

The aims of the Allies

The Paris Peace Conference began on January 12, 1919, the delegates having assembled with the accompaniment of teams of economists, lawyers, linguists, cartographers, and diplomats. Almost 40 "nations" were represented, including some that had never known independent nationhood before, such as the Arab delegation led by Feisal, and some that hoped to reestablish their ancient nations, such as Poland. The real power at the conference lay with the "Big Five"—Italy, Japan, Britain, France, and the United States—and negotiations were usually dominated by the latter

▲ *The Council of Four were the principal figures at the Paris Peace Conference. The council consisted of (from left to right) Italian prime minister Vittorio Orlando, British prime minister David Lloyd George, French prime minister Georges Clemenceau, and U.S. president Woodrow Wilson.*

three countries. The Germans were present as observers only, and there was one notable absentee: Bolshevik Russia did not attend.

As the victorious delegations began to state the aims that would justify the appalling suffering that had been inflicted on their people, it soon became clear that the nations that had been united in defeating the Central Powers were divided in determining the subsequent peace. There were disagreements over territorial demands, material compensation, and the conditions needed for future security. Hence much of the negotiating over the next 18 months consisted of intense wrangling over borders, money, and military obligations. There were also issues of principle at stake, and conflict among the Allies had much to do with their different visions for the postwar world.

The United States, in particular, brought a wider ethical vision to the talks. Its aims had been succinctly articulated in President Woodrow Wilson's famous Fourteen Points (see Volume 1, pages 310–311). Delivered in a speech to the U.S. Congress on January 8, 1918, the Fourteen Points were based on the principles of democracy and self-determination. At the time, with the war still raging in Europe, Wilson had hoped to keep the door open to a negotiated peace by convincing Germany that the United States sought "a peace without victors" and a peace without territorial gain for itself. Now that the United States had helped defeat Germany, the Fourteen Points became Wilson's ideal for a secure, lasting, and just peace.

Wilson demanded that "the world be made fit and safe to live in…for every peace-loving nation, which…wishes to live its own life, determine its own institutions, and be assured of justice and fair dealing by the other peoples of the world." Such a vision called for freedom of the seas, freedom of trade, and a worldwide reduction of armaments. Wilson also placed great stress on open diplomacy conducted in public view because he was convinced that the war had been caused by the secret dealings of Europe's governments. Wilson hoped that, in the future, the process of peace would be "absolutely open" and "permit henceforth no secret understandings of any kind."

The Fourteen Points contained specific, practical terms as well. The United States wanted German withdrawal from all Russian and Belgian territory; the return of Alsace-Lorraine to France; readjustments in the borders of Italy; "autonomous development" for the peoples of Austria-Hungary; the evacuation of Montenegro, Romania, and Serbia by the Central Powers; independence for the non-Turkish portions of the Turkish Empire; and a sovereign Polish state with access to the sea. All these developments were to be safeguarded by "a general association of nations" formed "for the purpose of affording mutual guarantees of political independence and territorial integrity to great and small nations alike."

In short, Wilson hoped for what would later be called a new world order, and the capstone would be a League of Nations to settle disputes and enforce the settlement. These lofty aims represented the liberal, democratic ideals of many in America—a young and idealistic country with few natural enemies and little of the bitterness caused by years of European rivalry. Various individuals and pressure groups around the world had been advocating the creation of such an international body during World War I, not least the U.S. organization, the League to Enforce the Peace. Wilson's aims also revealed the character of their author. He was a

---

POLITICAL WORLD

THE LEAGUE TO ENFORCE THE PEACE

The idea for the League of Nations came from a number of sources. In Britain, the Fabian Society, the Lord Bryce Group, the League of Nations Society, and Robert Cecil all promoted the idea. South Africa's Jan Smuts and France's Leon Bourgeois were also powerful proponents.

In the United States, the chief advocate was the League to Enforce the Peace. Formed at Independence Hall in Philadelphia in 1915, it worked for a League of Nations, a world court, and compulsory international conciliation. The league's president was the former U.S. president and Yale law professor William Howard Taft. Its other leaders included Hamilton Holt and Theodore Marburg.

When the United States entered World War I in 1917, the League gave its full support to the war effort. In February 1919 in Boston, as the peace talks proceeded in Paris, the league organized a National Congress for a League of Nations. The League to Enforce the Peace is usually seen as a significant influence on President Woodrow Wilson in his conversion to the cause of the League of Nations.

---

political scientist and college professor, with lofty moral principles and a theoretical approach rare in his more cynical and worldly European counterparts. The almost religious fervor of his political morality, together with his distance from the tarnished world of European politics, made Wilson very popular among the ordinary people of Europe. They saw him as a powerful and honorable crusader for justice, whose honesty and impartiality would lead them to a brighter future. The political elite of Europe, upstaged by Wilson, found him to be a pompous bore with a poor grasp of the hard realities of national ambition and ethnic hatred. As the British prime minister, David Lloyd George, put it: "The idealistic president regarded himself as a missionary whose function it was to rescue the poor European heathen from their age-long worship of false and fiery gods."

For France—its youth decimated, its finances in disarray, and its landscape deeply scarred—principles and fairness held less appeal. The war was won, but France still lay next to Germany, and it always would. One day the superior industries and larger population of Germany could once again be brought to bear on France's long and vulnerable eastern border. Invaded twice in half a century, France desired security and feared Germany more than ever. More important than fair national boundaries and future cooperation was the French need to weaken Germany to the point where it could never wage war again.

As well as the return of the provinces of Alsace-Lorraine (lost in the Franco-Prussian War, 1870–1871), the French prime minister, Georges Clemenceau,

wanted massive reparations (payments) and a *cordon sanitaire* (safe cordon) of territory around Germany. Reparations would serve the double purpose of forcing Germany to pay for the war while simultaneously weakening its military capabilities. The *cordon sanitaire*, in its full version, would have created a buffer state between France and Germany along the Rhine River. It also envisioned new allies for France in eastern Europe (Poland and Czechoslovakia) as a counterbalance to German power in the region. This French policy was never fully implemented. New nations were created in eastern Europe partly out of German lands, but Britain and the United States rebuffed French demands for a separate state on the east bank of the Rhine.

With hindsight, the French policy may seem misguided and vengeful. Annexation of German territory plus reparations added insult to defeat,

▼ Having served in various roles during the war, Winston Churchill (center) became British secretary of state for war in December 1918. He had misgivings about Bolshevik Russia and viewed Germany as a counterbalance.

caused economic chaos, and hastened the revival of German nationalism under Adolf Hitler—this time in a much more virulent and dangerous form—in the 1930s. It could be argued that this result stemmed from partial instead of full implementation of the plan to weaken Germany. If France had dictated the peace treaty and been able to enforce its provisions, Germany may have been much weaker and less dangerous for many decades.

The British had yet another set of priorities. Like France they wished to weaken and contain Germany to prevent another war. Britain too had suffered immensely, and it felt that Germany should pay for its aggression. Lloyd George, the British prime minister, had won reelection in December 1918 on a platform of squeezing Germany "until the pips squeaked." Yet the British government was unwilling to replace German dominance on the continent with French superiority. It sought a return to a balance of power in Europe and hoped to rehabilitate a weakened Germany as a liberal democratic partner. Some politicians, notably Winston Churchill, rapidly earmarked Germany as a future bulwark against Bolshevik Russia. As the treaty negotiations progressed, concerns about Germany's economic and political stability added the specter of a Bolshevik revolution there to an already complex equation.

Britain's worldwide imperial interests and detachment from the continent of Europe also gave it a broader, if no less self-interested, perspective than France. Britain was less concerned about permanently disabling Germany in Europe than it was about protecting the Royal Navy's superiority at sea, preserving British trade, and annexing German colonies. Britain's financial and territorial demands on Germany (excluding its colonies) were generally less severe than were those made by France. As negotiations between the Allies continued,

---

EYEWITNESS

WINSTON CHURCHILL

Britain's leader in World War II was minister for munitions during part of World War I and already a major political figure. The long, barbarous war had shattered society as Churchill knew it, and he took little joy in the final victory.

"What a disappointment the twentieth century has been," he noted. "How terrible and how melancholy is [the] long series of events [which] have darkened its first 20 years." This pessimism was a reaction to Bolshevism in Russia as well as to the war, both of which had led to "a dissolution, a weakening of those bonds, a challenge to those principles" on which the "structure and ultimate existence of civilized society depends."

During the peace talks he believed that Germany must be rehabilitated for the good of Europe. He saw a capitalist, democratic Germany as a barrier to Russian Bolshevism and bluntly declared that the Allies ought to "feed Germany; fight Bolshevism; make Germany fight Bolshevism." While in Paris, Churchill was walking with U.S. delegate Bernard Baruch, discussing the problems facing Europe. Baruch expressed concern at the weather, and Churchill stopped, pointed his walking stick to the east, and growled: "Russia! Russia! That's where the weather is coming from!"

Lloyd George moved toward a more just peace—providing this did not significantly impair British interests.

In the Fontainebleau Memorandum, written on March 25, 1919, Lloyd George infuriated Clemenceau by softening his stance on Germany. Instead of squeezing Germany until the pips squeaked, he spoke of a peace "with no causes of exasperation constantly stirring up either the spirit of patriotism, of justice, or of fair play, to achieve redress." He was especially worried about putting large numbers of Germans under the control of other states. Prophetically, he warned: "I cannot conceive any greater cause of future war than that the German people should be surrounded by a number of

▲ *The German delegates at Versailles in the spring of 1919, having been invited to receive the peace terms. When the terms were presented to the Germans on May 7, the reaction was one of outrage.*

small states, many of them consisting of people who have never previously set up a stable government for themselves, but each of them containing large masses of Germans clamoring for reunion with their native land."

The other major participant on the Allied side was Italy, which had been promised significant territorial gains by Britain, France, and Russia in the secret Treaty of London of 1915. As well as the predominantly German-speaking South Tyrol, which would give Italy a more secure northern border on the Alps, Italy was allotted Trieste, Istria (including Fiume, now Rijeka), and northern Dalmatia on the Adriatic coast—all to be carved out of the former Austro-Hungarian Empire. Italy was also promised Albania, colonies in North Africa, and, most cynically, a free hand in neutral, independent Abyssinia (Ethiopia). These promises had helped to bring Italy into the war on the Allies' side, but they were in direct conflict with the principles of President Woodrow Wilson's

Fourteen Points, as much of this land was occupied by Slavs, Germans, and independent Africans.

As if such divisions among the Big Four Allies (the Big Five minus Japan) were not enough, there were a host of competing claims from smaller members of the alliance as well as numerous areas of disputed territory in the new states that had risen from the ashes of the old Austro-Hungarian Empire. Such conflicts of interest led to intense friction among the Allies, and the reconciliation of claims to the satisfaction of all proved impossible. Furthermore, the Allies had to work fast to prevent uncertainty from creating even greater chaos in central Europe and the Balkans, where numerous Bolshevik-style soviets were being established.

The treaties that emerged from Paris were compromises that pleased nobody, especially the defeated powers, who were barely consulted. It was difficult enough to maintain a common public front among the Allies without the input of the defeated nations; it would have been impossible had the former Central Powers been allowed to negotiate, playing each of the Allies off against the others. Thus, the treaty took the form of a dictated peace, which later fed feelings that Germany had been harshly treated, and left festering territorial grievances all over Europe.

The peace terms

By May 1919 the United States, Britain, and France had agreed on the peace terms to be communicated to Germany.

The German government was outraged and initially refused to sign the treaty. However, the continuing Allied naval blockade and Allied threats of force left Germany with little choice but to comply. Germany would be starved into submission unless it acquiesced. So on June 28 Herman Muller and Johannes Bell of the new republican government signed the Treaty of Versailles in the Hall of Mirrors in the Versailles palace outside Paris. The signing took place in the same room in which the new German Empire had been proclaimed in 1871 after

▼ *French prime minister Georges Clemenceau gets to his feet to ask the German delegates to sign the Treaty of Versailles, June 28, 1919.*

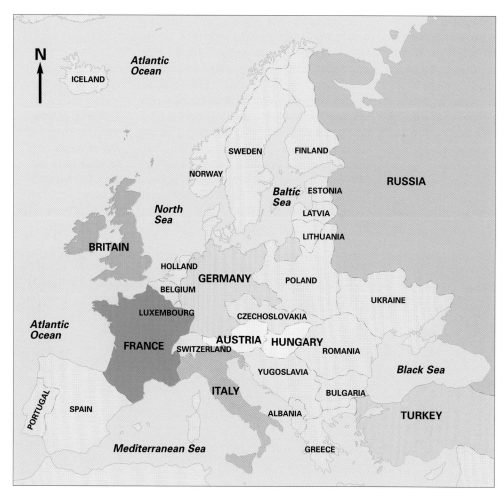

◄ *The postwar boundaries of Europe as seen after the Treaty of Versailles in 1919. Germans were the biggest losers, as large tracts of their eastern territories passed to Poland.*

Prussia's defeat of France. The symbolism was deliberate and to the French signified the settling of an old score.

The terms of the treaty contained three interwoven strands, all designed to weaken and punish Germany. The first strand was territorial reduction. Germany handed Alsace-Lorraine back to France and gave the districts of Eupen and Malmédy to Belgium. The German port of Memel (now Klaipeda) on the Baltic Sea was lost to the new state of Lithuania, which seized it with tacit Allied approval, and northern Schleswig was handed to Denmark after a plebiscite. The coal-rich Saar Basin was ceded to the League of Nations until 1935. This last was also an economic punishment designed to allow French exploitation of the Saar's coal as

compensation for the German exploitation and destruction of France's mines during the war.

Even more controversially, Poland was to be assured access to the Baltic Sea by the German surrender of the river port of Posen (Poznan) and part of Prussia (which became known as the Polish Corridor), while the predominantly German Baltic port of Danzig (Gdansk) became an international city under the control of the League of Nations. The Polish Corridor cut off East Prussia from the rest of Germany and, despite its population's 60 percent Polish majority, put significant numbers of Germans under Polish rule. Plebiscites were needed to resolve border disputes between Poland and Germany over Upper Silesia, which was split between the two countries, and in southern areas of East Prussia, which voted to remain German. Nevertheless, Germans felt aggrieved over the loss of large swathes of their eastern territories to Poland.

Germany's European losses were economically painful. It ceded 80 percent of its iron ore, 38 percent of its steel production, and 30 percent of its coal capacity, including all but 11 of the 61 coal mines in Silesia. Set against these forfeitures, its territorial and population losses were more moderate—only 13 percent of its prewar territory and 12 percent of its prewar population (about half of it non-German). The colonial losses, however, were complete: all the German colonies were handed over to new owners. Technically, most of these colonies became mandated territories of the League of Nations. Effectively, they were controlled by Britain, France,

▼ *French troops celebrate the liberation of Alsace in 1918. Along with Lorraine, it had been under German control since 1871.*

Japan, Belgium, and countries of the British Commonwealth. German East Africa became Tanganyika (Tanzania from 1961) and went to Britain. Cameroon and Togoland were split between France and Britain. German Southwest Africa (Namibia) went to South Africa, and German New Guinea to Australia. The small landlocked area of Rwanda-Urundi passed to Belgium, despite its scandalous record of colonial rule in the Belgian Congo. Germany's northern Pacific islands and its interests in the Shantung province of China were given to Japan, while its southern Pacific islands were distributed among New Zealand, Australia, and Britain.

Much to Clemenceau's disgust, the United States and Britain refused French demands for a new buffer state on the Rhine. Wilson, in particular, objected to such a flagrant violation of the principle of self-determination (the area in question was overwhelmingly German). Yet he did accept an Italian takeover of Austria's mostly German-speaking South Tyrol and the incorporation of the mainly German-speaking Sudetenland into the new state of Czechoslovakia. The Allies also rejected a distinct Austrian preference for *anschluss* (union) with Germany. This selective application of self-determination for security reasons struck most Germans, and many non-Germans, as hypocritical. It would prove a source of grievance that later gave fuel and propaganda opportunities to Hitler.

The second major strand of the treaty was military. Germany's army was limited to 100,000 volunteers, while its officer-training academies and general staff were disbanded. Germany was allowed no air force and only a small coastal naval force, with submarines specifically banned. The great fear among many senior figures in the German Navy was that its surface warships, interned at Scapa Flow in the Orkney Islands off the northeast coast of Scotland as part of the armistice terms in 1918, would

▲ On June 21, 1919, much of the German High Seas Fleet, interned at Scapa Flow, was sunk by its skeleton crews. Here salvage personnel of the British Royal Navy attempt to raise one of the scuttled vessels.

fall permanently into British hands. They acted to prevent this takeover from happening. Many of the interned vessels were scuttled by their skeleton crews on June 21, 1919.

Perhaps the most humiliating of the conditions laid down in the treaty was the demilitarization and occupation of the Rhineland. The entire area between the Rhine and France, as well as a 30-mile (50 km) strip on the east bank of the Rhine, was out of bounds to German troops, and much of the area was to be occupied by Allied troops. Germany was also prohibited from importing any arms, munitions, or war supplies, and its social organizations were forbidden to "instruct or exercise their members…in the profession or use of arms."

However, on top of all these conditions came the third strand—reparations based on war guilt. Article 231 of the treaty specifically laid the blame for the entire conflict and hence all the destruction caused by it at Germany's door. In the words of the treaty, Germany accepted "the responsibility of Germany and her allies for causing all the loss and damage to which the Allied and Associated Governments and their nationals have been subjected as a consequence of the war imposed on them by the aggression of Germany and her allies." The "war guilt" clause was perhaps the most controversial and contentious of all of the treaty's provisions. Not only did it open the door to potentially enormous financial claims on Germany, but it also appeared so unjust to Germans that it united the country in the desire to overturn the treaty, whether by negotiation or open defiance.

The amount of reparations to be paid could not be agreed upon at the conference. There was disagreement as to whether they should cover purely physical damage to France and Belgium or extend to the entire cost of the war to the Allies, an enormous and impossible sum to repay. In the event, Germany was ordered to pay 5 billion dollars immediately, the final sum to be determined by a reparation commission on which there would be no German representation. This unavoidable indecision led to years of wrangling, defaulting, and renegotiations. The commission reported in April 1921 and called for 132 billion gold marks (roughly $32 billion) to be paid in annual installments over a period of decades.

Germany claimed these sums to be impossibly high, but France, Britain, and other Allies needed capital from Germany to pay their own huge debts to the United States, particularly after Bolshevik Russia had renounced repayment of its own massive war debt of around $3.6 billion, most of it owed to Britain. The United States was eager to minimize German payments to allow its recovery but at the same time insisted on full repayment of U.S. wartime loans made to its Allies. Thus, reparations had very broad implications for the world

KEY FIGURES

JOHN MAYNARD KEYNES

The feeling that Versailles was too harsh on Germany was brilliantly expressed by the British economist John Maynard Keynes (1883–1946).

A member of the British delegation to Versailles and a financial adviser to the British government, Keynes had resigned in protest during the peace conference. His rapidly published critique, *The Economic Consequences of the Peace* (1919), became a best-seller. He criticized the unprincipled, secret deals of the Allies, describing Lloyd George as a man "rooted in nothing." More important, he won converts to the view that the reparations demanded of Germany would bankrupt the country, leading to an inability to make and buy goods.

For Keynes, the most serious problems at Versailles "were not political or territorial but financial and economic...the perils of the future lay not in frontiers or sovereignties, but in food, coal, and transport." By destroying the leading European industrial economy, Keynes argued, the peace treaty would both prevent the emergence of a liberal democratic Germany and slow down the recovery of the world economy.

financial system. Some believed, not least the British economist John Maynard Keynes, that an economically weakened Germany was likely to have disastrous consequences. It was a matter not simply of punishing Germany but of finding the money to meet wartime debts. Negotiations over reparations were tied to debt reduction, and the two would become central features of international politics in the 1920s. It is crucial to note that, despite their victory, Britain and France went from being creditor to debtor nations as a result of the war, with long-term consequences for the future power of both nations.

Another crucial fact that is often lost in the controversy over reparations is that because of repeated defaults and renegotiated plans, Germany ultimately paid off only a relatively small proportion to the Allies, about 12 percent of the total demanded, before reparations were abandoned in 1932. Hence, the traditional argument that the payment of reparations fundamentally destabilized Germany is probably overstated, although it is certainly true to say that the perception inside the country of a huge reparations demand contributed significantly to an unstable Germany.

After the Treaty of Versailles was signed, Wilson, Lloyd George, and the other heads of state returned home. It was left to the ministers, diplomats, and experts of the Supreme Council of the victorious powers to work out the fine details of a series of treaties with the other defeated powers. These treaties were all named after palaces in and

▼ *A view of the Alexandrovski Bridge across the Vistula River in the Polish capital, Warsaw. The peace treaties after World War I gave back Poland its independence for the first time since the eighteenth century.*

around Paris. The Treaty of Trianon with Hungary, signed on June 4, 1919, was followed by the Treaty of St. Germain with Austria on September 20. These two agreements confirmed the destruction of the Austro-Hungarian Empire. This huge multilingual and multiethnic empire had long maintained an uneasy economic and political order in much of eastern and central Europe. Austrians (Germans), Hungarians (Magyars), Czechs, Slovaks, Poles, Romanians, Ruthenians, Italians, Slovenes, Croats, Serbs, and Bosnian Muslims had lived within its borders.

From the ruins of Austria-Hungary, the peace treaties forged several smaller states. Two entirely new nations were born. Czechoslovakia was assembled from Bohemia, Moravia, and Slovakia, whereas Yugoslavia was an amalgamation of Serbia with the southern Slav lands of Slovenia, Croatia, and Bosnia. The existing Allied states of Italy and Romania received large tracts of land. The latter country doubled in size, having had the good fortune to be surrounded by defeated enemies. It was given a huge part of the old kingdom of Hungary and with it a large and aggrieved Hungarian population. A reborn Poland, which included the former Austrian province of Galicia, was also established. Hungary was given independent statehood but with a massively reduced territory, while Austria (the heart of the old empire) became a poor, small, landlocked country in search of an identity and on the brink of starvation. Its grand imperial buildings in Vienna sat like a crown on the head of a pauper—a constant mockery of former greatness.

Another defeated European power, Bulgaria, signed the Treaty of Neuilly on November 27, 1920. It lost western Thrace to Greece and South Dobrudja to Romania. After the implementation of the peace treaties, the enlarged Romania included significant minorities of Turks, Bulgarians, Hungarians, and Ukrainians. It was a good example of how the complex ethnic geography of eastern Europe and the Balkans prevented neat boundaries between nations and made Woodrow Wilson's principle of self-determination very difficult to apply. The situation in the region was further complicated by the need to reward Allies and create states large enough to act as counterbalances to Germany. As a result, self-determination was applied selectively and only when convenient or practical, a tactic that smacked more of Old World diplomacy than of a new world order.

The last set of borders to be resolved were those of Turkey. Long seen as the "sick man of Europe" because of its crumbling empire, Turkey was decimated by the Treaty of Sèvres signed in August

Iraq, and Palestine became mandates under British control. Istanbul had a Franco-British force of occupation, and Turkey was obliged to accept permanent League of Nations administration of the Dardanelles straits as a neutral zone. Turkey also lost Rhodes and the Dodecanese Islands to Italy.

Even more humiliating was Turkey's temporary loss of eastern Thrace and portions of Anatolia (Asia Minor) to its long-standing enemies, the Greeks. Even before the Treaty of Sèvres was signed, 20,000 Greek troops landed in Turkey with British encouragement. They occupied Smyrna (Izmir) and other areas that were to be transferred to Greece. The Italians also seized the southern Anatolian region of Cilicia. These conquests did not stand, and the treaty provisions were never fully applied. Nationalist Turks under Kemal Ataturk accepted neither the Greek invasion nor the sultan's signature. After raising an army, they pushed the Greeks off the Anatolian mainland and toppled the sultan. Eventually, their successes were recognized in the more favorable Treaty of Lausanne in 1923.

The various peace treaties had changed the face of Europe. Nine new states had come into being or been revived; other borders had been radically redrawn; and the collapse of four empires was effectively confirmed. In establishing the League of Nations, the treaties had also created a new mechanism for the resolution of international disputes, and the league's mandate system had given the first indications that the days of colonialism were numbered. However, the treaties left much unresolved and many unhappy, and in the postwar years Italy, Japan, Soviet Russia, and Germany all sought to revise them by both diplomacy and force.

Problems with the peace

Italy became the first state to actively challenge the peace, despite having been on the winning side. When the

▲ *The former Turkish capital, Constantinople (Istanbul). Turkey was given harsh terms under the Treaty of Sèvres but achieved some revisions in 1923.*

1920. With the exception of the issue of reparations, Turkey was in many ways treated more harshly than Germany. It suffered the loss of its vast Middle East empire. Hejaz (now part of Saudi Arabia) became independent. Syria and Lebanon became mandates of the League of Nations under French control, while Transjordan (Jordan),

▼ *Italian national-ist poet Gabriele D'Annunzio is forced to leave Fiume (Rijeka) at the end of the unofficial 16-month Italian occupation of the city. D'Annunzio is the bald figure, center right, being held aloft by the crowd.*

other major Allies denied Italy the Adriatic port of Fiume (Rijeka) in April 1919, the Italian delegation left the talks, and a myth of "mutilated victory" was born. Italy returned to sign the Treaty of Versailles, but Italian public opinion was further outraged when territorial claims on Albania, northern Dalmatia, and Abyssinia were also refused. The resulting sense of injured national pride led an unofficial volunteer army under Italian nationalist poet Gabriele D'Annunzio to seize Fiume from Yugoslavia in September 1919 and hold it until evicted by Italian warships in January 1921. The same feeling of outrage also contributed to the rise of fascism under Benito Mussolini, who in the aftermath of the March on Rome by his supporters in October 1922 was granted dictatorial powers the following month. In 1935 Mussolini invaded Ethiopia, signifying contempt for the League of Nations, a break with the Allies, and Italy's realignment with the Axis powers of Germany and Japan.

Japan initially appeared more satisfied with the peace and participated constructively in the 1921 Washington Conference, the first major attempt at arms reduction after the war. Japan signed an agreement that seemingly pre-

The League of Nations

The League of Nations was designed as the lynchpin and crowning achievement of the peace. Its covenant preceded each of the individual peace treaties, and Woodrow Wilson threw all his moral weight behind it.

The basis of the League was collective security, the peaceful resolution of disputes, and the protection of the status quo after the peace conference. Its central pillar was Article 10, which read: "The members of the League undertake to respect and preserve as against external aggression the territorial integrity and existing political independence of all members of the League." Furthermore, in Article 16, any act of aggression against a member was viewed as "an act of war against all other members of the League."

The Council of the League was to be made up of five permanent members (the United States, Britain, France, Italy, and Japan) and four members selected by the Assembly, which consisted of all members. All neutral nations and almost all of the defeated countries were invited to join, but there were two important omissions: Germany and Soviet Russia. Then, when President Woodrow Wilson

failed to gain ratification of the Treaty of Versailles at home, the United States withdrew. The League was left without the most powerful nation, the United States, and in terms of potential probably the two next most powerful nations, Germany and the Soviet Union. This situation created a fundamental weakness in the organization from the out-set, with direction defaulting to Britain and France, both of which had been permanently weakened by the war.

There were other crucial flaws. Against the strong arguments of France for a League backed by a military force, the United States and Britain refused to commit to

either a standing army or dedi-cated national contingents under League control. The result was that when the League was really needed in the difficult circum-stances of the 1930s, it lacked the might to act effectively. When confronted with powerful revi-sionist states such as Italy and Japan that were not prepared to play by the rules in Abyssinia and Manchuria, respectively, the League was revealed as toothless and spineless.

However, that the League was doomed to ultimate failure was not as clear at the time as it became with hindsight. In the 1920s the League had a number of small successes. It settled a dispute over the Aaland Islands between Sweden and Finland

▲ U.S. observers standing outside the conference hall during a ses-sion of the League of Nations. The League was fatally weakened by the U.S. failure to join.

and supervised plebiscites that gave Vilna (Vilnius) to Poland rather than Lithuania and saw Carinthia vote for Austria over Yugoslavia. It also successfully established and administered Danzig (Gdansk) as a free city in difficult circumstances.

The League's subsidiary bodies had genuine successes, too. The International Labour Organization, for example, persuaded governments to fix maximum working hours and minimum wages, and the Refugee Organization helped to settle half a million refugees. However, the League's chief func-tion was to ensure world peace and security, and in this respect it failed to match the expecta-tions placed on it in Paris.

◀ The first session of the League of Nations takes place in the Salle de Réforme, Geneva, November 15, 1920. The league continued in existence until 1940.

▲ *Japanese and U.S. sailors on board the USS* Mayflower, *the president's yacht, in Washington, D.C., July 1922. Japan's ambition in Asia and the Pacific eventually soured relations with the western Allies.*

vented a naval arms race between the United States, Britain, and Japan by limiting the size of their navies in the ratio of 5 to 5 to 3, respectively. However, rivalry with the United States in the Pacific, plans for a Japanese-dominated East Asia Coprosperity Sphere, and long-standing ambitions in the Chinese province of Manchuria would eventually separate Japan from the western Allies. In 1931 Japan invaded Manchuria, setting up the puppet state of Manchukuo. This act was followed by Japan's withdrawal from the League of Nations in 1933, after the latter ineffectually condemned its conduct regarding Manchuria, and eventually by conflict with the United States and Britain in World War II.

Bolshevik Russia was effectively ignored by the treaties, but it was never reconciled to its revised western border with newly reestablished Poland, which was settled in 1921 after a conflict with Poland and not by the Peace of Paris. Nor did Russia accept the creation of

the independent states of Finland, Latvia, Lithuania, and Estonia—all of which had been parts of czarist Russia before World War I. When war broke out again in Europe in 1939, Soviet Russia used the opportunity to seize eastern Poland and then Latvia, Lithuania, and Estonia. It also fought a costly war with Finland during 1939 and 1940 to revise its northern borders around Leningrad (St. Petersburg).

Germany remained the major problem, though. The war guilt clause and the perception of an unjust peace gave rise to "stab in the back" theories that denied that Germany had been beaten militarily and placed the blame for Versailles on domestic enemies such as socialists, liberals, and Jews. Militarism and nationalism were still alive in postwar Germany, as the French politician Aristide Briand realized when he quoted the theories of the still-popular General Erich Ludendorff, beliefs expressed more than a year after the armistice: "War is the cornerstone of all intelligent policy. It is the cornerstone of every form of future event, and chiefly of the future of the German people.... The warlike qualities of the Prussian and German Armies have been put to the proof on the bloody battlefields. The German people need no other qualities for their moral renovation. The spirit of the former Army must be the germ which will allow this renovation to take place."

Ultimately, renewed German nationalism led to the rise of Adolf Hitler in the early 1930s. Later that decade, as Lloyd George had predicted, the German minorities in the Sudetenland and the Polish Corridor provided a pretext for German aggression that led to World War II. After bullying Czechoslovakia, France, and Britain into accepting the annexation of the Sudetenland in 1938, Germany invaded Czechoslovakia in March 1939. Finally convinced of Hitler's ambitions, Britain and France offered guarantees to Poland, thus making another European war inevitable when Germany invaded Poland in September 1939.

The World War I peace treaties pleased no one and aggrieved many. They divided the world into victors hoping to hold on to what they had and revisionists hoping to break their grip. German perceptions of a harsh peace laid foundations for future conflict. Compromise among the Allies had confused the principles of the peace without satisfying the security needs of France or the national aspirations of Italy and Japan. Intense national rivalry was not soothed by peace; if anything, the creation of sizable ethnic minorities on the wrong side of new national borders made rivalries worse. The new frontiers also dislocated economies, separated producers from markets, and cut lines of communication. This situation prompted floods of emigrants and refugees, further destabilizing fragile postwar societies. However, the flaws in the settlements must be seen in the context of Bolshevik revolution, economic collapse, intense nationalism, and an unrepentant Germany. To place too much blame on the Allied governments for the failure of the treaties is to underestimate the challenges they faced.

▼ *German troops returning from the western front after the armistice cross the Moselle River in Koblenz. After Versailles, the view arose that the German Army had not been defeated in World War I but had been sold out by the civilian politicians.*

Peace and the Allies

The Allies were victorious in World War I but at great cost. For many of the European Allies, peace brought neither security nor prosperity as many political, social, and economic problems remained unsolved.

As the European Allies reflected on their victory, it seemed that their power had risen to new heights. They had emerged from the war with their institutions intact and their empires enlarged. France had reemerged as the leading power on the Continent; Britain's navy still ruled the waves; Italy stood on the brink of achieving great-power status a little more than half a century after its creation as a unified and independent state; and constitutional democracy had triumphed over military autocracy. In London, jubilant crowds roamed the streets, chanting "Who won the war?" The reply would thunder back, "We won the war!" However, what exactly had the European Allies won?

Although the war accelerated the rise of the United States to economic and political world supremacy, for the European Allies the meaning of victory in the conflict was less clear. Not only had the war killed and maimed millions of their young men, it had consumed vast resources, cost them much of their national wealth, and disrupted the economic systems that produced that wealth. Between 1914 and 1920, industrial production declined by 12 percent in Britain, 26 percent in Italy, and no less than 34 percent in France. World trade had stagnated, and the Allies' traditional markets had been lost to the United States and Japan. Before 1914 Britain and France were the world's great creditor nations. Britain provided 43 percent and France 20 percent of all the world's exported capital. The global financial and economic system was centered on London, the British capital, in which city were processed the transfers of money, goods, and services that kept the world economy working. London was effectively the world's bank, and the British pound its currency of last resort. The war changed all these things.

France, Britain, and Italy now had huge national debts. Between 1914 and 1922 the national debt of France rose from $6.5 billion to $27.8 billion. In Italy

the debt rose from $3 billion to $8.7 billion, while in Britain it soared from $3.4 billion to $34.2 billion—an increase of 1,000 percent in eight years. The United States was owed over $10 billion by its European Allies; Britain was owed large sums by France and Italy; and Russia, having borrowed $2.5 billion from Britain and $900 million from France, refused to repay its outstanding loans. This web of debt had inevitable consequences for the world role of these nations, and it raised a new question for their expanded empires: How long could their colonies be controlled with diminished financial resources?

▼ A children's street party in Tewkesbury Street, north London, to celebrate the end of World War I. Euphoria today, but what did the future hold?

These financial costs of the war had profound long-term consequences, but they should not conceal the incalculable toll in human lives—1.5 million dead in France, 750,000 in Britain, and 600,000 in Italy. Machines can be replaced; individuals and the relationships they create cannot. The war ripped through the fabric of society, leaving millions of grieving widows, orphaned children, and disabled men, not to mention millions of women who would never marry and parents whose lives had been shattered by the loss of their sons. This legacy generated emotional responses that were just as important in the aftermath of war as the economic difficulties. Aside from the lasting bitterness toward Germany, in particular in France, there was an increasing tendency toward pacifism and restraint in international affairs. Ironically, this natural desire to avoid another war would evolve into appeasement of Adolf Hitler and the Nazis in the 1930s, thereby paving the way for an even more destructive conflict in 1939.

France: reconstruction and recovery

After the war, two issues dominated French public life: the search for security and the need for economic reconstruction. The more pressing of the two was reconstruction, particularly the rebuilding of the shattered towns and industries of the northeast that had been occupied by Germany or fought over for much of World War I. France hoped that German reparations would pay for this work, but the payments did not come quickly enough. So reconstruction was financed primarily by loans. As France had also paid for the war largely with loans rather than taxation, its already huge war debt to Britain and the United States expanded. The French government then started printing more money to meet its expenditures, thereby causing serious inflation and a falling franc. The historically solid franc, traditionally founded on

▲ *French president Raymond Poincaré (center) and prime minister Georges Clemenceau review troops in Metz in December 1918. In 1920 Clemenceau ran for president but was defeated, partly perhaps because of his atheism but partly because it was thought he had not been hard enough on Germany at the Paris peace talks.*

huge gold reserves, had already halved in value against the U.S. dollar during the war, and this trend continued. High inflation also drained real value from middle-class savings, although on nothing like the scale experienced in eastern Europe and Germany. The French middle classes had lost 75 percent of their savings by 1926, and the French currency had fallen to 48 francs to the dollar, just 10 percent of its prewar value.

However, in other respects France recovered well. Unemployment was lower than in Britain, industrial growth was faster, and devaluation of the franc at least allowed French exports to become more competitive. Also, by replacing its old, damaged industrial base with new plants and machinery, France was able to increase productivity rapidly, leading to genuine advances in prosperity during the 1920s. The franc

was eventually stabilized by Prime Minister Raymond Poincaré in the late 1920s, and despite high inflation, incomes and consumption rose significantly. In 1921, for example, there were 236,000 registered cars in France; by 1926 there were 891,000. Most important, France's economic recovery was strong enough to ensure relative political stability. Unlike many European countries, France did not have to contend with a serious revolutionary challenge or widespread poverty.

On the social front, reconstruction was less dramatic. The war had initiated a series of social changes, but there were few postwar welfare reforms of note. Many women had been liberated from long skirts and long hours in the home by working in factories, offices, and hospitals across the land. This wartime mobility and independence had set new precedents and raised expectations. Even so, the pace of modernization and urbanization was slow. Most women went back to their prewar roles, and unlike those of many other European nations, French women were denied the vote until the aftermath of the next world war in 1945. Moreover, despite reconstruction and increased industrial output, much of France after World War I was still very rural. Country life simply returned to the age-old rhythms of the peasant farmers, who were fiercely protective of both their traditions and of their small plots of land. More fundamental modernization and social reform would have to wait until after World War II.

The Third Republic

The French state emerged from the war in a fairly stable condition, a remarkable state of affairs given the number of constitutions and uprisings that France had gone through since the revolution in 1789. The Third Republic, established after the Franco-Prussian War in 1870 and 1871, was a fragile constitutional solution that could barely contain the prevailing political divisions between right and left, royalists and republicans, the Catholic Church and anticlerical radicals. By the end of World War I, however, patriotic unity had diminished these divisions. Church-state relations were still capable of arousing strong passions, but dwindling attendances made the Church's power less threatening to radicals and socialists, and few royalists seriously expected a revival of the French monarchy.

In the election of November 1919, the French parties of the right formed the Bloc National and achieved a landslide victory under Georges Clemenceau. The Bloc National secured 433 seats to only 190 seats for the socialists and radicals, and the new Chamber of Deputies contained so many war veterans in their blue uniforms that it became known as the *Chambre bleu horizon* (the sky-blue Chamber). However, the Bloc's success masked continuing rivalry and instability in party politics. Proportional representation allowed many small parties to flourish, and so elections were fought between loose coalitions that often fell apart after brief spells of government.

An example of this instability was the fate of wartime leader Clemenceau. Having led the right to victory in 1919, he asked the National Assembly to make him president—a powerful post, although the prime minister dealt with most government business. However,

▼ *A woman stacks crops on her plot on the Chemin des Dames ridge, which had been on the western front during the conflict. After the war, rural life in France returned to its ancient ways.*

Clemenceau's enemies within the Bloc National turned on him, partly because of his atheism, and he was defeated by Paul Deschanel. Clemenceau, humiliated, resigned from government. In September 1920 Deschanel himself was replaced by Alexandre Millerand. It was only after January 1922, when Millerand appointed the veteran conservative and nationalist Raymond Poincaré as prime minister, that France enjoyed a measure of governmental stability.

The French search for security

The other great issue of postwar French politics was security. Two schools of thought developed in the early 1920s. The first sought strict German adherence to the terms of the Treaty of Versailles and full payment of reparations. This view was based on a fundamental mistrust of Germany, and its goal was to keep France's neighbor as weak as possible. The second school of thought sought limited reconciliation and accommodation with Germany, while remaining wary of its intentions. The French were right to be concerned. Invaded twice in half a century, France had a population of only 40 million to Germany's 60 million, and its industrial base had been severely damaged while Germany's superior productive capacity was largely intact because the war on the western front had been fought in France and Belgium, not Germany.

In its favor, France did have a large, well-equipped military that dwarfed the German Army after its disarmament, but French politicians knew that long-term security depended on either prolonged German weakness or military support from Britain and the United States. Neither of these requirements materialized. First, the U.S. refusal to ratify the Treaty of Versailles amounted to a refusal to guarantee French borders. This decision gave Britain the opportunity to renounce its own commitment on the grounds that it had only agreed to commit with U.S. help.

KEY FIGURES

ARISTIDE BRIAND

Aristide Briand (1862–1932) was one of the leading French politicians of his generation. He served 11 times as prime minister between 1909 and 1932 and was an influential French foreign minister during World War I and from 1925 to 1932.

Briand began his political career as a socialist but spent most of it as a moderate after his expulsion from the Socialist Party for taking office in a "bourgeois" government in 1906. As prime minister, Briand expressed French frustrations with Germany at the Washington Conference in 1921: "Since the armistice we have had many disappointments. She has refused to pay compensation due for the devastated regions. She has declined to make the gesture of chastisement that, after all, every man of sense would expect after the horrors we have witnessed. Germany has refused to disarm."

However, Briand was no hawk. He is best known for his support of the League of Nations and for his role in promoting international peace. His efforts led to the Locarno Treaty of 1925 and the Kellogg-Briand Pact of 1928, which renounced war as an instrument of national policy. In 1926 he was awarded the Nobel Prize for peace.

Germany was still weak in the early 1920s, but this situation changed in the 1930s. Furthermore, it was clear that Germany sought a revision of the treaty from the moment it was signed—whether by diplomacy or force.

To replace Anglo-American support, France made alliances with Romania, Poland, Czechoslovakia, and Yugoslavia. Any alliance with its traditional partner Russia was ruled out on both practical and ideological grounds, and so the so-called Little Entente with these new eastern European states was the only realistic option. However, these agreements were as much a liability as an advantage. France was committed to help resist a German attempt to reclaim its eastern territories lost under the conditions of Versailles, yet it was unclear how much help these fledgling countries could give their western ally should Germany invade France again.

Faced with German evasions on reparations, France was reluctant to disarm and eager to enforce Versailles in full. Commentary on the treaty often focuses on the harsh treatment of Germany and how it contributed to the rise of Adolf Hitler and the Nazis. However, the frustration and fear of France is equally noteworthy. When Germany defaulted on coal shipments to France in January 1923, Poincaré lost patience and occupied the steel and coal region of the Ruhr, without the support of the United States or Britain. Passive German resistance, strikes, and sabotage obstructed French attempts to force the resumption of coal deliveries, and the French and Belgian occupation achieved little for France besides diplomatic isolation. Poincaré's uncompromising stance on reparations alienated the United States and Britain and ran counter to the more sympathetic attitudes toward Germany that were developing there. France's reluctance to disarm also made it look power hungry and militaristic. Given that France's search for security depended on these former Allies, a satisfactory solution was difficult to reach in the immediate postwar years.

However, in September 1923, German chancellor Gustav Stresemann put an end to passive resistance and resumed reparations. This move allowed the U.S.-inspired Dawes Plan to be enacted in 1924, by which Germany agreed to reschedule reparations at a reduced rate and France agreed to remove troops from the Ruhr, commencing in July 1925. Meanwhile, the discredited nationalist policies had split the Bloc National and led to the defeat of the right-wing coalition at the polls in 1924. The Cartel des Gauches (Cartel of the Left) won a close election and formed a new, more conciliatory government of socialists and radicals led by Edouard Herriot. Tensions with Germany eased, and the new foreign minister, Aristide Briand, secured the Locarno Treaty (or Pact) of 1925, by which Britain and Italy guaranteed the existing frontiers of France, Germany, and Belgium.

In the latter half of the 1920s, a feeling of qualified optimism about international affairs, often called the spirit of Locarno, spread across Europe. Improved economic conditions also gave France a sense of renewed hope for the future. Nevertheless, the perceived threat of Germany never disappeared. The fact that in 1929 France began construction of the Maginot Line fortifications to deter a new German

---

POLITICAL WORLD

THE LOCARNO TREATY

The Locarno Treaty of 1925 supposedly guaranteed the borders of France, Germany, and Belgium. In return for a permanent seat on the Council of the League of Nations and the withdrawal of Allied troops from German soil, Germany recognized its western frontiers as inviolable and agreed to the permanent demilitarization of the Rhineland.

The Locarno negotiations also generated separate agreements between Germany and Poland and Germany and Czechoslovakia that pledged to settle all disputes by peaceful arbitration, although these agreements did not guarantee these eastern borders.

The treaty seemed to solve French security worries by ensuring Italian and, more important, British support in the event of a German invasion. In theory, Britain and Italy would also aid Germany in the event of a French invasion, but the treaty was essentially a guarantee for France. It was also a personal triumph for Germany's chancellor, Gustav Stresemann, and France's Aristide Briand, who received the Nobel Peace Prize along with Britain's Austen Chamberlain. Locarno seemed to herald a brighter future for Europe, but it proved a false dawn. Franco-German relations began to deteriorate again in 1929, Germany never abandoned its desire to reclaim its lost eastern territories, and in 1936 Hitler simply ignored the treaty when he reoccupied the Rhineland.

KEY EVENTS

THE MAGINOT LINE

The Maginot Line, named for André Maginot, French minister of war at the time construction began, was a series of fortifications on the Franco-German border from Switzerland to Belgium. It symbolized the defensive character of French military planning between the world wars and the country's fear of renewed conflict with Germany.

The Maginot Line consisted of bombproof artillery emplacements, antitank defenses, and fortified machine-gun posts. The costly construction began in 1929, but the whole rationale behind the creation of a fixed defensive position, even one of considerable strength, was flawed. The Maginot Line was based on the belief that the next war would be fought in the same manner as World War I had been.

Aside from the psychological limitations this defensive-mindedness placed on the French Army (in the event of war, the troops planned to sit tight and let the Germans bleed to death in futile assaults on the line), the Maginot Line contained one catastrophic flaw—it stopped at Belgium, partly for political reasons. In May 1940 the Germans simply went around the Maginot Line by attacking through the Ardennes forest in the south of Belgium—violating Belgian neutrality just as units of the German Army had done 26 years earlier in the first days of World War I.

Artillery gun ports on the Maginot Line, a system of defenses that cost some 7 billion francs to build.

---

invasion testified to continuing insecurity in France concerning the intentions of its eastern neighbor.

The French colonies

In the aftermath of World War I, France extended its colonial empire but also heard the rumblings of discontented nationalism. Continuing its prewar policy of expansion in Morocco, France embarked on a major campaign against the tribes of the Rif Mountains led by Abd el-Krim. By 1925 France was engaged in joint military operations with Spain, also a colonial power in the region, that involved 160,000, mostly Moroccan, troops. The Franco-Spanish force defeated Abd el-Krim in 1926.

During World War I, conscription of colonial soldiers and laborers had caused riots and disturbances in French Africa and French Indochina (now Vietnam). These protests were put down severely, but in Indochina the nationalist movement grew, and a communist party was founded in 1925. A poorly coordinated rebellion broke out in 1930 that resulted in the execution of most of its leaders, but one of them, Ho Chi Minh, escaped to Hong Kong. He would later return to head the independence movement against France and eventually the United States.

France was also granted League of Nations mandates in Syria and Lebanon with the intention that it guide these two territories toward self-government. However, the French ruled these thinly veiled colonies with such a firm grip that discontent in Syria led to serious disturbances in Damascus in 1925. These uprisings were suppressed only after two days of shelling supported by troops and tanks. The severity of the French response in Syria provoked criticism at home, but French governments showed no desire to begin a gradual withdrawal from their colonies until well after World War II.

British economic and social problems
The main domestic concerns facing postwar Britain were economic recovery and social reform. A brief boom in 1919 helped to get some demobilized soldiers back into civilian life. However, disillusionment set in almost as soon as the war ended—returning soldiers and industrial workers soon realized that victory had not cured Britain's serious social problems. Poor housing, poverty, and unemployment blighted many urban areas, where diseases such as tuberculosis were common, and slum-dwelling children were often malnourished and underschooled.

Between 1918 and 1920 the coalition government led by David Lloyd George addressed some of these issues. An Education Act (1918) raised the school-leaving age to 14 and made school free. The Housing Act (1919) made local authorities responsible for the quality and quantity of housing. The range of insured workers eligible for benefits was expanded under the Unemployment Insurance Act (1919), and a new Ministry of Health took the first, hesitant steps toward a public health service available to all. These measures built on the welfare foundations laid down by Lloyd George and the Liberals from 1906 to 1911, which included old-age pensions, state-funded housing, labor exchanges to help the jobless, and a National Insurance Act that provided some workers with basic unemployment and sickness benefits.

▼ *Volunteers man a pump at a coal mine in northern England during the miners' strike of 1921. That year, 86 million work days were lost in Britain to strikes of one kind or another.*

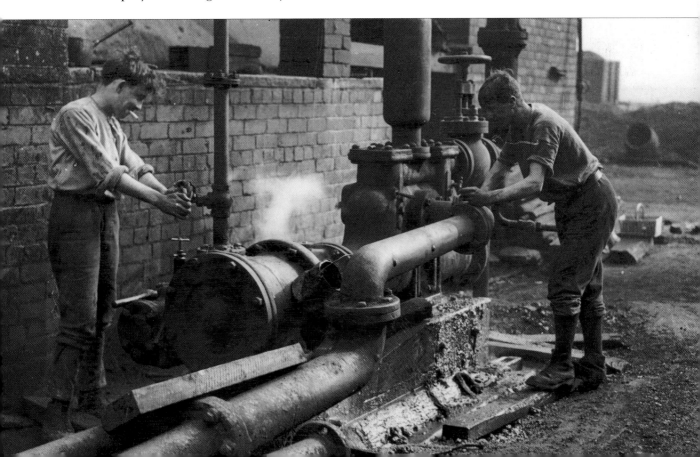

▲ *Police move in against strikers in south London during the British General Strike of 1926. Despite the amount of strike activity in Britain during the 1920s, political stability was preserved, and there was no slide into revolution.*

The position of women in Britain also improved in these years. Wartime employment had transformed the role of women in society. Having had women working alongside them in factories and offices, as well as nursing them at the front, did more to convince men of women's abilities than did years of campaigning. By 1918 there was a widespread feeling that women should now have the right to vote in general elections. A measure that provoked violent controversy only five years earlier now passed parliament with relative ease. The 1918 Representation of the People Act extended voting rights in national elections to all women over 30 who paid property tax and to all males over 21. This legislation expanded the electorate from 8 million to more than 21 million. Discrimination against women in terms of voting rights finally ended in 1928, when all women aged over 21 were given the vote, making Britain a truly democratic country for the first time.

These measures can be seen as the most important examples of a general democratization of British society caused by wartime experience. Britain's wars in the previous century had been fought by an aristocratic male military elite and a small professional army usually a long way from home and had limited direct impact on the vast majority of ordinary people. In contrast, World War I had required sacrifices from both sexes and from all social classes in Britain. As the sacrifices grew, a great many people naturally thought that postwar society would need to reflect this fact.

However, these items of legislation did not go far enough for those who sought to make Britain a land fit for the survivors of the war, and the brief boom did not prevent large-scale labor unrest.

In 1919, 2.4 million workers took part in strikes, including the railroad workers, coal miners, and even the police. The economy then plunged into recession at the end of 1920. The cost of living was three times higher than it had been in 1914, and inflation was running at about 20 percent. In 1921 unemployment reached 17 percent, and union membership 8 million. The combination of economic recession and union power fueled a continuing wave of industrial unrest. In 1921, 86 million workdays were lost to strikes.

These events seemed revolutionary to some, especially set in the context of the ongoing turmoil in Bolshevik Russia and riots by conscripts against delays in their demobilization. The scale of strike activity in Britain from 1919 through 1921 was much greater than in revolutionary Germany, and class hatreds were intense in areas with declining industries such as textiles, shipbuilding, and coal mining. There was also significant communist sympathy in areas such as South Wales and the Scottish city of Glasgow, which gained the epithet Red Clydeside. Yet class conflict in Britain never amounted to a genuine threat of communist revolution. The Labour Party, the new voice of the working class, was reformist rather than revolutionary. When it briefly achieved power for the first time in 1924, it sought few radical changes. When a full-blown general strike did break out in 1926, it was shortlived, unsuccessful, and remarkably peaceful. Essentially, although socialists, union members, and the poor were aggrieved at postwar poverty and the pace of reform, there was sufficient consensus among the more affluent members of the middle and working classes to ensure political stability.

The fact that large numbers of the working class continued to vote for both the Liberals and the Conservatives, parties of the center and center right, also showed the weakness of the revolutionary threat. British politics was never purely class based. Religion, patriotism, regional identity, and local circumstances always played an important part. By forging a coalition of middle-class and upper-working-class English voters, the Conservatives emerged as the strongest party during the 1920s. The Conservatives formed the bulk of Lloyd George's reelected coalition government after January 1919, and they were elected to office on their own after breaking the coalition in 1922, with Andrew Bonar Law as prime minister. Bonar Law retired because of illness shortly afterward and was replaced by Stanley Baldwin, a cautious, moderate politician who generally took a conciliatory approach to class relations. He would lead Britain for much of the period between 1923 and 1937, a period in which, despite the Great Depression, Britain achieved modest

▼ *Stanley Baldwin, British prime minister during the General Strike of 1926, leaves his official London residence, No. 10 Downing Street. His government prevented the country from coming to a standstill by using troops and volunteers to maintain services and deliveries of food.*

▲ *Miners emerging after a shift at the coal face. The General Strike was called in support of the miners' unions and lasted from May 4 to May 12, 1926, although the miners remained on strike until August.*

increases in prosperity in the southeast and in parts of the Midlands outside the areas of declining industries.

However, the British economy was facing serious challenges. Britain was not in decline in any absolute sense, but it was slowly losing ground relative to key competitors. Its share of world trade dropped steeply, and after 1918 the pound was replaced by the dollar as the leading world currency. Britain desperately struggled to maintain its financial preeminence, and in 1925 it returned to the gold standard at the dollar-pound exchange rate of $4.79. By backing the pound with its value in gold and by pegging it to the U.S. dollar near the prewar rate of $4.86, Britain hoped to reestablish the prestige of its currency. This attempt to turn back the clock ignored harsh new economic realities. London remained a key financial center, but the United States had become the world's leading banker. Wall Street now provided most of the loans that rebuilt Europe and kept an unbalanced world economy functioning.

Moreover, the pound was clearly overvalued after the war, and so British exports became too expensive to compete, and unemployment remained stubbornly high. By 1921 the volume of British exports was half the 1913 level. The economy recovered in the late 1920s, with output and consumption rising, but unemployment remained over 10 percent before rising sharply again in the depression of the 1930s. In short, the war had dealt Britain a severe financial blow, and it never fully recovered its place in the world economy.

Britain and Ireland

After the war, Britain faced some difficult foreign and imperial issues, most notably disturbances in India, the Chanak Crisis in Turkey, and uprisings in Egypt and the Middle East (see pages 621–626). None was more testing than the crisis that developed in Ireland. World War I had an immense impact on Ireland, creating the conditions that led to independence after 750 years of English and later British involvement.

Independence, though, came with partition, and six of Ireland's 32 counties remain part of Britain to this day.

Before the war, most Irish Catholics, some 80 percent of the population, wanted home rule, not independence. Home rule would leave Ireland part of the United Kingdom under the British crown but with an Irish parliament to deal with Irish affairs. However, home rule was violently opposed by Irish Protestants, who threatened to block it by force. From 1910 to 1914, British and Irish Protestant Unionists struggled with Irish home rule supporters and the Liberal government. As Europe drifted into war, the government finally pushed through a Home Rule Bill. Implementation would have caused chaos in the Irish province of Ulster, the Protestant stronghold, so home rule was suspended for either 12 months or until the war ended.

Failing to anticipate the scale and length of the war, most expected home rule to be introduced in September 1915 with unspecified concessions to sweeten the pill for Protestants in Ulster. The government seemed to have defused a potentially explosive situation, but it had only deferred difficult decisions to a later date. As the war progressed, those decisions became more difficult as the demands of nationalist Ireland escalated. The execution of the leaders of the 1916 Easter Rising (a pro-independence rebellion in Dublin) and the threat of conscription in Ireland in 1918 turned Irish opinion away from home rule toward separatism. By the war's end, most British politicians were willing to concede home rule, but a majority in Ireland no longer found this arrangement acceptable. This situation led to a period of political upheaval, division, and civil war.

▲ *Civilians look on as British troops conduct a raid on Dublin Park, Ireland, February 1921. The fighting in Ireland escalated that year, its first six months witnessing 70 percent of the total deaths recorded in the conflict.*

Ireland: Partition and Independence

From late 1918 Ireland was rent by political violence as supporters of continuing union with Britain fought those who desired complete independence. The country was eventually partitioned between the two groups, and independence for the major portion of Ireland was finally settled in 1922.

In the British general election of December 1918, the new voice of Irish nationalism, the Catholic nationalist party Sinn Féin (We Ourselves) replaced the old Home Rule Party by winning 73 of Ireland's 105 seats. The Home Rule Party won only six seats, and the Protestant Unionists, who wished to maintain absolute ties with Britain, won 26. Sinn Féin refused to take part in mainstream British politics, and on January 19, 1919, its members formed the Irish Assembly (Dáil Éireann), which declared an independent republic. With two competing governments—one in Dublin, one in London—Ireland stumbled into a bitter civil war. The Irish nationalists were led by Éamon de Valera, the Brooklyn-born new leader of Sinn Féin and president of the Dáil, and Michael Collins, who rapidly emerged as the key financial, intelligence, and military leader of the new Irish Republican Army (IRA). The British outlawed the Dáil, but this underground assembly and its loosely controlled forces made parts of Ireland ungovernable.

The Government of Ireland Act of 1920 tried to revive home rule by allowing for the creation of separate parliaments in Dublin in the south and Belfast in the north. Northern Protestants reluctantly used the act to set up a Protestant-dominated system in six Ulster counties that would trample on the rights of a large Catholic minority. The act was rejected in the south of Ireland, and violence escalated in late 1920, with Collins orchestrating an efficient and ruthless campaign. Ambushes, assassinations, and raids on barracks by the IRA led to more than 400 policemen and 160 soldiers being killed. Intimidation and murder of those supporting British rule became commonplace.

In response, the British embarked on an increasingly brutal campaign of coercion aided by the formation of the Black and Tans and the Auxiliaries. Recruited from among former soldiers, these units were officially controlled by the police, the Royal Irish Constabulary, but they brought the indiscriminate brutality of the trenches to the streets and country lanes of Ireland. By the fall of 1920, southwest Ireland was under martial law, government forces had wide powers of search and arrest, and reprisals

were official policy. Towns and villages were being shot up and burned, while suspects were tortured, beaten, and occasionally killed. The most infamous episode in this vicious circle of IRA attacks and indiscriminate reprisals was Bloody Sunday. On November 12, 1920, 12 British agents were killed in a dawn raid by a handpicked group of Collins' men. In revenge, a group of Auxiliaries fired into the crowd during a Gaelic football game at Croke Park in Dublin—12 innocent people were killed and 60 wounded.

In 1921 the conflict intensified, with more than 1,000 of the 1,400 deaths resulting from this bout of troubles taking place in the first half of that year. Then, suddenly, the fighting stopped on July 9, 1921. Critics in Britain and abroad, especially in the United States, had expressed outrage at the methods of the government forces in Ireland for some time, and the military were tired of a war that showed no sign of ending. Britain sought a compromise, Ireland was sick of the chaos, and so the IRA, nearing exhaustion, accepted the British offer of a truce.

The Anglo-Irish Treaty of 1921 gave Ireland dominion status. This new Irish Free State had its own government based in Dublin with full powers within Ireland. However, the free state did not include the whole of Ireland: the six counties of Northern Ireland were allowed to remain part of Britain. Politicians in the new free state also had to swear allegiance to the British monarch. IRA extremists and a large minority of the Dáil rejected the treaty, including de Valera, who resigned as president of the Dáil. Collins became head of the transitional Provisional Government and the new Free State Army. Sinn Féin and the IRA split into pro- and antitreaty factions, and Ireland drifted toward civil war.

Protreaty Sinn Féin won a large majority in the Free State elections in June 1922, and the new government quickly overran antitreaty forces, but not before Michael Collins had been killed in an ambush in August 1922. After a futile guerrilla war, de Valera (a future prime minister and later president of Ireland) ended the antitreaty campaign in April 1923. The new Irish Free State finally united under the conservative leadership of William Cosgrave.

◀ *Women protesting against Irish executions in 1921. That year, a treaty enabled the formation of the Irish Free State, but Ireland's troubles were far from over.*

▲ *Benito Mussolini as a young fascist in the postwar years. In November 1922 Mussolini engineered the rise to power of himself and his fascist supporters. He proceeded to create a totalitarian state in Italy.*

Italy: the road to fascism

If the trauma of war shaped the postwar national lives of Britain and France, it completely defined that of Italy. The strains of the war and the disappointment of the peace treaties caused a period of crisis and instability that led to the subversion of the constitution and the creation of a fascist dictatorship under Benito Mussolini. These developments partly stemmed from the nature of Italian political life. Whereas Britain and France had long traditions of constitutional government and unified statehood, albeit a turbulent one in the French case, Italy had emerged as a uni-fied constitutional monarchy only in the 1870s. Its national political culture had shallow foundations and was ultimately unable to withstand the after-shocks of the war.

The first problem lay with the way governments were formed. Since 1900 Italian governments had often been unstable coalitions that underwent frequent changes in personnel. Traditions of *combinazione* (combination) and *trasformismo* (transformism) arose, according to which shifting combinations of prominent leaders made deals before and after elections so as to form governments. Yesterday's bitter political foe became today's ally for a time as electoral arithmetic dictated. Often held together by the wily Liberal leader Giovanni Giolitti, the system allowed socialists and Catholics to be coopted into governments led by the antirepublican and anticlerical Liberal party. This was a logical, if somewhat cynical, solution to the deep divisions in Italian society, and it lulled politicians into thinking that any new political force, no matter how radical or unpleasant, could be neutralized with a share of power. This false assumption would lead to the destruction of Italian democracy.

The rise of fascism also owed much to the deep divisions in Italian society. In the poor south, landlords and peasants often despised each other. The more industrial north, in turn, looked down on what it regarded as a backward and corrupt rural south. Labor relations between industrialists and workers were tense, and the state itself was founded on a fierce anticlericalism that placed it in conflict with the Catholic Church, which was perhaps the most influential institution in Italian life. Although the war imposed a measure of discipline and patriotic unity on Italy, these divisions soon reopened as disillusionment with the peace and anger at economic problems grew. Inflation began to soar, reducing the real wages of workers and returning soldiers, and angry peasants came back from the war to the same poverty under the same landlords. More than 600,000 Italians had died, it seemed, for very little.

This dissatisfaction soon plunged Italy into a deep political and economic crisis. In 1919 union membership rose rapidly, and more than 2,000 strikes broke out in all. Railroad workers, postal staff, unskilled agricultural laborers, and government clerks withdrew their labor. Southern peasants seized and broke up estates; northern peasants of the Po Valley combined in large associations; workers demonstrated against rising prices; and a general strike took place in July. In the November 1919 election (the first in Italy to be based on universal male suffrage; women still did not have the vote), the Italian Socialist Party (PSI) won 156 seats to become the largest party in the Chamber of Deputies for the first time. When armed workers seized factories in many northern cities in September 1920, a socialist revolution seemed imminent.

▼ *Giovanni Giolitti, five times Italian prime minister, invited the fascists into his election-fighting coalition in 1921 but opposed them after 1924.*

However, the left was weaker than it appeared. The Red Scare of 1919–1920 may have convinced the wealthy and the middle classes that a socialist revolution was at hand, but, as Giolitti realized, the socialists had neither the organization nor the resolve to seize power. Riddled with divisions between Marxists and moderates, the socialists lacked a coherent plan and a charismatic leader. Furthermore, their proposal to nationalize the land also alienated the peasants, who were fighting landlords to acquire their own land, not to hand it over to the state. This peasant disenchantment helped the new Catholic Popular Party to establish itself, cutting the socialists off from a large base of potential support. By January 1921 the PSI had split into communist and socialist factions, and the revolutionary wave was ebbing.

Utilizing a surge of popular nationalism whipped up by fear of communism, Benito Mussolini created a new political force that openly employed violence to establish order and gain power. Before the war, Mussolini had been a prominent Marxist in the PSI, editing their official newspaper. During the war, he split with the party by calling for intervention on the Allied side (the socialists sought nonintervention). He founded a pro-war newspaper and later joined the Italian Army; he was wounded in training and discharged without seeing active service. In March 1919 he founded the *Fasci di Combattimento* (Fighting Leagues), and by November 1920 armed gangs of black-shirted fascists were beating and killing socialists and trade unionists. A common tactic was to force opponents to drink castor oil and then "ban" them from their towns. The next two years saw violent feuding in many areas, culminating in the fascists' forcible expulsion of elected socialist governments in Milan and elsewhere.

Mussolini expertly used this engineered crisis to move the fascists closer and closer to power. Playing on middle-class fears of bolshevism and drawing financial support from wealthy industrialists and landowners, he essentially destabilized the state under the pretence of restoring order. The Liberal Party failed to prevent or punish fascist beatings and intimidation, seeing the fascists as a useful antidote to socialism. Indeed, Giolitti and Prime Minister Ivanoe Bonomi believed they could safely allow the fascists to weaken the socialists and then control them by the old methods of *combinazione* and *trasformismo*. In 1921 Giolitti invited the newly formed National Fascist Party to fight the election as part of a center-right coalition. The fascists won 35 seats but refused to be bought off by a ministerial post for Mussolini, known by now as Il Duce (The Leader).

The crisis came to a head in the fall of 1922. The socialists called another general strike, and the violent reaction of the fascists reached new heights. Local party leaders urged Mussolini to seize power, and many Italians saw a Mussolini-led government as the only solution to the seemingly endless cycle of chaos, especially since Mussolini had been courting traditional conservatives and cultivating a more "respectable" image since 1921. Ironically, the more Mussolini's supporters created chaos, the more Mussolini was seen as the only person who could bring order.

By October the Socialist Party had split again and fallen out with the trade unions. Meanwhile, the church was pulling away from the Popular Party. With their enemies divided, the fascists planned a march on Rome, essentially blackmailing the government to hand them power or risk civil war. A united political elite backed by a loyal Italian Army could easily have dealt with this theatrical coup by less than 50,000 fascists. However, when the Liberal prime minister, Luigi Facta, finally asked King Victor Emmanuel III to declare martial law, he refused. Facta resigned, and the king invited Mussolini to form a new

government on October 29, 1922. The Chamber of Deputies, still not fully aware of the ultimate consequences of its actions, confirmed the appointment of Mussolini as premier by 306 votes to 106. Many leading liberal statesmen voted for him, including wartime leader Vittorio Orlando and Giolitti.

In the end, Mussolini had merely needed to threaten violence to be installed as prime minister with all the formality and legitimacy of the royal request and a confirmation in the chamber. Failure of nerve, a weak king unsure of the loyalty of the Italian Army, and the inability of politicians to unite across party lines in the face of a threat to the system had led to the demise of the short-lived Italian democracy.

Over the next three years, Mussolini gradually shed his constitutional façade to create a totalitarian state. Two key events stand out. The first was the Acerbo Law of 1923, which guaranteed two-thirds of the chamber's seats to the fascists if they won more than 25 percent of the votes. In the 1924 election they easily passed this figure, although partly with the help of intimidation at the polls. This election victory gave the fascists control of the chamber for the first time. The second event was the

▼ *The fascist March on Rome, October 1922, which preceded the transfer of power in Italy to Mussolini. Il Duce did not take part in the march himself; he traveled from Milan to Rome by train.*

Matteotti Crisis of 1925. The socialist deputy Giacomo Matteotti openly criticized the electoral methods of the fascists on the floor of the Chamber of Deputies. A few days later he was kidnapped and stabbed to death by fascists. The country was appalled, and nonfascist deputies of all persuasions called for Mussolini's dismissal, before walking out of the chamber in protest.

For a few months Mussolini seemed to lose his nerve, and even the king wavered in his support. However, on January 3, 1925, Mussolini confronted the chamber, taking responsibility for fascism and challenging those present to impeach him. The Chamber of Deputies backed down and effectively signed its own death warrant. Over the next few years, Mussolini abandoned any pretense of parliamentary government. He ruled by decree, censored the press, controlled the radio, banned independent trade unions, imprisoned opponents (and occasionally had them

▲ *Socialist deputy Giacomo Matteotti (center) paid with his life in 1924 for crossing Mussolini. His killers received only light sentences, but the crisis the Matteotti murder created almost toppled the fascist regime.*

killed), and generally harassed any source of political opposition into obedience or exile.

Italian fascism was primarily an emotional movement rather than a rational one. It was a style of politics that had no coherent political philosophy but worshiped power, violence, and order for their own sake. At best, it was ambiguous; often it was simply contradictory and ludicrous. Mussolini's fascism randomly combined the populism of socialism, the emotionalism of nationalism, and the conservative love of order with a desire to bring capital and labor together through "corporate" control of the economy. All was loosely held in place by a violent hatred of communism and the glorification of the nation-state as the vehicle for individual and collective fulfillment. Fascism denied individual rights, derided democracy as weak and decadent, and embraced the idea of war and self-sacrifice. Fascism was an Italian invention, but the conditions that gave rise to it were reproduced in other countries in postwar Europe. Its ideas, combined with a virulent racism largely missing from the Italian brand, would reach their fullest and most destructive expression in Nazi Germany between 1933 and 1945.

Japan becomes a world power

Japan profited prodigiously from the war, which helped it establish itself as a top-ranking world power that could negotiate as an equal with the United States and Britain. With Germany fighting a war on two fronts in Europe, its Chinese and Pacific possessions became easy pickings for the Japanese, who gained the Chinese port of Tsingtao on the Shantung Peninsula, along with the German northern Pacific islands—the Carolines, Marianas, and Marshalls. Germany also gave up to Japan all its rights and privileges in China, which included railroads and coal-mining interests that were desperately needed for Japan's industrial expansion.

Together with Korea, under Japanese control since 1895, these spoils of war gave Japan a firm foothold on the Asian mainland. Moreover, Japan's wartime trading had increased its gold reserves by nearly $900 million, a total gain second only to that made by the United States. After the war, to secure its place in Asia, Japan intervened on a significant scale in the Russian Civil War. Its forces occupied a large area of eastern Siberia and the Russian east coast, including the port of Vladivostok.

The expansion of Japanese power in Asia came largely at the expense of Russia and China, upsetting a delicate balance in the Far East and raising alarms in the United States. The United States feared that Japanese dominance of East Asia would close the region to its trade and influence. Furthermore, the alliance between Japan and Britain, in operation since 1902 and originally intended to counterbalance Russian expansion in East Asia, now seemed to threaten U.S. interests. These arguments soured Anglo-American relations, fueled a naval arms buildup, and contributed to the U.S. rejection of the Treaty of Versailles.

The Washington Conference of 1921–1922 soothed these concerns in the short term. The Anglo-Japanese alliance was expanded into a four-power pact between the United States, Britain, Japan, and France, whose navies were fixed in the ratio of 5 to 5 to 3 to 1.75, respectively. Pacific and East Asian territorial disputes were to be settled by peaceful negotiation, and Japan would withdraw from the Shantung Peninsula and the Russian east coast. However, the balance of power in the region had tilted firmly in favor of Japan, whose expansionist designs would be revived in the 1930s, eventually provoking the U.S. entry into World War II in 1941.

▼ *Japanese troops fighting for the Whites charge Bolshevik positions in Siberia during the Russian Civil War. Japan's gains from World War I and its aftermath helped to propel the country into the top rank of world powers.*

The Defeated Powers

At the armistice on November 11, 1918, Germany was in a state of political confusion and economic collapse. This situation took millions of ordinary patriotic Germans entirely by surprise. Even as recently as July, most had shared the overconfident convictions of the country's military leadership, Field Marshal Paul von Hindenburg and his chief of staff, Erich Ludendorff, that Germany was on the point of victory. It came as an especially bitter blow when the citizens of Germany realized it was not. Their country had suffered great hardships and made immense sacrifices. It had defeated Russia in the east while at the same time resisting the combined might of France and the British Empire in the west.

All of the powers defeated in World War I were confronted by deep-seated problems that produced widespread economic, political, and social unrest during the 1920s and beyond.

Yet by August 1918 the combined manpower and productive resources of France, Britain, and the United States had worn down the militarily superior but ultimately overstretched German Army. Moreover, because its economy had been shifted away from food toward munitions, malnourished Germany was running out of food. When Germans realized that victory was impossible, faith in Emperor Wilhelm II, the military leadership, and the country's social and political systems disintegrated. Almost overnight, the once-powerful German state began to fall apart.

Germany's political turmoil

Even before the armistice, councils, or soviets, of soldiers, sailors, and workers were springing up all over Germany and in the German Army. On November 3, the naval personnel at Wilhelmshaven and Kiel on the north German coast mutinied (see page 512), and the sailors set up soviets on the Russian model. On the 8th Bavarians in southern Germany followed suit, forming revolutionary councils under the leadership of Kurt Eisner. The following day the emperor abdicated, and in Berlin, the German

capital, leading social democrats and independent socialists established the Council of People's Commissars. This body declared the country a republic and secured the support of the capital's workers' and soldiers' councils for the new German government.

Germany seemed to be following Russia toward revolution, but the events that had overtaken the central government seemed more revolutionary than they really were. The emperor, along with the members of the other ancient German royal families, had

▲ *Bavarian socialist journalist and politician Kurt Eisner (right) at a conference in Bern, Switzerland, in 1919, the year of his assassination. He is with the leader of the Swedish Social Democratic Party, Hjalmar Branting.*

◄ *After the war, Germany suffered crisis upon crisis, including food shortages, inflation, and political instability. These Germans, pictured in 1922, are paying for potato peelings with wood, which was more valuable than money.*

been removed overnight, yet Wilhelm II had been an unpopular and weakened figure since early in the war. Despite the revolutionary sound of its name, the Council of People's Commissars had as its key figures long-standing moderate social democrats who were desperate to maintain order while reforming the government along more democratic and socially just lines.

In fact, the two crucial events in Germany's transformation from monarchy to republic had taken place before the armistice. First, a center-left coalition of independent socialists, social democrats, and the Center Party had come to power. It was effectively handed power by General Erich Ludendorff when he and his senior officers realized that they had lost control of the western front. This was the first time that the parties of the middle and working classes had been in control of Germany, and in a practical sense this event was more revolutionary than the formal abdication of the emperor. Second, the Allies had made it clear that they would negotiate only with democratically chosen representatives. This condition made it necessary for Germany to replace Emperor Wilhelm II and to push the ruling military elite into the background before peace could be concluded.

The new chancellor was Friedrich Ebert. He immediately introduced reforms to help the working class, such as a 40-hour working week and unemployment benefits, but he despised bolshevism. He feared that Germany's advanced and complex industrial society would collapse into poverty and civil war if the communists succeeded—a scenario that would hurt working families as much as anyone else. Indeed, he initially hoped for a constitutional monarchy to maintain some continuity, but when that outcome proved impossible, he turned to the other source of order in Germany, the armed forces.

The key moment for the new government was a telephone conversation between Ebert and the new chief of staff, General Wilhelm Groener. Ebert

▼ Spartacist troops occupy the offices of the majority socialist newspaper Vorwärts, Berlin, 1919, during the Spartacist revolt. Led by Karl Liebknecht and Rosa Luxemburg, the Spartacists were a revolutionary communist group.

assured Groener that he would fight bolshevism and strive to preserve law and order. Groener then agreed to put the German Army at the disposal of the new government. This alliance turned out to be the crucial difference between the events in Germany in 1918 and the 1917 revolution in Russia, where the moderate socialist revolutionary government of Alexander Kerensky did not have the support of the Russian Army under Lavrenti Kornilov. In Germany, the aristocratic military class knew that the old days were over but knew also that a moderate and democratic republic under reform-minded leaders would allow them to retain much of their wealth and some of their influence—not to mention their lives. Given the choices available and the immediate threat of communism or chaos, Ebert's regime was their best option.

For Ebert and the social democrats, there was the problem of keeping the government out of the hands of revolutionary independent socialists and Spartacists. The Spartacus League (named after the leader of a slave rebellion in the Roman Empire) was a revolutionary communist group led by Karl Liebknecht and Rosa Luxemburg. On January 1, 1919, the Spartacists formed the German Communist Party, and on the 6th a large crowd gathered in Berlin, to demand a revolution. Luxemburg called for restraint, realizing that the party did not yet have majority support. However, the crowd declared a German soviet republic, seized public buildings, and raised the red flag.

The reaction was severe. The German Army put down the revolution with machine guns, artillery, and the assistance of Freikorps (Free Corps). These unofficial groups of soldiers were common in Germany in the postwar years. Many were right-wing nationalists, and many were simply unemployable adventure seekers brutalized by their experiences at the front and unwilling to return to uneventful poverty. Around 1,200

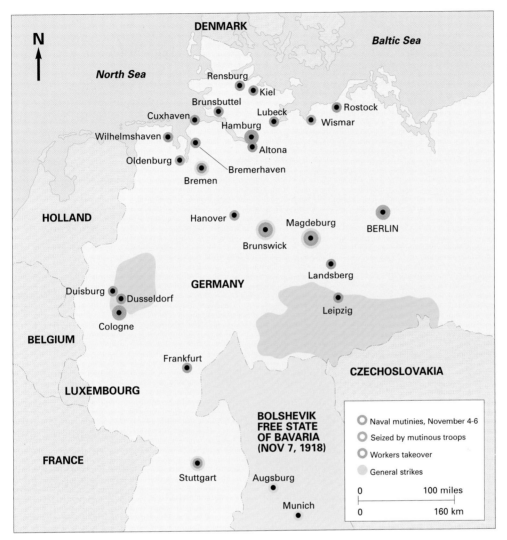

N

DENMARK

Baltic Sea

North Sea

Rensburg
Kiel
Brunsbuttel
Lubeck
Rostock
Cuxhaven
Wismar
Hamburg
Wilhelmshaven
Altona
Oldenburg
Bremerhaven
Bremen

HOLLAND

Hanover
Magdeburg
BERLIN
Brunswick

GERMANY

Landsberg

Duisburg
Dusseldorf
Leipzig
Cologne

BELGIUM

Frankfurt

CZECHOSLOVAKIA

LUXEMBOURG

BOLSHEVIK
FREE STATE
OF BAVARIA
(NOV 7, 1918)

FRANCE

Stuttgart
Augsburg

Munich

○ Naval mutinies, November 4-6
◎ Seized by mutinous troops
◉ Workers takeover
⬤ General strikes

0   100 miles
0   160 km

◀ As World War I reached its conclusion, Emperor Wilhelm II abdicated, and Germany was racked by political instability. Strikes, mutinies, and uprisings became the order of the day, as moderate politicians struggled to get the Weimar Republic up and running.

communists were hunted down, arrested, and killed. Among them were Liebknecht and Luxemburg, who were shot and dumped in the Landwehr Canal in Berlin's city center in broad daylight. To many on the left, these events were horrors bordering on insanity. Ebert's socialist government was allowing the army and right-wing Freikorps thugs to murder fellow socialists. The German left never recovered, and its divisions prevented it from strengthening the new democratic regime against its right-wing enemies.

Chaos in Bavaria

Another brutal episode of this postwar drama occurred in Bavaria, Germany, in 1919 and especially in its capital, Munich. Bavaria was one of the largest and most independent of the states that made up Germany. It was also a state that was full of contradictions. It was jealous of its autonomy and suspicious of the Prussian-dominated central government. Yet many Bavarians regarded themselves as true German patriots. Most workers in Munich itself wanted a democratic and socialist regime, but the city was also a center of right-wing nationalism and of anti-Semitism. The peasantry who lived in rural Bavaria, moreover, was deeply conservative. These tensions mirrored divisions all over Germany.

▲ Members of the Ehrhardt Brigade of the Freikorps in the Potsdamer Platz, Berlin, during the Kapp Putsch, March 1920. The brigade, the proposed disbandment of which was a trigger for the putsch, took over the capital on the 13th, but a general strike by workers brought the right-wing revolution to an end.

When the breakdown of government came in early November 1918, troops in Munich showed little interest in maintaining the existing order. Indeed, many had already organized into radical soldiers' councils. The Wittelsbachs, the Bavarian royal family, sensibly fled on November 7 after over 700 years on the throne, and a revolutionary socialist government was quickly established. The new government in Bavaria, like that in Berlin, was formed by social democrats and independent socialists, but on the other hand, the more radical independent socialists had the upper hand in the Bavarian capital, with Kurt Eisner becoming minister president of the new National Council. A confused and chaotic few months followed. The new government unsuccessfully sought to extend its control into the countryside, and socialists of various persuasions vied for supremacy in Munich.

On February 21, Eisner was assassinated by Count Anton von Arco-Valley,

an aristocrat, student, and former officer. The revolution turned from confusion to chaos. On April 6, independent socialists and anarchists proclaimed a new Councils' Republic, under the leadership of the writer Ernst Toller. An alternative Bavarian government of social democrats, based in Bamberg under Johannes Hoffman, sent troops in a vain attempt to overthrow the new government. By the 13th, a Second Bavarian Socialist Republic had been declared. This Bolshevik-style Bavarian Soviet was led by the communists Eugen Leviné and Max Levein.

This confusion was all too much for the German Army and the national government in Berlin. Assisted by lawless bands of Freikorps, troops descended on Munich. Food supplies from the countryside dried up, and Toller quarreled with Leviné and Levein. The army crushed a hastily assembled Red Army of workers and soldiers. Both sides committed atrocities, but the regular army and the Freikorps were especially brutal, killing hundreds of innocent civilians and even a group of priests. The Bavarian Soviet was dead, and over the next few years Bavaria evolved into a bastion of right-wing nationalism.

The "enemy within"

These months of revolutionary chaos followed by a short, bloody civil war and reprisals had important consequences for Germany. Not only did they show up the divisions on the left and the left's ultimate failure to secure a lasting social revolution, they also fed the myths that later formed the heart of Nazism: first, that communism and socialism in any form would lead to destructive anarchy that must be put down by force; second, that democratic government was weak, unpatriotic, and incapable of stamping out communism by itself; third, that the communist chaos was all part of an international Jewish conspiracy to undermine Germany.

Anti-Semitism had been strong in Bavaria, Austria, and many other parts of the German-speaking world before World War I. It reemerged when condi-

tions in Germany worsened and people were in need of scapegoats. Anti-Semitism was also often connected with anticommunism and nationalism. Many of the leaders of the revolutions in Berlin and Bavaria, such as Eisner, Luxemburg, Toller, and Leviné, were Jews, and Leviné and Luxemburg were non-German Jews. That such was the case lent a superficial plausibility to claims of an international Jewish conspiracy and encouraged outrages like the assassination in 1922 of Walther Rathenau, the minister for reconstruction, who was a wealthy Jew. The fact that Rathenau, a German by birth, had successfully directed the country's industrial production for the government during the war did not seem to matter.

The Bavarian episode also connected with the central nationalist myth of the postwar era—that Germany had not really lost the war but had been stabbed in the back by Jews and socialists on the home front. This theory did not just obscure the facts, it also turned them on their head. It was the German Army's high command that had insisted on an armistice after the failure of

▼ *The leader of the Spartacus League, Karl Liebknecht. addresses the crowds in Berlin, 1919. In the aftermath of the Spartacist revolt in January of that year, Liebknecht and the group's coleader, Rosa Luxemburg, were murdered.*

▲ The harsh terms of the Versailles peace treaty caused outrage in Germany when they became known and led to smouldering resentment. Here, former German inhabitants of Alsace and Lorraine, provinces returned to France under the treaty, protest at a rally in the Königsplatz, Berlin, 1919.

major offensives in the spring and summer of 1918. The generals had gambled everything on one last attack, and when their exhausted forces were pushed back by an Allied counteroffensive, Ludendorff had called for an armistice. The new chancellor at the time, Prince Max of Baden, wanted Germany to keep fighting long enough to negotiate a compromise peace. Ludendorff failed to realize that asking for an armistice was as good as admitting that the German Army was finished. He naively hoped to withdraw his forces to lick their wounds while the politicians negotiated an acceptable peace.

Effectively, Ludendorff and the military elite simply walked away from the disaster they had caused and then savaged the politicians who reluctantly picked up the pieces on entering office for the first time. The men who had led Germany throughout the course of the war managed to lay the blame for the harsh peace treaty that was concluded at Versailles at the door of the parties who had done nothing to create the crisis.

The Weimar Republic
While chaos reigned in Bavaria, Germany was creating a new constitution for the new republic, to be known as the Weimar Republic after the town in which the new government first met. On paper, the Weimar constitution was a model of advanced democracy. All men and women over the age of 20 could vote. The new president, who was to be elected by popular vote, would appoint the chancellor, who in turn needed the support of the Reichstag (parliament) to stay in office. The central government now had greater powers over the old states (now renamed *Länder*). There were provisions for referenda on important issues, and the proportional representation voting system would ensure that the parties in the Reichstag accurately represented the spectrum of opinion in the country.

Ebert was elected the first president on February 11, 1919, and he appointed Philipp Scheidemann, a fellow social democrat, as his chancellor. To these men fell the horrendous responsibility of accepting or rejecting the Treaty of Versailles, which all Germans thought a gross injustice and a calculated insult. The new government protested the treaty and asked for revisions to parts, such as the war guilt clause, but only inconsequential changes were made. However, in the end the German government had little choice but to sign the treaty, although Scheidemann tendered his resignation rather than put his name to it. Not only had the Allied naval blockade been maintained that could starve Germany into submission, but it was made clear that further force would be used if necessary. By signing, though, the Weimar Republic inevitably linked itself to the failure and humiliation of Germany's defeat.

These associations made the Weimar Republic unpopular with the political right from its inception. It had also alienated the far left by its actions in Berlin. High unemployment and infla-

tion did not endear Germans to their new constitution, and proportional representation made matters worse by returning numerous small parties to the Reichstag. Often the parties that supported the republic were in the minority, trying to keep together multiparty governments in the face of violent opposition from communists and nationalists. From 1919 to 1928, there were 15 different governments.

In March 1920 there was a right-wing attempt to overthrow the new republic. Wolfgang Kapp, leader of the far-right Fatherland Party, briefly seized Berlin with the help of 12,000 troops from the Ehrhardt Brigade and the Baltikum Brigade under General Lüettwitz and with the approval of Ludendorff. The government fled to Dresden, but the workers refused to be cowed. They organized a general strike that brought the capital and many other cities to a standstill. Bureaucrats also refused to follow Kapp's orders, and it soon became clear that Kapp did not have the support of the country or even of most of the German Army. After four days, the leaders of the Kapp Putsch fled. Kapp

▼ *Field Marshal Paul von Hindenburg was appointed chief of staff of the German Army in August 1916 and continued in his post beyond the armistice, retiring in 1919. He remained a national hero in Germany and in 1925 was elected president of the German republic.*

escaped to Sweden, but later returned and died in prison before he could be brought to trial. The other leaders were treated with remarkable leniency by the courts. Lüettwitz was merely dismissed from the German Army.

The chaos unleashed by Kapp was then used by the left, as communists turned the general strike into a revolution in the Ruhr. The new army chief of staff, General Hans von Seeckt, had refused to confront Kapp, declaring that "troops do not fire on troops." He felt no qualms about firing on communists, however, and ruthlessly carried out the government's request to put the rising down. Regular units and bands of Freikorps were involved in the action. For the next few years, Germany existed in a state of intense instability.

German economic problems
Germany found it hard to meet its reparations payments. This difficulty was partly the result of crippling inflation, although inflation also helped the government by effectively wiping out its debt to its own people in the form of war bonds. The inflation was brought about by the German government's having printed money instead of raising taxes. The former practice had funded the war and had been carried on in the postwar period. Indeed, it seems clear that Germany deliberately fueled inflation to reduce its debt and to prove to the Allies that it could not pay. The Reparations Commission, set up to apportion payments, finally reported in 1921, fixing Germany's share at 132 billion marks. Germany never made a serious effort to make the full payments on schedule. The country also annoyed the Allies by concluding a military cooperation agreement with Soviet Russia in 1922. Known as the Treaty of Rapallo, this agreement was not an alliance, but it allowed Germany to evade many of the restrictions of Versailles by, for example, training pilots in Russia.

POLITICAL WORLD

THE DAWES PLAN

The Dawes Plan was an attempt to resolve the economic and diplomatic crisis that resulted from Germany's failure to pay reparations and the subsequent French invasion of the Ruhr in 1923.

Although the United States was not a member of the League of Nations, it could not avoid the consequences of Germany's defaults, as they were tied to its former Allies' inability to repay their wartime debts to America. Thus, two U.S. bankers, Charles Dawes and Owen D. Young, prepared a report on how best to stabilize Germany's currency, how to balance its budget, and how to secure regular reparations payments at a sustainable level.

The result was the Dawes Plan (1924), which formed the basis of a solution to the Ruhr crisis. The plan recommended a new currency, controlled by a board containing seven German and seven foreign advisers. This currency would be backed by foreign loans and a mortgage on the German state railroad. Germany would pay annual reparations on a sliding scale from 220 million marks to 2.5 billion over five years, but the total amount of reparations would remain unchanged. The plan was not especially popular in Germany, but it went some way to stabilizing the economy, reducing the massive unemployment, and, most important, removing French troops from the Ruhr. In these regards, it was a success.

When Germany defaulted on its reparation coal payments again in January 1923, French and Belgian troops occupied the rich iron and coal region of the Ruhr. An effective campaign of passive resistance and sabotage minimized the benefit to France. The effects of the occupation on Germany, however, were profound. The German economy was still fragile, and now deprived of 85 percent of its coal, it virtually collapsed. When combined with the irresponsible financial and monetary policy of the German government, the Ruhr occupation caused unemployment and hyperinflation that wiped out the savings of the middle class and deeply destabilized the Weimar Republic. The real value of wages plummeted, and by November 1923 bank notes were virtually worthless. One U.S. dollar was now worth four billion marks.

The financial and diplomatic efforts of Chancellor Gustav Stresemann eventually restored some order. Stresemann called off resistance and decided to resume payments in September 1923. A new currency (backed by the value of land) was issued at one Rentenmark to a billion Reichsmarks, and the French began to leave the Ruhr. Matters also improved when Charles Dawes, an American banker, suggested a U.S.-financed plan by which Germany could meet its reparations. However, the previous instability, unemployment, and inflation had led to the increasing popularity of extreme right-wing nationalist groups such as the German Workers' Party and its offspring, Adolf Hitler's German National Socialist Workers' Party (Nazi Party).

Hitler, a wartime corporal and holder of several awards for bravery, rose to prominence with his violent oratory. When Anton Drexler, the leader of the German Workers' Party, heard Hitler speak for the first time in 1919, he commented: "Goodness, he's got a big mouth. We could use him." On November 8, 1923, Hitler attempted a putsch in Munich, but it failed. For the moment he retired from public view, but the failed coup had taught him one valuable lesson. If Germany was to be transformed by the Nazis, the party would have to cynically exploit the state's existing democratic system and the tensions between its various classes.

After the economic successes of the U.S.-inspired Dawes Plan, the Weimar Republic appeared to recover, and Germany entered a period of growth and relative prosperity. The republic also enjoyed a blossoming in the arts that gained widespread recognition. Writers and playwrights such as Thomas Mann and Berthold Brecht gained

EYEWITNESS

ADOLF HITLER

The end of World War I and its aftermath were central to the ideological development of Adolf Hitler, the future Nazi dictator of Germany. He heard the news of the armistice and the abdication of Emperor Wilhem II in a hospital bed, where he was recovering from a British mustard gas attack on the western front. He later wrote of his violent reaction to the shattering events:

"And so it had all been in vain... Did all this happen only so that a gang of wretched criminals could lay hands on the Fatherland?... The more I tried to achieve clarity on the monstrous event in this hour, the more the shame of indignation and disgrace burned in my brow. What was all the pain in my eyes compared to all this misery? There followed terrible days and even worse nights—I knew that all was lost... In these nights hatred grew in me, hatred for those responsible for this deed."

Extract taken from Hitler's personal political manifesto Mein Kampf (My Struggle), first published in 1925.

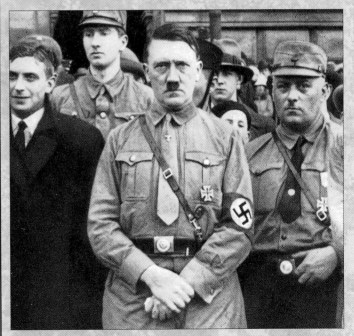

Adolf Hitler in the company of Nazi paramilitaries, or brownshirts, of the SA (Sturmabteilung, or storm division).

The Munich Putsch

Adolf Hitler and his Nazi Party followers launched an unsuccessful coup in Munich in late 1923. Its failure caused Hitler to consider an alternative path to power in Germany through the existing democratic political system.

The German National Socialist Workers' Party (NSDAP, or Nazi Party), led by Adolf Hitler from 1920, rose to prominence in the Bavarian capital, Munich, on the back of Germany's hyperinflation, its economic difficulties, and the French occupation of the Ruhr industrial region. However, in the Bavaria of the early 1920s,

Nazism was just one current in a maelstrom of separatism, anti-Semitism, and extreme right-wing activity. Indeed, Hitler's putsch was partly an attempt to channel this disaffection toward the overthrow of the Weimar Republic before the Bavarian government used the discontent to break away from Germany.

The so-called Beer-Hall Putsch in Munich took place on November 8, 1923, exactly five years after the foundation of the Weimar Republic. Hitler and 600 Nazi supporters, known as brownshirts, broke into a beer hall in Munich where an important meeting of right-wing and Bavarian nationalist parties was

taking place. Hitler hoped to seize power in Bavaria and install the wartime military leader General Erich Ludendorff as head of the military before marching on Berlin. In Munich, Hitler declared himself head of a new national government and forced the Bavarian prime minister, Gustav Ritter von Kahr, to promise loyalty to this national revolution from the platform. The following morning, without a gun in his back, the prime minister was less supportive. In a desperate attempt to rally support and retrieve the situation, Ludendorff and Hitler marched through Munich at the head of 3,000 Nazis.

The local police, however, were unimpressed by this gesture and fired on the marchers, killing 16 brownshirts. Ludendorff kept marching right through the police cordon; Hitler fled but was captured two days later. The attempted coup thus ended in failure at the first obstacle, primarily because there was only limited support in the local military and police. Ten of the putsch's leaders, including Hitler and Ludendorff, were put on trial. Ludendorff was acquitted, to the disgust of both himself and his opponents. Hitler was given the minimum sentence of five years but was only required to serve 13 months. While in prison, he composed *Mein Kampf* (My Struggle)—his infamous autobiography and justification of subsequent actions—which he dictated to Rudolf Hess.

◄ *Cavalry clear a Munich street on November 9, 1923, after Hitler's abortive putsch. Beside 16 Nazis, three policemen died in the clash near the Marienplatz.*

▲ *Nazi storm troopers await the putsch. Conceived along the lines of Mussolini's blackshirts, the brownshirts survived a ban imposed on them after the coup.*

international reputations, while the artists, architects, and designers who coalesced around the Bauhaus movement, begun in 1919 by Walter Gropius, strove both to enlighten and to break down the barriers between art and everyday life.

The superficial political stability and artistic experimentation of the Weimar Republic was destined not to survive, however, nor was its brief period of economic recovery. The Wall Street crash of 1929 plunged Germany into a massive recession, one that once again fueled political extremism. The inherent instability of the German political system was intensified as the parties of left and right struggled to win power and laid the foundations for Hitler's rise to power in 1933.

Austria-Hungary: an empire shattered

The collapse of the Austro-Hungarian Empire was perhaps the most potent symbol of the Central Powers' defeat in 1918 and of change in postwar Europe. Germany and Russia both lost dynasties and territories, but they retained their integrity as great nations. The Austro-Hungarian Empire was torn to pieces. Although a small, poor Austria did survive as one of the new states of Europe, it had lost most of its territory and all of its empire. In fact, in terms of land and people forfeited, no nation emerged from the war as badly as Austria. The rump of German-speaking Austria that remained in September 1919 after the Treaty of St. Germain was signed contained only 6.5 million people, compared with 50 million in the former Austro-Hungarian Empire.

In the process, Austria also lost most of its industry, much of it to the new Czechoslovakia, and most of its food-producing areas, many of which had been located in Hungary. Economic dislocation in the entire Danube basin was severe, and Vienna, the Austrian capital, was like a tree severed from its roots. As a result, Austria began to starve. At one point, the weekly bread ration was down to just 4 ounces (113 g), and even poverty-stricken Germany felt obliged to help. Substantial relief also arrived from Britain and especially the United States, which staved off mass starvation but could not prevent considerable suffering and many deaths.

Politically, Austria was also in turmoil. This new state, shorn of greatness, experienced a full-scale identity crisis, a crisis deepened by the refusal of the Allies to allow the one thing that almost all Austrians wanted—*Anschluss* (union) with Germany. Unable to submerge their trauma in a greater Germany, Austrians disagreed violently over the nature of a state that few of them even wanted. Vienna, containing a third of the population, became strongly socialist and was commonly referred to as Red Vienna, while the countryside was Catholic and conservative.

After feeble and failed attempts at a communist revolution had taken place, elections in February 1919 led to moderate socialists forming a government. By October the following year Austria had become a democratic, parliamentary republic, albeit a somewhat unstable one. By the mid-1920s the rural conservative elements had gained power under the leadership of Anton Seipel, a priest turned politician who became the dominant political figure in 1920s Austria. A measure of prosperity returned late in the decade, but the country remained ill at ease with its identity. Anti-Semitism and Nazism were strong forces from the mid-1920s (Hitler was Austrian by birth), and when Nazi Germany annexed Austria in 1938, it did so with popular support.

Hungary, the other dominant state in the old Austro-Hungarian Empire, also fared badly at the Paris peace talks. Although a new, purely Magyar state of eight million was created, large numbers of Hungarians were handed to Romania and Czechoslovakia. In the turmoil that ensued, a Hungarian soviet

government was established in March 1919. Its leader, Béla Kun, sanctioned invasions of Slovakia and Transylvania (now in Romania) to recover lost territory, but these acts merely hastened the demise of the Hungarian soviet. The Romanians counterattacked and soon reached Budapest, the Hungarian capital. Béla Kun resigned on August 1 and fled to Germany, a wise decision given the severity of the terror that followed. There were 400 executions and assassinations of Hungarian communists, with Jews especially targeted.

As communists were being hunted down and executed, the Hapsburgs, the ruling dynasty of the old empire, briefly reappeared on the European stage. In 1921 Archduke Joseph, a cousin of the former emperor, Charles, twice tried to establish himself as ruler of Hungary, but he was forced to withdraw under Allied pressure. Admiral Miklós Horthy, the former head of the Austro-Hungarian Navy, emerged as regent and succeeding in establishing in Hungary an authoritarian regime with fascist tendencies.

Turkey: the end of the Ottoman Empire

In the aftermath of World War I, Turkey was reduced to Asia Minor and a small area around Constantinople (Istanbul). It lost all of Arabia and a large swath of the Middle East from Palestine to Iraq. However, the humiliating terms of the Treaty of Sèvres, signed on August 10, 1920 (see pages 543–544), never came into full effect. They provoked a nationalist backlash and effective resistance led by a modernizing nationalist general, Mustafa Kemal, later named Atatürk (Father of the Turks).

Mustafa Kemal's Turkish national movement grew in strength during 1920 and 1921, controlling most of central and eastern Turkey from a new capital in Ankara. It accepted neither the Greek invasion of western Asia Minor nor Allied control of Constantinople

▲ *The Bauhaus workshop building in Dessau, Germany, designed by Bauhaus founder Walter Gropius. The name* **Bauhaus** *is an inversion of the German word* **Hausbau,** *meaning "building of a house"; hence it means "house of building."*

and the Dardanelles Straits. The Treaty of Sèvres, signed by the sultan, was rejected, and after raising an army, Mustafa Kemal defeated the Greeks and forced them to leave the Anatolian mainland. The nationalists' success brought them into direct contact with the British forces at Chanak on the Dardanelles and threatened Allied control of Constantinople and the vital seaway. In a humiliating reversal for the disunited Allies, France and Italy refused to back Britain in a fight to defend their position in Turkey, thereby forcing Britain to negotiate. Eventually, Turkish successes were recognized in the Treaty of Lausanne in 1923. This document, which replaced the Treaty of Sèvres, restored some lost territory to Turkish control.

On November 1, 1922, the Turkish National Assembly voted to abolish the centuries-old sultanate. The Ottoman Empire was formally buried, and a new, secular, modern Turkish republic began to emerge. Mustafa Kemal became a virtual dictator, although a benevolent one in many respects. The Ottoman Empire's religious leader, the caliph, was exiled, and Islam lost its formal position in the state. Education and literacy became central goals, even for women, who achieved unprecedented rights in an Islamic country, including the vote in the 1930s. Dress was westernized, and a Latin alphabet replaced the Arabic script for writing Turkish. Kemal and the national movement effected a major social and religious revolution in a few short years.

Turkish policies toward the Kurds and Armenians in the country's eastern provinces and borderlands were less

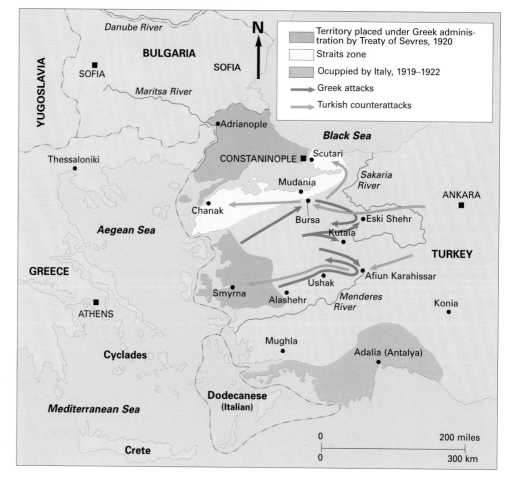

▶ *Turkey as partitioned by the Treaty of Sèvres, signed on August 10, 1920. Mustafa Kemal rejected the terms of the settlement, however, and eventually obtained revisions under the Treaty of Lausanne, 1923.*

enlightened, however. Having massacred up to 1.5 million Armenians during World War I, Turkey colluded with Soviet Russia to snuff out the new Armenian state planned by the Allies. Armenia was to be a U.S.-protected mandate, and U.S. loans were made on the assumption that there would be an Armenia to pay them back. However, the U.S. Congress's failure to ratify the Treaty of Versailles, as a result of which the United States stayed out of the League of Nations, killed the plan. Consequently, the Armenians were subject to further massacres and forced emigration by the new Turkish government, as well as receiving rough treatment from the Russian Bolsheviks.

The new Turkey also overturned the new Kurdish state that the British had established in southeastern Anatolia. Turkey claimed the Kurds as Turks. The Kurds disagreed and voted with their feet by fleeing south when Turkey invaded the Kurdish Mosul region, which had been occupied by Britain since the war. Given the choice, the Kurds preferred British colonial rule in northern Iraq to being governed from Ankara. Britain briefly considered setting up a Kurdish state in northern Iraq but was reluctant to loosen its control of the Mosul oil fields. The problem was never resolved. The Kurds still straddle the border between Turkey and Iraq and are still persecuted by both nations.

Russia in turmoil

No nation suffered more grievously from World War I and its immediate consequences than Russia. Not only were its casualties extremely high, but the trauma of war plunged Russia into revolution, civil war, terror, and famine from 1917 to 1922. The stark figures tell the story best. About two million men were killed in the world war; a much larger, unknown figure perished in the subsequent civil war and the accompanying terrors; and three million may have died during the famine of 1921.

Indeed, historian Norman Davies suggests, "If the victims of the fighting, of the White and Red Terrors, and of the terrible Volga famine are all added together, the total number of deaths would not be lower than the mortality on all fronts of the Great War." Some estimates put the total Russian death toll for these years as high as 13 million.

Russia was clearly the biggest loser of the war. This fact is obscured by the eventual victory of its former Allies but confirmed by the humiliation heaped on it by Germany in the Treaty of Brest-Litovsk of March 1918. Ultimately, Germany's defeat allowed Soviet Russia to escape Brest-Litovsk's full effects, but the agreement's terms make the Treaty of Versailles seem benevolent. The former Russian Empire was shorn of the Baltic states, Finland, Russian Poland, and much of the Caucasus, as well as all of Ukraine. These forfeitures translated into 33 percent of its crops and factories and 75 percent of its iron industries and coal deposits and were then compounded by the enormous dislocation of the civil war, which led to almost complete economic collapse. Industrial production in Russia in 1920 was only 13 percent of its 1913 level.

▲ *Greek troops prepare for an attack during their war against Turkey, August 1921. The conflict lasted from the Greeks' seizure of Smyrna (Izmir) in 1919 until their ejection from Turkey in 1922.*

The Russian Civil War

By the time the fighting stopped on the western front in November 1918, a new conflict had already started in Russia to oust the recently installed Bolshevik regime. The Russian Civil War was really a series of conflicts fought out between the Bolshevik Red Army and an array of separate forces that defy easy classification. The Bolsheviks' main enemies were the three White armies fighting for control of the Russian heartland and government. These forces were led by General Anton Denikin, who was pushing north from Ukraine with Cossack support; Admiral Alexander Kolchak, pushing west from Siberia; and General Nikolai Yudenich, pushing east from Estonia. The war was also a struggle between Russians and the nations that lay on the fringes of the former Russian Empire. Therefore, the Bolsheviks had to fight against armies from Ukraine, the Caucasus, and the Baltic states, in some of which areas there were also rival nationalist groups. Complicating matters further were anarchist peasant armies, which were reacting to the seizure of crops by the Bolshevik government.

The Russian Civil War was also an ideological struggle between the half-hearted, war-weary capitalist nations and Russian communists fighting for survival. More than 180,000 Allied troops from Japan, Britain, the United States, France, Italy, Finland, Serbia, Canada, Greece, and Korea helped the Whites. The Japanese intervention was particularly substantial and can be seen as a continuation of earlier Japanese-Russian conflict in Manchuria and eastern Siberia. The Bolsheviks even had to contend with an army of Czech prisoners of war trying to fight their way home along the Trans-Siberian Railway. In Ukraine alone there were 11 different armies operating at various points between 1918 and 1921.

In October 1919 the Bolsheviks were near to collapse. Denikin's forces were closing in on Moscow, having reached a point just 100 miles

▼ *U.S. sailors from the warship USS Albany parade through the streets of the Russian Pacific port of Vladivostok. U.S. personnel were among the Allied forces that took part in the Russian Civil War on the side of the anti-Bolshevik Whites.*

(160 km) from the city. Meanwhile, Yudenich was within artillery range of Petrograd (St. Petersburg), Kolchak was 200 miles (320 km) east of Moscow, and an invading Polish army under Marshal Józef Pilsudski was a similar distance west of Moscow near Smolensk. A coordinated effort might well have toppled the communists, but there was no unity of purpose. The Whites ranged from left-wing socialist revolutionaries to right-wing supporters of the czar. They disagreed over the nature of the government that should replace the Bolsheviks and over the independence of Poland, Georgia, and the Baltic states of Lithuania, Latvia, and Estonia.

Soon the tide began to turn. The Red Army defeated Kolchak heavily in late 1919, and he was captured and executed in February 1920. Yudenich was driven off by Leon Trotsky's brilliant defense of Petrograd, and Denikin was driven back to southern Ukraine by the end of March 1920, at which point he passed command of his forces to General Piotr Wrangel. The Russians also embarked on a campaign to reconquer Poland and came close to capturing its capital, Warsaw, in July. However, a magnificently conducted Polish counterattack by Pilsudski, later known as the Battle of Warsaw, or the Miracle of the Vistula, took place between August 16 and 25. The Russian invaders were crushed and in March 1921 reluctantly agreed to the Treaty of Riga, under the terms of which Russia in effect accepted Poland's territorial claims.

Many White units in Russia fought on until the end of 1921, but they were effectively finished by the end of 1920. The civil war had been incredibly complex, with multiple strands, local conflicts, and an international dimension. The Bolsheviks survived but with a lasting legacy of both paranoia and legitimate distrust of the outside world. Against all the odds, the Whites and the capitalist West had failed to strangle Soviet Russia at birth.

KEY EVENTS

THE BATTLE OF WARSAW

Responding to the Polish invasion of Ukraine, the Red Army under Marshal Mikhail Tukhachevski counterattacked into Poland with remarkable speed in 1920. The Polish capital, Warsaw, was soon under threat.

Tukhachevski launched the campaign with the cry "To the West. Over the corpse of White Poland lies the road to worldwide conflagration." He even boasted of sweeping on to Paris. By August 14 the Red Army was within 12 miles (19 km) of the Polish capital on the Vistula River. It seemed that Warsaw would inevitably fall, and with Germany in political chaos the threat of a Russian-led German revolution was a very real one. Berlin was only a few days march from Warsaw. The British and French sent arms and advisers led by General Maxime Weygand, while their politicians anxiously awaited the fall of Poland and the possibility of a communist-dominated Europe east of the Rhine River. Britain's Winston Churchill wrote in his diary, "Nothing can save Poland now."

Then, on August 16, the Polish Army counterattacked. Under the command of Marshal Józef Pilsudski, the Polish head of state, the army quickly stemmed the Russian advance and began a rapid reconquest of eastern Poland. The consequences of this battle were immense. Central Europe was spared the prospect of Soviet revolution, and Russia was forced to abandon immediate hopes of world revolution in favor of communism in one country. The British ambassador to Germany, Lord D'Abernon, who witnessed the fighting outside Warsaw, later wrote: "Had Pilsudski and Weygand failed to arrest the triumphant march of the Soviet Army at the Battle of Warsaw, not only would Christianity have experienced a dangerous reverse, but the very existence of western civilization would have been imperilled." To the Poles, the battle was quite simply the Miracle of the Vistula.

Communism in Russia

The actions and reactions of the new Soviet government can be understood only in terms of the condition of Russia at the time and of the regime's philosophy of Marxism as filtered through the mind of Vladimir Lenin, the Bolshevik leader. For Marxists, the material world is all that exists. This materialism makes most Marxists fundamentally hostile to religion and obsessed by economics, which they see as the driving force behind all social and political systems. Moreover, human experience before the revolution was essentially one of exploitation, with the world divided between labor and capital. Thus all human history was a history of constant class struggle that would ultimately lead to revolution.

Lenin's contribution to Marxism lay in modifying the roles of the party, the peasantry, and the proletariat, or workers. Russia was not the most advanced industrial society and did not have a large industrial working class. It should not have been the leader of the world revolution. This uncomfortable fact necessitated serious modification of Marxist theory. So for Lenin, the Communist Party became an elite of professional revolutionaries that would direct and protect the revolution from above. The situation in Russia also required an expanded role for the peasantry. Marx regarded the peasantry as exploited but reactionary individualists at an earlier stage of political consciousness. For Lenin, the peasantry should stand alongside their urban compatriots in the creation of a communist state. Karl Marx proved to be nearer the mark than Lenin. The Soviet state would have to starve and imprison millions of peasants in order to try to convince them that the seizure of their crops and the collectivization of their farms were a good thing for Russia as a whole.

Furthermore, the fact that Russia was unprepared for an immediate transition to communism required a long dictatorship of the proletariat led by the party (in this case the Bolsheviks and later the Communist Party) to resist the counterrevolutionary attempts of the bourgeoisie. The classless society and the withering away of the state that Marxist theory promised would be a

long time in coming—indeed it never came. The Marxist-Leninist philosophy did not breed respect for individual rights or acceptance of dissent. When combined with the incredibly difficult circumstances of civil war and a fight for survival against foreign and domestic foes, it led to intolerance and inhumanity on a grand scale.

The political system that emerged reflected this philosophy. It was democratic in principle. Local soviets elected delegates to provincial soviets, who in turn sent delegates to the All-Russian Congress of Soviets, which would then elect an executive committee and the Council of People's Commissars. In practice the system was dominated by the Communist Party, aided by an apparatus of secret police, state control of the media, and terror from above. Despite hopes for a genuine democracy of workers and peasants, Russia quickly became a dictatorship of the party elite, with Lenin at its head.

The new Russian economy

Almost immediately after the revolution in October 1917, the Bolsheviks began to take control of the factories, mines, and other productive units of the economy, including, in theory, all land. Civil war needs merely accelerated this rapid expansion of state control, which was known as war communism. The peasants were still allowed to farm the land as their own but were forced to give up ever larger portions of their crops. These methods served the short-term purpose of providing enough food and munitions to win the civil war, but they brought the economy to a standstill.

Throughout this period hunger and shortages were endemic in Russia. However, when the dislocation of war combined with drought in the Volga basin in 1921, a new depth of scarcity was reached. Millions starved to death, and many more were saved only by the intervention of the American Relief Administration led by Herbert Hoover.

▲ *Senior members of the Russian Communist Party take the air in Moscow in June 1925, some 18 months after Lenin's death. They are, from left to right, Josef Stalin, Alexi Rykov, Leo Kamenev, and Grigori Zinoviev. Stalin, the "man of steel," was to emerge as the long-term successor to Lenin, crushing all opposition along the way.*

The New Economic Policy (NEP) kept the "commanding heights" of the economy in the state's hands. Among the concerns covered by this description were large and medium factories of all kinds, power generation, railroads, and mining. The NEP allowed small manufacturers, retailers, and farmers to produce and sell for the market. Forced confiscation of crops was replaced by a tax in kind, and a class of successful landowning peasants, the kulaks, soon emerged. The policy was mostly a success. By 1928 both industrial and agricultural production had returned to prewar levels. Nevertheless, the majority of communists, including Lenin and Josef Stalin, his successor, always viewed the NEP as a temporary expedient.

On January 21, 1924, Lenin died. He had been increasingly incapable of governing due to a series of strokes, and his last months saw a struggle for power between his likely successors. The hero of the civil war, Trotsky, seemed best placed, but Stalin (an adopted name, meaning literally "man of steel") cleverly used his position as general secretary of the Communist Party. He gradually gained almost total control of the party and with it the state. His basic philosophy of socialism in one country also held more appeal than Trotsky's call for permanent revolution, which seemed to make the ultimate success of the Russian experiment dependent on international revolution.

Gradually, Stalin consolidated his power and moved away from the New Economic Policy toward full state direction of the economy. He enforced his will by terror and periodic purges. In 1928, the first of the five-year plans was launched. The expansion of industry and the collectivization of farming were the new goals, and in terms of increased industrial output, the success was spectacular, but so was the human cost. Many millions of his country's citizens were killed or starved to death to achieve Stalin's goals in the 1920s and 1930s.

Hoover's aid program had been saving lives in Poland, Ukraine, Germany, western Russia, and the former Austro-Hungarian Empire since 1919. Huge quantities of food and supplies arrived in Europe that year. In response to the Volga famine of 1921 through 1923, U.S. aid fed half a million people a day in 3,000 kitchens across Russia.

After all this deprivation and starvation, Lenin persuaded a reluctant Communist Party to take a step back on the path to full communism. The farms, factories, and transport systems of Russia were in disarray, and the party was extremely unpopular. The rising by discontented sailors at Kronstadt naval base in March 1921 brought home the need to compromise. The sailors that rebelled were the very people who had supported the October Revolution— the communists were alienating their natural supporters.

The U.S. Legacy

Prior to World War I the United States was relatively uninvolved in political affairs outside Latin America and the Pacific. This situation had more to do with political attitude than it did with national power. In the words of the historian Paul Kennedy, "The United States had definitely become a great power. But it was not part of the Great Power system." By declaring war on Germany in April 1917, everything changed, and the United States became a major part of the international power system with sudden effect, and it seemed set to take up the leading role among the Great Powers.

The United States was unquestionably the leading economic and financial power in the world by the outbreak of World War I. Since the Civil War (1861–1865), the rapidly expanding U.S. population had tamed and exploited the country's enormous resources with remarkable energy and ingenuity, and for the two decades after 1900, the country had enjoyed a period of unparalleled prosperity. By 1919 the United States stood before a broken Europe as a continental colossus of seemingly boundless agricultural and industrial strength. After World War I, the U. S. economy reached even greater heights—a position that was symbolized so aptly by those metaphors

World War I confirmed the United States as the world's dominant power, yet the country's growing prosperity in the 1920s took root against wide-ranging political, social, and cultural changes that provoked often violent responses.

► Jubilant Americans in Washington, D.C., show newspaper headlines that announce the surrender of Germany on November 8, 1918, ending World War I. The official end of the war came three days later, on November 11, at 11:00 A.M. However, the celebrations were brief and muted as the true cost of the conflict became more and more evident.

of modernity, the skyscrapers of New York and Chicago. With this economic strength came cultural and social confidence, and in the 1920s U.S. citizens stopped following European fashions and started setting them. U.S. movies, music, and automobiles redefined popular culture, and the rest of the world watched enviously as the United States seemed to revel in conspicuous consumption. In the field of citizens' rights, great strides were made in the emancipation of women with the passing of the Nineteenth Amendment, in part thanks to the efforts of suffragists, including Carrie Chapman Catt, and also to the wider role women played in World War I, although other sectors of U.S. society continued to face discrimination or outright hostility.

Yet the United States that emerged from World War I was not entirely at ease with itself or its new position in the world. Apart from the obvious disparities of wealth between rich and poor, it

KEY FIGURES

CARRIE CHAPMAN CATT

Carrie Chapman Catt (1859–1947) dominated the women's suffrage movement in the United States for much of the early 20th century. Born in Wisconsin, she grew up in Iowa and became a local teacher and then a reporter in San Francisco.

Catt joined the Iowa Women's Suffrage Association and by 1890 was active in the National American Women's Suffrage Association. She took over as president from Susan B. Anthony in 1900 and helped to found the International Woman Suffrage Alliance in 1902. The deaths of her second husband, Susan B. Anthony, her brother, and her mother in quick succession between 1905 and 1907 left her heartbroken, and Catt spent much of the next eight years promoting the cause abroad. She returned from Europe in 1915 to reunite a divided suffrage movement.

Catt helped secure the support of both main parties in 1916 and voting rights in New York State after leading a highly effective campaign in 1917. By 1919 the Nineteenth Amendment had passed the House, and female voting rights were finally guaranteed in 1920. Catt then campaigned against child labor and founded the National Committee on the Cause and Cure of War. This pacifism marked her out as a dangerous radical in the eyes of many government agencies, including the fledgling FBI.

Catt was a talented speaker, writer, and political organizer. She was also a pragmatist who campaigned at both the state and national level and who was prepared to fight for partial suffrage in less progressive states. She was arguably the single most influential person in the campaign for a woman's right to vote.

The Red Scare

Just after World War I suspicion of foreigners and fear of socialist revolution in the United States erupted into a mass public paranoia called the Red Scare.

Widespread labor unrest had already unsettled many conservatives in early 1919, but the trigger came on June 2, when the attorney general, Mitchell Palmer, had his home in Washington bombed. High-ranking government officials in other cities were also bombed, and the following day's *New York Times* blamed the attacks on Bolsheviks. These incidents provoked a government crackdown on a wide variety of recent immigrants, socialists, trade unionists, radicals, and peace campaigners, almost all of whom were innocent of any normally recognized crime. Palmer created a special task force within the Department of Justice to deal with the "crisis." At its head was 24-year-old J. Edgar Hoover, the future founder of the FBI. By November he claimed to have found 60,000 Bolshevik agitators in the United States.

The Red Scare reached its peak in January 1920, when the Justice Department arrested

around 10,000 "subversive aliens," often without a warrant or without informing them of their right to legal counsel. Many were beaten. The vast majority could not be brought to trial for lack of evidence, and they were eventually released. Nevertheless, around 600 were deported to Bolshevik Russia, and although Palmer's tactics raised objections in Congress, he was allowed to continue his

◄ *Carrie Chapman Catt, the prominent U.S. suffragist, seen taking part in a New York parade. Catt was one of the strongest voices for the abolition of war.*

▲ *The Red Scare of 1919–1920 saw much social unrest in the United States. Troops were often called in to restore order in trouble spots across the nation.*

activities. Newspapers teemed with patriotic and anticommunist cartoons, and vigilante groups targeted recent immigrants. Ironically, in a largely sincere bid to protect a particular idea of democracy, the government, leaders of industry, and many ordinary Americans resorted to distinctly undemocratic methods.

The origins of this reaction go back to the war, which had released an outpouring of patriotic xenophobia. "Hyphenated" Americans with recent origins in Germany, eastern Europe, and Russia were especially suspect, and President Woodrow Wilson

had given legal form to these feelings through the Espionage and Sedition Acts of 1917 and 1918. The latter punished any opinions which were judged to be "disloyal, profane, scurrilous, or abusive" of the U.S. flag, government, or uniform. It resulted in prosecutions for criticism of the budget and even the YMCA. Socialist leader Eugene V. Debs was imprisoned under these provisions, and the end of

hostilities did little to dampen the paranoia. Politicians scurried to emphasize their sound lineage. British, Scots-Irish, Dutch, Scandinavian, and (if distant enough) German were acceptable. Anyone else was suspiciously "un-American."

When Carrie Chapman Catt, the respected suffragist, discovered that her peace organization had been investigated as part of a government probe in 1920, Catt, who was never a communist and hardly a dangerous radical, responded in an article called "Poison Propaganda." Catt argued that these activists were merely law-abiding citizens "speaking, arranging meetings, petitioning, reading, investigating, thinking how to abolish war, the world's greatest crime." With some justification she asked rhetorically, "Is this America or Russia? Is this the 20th century or the Middle Ages?"

By the end of 1920, the paranoia was subsiding, and opposition to Palmer and Hoover was growing. President Harding, who was never a vindictive man, discouraged further witch-hunting. He released Debs, along with 23 other radicals and socialists imprisoned under wartime legislation. Harding realized that Debs was more dangerous in prison as an icon of injustice. In 1921 Palmer and Hoover were given a rough ride by the Senate Judiciary Committee, and the Red Scare fizzled out. However, by that time it had frightened many liberals into silence, encouraged trade unions to purge their socialist members, deprived communists of their First Amendment rights, and destroyed several radical organizations completely.

▲ Immigrants being served drinks in the reception center on Ellis Island in Upper New York Bay, New York, in 1920. In the years following World War I, the United States became increasingly isolationist, and immigrant numbers were greatly reduced.

was a nation full of contrasts and contradictions. The most powerful nation in the world, the United States became the least willing to engage in foreign affairs when the world needed its influence the most. The country best able to profit from free trade increased tariffs (tax barriers) to discourage foreign imports and hence the ability of foreigners to buy U.S. goods. The land that had built its prosperity on the hard work of immigrants rapidly closed its doors to mass immigration. Having earned a reputation for tolerance, democracy, and freedom of speech, the United States turned a blind eye to racism and actively persecuted political dissent. In short, the country was a troubled giant, torn between its traditional values and its newfound urban prosperity.

U.S. power in a global context

Before the war, the United States already had the world's richest and largest industrial economy. In 1914 its national income was more than three times larger than either of its nearest rivals, Germany and Britain. Its per capita income was over twice that of Germany and over 50 percent higher than in Britain. After Russia, which was much poorer, it had the largest population among the world's leading nations, with around one hundred million citizens.

World War I accelerated the growing gap between U.S. economic strength and that of other nations. Demand for U.S. food, munitions, and goods soared between 1914 and 1918, boosting the country's economy and helping to increase its gold reserves by $1.3 billion.

The conflict also fundamentally changed the world's financial system to leave the United States as the world's leading financier. Before 1914 much of the capital needed for U.S. economic expansion came from Britain, France, and Germany. After 1918 Europe was massively in debt to the United States. Britain, for example, owed the United States around $4.2 billion, and Germany was dependent on U.S. loans for its economic survival.

A brief postwar depression temporarily halted growth as the wartime orders dried up, but it soon gave way to further economic expansion and rising prosperity. Manufacturing production in 1920 was already 22 percent higher than in 1913, and by 1925 it was 48 percent higher. U.S. industrial growth was so spectacular that by 1929 its industrial output surpassed that of the combined total of the six next biggest producers. All this growth was obviously good for the United States, but owing to the structure of the U.S. economy it had some negative consequences for the rest of the world. First, the United States was protectionist rather than free trading. Second, it lacked a powerful central bank that could control and calm its financial markets. Third, its economic cycles were more volatile than those of Britain. Finally, its economy was less integrated in the world trading system, with less than 10 percent of U.S. manufactured goods being exported. In short, while the size and strength of the U.S. economy ensured its financial preeminence, its institutions and attitudes to trade were not well suited to leading and regulating the world's economy.

For most of the 1920s, this disparity mattered little as the expanding U.S. economy made loans available to Europe at low interest rates. However, the Fordney-McCumber tariffs, introduced in 1922, made it hard for European countries to earn enough through their exports to the United States to repay their loans. The system began to break

---

EYEWITNESS

CARL SANDBURG

Carl Sandburg was one of America's most popular poets in the 1920s. The son of Swedish immigrants, raised in Illinois, he worked as a laborer, soldier, journalist, and secretary to the socialist mayor of Milwaukee before moving to Chicago in 1913.

In four volumes of poetry, between 1914 and 1922 Sandburg produced a panorama of contemporary America in simple language and with a feel for the common person. His most famous poem, *Chicago*, memorably personifies the bustling, working city he settled in:

Hog Butcher for the World,
Tool Maker, Stacker of Wheat,
Player with Railroads and the Nation's Freight Handler;
Stormy, husky, brawling,
City of the Big Shoulders.

In a lesser-known poem that was written in 1920 called *Manual System*, Sandburg illustrated the increasing pace of life, the growth of technology, and the tedium faced by the new breed of working women who were harnessed to this technology:

Mary has a thingamajig clamped on her ears
And sits all day taking plugs out and sticking plugs in.
Flashes and flashes—voices and voices
 calling for ears to pour words in
Faces at the ends of wires asking for other faces
 at the ends of other wires:
All day taking plugs out and sticking plugs in,
Mary has a thingamajig clamped on her ears.

---

down in 1928. Rising interest rates and a stock market boom made U.S. investments more attractive to U.S. banks and financiers than foreign investments, so U.S. credit to Europe began to dry up. It collapsed completely when the Wall Street crash of October 1929 brought a sudden end to U.S. loans. The world then suddenly entered a decade of economic contraction, with the United States among the worst affected.

▲ *Workers flood the streets in the aftermath of the Wall Street crash, October 29, 1929. This financial collapse ended U.S. credit to Europe and heralded the beginning of the Great Depression of the 1930s that would sweep both the United States and much of the rest of the world.*

Wilson and the League of Nations

With the armistice of November 1918, President Woodrow Wilson's authority and prestige were at their height. He was in the middle of a successful second term, and he had just led the U.S. people to victory in World War I. In Europe his popularity was especially high, and he was optimistic that he could enforce his political will on his Allies, chiefly Britain and France, at the Paris peace talks, which began in January 1919. However, even at this early stage, even before the Treaty of Versailles had been finalized, there were several problems to be faced.

First, the simple act of attending the peace talks offended many U.S. citizens, who thought that the president should not leave the country. (Wilson was the first president to visit Europe.) Second, Wilson failed to take either prominent Republicans or any men of outstanding abilities with him to Paris, which left him open to partisan criticism. Third, he had mistakenly tied his fortunes too closely to the Democrats in Congress by asking the nation to vote for Democrats in the 1918 congressional elections. He sought a mandate for his negotiations and a cooperative Congress to ratify the peace treaty that he would return with. However, when the Democrats did poorly and lost control of both Houses, his mandate and prestige were obviously in question. Former president Theodore Roosevelt sent him on his way with a warning to the Europeans that Wilson had no authority to speak for the United States. This statement was an exaggeration as Wilson was still a popular and respected president, but it foreshadowed the problems he would face on his return from France.

As the peace talks progressed, some Americans were further dismayed that Wilson seemed to give so much ground to France and Britain. To them, it seemed that Wilson was acquiescing in a vengeful peace. Liberal Democrats in particular thought the final Treaty of Versailles unfair, criticizing the heavy reparations and colonial gains that Britain and France made at the expense of Germany. The reality was that Wilson did have to compromise, but he was willing to do so in return for support for the League of Nations—a project dear to his heart and one that he had outlined in his Fourteen Points in 1918 (see Volume 1, pages 310–311). While Wilson was away he also lost touch with the mood of the nation, which was moving away from generous internationalism toward suspicious isolationism. By the time he finally returned to the United States in mid-1919, there was considerable opposition in the Senate and in the country to the Treaty of Versailles in its final form.

Furthermore, powerful ethnic groups threw their weight behind the opponents of the League. Italian Americans were annoyed at Wilson's failure to secure territorial gains for Italy, one of the Allied victors. German Americans were opposed to any treaty that would punish their former homeland so severely. Irish Americans were angry at the failure of Irish claims for independence and a seat at the conference table. They saw Wilson as a hypocrite who advocated self-determination only when convenient. This view was somewhat unfair as the British government would never have given in to Irish demands, and Wilson was understandably reluctant to aggravate a major ally over a dispute that it regarded as a purely domestic issue. However, Wilson's Scots-Irish lineage did make him more sympathetic to the Ulster Protestants concentrated in the north of Ireland, who wished to remain British, than to the Catholic Irish in southern Ireland who sought independence. Irish Americans naturally resented this prejudice.

▼ *The U.S. delegation at the Versailles Peace Conference of 1919. President Wilson is seated in the center. The punitive terms imposed on the defeated Central Powers, particularly those concerning Germany, caused much resentment in the United States and were at the heart of the causes of World War II.*

KEY FIGURES

HENRY CABOT LODGE

A powerful and respected Republican senator from Massachusetts, Henry Cabot Lodge (1850–1924) played a crucial role in the U.S. rejection of the Treaty of Versailles as chairman of the Senate Foreign Relations Committee.

Henry Cabot Lodge was instrumental in the failure of the United States to ratify the treaty and partly responsible for the destabilizing effects of the U.S. absence from the League of Nations. However, he was not an isolationist, and he was not the chief villain of this episode. It was rather President Woodrow Wilson's intransigence in forcing the Senate to take the treaty whole or not at all that precipitated the crisis.

Like most Americans, Lodge was in favor of some kind of League of Nations, but he wanted a treaty that would reduce U.S. commitments to more realistic levels. He did not think the United States should be committed to defending any and all borders even if they were morally unjustifiable or irrelevant to U.S. interests. He proposed a set of amendments that were appealing to most Americans and broadly acceptable to the European allies.

Given that Lodge was able to command most of the Republican votes in the Senate, about 49 compared to Wilson's 23, the president would have been wise to compromise, but Wilson found Lodge irritating (he was said to

have a voice "like the tearing of a sheet"), and he refused to vote for Lodge's amendments. Lodge's supporters then refused to approve the treaty as it stood, and the league went unratified, despite the fact that there was a large majority in Congress that wanted some kind of league.

By the time of the Senate debates of August 1919, ratification of the Treaty of Versailles was an issue of party politics, and Republicans used the changed mood of the country to score a political victory over Wilson and the Democrats. Led by Henry Cabot Lodge, the senator from Massachusetts and chairman of the Senate's Foreign Affairs Committee, Republicans in the Senate already had a slight edge over the Democrats with 49 senators to 47. With liberal Democratic opponents to Versailles led by Thomas Gore and David Walsh taking more votes from Wilson's own party, the outcome suddenly looked doubtful for the president. Most Americans were still willing to see some sort of U.S. cooperation in the resolution of international problems and in the promotion of peace, and there was enough support in Congress and in the country to secure ratification of the League of Nations with reservations. However, there was clearly a deep fear of committing the United States to unending overseas entanglements.

A series of amendments were tabled in an attempt to pass a modified ratification. The key stumbling block was article 10 of the league's covenant. This required members to submit all disputes to arbitration and committed them to economic and military sanctions against nations who transgressed. Many senators saw this article as an infringement of U.S. sovereignty, but Wilson saw it as the backbone of the treaty, without which the League of Nations would be little more than "an influential debating society." He would not give way on any amendments.

Realizing that he did not have the votes in the Senate, Wilson took his campaign to the country. In 22 days during September 1919, he traveled 8,000 miles (12,800 km) across the United States, giving 42 speeches. Wilson's health was not good to start with. He had suffered a stroke while in Paris that had been concealed from the public, and the strain now took its toll. On September 25 he suffered another stroke and was forced to return to Washington. On October 10 he had a third stroke that paralyzed his entire left side. He never fully recovered, and thereafter Wilson was a sad, stubborn figure who was barely in control of the White House. His wife, Edith, effectively became the country's first female president, making cabinet appointments and forging the president's signature on bills.

On November 19, the Senate voted against the treaty by 55 votes to 39. Ironically, 23 of Wilson's supporters voted against an amended treaty on his instructions rather than accept it with Lodge's reservations. A second attempt to ratify the treaty failed in March 1920, and by then the League of Nations had been born, but with the father absent. The United States never joined the League of Nations, and the Wilson presidency, one of the most important administrations of the era, ended in disappointment and deception. Wilson died on February 3, 1924.

Immigration, patriotism, and xenophobia

In the arena of foreign policy, the return to isolationism symbolized the U. S. turning of its back on the world

▼ *President Woodrow Wilson addressing the public at Tacoma, Washington, on his League of Nations Peace Tour in September 1919. Although Wilson's long-cherished notion of an international forum for settling disputes came into being, it did so without the United States.*

cogs in the capitalist system. Ironically, many unions supported the new quotas in their anxiety to stop cheap immigrant labor from undermining their hard-won wage levels. Often recent immigrants themselves, in effect they helped to kick away the social ladder that they had only recently climbed. The country was swept by a so-called Red Scare between late 1919 and May 1920 that resulted in beatings, unwarranted arrests, and deportations.

However, the war and a strong fear of communism also tapped into older sources of prejudice, often called nativism. This outlook dated to the early days of mass immigration in the mid-19th century, and the phenomenon originally focused on Protestant Anglo-Saxon dislike of Catholic Irish immigrants. However, through the postwar period

after the horrors of war and the disillusion of the peacemaking process. This impulse had its counterpart in domestic policy as the country began to close its doors to immigrants. The Immigration Act of 1917, the Emergency Quota Act of 1921, and the National Origins Act of 1924 all restricted immigration. After 1924 annual immigration rates plummeted to 15 or 20 percent of their prewar levels, and of these immigrants, 80 percent had to come from western and northern Europe.

The fear and suspicion of foreigners had both short- and long-term causes. In the short term, the war had generated antiforeigner feeling, much of which had been directed against German Americans, and the socialist revolutions in Europe had raised suspicion of radicals abroad and at home. As a result, emigrants from eastern, central, and southern Europe were suspected of bringing communistic, unpatriotic, and "un-American" ideas into the country. Because many recent immigrants were active in socialist and labor organizations, this fear had some plausibility, but it obscured two key facts: most prominent radicals were homegrown Anglo-Saxon Protestants, and most immigrants were hardworking

▲ *Immigrants on Ellis Island, August 1923. A series of new laws in the decade following World War I saw the number of immigrants cut from more than four million in 1920 to 528,400 in 1930. These new laws favored European immigrants over those from the rest of the world.*

nativism expanded to include (or rather to exclude) Jews and any immigrants from outside northern and western Europe, particularly those from China and Japan. These years also saw a marked increase in organized racism directed against African Americans. The Ku Klux Klan was reborn as a nationwide body in Atlanta, Georgia, in 1915 by William Simmons. This time around it also targeted Catholics and Jews. It had strong support outside the South in states like Indiana, and it claimed five million members at its peak in the mid-1920s. Once again, African Americans were its main victims. Hundreds were lynched or even burned alive in these years, with the tacit or active approval of some in the white community. Photographs from this era show large crowds of well-dressed white people posing for the camera next to African American bodies that are charred or swinging from a tree. From their expressions (and their picnics), the participants were apparently enjoying a family day out.

Experiences such as these gave a push to massive internal migration. The pull was the need of factories in the Northeast and Midwest for labor. The need was intense during the war, and it continued well into the 1920s. With immigration blocked by the war and then afterward by Congress, African Americans in the South moved to northern cities to fill the gap. The immediate effects were race riots and turf wars in many major cities. Fleeing from intolerance in the South, blacks who moved north found plenty more of it in St. Louis, Chicago, Detroit, Kansas

▼ *A man kneels at a burning cross as a hooded Ku Klux Klan member stands over him with a chalice during a nighttime initiation ceremony in the 1920s. Originating in the 1860s, the Ku Klux Klan was revived in 1915 and both fueled and was fueled by the climate of intolerance that swept the United States following World War I.*

The Nineteenth Amendment

Securing the vote for women in the United States was a long and arduous struggle that stretched over many decades, but the campaign finally reached fruition with the Nineteenth Amendment in 1919, partly due to women's support for the U.S. efforts in World War I.

Beginning in the mid-nineteenth century, several generations of women wrote pamphlets, gave lectures, organized marches, lobbied politicians and practiced civil disobedience to achieve this change to the Constitution. Few early supporters, like Susan B. Anthony and Elizabeth Cady Stanton, lived to see the final victory, but piecemeal victories were achieved at the state level. Wyoming led the way in 1869, and by the outbreak of World War I, 11 western states allowed women to vote, nine of them having done so between 1910 and 1914. In the East and South advocates despaired of attaining their goal through modification of individual state laws. Judicial efforts had also failed, including an attempt to secure votes for women under the Fifteenth Amendment, which prohibited discrimination against African Americans, but the political tide was in the suffragists' favor.

▶ *Suffragists parade down Bedford Avenue in Brooklyn, New York, to call for votes for women. The campaign began in 1848 and achieved final success in 1920.*

There were two deciding factors. First was the pressure that women voters could exert on the parties in the West. Poor performance by the Democrats in these states in the 1914 election led to their conversion. This switch in turn dictated that the Republicans support the cause to avoid losing the female vote. By 1916 both Republican and Democrat parties officially endorsed the amendment. Second, the respect earned by women during World War I for their work in jobs previously reserved for men cannot be underestimated in converting men to the cause. For some time women had been slowly entering the professions as teachers, then doctors and lawyers, and even architects, such as Julia Morgan. Proof of their competence had been slowly wearing down male objections, but female war work was even more effective by combining patriotism with competence.

The suffrage movement won the support of President Woodrow Wilson in 1918, and in early 1919, the House of Representatives passed the Nineteenth Amendment by 304 votes to 90. The Senate approved it by 56 votes to 25 later in the year. The amend-

▶ *A poster from the League of Women Voters urges women to use the vote that the Nineteenth Amendment had given them.*

ment, which guarantees the right of all women to vote, was generally known as the Anthony Amendment, after its author, Susan B. Anthony. It states:

1) The right of the citizens of the United States to vote shall not be denied or abridged by the United States or by any state on account of sex.

2) Congress shall have power to enforce this article by appropriate legislation.

The states began to ratify the amendment, starting with Illinois, Wisconsin, and Michigan, but antisuffrage sentiment was very strong in some states, and as with any other

League of Women Voters

constitutional amendment, three-quarters of them had to ratify it. Tennessee witnessed a particularly hard-fought battle, as antisuffrage legislators fled the state to avoid a quorum while their associates held massive antisuffrage rallies. At one point, the vote hinged on 24-year-old state legislator Harry Burn, who converted to the suffragists' cause at the insistence of his elderly mother. Eventually, in August 1920, Tennessee affirmed its vote for the amendment and delivered the crucial 36th ratification that was necessary for final adoption.

▲ *The Republican U.S. president Warren Harding (left) with Vice President Calvin Coolidge. Their landslide election victory in 1920 was the start of a new pro-business era and saw the United States begin to concentrate on domestic rather than international issues.*

City, and New York. In 1917, 39 blacks were killed in a race riot in East St. Louis, and simmering violence in Chicago erupted two years later in five days of rioting that claimed 38 lives, after an African American had been killed for swimming from a white beach on Lake Michigan while the local police looked on. Both incidents were essentially an attempt by poor whites to keep blacks out of their neighborhoods, and they were repeated on a smaller scale in many other cities in 1919.

Harding, Coolidge, and Hoover

Wilson's physical state prevented any attempt at a third term as president, so two new men took the field for the 1920 presidential election. The Democrats ran with James M. Cox, the governor of

Ohio, and the Republicans with Warren Harding, who was a senator from Ohio. Both were conservatives. Wilson saw the election as a referendum on the League of Nations, but most Americans disagreed. They were tired of international problems and voted on domestic issues. Harding captured the mood perfectly with his call for a return to "normalcy." This vague term was less innocent than it sounded. His normalcy essentially meant a free rein for big business, low taxes for the wealthy, and an end to the progressive program of social reform. However, his policies sounded soothing to a nation that had been disturbed by the Red Scare and was now suffering from postwar inflation and recession. Harding won a landslide victory, capturing over 16 million votes to Cox's 9 million. The Progressive Era of Teddy Roosevelt and Woodrow Wilson was over. Most Americans now focused on the peaceful pursuit of prosperity.

The new administration, as well as those of Coolidge and Hoover that followed, was openly sympathetic toward big business—a fact shown by both cabinet appointments and the government's policies. Andrew Mellon, the second richest man in the United States, was also the treasury secretary from 1921 to 1932. Herbert Hoover, a very capable and energetic man, was a self-made millionaire in the mining industry when he was appointed secretary of commerce in 1921. Over the next few years Mellon lowered estate taxes and surtaxes and abolished the excess-profits tax. His actions stimulated the economy but also fueled an unsustainable stock market boom. At the same time, anti-trust activity virtually ceased, and the government supported employers in the violent suppression of strikes.

The election of Harding had ushered in an era without presidential activism, but his pro-business stance was not truly based on the free market. First, the government gave many subsidies to private firms and handed them property at rock-bottom prices, such as merchant shipping built during the war. Second, tariffs were increased massively, preventing free trade with the rest of the world and keeping prices artificially high for U.S. consumers. Wilson had vetoed a tariff increase shortly before leaving office, pleading with Congress not to prevent European access to U.S. markets by making their exports too expensive. Nevertheless, the Republican Congress passed the Fordney-McCumber Act in 1922. It raised tariffs by an average of 38 percent and gave particular protection to the chemical and drug industries, a decision that hurt key export industries in an already impoverished Germany.

Warren Harding was a reluctant internationalist but not a strict isolationist.

Nor for that matter were his Republican successors, Coolidge and Hoover. Harding's administration initiated the Washington Naval Conference of 1921–1922, which attempted with some success to limit the size of the world's major navies. Coolidge oversaw the Dawes Plan of 1924 that rescheduled German reparations, as well as the Kellogg-Briand Pact of 1928 that renounced war. Hoover encouraged the Young Plan in

▼ *Andrew Mellon became U.S. treasury secretary in 1921, a position he held until 1932. Under his stewardship the U.S. economy experienced rapid growth until the Wall Street crash in 1929.*

▲ *President Warren Harding delivers his first annual message to Congress, July 12, 1921. The session was attended by delegates to the Washington Naval Conference of 1921–1922, which succeeded in limiting the size and strength of the world's major navies.*

1929 that further reduced German reparations and European debt to the United States. In essence, the United States in the 1920s was happy to help find peaceful resolutions to international problems, but it did not commit itself to formal security agreements.

The majority of Americans supported these policies, and few could foresee the difficulties that lay ahead. Protectionism pleased big business, farmers, and organized labor by preventing competition, and Harding presided over a turnaround in the U.S. economy from the postwar slump to the boom that lasted from 1923 to late 1929. Furthermore, Harding was a congenial character who was very popular with the public. Indeed, few presidents have been so popular in their own lifetime, and his death in San Francisco in August 1923 produced a massive and spontaneous

outburst of genuine grief. Thousands lined the streeets to pay their respects as his body was transported back to Washington by train.

Within weeks, however, Harding's reputation went into permanent decline as news of corruption in his administration came out. Harding himself was merely negligent rather than personally corrupt, but his choice of colleagues was poor. A number of his appointees had been involved in serious corruption scandals, the two most famous being the Teapot Dome and Veterans Association cases. In the former, a government oil field under a hill in Wyoming was sold off by Albert Fall, secretary of the interior, in 1921 to someone who had given him a loan. In the latter, Charles Forbes abused his position as head of the newly formed Veterans Association to steal money intended for military pensions and medical benefits.

News of the death of Harding took many hours to reach Vice President Calvin Coolidge at his home in rural Vermont, which had no telephone. Coolidge was sworn in by his own father, a public notary, by the light of an oil lamp in the middle of the night. This image of New England rural simplicity did wonders for the corrupted administration, which Coolidge immediately set about reforming. Coolidge was a strong-willed, hardworking man of few words. His basic philosophy of governmental minimalism was similar to that of Harding, but his style was very different. Gone were the late-night poker parties with cronies in the White House. "Silent Cal" ran a tighter ship. He also presided over a period of unbroken economic progress, encapsulated in his pithy remark that "the business of America is business."

Coolidge secured his own election in 1924 with remarkable ease, given the scandals of Harding's administration revealed barely 12 month earlier. He chose not to run again in 1928, leaving his colleague Herbert Hoover to win his own landslide against Democrat Al Smith. Hoover polled 21.4 million votes to Smith's 15 million votes, winning in all but six southern states. However, the boom of the 1920s would soon turn to bust. Coolidge had stepped down just in time, and Hoover was left to deal with the Wall Street crash and the Great Depression that followed a year later. It was the end of an era.

Prosperity and the automobile

In the immediate postwar period the United States suffered a recession, which was partly due to global overproduction

▼ *President Warren Harding's funeral procession down Pennsylvania Avenue in Washington, D.C., August 8, 1923. Harding's reputation as a trustworthy leader did not survive for long after his death.*

▼ *The 15 millionth Model T Ford rolls off the production line, May 26, 1927. Henry Ford was a pioneer of mass-manufacture and his revolution in factory efficiency made the automobile affordable to millions of American workers and families.*

in agriculture and certain key industries, like steel, and partly due to the short-term problems of adjusting from military to consumer production. Inflation was high (prices rose by 40 percent between 1918 and 1920) and unemployment was growing. Even when the economy was booming from 1922 to 1929, the resulting wealth was very unevenly spread around. Politicians boasted of "a chicken in every pot," but such was not the case. Farmers in particular had a hard time, with prices falling by 60 to 70 percent for some crops over the course of the decade. For many people, agricultural life became unsustainable and these years saw a decrease in rural population while that of the cities boomed. Nor did labor disputes and unemployment disappear.

Strikes were common throughout the period, and they were often dealt with very harshly by the employers.

However, the overall picture of the 1920s was one of impressive leaps in productivity based on hard work and major technological advances. The war had stimulated both the level of demand and the pace of innovation. There were major improvements in oil production and refining, electrical engineering, chemical and dye production, alloy, aluminum, and steel production, refrigeration, and canning. These gains soon found their way into new and improved consumer goods. Washing machines, refrigerators, radios, telephones, and electric lighting became commonplace in U.S. homes. No product symbolizes this industrial expansion and innovation

so much as the automobile. This was the great era of Henry Ford's assembly line, the Model T, and mass automobile ownership. Increasingly efficient production methods brought the price of a Model T Ford down to $260, and by the time the last one rolled off the line in 1927, more than 15 million had been built.

The significance of the automobile is most clearly shown by the growth of the corporations that built them. Before the war J. P. Morgan's mighty U.S. Steel was still the country's largest corporation. By the late 1920s it had been surpassed by three automobile companies, Ford, General Motors, and Chrysler. The sheer number of automobiles produced was also impressive. In 1920, 1.9 million were sold in the United States. In 1929, 4.5 million were sold. They brought mobility and freedom to ordinary Americans, letting them go where they wanted when they wanted. In doing so, they also transformed the face of the United States. No longer did wage earners need to live around railroad stations and factories in dirty, overcrowded cities. They could move out to new homes on green-field sites outside the city. Suburbs sprang up everywhere as wealthier workers moved away from the inner cities.

The automobile also allowed California and other states to realize their full potential. Blessed with space, sunny weather, and cheap electricity from new and ambitious hydroelectric power projects, California boomed in the 1920s. Los Angeles in particular grew at a phenomenal rate. Its population was around half a million at the war's end. During the 1920s 100,000 new people a year were settling there, and the population rose to 2.2 million by 1930, thanks in part to the lure of its most important industry—the movies.

Hollywood and the Jazz Age
In the 1920s Hollywood *was* the United States to the outside world. Along with

jazz, it redefined popular culture, and the styles and story lines of its movies became the most powerful cultural influence of the twentieth century. Millions of ordinary people across the world were inspired, entertained, and emotionally manipulated by the big Hollywood studios. Movie stars became the most admired and imitated people on the planet. The popular models of ultimate success were no longer world leaders, landed aristocrats, or captains of industry, but movie stars. In the movies,

▲ *The young jazz legend, Louis Armstrong, photographed in 1927. The 1920s were dubbed The Jazz Age by F. Scott Fitzgerald, and young people embraced jazz music as an expression of a new national mood.*

609

▲ An FBI agent destroys barrels of illicit liquor in 1920. Scenes like this were reenacted all over the United States for more than a decade, but Prohibition was eventually seen as a mobsters' charter, and it was repealed in 1933.

almost everyone was beautiful, good always triumphed over evil, and virtue invariably had its reward. The movies offered glamour and an escape from harsh reality. The United States and the rest of the world lapped it up.

Of course, not everyone loved Hollywood. The things that appealed to some—luxury, glamour, and even decadence—did not make it popular with evangelicals and progressives. Nor was the power of recently arrived Russian and European Jews within the industry appreciated in these xenophobic times.

To satisfy the U.S. Bible Belt, the entertainment industry brought in William H. Hays, former postmaster general, to establish a code of conduct. The Hays Code banned the depiction of sexual and criminal immorality and effected an uneasy truce between Protestant moralism and unfettered creativity that lasted until the 1960s.

The other important cultural development of the Roaring Twenties was sparked by the internal migration of African Americans from south to north. It was the creation of jazz. The social and artistic significance of jazz for the United States remains immense. First, it was the first new art form that was truly American. Second, it brought African American artistic ability into mainstream U.S. culture for the first time, providing for a reevaluation of the role of African Americans in wider U.S. society. Third, it changed both popular music and musical theater forever. Nightclubs like the Cotton Club in New York became all the rage, and jazz artists who had recently decamped from the southern states played, danced, and sang nightly to packed, all-white audiences in major northern cities. Duke Ellington, Louis Armstrong, Fats Waller, Ethel Waters, and Josephine Baker were the stars. As African American writer Langston Hughes put it, "the Negro was in vogue."

The jazz and nightclub scene became part and parcel of the illegal trade in alcohol, which had been under widespread prohibition since 1918, forcing the glamour and excitement of this vibrant cultural development into the pocket of sordid underworld bosses like Al Capone in Chicago and Dutch Schultz in New York. The movements, rhythms, and venues of jazz naturally offended many evangelicals and conservatives, who thought that jazz released instincts and impulses that were better kept under control. It was also blamed for a perceived general lowering of moral standards among women that saw them drinking and smoking in public, as well as wearing short hair, short dresses, and too much lipstick.

Jazz was one of the more positive developments of the postwar period, and it epitomized the popular and enduring image of the era. After a period of war, recession, and political paranoia, many Americans simply wanted to enjoy the music and join the party. It was a party that would last until October 29, 1929, when the Wall Street crash left the United States and the rest of the developed world facing a very different future.

POLITICAL WORLD

THE EIGHTEENTH AMENDMENT

The prohibition of the manufacture, sale, and use of intoxicating liquors was one of the most controversial attempts to modify social behavior in modern U.S. history. The struggle between "wets" and "drys" was an urban-rural struggle that pitted working-class men and the cosmopolitan upper classes against puritan fundamentalists in Middle America and their allies in the Progressive Movement.

The origins of Prohibition came from three major sources: evangelical Christianity, with its roots in the Great Awakening of the nineteenth century and its desire for moral improvement; large capitalists and factory owners, who wished to improve the efficiency of their workers by preventing them from drinking; and millions of ordinary women, who sought relief from irresponsible husbands who were drinking away their wages and savings. This powerful combination of forces became unstoppable once the war had encouraged a spirit of disciplined self-denial and once politicians started competing for the female vote. (The fact that many brewers were of German origin made matters worse.)

The Eighteenth Amendment was passed by Congress in 1917 and ratified by the required number of states, 75 percent, in just over a year. The amendment and the 1919 Volstead Act which enforced it did have a short-term impact on alcohol consumption, but in the long term it merely made drinking more expensive and more dangerous. The rich still drank, thousands of speakeasies (illegal drinking dens usually associated with gambling) soon opened, and lawlessness rapidly soared as organized crime filled the production, distribution, and retail vacuums previously filled by legitimate businesses and gave rise to the term "bootlegger." Prohibition essentially launched organized crime in the United States, creating violent mobsters, corrupt judges, and crooked cops in cities across America. The failure of the policy was evident, and national Prohibition was eventually repealed by the Twenty-First Amendment in 1933, with powers of liquor regulation being returned to the individual states.

The Wider Impact

Europe's powers drew men and resources into the conflict from distant shores, and their preoccupation with war for four years created opportunities for change elsewhere. For example, World War I significantly shifted patterns of world trade and international economics, with non-European nations such as Japan and Canada emerging from the war with much larger shares of world exports. Between 1913 and 1925 Canada's share rose from 2.4 to 4.4 percent, and Japan's from 1.7 to 3.0 percent. The inability of Europe's major trading nations to satisfy their previous export markets during the war also led to a number of opportunities for other overseas industries to carve out new or larger international markets, particularly in the case of Latin America and the British Dominions (Australia, Canada, and New Zealand), which began to complement their high levels of food exports with manufactured goods.

Latin and South America were barely touched by the war in a physical sense. However, changing trade patterns and

While the bulk of the fighting had taken place in Europe, World War I had significant consequences for the rest of the world, not least in India, the Middle East, and China.

▶ *A coffee drying facility in Costa Rica, 1922. Latin American countries increased their exports of foodstuffs and raw materials after the war ended in 1918.*

◀ *Japanese workers winding induction regulator coils in an engineering plant, 1927. Japan's industrial base grew rapidly following World War I, and exports to the lucrative European markets increased. Japan's economic growth was mirrored by its military expansion in the 1920s and 1930s.*

European ideological influences did have some impact. In Brazil, for example, there was a brief socialist uprising in Rio de Janeiro, the capital, after an unsuccessful three-day general strike in January 1919. Argentina did well from the war, building on its existing power as a major exporter of food, especially of beef and corn. Mexico was gripped by revolution in 1920, but it was largely a domestic struggle that dated back to 1910 and in no way primarily related to the outcome of World War I. There were anti-British riots in Trinidad, Jamaica, and British Honduras, but none of these left lasting marks that were primarily attributable to the war.

Africa was directly affected by the large number of territorial transfers following the war, with former German colonies—Southwest Africa, German East Africa, Cameroon, and Togoland—being taken over by Britain or France. However, this upheaval was merely a change of colonial master for most ordinary Africans. This chapter, therefore, looks at the consequences of World War I on those non-European regions that were most powerfully affected in the long term, namely India, the Middle East, and China.

India and Britain

The British Empire was never larger than after the signing of the World War I peace treaties, but it quickly became clear that the conflict had seriously weakened Britain's ability to maintain control of its vast empire. Apart from the obvious fact that Britain had fewer resources, other factors, most notably war weariness, liberal ideals, and widespread pacifism, led to diminished domestic support for continuing the sacrifices needed to defend the empire. Overstretched by commitments abroad and undermined by economic problems at home, some began to view the empire's far-flung colonies as a moral embarrassment and a military liability rather than a prestigious resource. One

▶ *Buenos Aires, the capital city of Argentina, seen in 1920. A major exporter of foodstuffs such as beef and corn, Argentina exploited the increased demand for these staples in Europe in the postwar years to build up a thriving economy.*

▲ *An Indian volunteer lies in front of a cartload of imported British goods being taken for sale in Bombay. This form of peaceful protest against British rule in India was widespread in the years between World Wars I and II, inspired by the leadership of Mohandas Gandhi.*

such individual was socialist Annie Besant, who became president of the British-based Indian Home Rule League in 1916. Yet many Britons clung to the ideal of empire as if the very survival of Britain itself depended on it, and for the imperialists and conservatives, India was the lynchpin of the whole empire, the "jewel in the crown," whose loss was inconceivable.

The short-term need for colonial troops and resources in World War I had long-term consequences for the integrity of the empire in India and elsewhere. India already had a strong, constitutional nationalist movement before the war, led by the Indian National Congress, which had been founded in 1885. However, the sacrifices and experiences of Indians during the war fueled and radicalized the independence movement as never before. The reasons were manifold. First, many Indians saw greater independence as the price Britain had to pay for Indian help in the war. Indian nationalists believed that the wartime shortages and increased taxation, as well as the strict censorship laws the British had introduced, were the price of future progress toward devolved self-government and eventual independence.

Second, the prejudice that was suffered by Indian soldiers in the Middle East and on the western front made it clear that the war was not a struggle of imperial equals against a common enemy, but a European-centered war for which an ungrateful Britain needed temporary Indian help. Once the war was over, India's contribution to victory was acknowledged but not rewarded.

Finally, witnessing at first hand white Europeans being killed in huge numbers diminished the prestige of the British in Indian eyes and clearly demonstrated that the British were less than invincible. Therefore, the war changed the attitudes of many previously loyal Indian soldiers and civilians, causing them to question the ideal of empire in a fundamental way.

▼ *Not all Indian nationalists embraced the methods of passive resistance urged by Gandhi. Riots, such as one here in Peshawar in 1930, were put down by British and Indian troops.*

▼ *The Golden Temple at Amritsar, the holiest of Sikh shrines. Amritsar was the scene of the massacre of almost 400 Indians by British-led troops on April 13, 1919. The massacre was a watershed in Anglo-Indian relations and marked the beginning of a sustained campaign for Indian home rule.*

When the war ended, wartime restrictions such as press censorship and imprisonment without trial were not repealed. The Rowlatt Act (or the Anarchical and Revolutionary Crimes Act) deliberately extended this denial of civil rights in 1919. Many Indians felt betrayed, and support for Indian nationalism grew. Protests in the province of Punjab were especially violent and led to the imposition of martial law in an area that had traditionally supplied many recruits to the British-officered Indian Army and local police. This reaction to the Rowlatt Act, which saw unusual levels of cooperation between Hindus, Muslims, and Sikhs, led to the key event in postwar India—the Amritsar massacre.

The massacre was a deliberate attempt by an overzealous British officer to intimidate the increasingly rebellious Punjabis into submission. Tensions in Amritsar, the Sikh holy city, were high after an attack on a group of Europeans left five dead and a female missionary, Frances Sherwood, severely beaten. The local military commander, Brigadier-General Reginald Dyer, issued a number of humiliating communal punishments, including the infamous "crawling order" that required Indians passing the place of the attack to crawl on their hands and knees. A few days later, on April 13, 1919, an unarmed demonstration of around 10,000 people entered the large walled area of Jallianwallah Bagh in

Amritsar. Without any warning, Dyer ordered his 50 Gurkha and Indian troops to fire on the crowd. They kept firing for nearly 10 minutes while the crowd was unable to escape. At least 379 men, women, and children were killed, around 1,200 were wounded, and Dyer made no attempt to offer medical assistance to the injured. Adding insult to injury, he was hailed by imperialists in Britain as the Savior of the Punjab. Dyer was eventually reprimanded by a commission of inquiry and forced to retire on half pay, but he was not court-martialed, and some senior politicians actually passed a resolution condemning his forced retirement.

Indian nationalists saw the failure to punish Dyer adequately as a reflection of British insincerity, despite its rhetoric of reform and devolved power. In the very English words of Jawaharlal Nehru (the future Congress Party leader), Dyer's deed was "absolutely immoral, indecent...the height of bad form." Yet the mixed reaction to Dyer revealed that many in Britain still held a very old-fashioned and authoritarian view of India and how to keep hold of it.

Dyer's massacre was also a frustrated reaction to the most effective demonstrations against British rule in India for decades. A new and inspiring Indian leader, Mohandas Gandhi, had developed a form of peaceful resistance known as the *satyagraha* (truth force). This nonviolent resistance included fasting, demonstrations, the deliberate courting of arrest, the boycott of British goods, and one-day strikes in which all work and commercial activity ceased. These activities intensified after the massacre, developing into a full-fledged noncooperation movement that lasted two years, from 1920 to 1922. By boycotting schools, courts, and other institutions of British power, the movement hoped to achieve self-rule. British control of India came closer to collapse than at any time since the Indian Mutiny of 1857. However, the Rowlatt

KEY FIGURES

MOHANDAS GANDHI

Gandhi (1869–1948) pioneered nonviolent tactics while campaigning for the rights of indentured Indian laborers in British-controlled South Africa. When he returned to India in 1915, he developed a philosophy of *satyagraha* (truth force), which became the cornerstone of his efforts to achieve Indian independence.

It was in the immediate postwar years that Gandhi emerged as the unlikely, but charismatic, spiritual and political leader of India. This passage from his writings summarizes his central belief of *satyagraha*: "Violence is the negation of this great spiritual force, which can only be cultivated or wielded by those who will entirely eschew violence. It is a force that may be used by individuals as well as by communities. It may be used as well in political as in domestic affairs. Its universal applicability is a demonstration of its permanence and invincibility.... Only those who realize that there is something in man which is superior to the brute nature in him and that the latter always yields to it, can effectively be Satyagrahis. This force is to violence, and therefore, to all tyranny, all injustice, what light is to darkness. In politics, its use is based upon the immutable maxim that government of the people is possible only so long as they consent either consciously or unconsciously to be governed."

▲ *Mohandas Gandhi (center) was a lawyer by profession who, from 1915 onward, took a leading role in the struggle for Indian home rule. A passionate believer in nonviolent methods, he became the spirit and soul of Indian nationalism. He was assassinated in 1948, months after independence had been achieved.*

protests and the noncooperation movement often generated violent riots and murders that were not part of Gandhi's strategy. To the surprise of many, Gandhi suddenly called off the protests and subjected himself to three days of fasting as a penance for the violence he had unwittingly unleashed.

However, Gandhi and the *satyagraha* had shaken British rule in India, and both would reemerge as key forces in the eventual independence of the subcontinent. Before Gandhi, Indian nationalist leaders were British-educated, upper-middle-class professionals who wore suits and gave speeches in English. Gandhi, although he was educated as a lawyer in London, added a new Indian and spiritual dimension to the movement. In doing so he broadened its appeal to the masses. Gandhi wore Indian dress at all times, studied the sacred Hindu text, the *Bhagavad Gita*, every day, and steadfastly rejected Western industrialism and materialism in favor of cottage industry and religious communities.

While Indians campaigned for self-rule, the British were trying to implement the Montagu-Chelmsford reforms of 1919. This was the first significant, albeit limited, gesture toward Indian self-rule. Central and provincial assemblies were freely elected by about 10 percent of the male population, and a system of joint Anglo-Indian administration was set up at the provincial level.

Indians usually controlled areas like health, education, and local government affairs, while control of judicial, foreign, military, and most financial matters remained firmly in British hands. This reform and many others that followed were motivated more by a desire to hold on to India for as long as possible than a genuine commitment to eventual independence. Nevertheless, they represented real changes in the nature of government. India received a further measure of self-rule in the Government of India Act of 1935 and then outright independence in 1947. However, this came at the cost of partition into Muslim Pakistan and mainly Hindu India, as well as the deaths of more than a million people in clashes between Hindus and Muslims.

The Middle East

World War I profoundly affected the whole of the Middle East, from Egypt to Iran. The fall of the Turkish Empire created the conditions for new states, new colonies, and new conflicts throughout the region. There was little agreement among the powers that had taken over Turkey's role in the region or the local peoples themselves on the form that the new order should take. Thwarted ambition, contested territory, and thinly disguised imperial self-interest dominated the region's political future.

The Turks had held sway over most of the Middle East for centuries. Their empire's collapse led to conflicting demands for Arab independence, a new Jewish homeland, and a claim on the spoils of victory by Britain, France, Italy, and Greece. Britain and France were the main short-term beneficiaries. Both received mandates from the League of Nations to guide the peoples of the region to independent statehood in Syria (France) and Palestine and Mesopotamia (Britain). This carve up was the result of the prearranged Anglo-French Sykes-Picot agreement of 1916, which flatly contradicted promises made by Britain during World War I to

▼ Lord Louis Mountbatten, the last British governor of India, addresses the Indian parliament as India gains independence, August 15, 1947. Partition of the subcontinent into Muslim and Hindu states (Pakistan and India) followed, amid much violence and bloodshed.

the Arabs as part of Britain's attempt to turn them against their Turkish masters.

Both Britain and France behaved irresponsibly and dishonestly in their new mandates. France arbitrarily carved a new country, Lebanon, out of Syria to create an artificial future state for the local Christians, who were barely in a majority within the new borders. The French subsequently had to face and put down various Arab risings. Britain was happy to concede independence to the Arab tribes of the barren interior of central and southern Arabia, which had few resources and limited strategic significance. This area became an independent Arab kingdom (Saudi Arabia) under Husein, who was the sherif of Mecca. Conversely, in Mesopotamia and near the Persian Gulf, the strategic importance of the region's oil reserves and nearby India to Britain and others complicated the picture.

Britain established Husein's son, Feisal, as a puppet ruler in Mesopotamia (Iraq) to maintain control of its vast oil fields, as well as the strategic overland connection to India. Feisal had wanted to rule in Syria, but this land had been given to France. His brother, Abdullah, was proclaimed emir of Transjordan (Palestine east of the Jordan River), but again under British supervision. This British betrayal of their Arab allies led to an ongoing conflict with Arab tribes. The British also faced a Kurdish rebellion in northern Iraq during this period. In both cases British bombers were used to destroy villages suspected of holding rebels as a new method of "cheap" imperial policing. When combined with considerable concessions in Persia (Iran), Britain emerged from the war in control of huge new oil reserves.

Palestine, where there was no oil and little strategic importance, was divided along the Jordan by the British to create a possible future homeland for the Jews west of the river. By encouraging a Jewish national home in Palestine and promising independence to the Arabs, the

---

POLITICAL WORLD

ZIONISM

In the two decades before World War I, Zionism emerged as a powerful force among European Jews. Its main aim was the creation of a Jewish nation in Palestine beyond the reach of European persecution.

Zionism was a reaction both to increasing anti-Semitism and to the fear that assimilation into the national cultures of Europe would destroy the distinct Jewish identity. In the late nineteenth century, pogroms (Russian for "devastation") were encouraged by Czar Alexander III in Russia and Russian Poland. Pogroms killed thousands of Jews, destroyed their property, and drove over two million to emigrate, mainly to the United States. Anti-semitism was widespread throughout Europe, although less severe in western European countries like Italy and Britain, which both had Jewish leaders before 1914 .

Theodor Herzl was the founder and leading advocate of Zionism until his death in 1904. A highly assimilated Hungarian Jew who had once urged the mass conversion of Jews to Catholicism in the Austro-Hungarian Empire, his latent Jewish identity was roused by the anti-Semitism he witnessed in France. In 1896 he published *The Jewish State: An Attempt at a Modern Solution of the Jewish Question*, which was the founding document of Zionism. The other key figure in early Zionism was Chaim Weizmann, who helped to persuade the British government to issue the Balfour Declaration in 1917. Weizmann became leader of the World Zionist Organization in 1920 and eventually presided over the realization of the Zionist dream when he became the first president of the new state of Israel in 1948.

British had effectively offered the same territory to two different groups, but then remained in charge themselves. The consequences were predictably problematic and often violent. Many European Jews, supporters of the cause of Zionism, advocated the creation of a wholly Jewish state in Palestine. Clashes between Arabs and Jews followed.

The ideals of nationalism endorsed by U.S. president Woodrow Wilson, encouraged the peoples of the Middle East to expect independence after the war. This hope was especially high among the Egyptians, who had existing traditions of independent statehood. Egypt had long been a semi-independent province of the Turkish Empire until creeping British influence had undermined its sovereignty in the 1880s. Because of the Suez Canal, a "friendly" Egypt was deemed essential to Britain's lines of communication to India. By World War I it had become a British colony in all but name, a position that was formalized when Egypt became a British protectorate on the outbreak of war with Turkey in 1914. Seeking real independence from Britain, many Egyptians rebeled in March 1919.

The rising was sparked by the deportation of leaders of the nationalist Wafd (Delegation) movement in March 1919, including their leader Said Zaghlul. This was the movement of the educated class and students that demanded the expulsion of the British and Egypt independence, but poor city dwellers from Cairo, the capital, and Bedouin tribesmen also participated. This national uprising saw rioting, sabotage, and violent mobs in the streets. Britons and other Europeans were attacked all over

▼ *Jewish immigrants from Europe arrive in Haifa, Palestine, 1929. The movement for an independent Jewish state in the region had been gaining momentum since the final decades of the nineteenth century.*

Palestine

At the end of World War I, Britain took charge of Palestine, formerly part of the Turkish Empire. The region was home to a large Arab population but was also claimed by European Jews as their ancestral homeland. Friction between the two groups steadily grew.

Palestine is a narrow strip of land bounded by the Jordan River to the east, the Mediterranean Sea to the west, Lebanon to the north, and the Sinai Desert to the south. It roughly corresponds to the ancient Holy Land and includes Bethlehem, Jerusalem, and Nazareth. Part of the Turkish Empire before and during World War I, Palestine was given to Britain as a mandate after the war. In 1918, it was inhabited mostly by Palestinian Arabs, some 700,000. However, the area was also the ancient homeland of the Jews before they were scattered in the Diaspora during the second century C.E. By 1918, 56,000 Jews remained in Palestine.

Inspired by Zionism, the Jewish movement to reestablish their ancient homeland, Jews began emigrating from Europe to Palestine well before World War I, and their plan received the unexpected support of the British government in 1917. The Balfour Declaration (see Volume 2, page 371) favored "the establishment in Palestine of a national home for the Jewish people," while also promising that "nothing shall be done which may prejudice the civil and religious rights of existing non-Jewish communities in Palestine."

Arthur Balfour, the British foreign secretary, made the promise partly out of a genuine sympathy for the plight of the Jews, partly in an attempt to

▲ *A view of the Jewish quarter in the old city of Jerusalem, seen in 1938. The two synagogues, Tiferet Israel (left) and the Hurva, were destroyed in fighting in 1948.*

gain U.S. Jewish support for the war effort, and partly to encourage revolutionary Russia's continued participation in the conflict. The United States had a small but influential Jewish community, while several Russian Jews were key figures in the Russian Revolution.

As a Jewish state in Palestine would lead to the displacement of local Arabs from land they had occupied for centuries, conflict was inevitable. Jewish settlement in Palestine continued as a small but steady stream in the postwar years, but the

Arabs, who wanted independence after helping Britain defeat their former Turkish rulers, had also developed a strong sense of nationalism. They rejected British rule and began attacking Jewish settlements in 1920. The Jews formed their own self-defense force, the Haganah, in response, and a cycle of inter-communal violence was established. The combination of Zionism and confused British

▲ *The Russian born chemist and Zionist leader, Dr. Chaim Weizmann (1874–1952), the first president of the new nation of Israel, which was established on May 14, 1948.*

signals to both Arab and Jewish nationalists had created a conflict between an increasingly dominant minority immigrant group and a dispossessed indigenous people that continues to the present day.

Egypt. In reaction, 1,500 Egyptians were killed in two months of ferocious policing by the British, who still had considerable numbers of troops in Egypt.

Racial contempt for Egyptians, by both ordinary British soldiers and by their officers, was strong in postwar Egypt and further heightened tensions. The attitude was summed up by General Walter Congreve, who wrote of the Egyptians: "When you talk politics to an Easterner you may be sure you will get the worst of it. Kick him and he loves and respects you." In short, many Egyptians received rough treatment, and the uprising was only fully quelled by the return of Viscount Allenby of Megiddo, who, as General Edmund

▼ *Egyptian soldiers commanded by British officers were used to quell the rioting of Egyptian nationalists in the postwar years. In Egypt, as in India, those who demanded independence from Britain could expect rough treatment.*

Allenby, had defeated the Turks in Palestine during the war. Allenby allowed four Wafd leaders back from exile in a gesture of compromise. He also organized Egyptian "independence" in 1922, but it was subject to British control of the country's defenses and the Suez Canal.

Revolution in China

The war itself had little direct effect on China, but the ideological and diplomatic changes it caused had profound

effects on the country's ongoing struggle for reform, for sovereignty, and for national unity. Since the mid–nineteenth century, China had been subject to unequal treaties with the Western powers, which gave them such wide commercial and legal concessions that they seriously undermined Chinese sovereignty. Dissatisfaction with this state of affairs had led to sporadic outbursts of antiforeigner, nationalist activity.

The Chinese Revolution of 1911–1912 drew on this tradition. It was a nationalist, republican reaction to decades of foreign intervention and an unpopular imperial government compromised by its dealings with the Western powers. The Chinese nationalist republicans, who became the Guomindang in 1912, overthrew the Qing dynasty with the help of Yuan Shikai, the imperial military leader sent to crush them. Yuan Shikai was set up as president of the new republic on March 10, but he immediately quarreled with Sun Yixian (Sun Yat-sen), the head of

▲ *The Chinese revolutionary Sun Yixian (Sun Yat-sen) and his entourage visit the Ming tombs in 1923. The leader of the Guomindang republicans, Sun Yixian was an influential voice for the unification of China.*

627

▲ Sun Yixian, the first president of the Republic of China, with his wife and staff officers shortly before his death in 1925. Sun Yixian had joined with the communists to take on the Chinese warlords. However, his successor, Jiang Jieshi, broke with the communists, leading to two decades of internal strife in China.

Guomindang republicans, after accepting a foreign loan to stabilize the new regime. Following a brief struggle, the nationalists were defeated, Sun Yixian fled the country, and the Guomindang was banned, despite the fact that it was the majority party in both houses of the new parliament.

But Yuan's hold on power was tenuous, and he became extremely unpopular when he accepted almost all of Japan's 21 Demands in 1915 (see Volume 1, page 258). This humiliating package of concessions and privileges threatened to make China a satellite of Japan. Yuan's attempt to make himself emperor then caused the breakaway of several southern provinces, and by his death in June 1916, China had been plunged into chaos. From 1916 to 1928, warlords and regional governors, controlling large areas of China, paid little heed to what remained of the central government in Beijing.

By the end of World War I, the nationalists had destroyed the old government but had not replaced it with their own. Neither had they been able to assert China's independence from the European powers, Japan, and the United States. China had been on the Allied side in the war since 1917, but it was ill rewarded at the Paris peace talks. Its fellow ally Japan had been allowed to take over Germany's concessions in China. In protest, China walked out of the talks, and domestic outrage gave rise to the May Fourth Movement—named after the spontaneous demonstrations on May 4, 1919, that followed news of the Japanese gains at Versailles.

Students, workers, and even the middle classes took part in nationwide strikes, demonstrations, and a boycott of Japanese goods. The movement was a specific example of a widespread reaction to Chinese backwardness and subservience. The traditional Confucian outlook placed great emphasis on respect for authority and little on democracy or scientific inquiry. Reformers sought to industrialize and modernize China in order to resist foreign interference, much as Japan had done a generation earlier. Thus, World War I had both direct and indirect consequences for China. It allowed increased involvement in its affairs by Japan, but the ideals of self-determination that came out of the war also inspired movements for national regeneration and unity.

The Chinese mines and railroads given to Japan were eventually handed back as part of the Washington Agreement in 1922, but foreign involvement in China continued. When Sun Yixian, who reformed the Guomindang in 1920, estab-

▼ *The Japanese Imperial Army was a major force in China, where it took over German concessions at the conclusion of the Treaty of Versailles. China resented the fact that its own efforts in the Allied cause during the conflict had largely gone unrewarded.*

▶ *Jiang Jieshi (Chiang Kai-shek) stands next to Sun Yixian. In 1923, when this photograph was taken, Jiang was rapidly becoming Sun's most trusted young commander, a man who had a reputation for dealing with the renegade warlords who Sun believed had to be crushed if China was to become a fully unified nation. Jiang eventually succeeded Sun as leader of the United Front.*

lished a stronghold in Canton in 1923, his attempts to seize the customs revenues there met with French and British opposition. This money was designated for repayment of loans, and China's recent allies had no intention of renouncing them. The Beijing government had earlier faced similar prob-

lems. China had been granted a suspension of "reparations" payments for the antiforeigner Boxer Rebellion of 1900 while the war lasted, but Beijing came under pressure to resume indemnities in 1919.

Internally, the immediate aftermath of World War I was an especially confused and lawless period in China. Warlords, private armies, and bandits held sway over vast territories and offered little to the peasants but extortion and violence. The most infamous example of lawlessness was the kidnapping of 300 passengers, including 20 foreigners—mostly U.S. citizens—from a train at Lincheng on the main Shanghai-Peking line in 1923. Bizarrely, the weak government was unable to secure their release for a month until they allowed the bandits to become a unit in the Chinese Army. The Western powers then demanded compensation simply because they could. This sort of anarchy and foreign bullying epitomized the problems of early twentieth-century China. It also naturally strengthened support for the nationalists and for the small but growing Chinese Communist Party.

The Guomindang increasingly turned to Moscow for help in the face of Western imperialism, and in return for Soviet assistance they permitted Chinese Communist Party members to join the Guomindang. The two parties created the United Front against the warlords, and Communists like Mao Zedong rose to prominent positions in the Guomindang. When Sun died in 1925, the leader of the Guomindang's military academy, Jiang Jieshi (Chiang Kai-shek) assumed control. The party became less radical, and relations with the communists began to sour.

Jiang Jieshi then led the Northern Expedition in 1926 which was an operation intended to topple the lawless warlords and to unite China. After taking Shanghai, he turned on his communist allies in the Shanghai Coup of 1927, murdering any communist he could capture. Beijing was taken the following year, but the new nationalist government never established full control over the warlords or the communists. Jiang's treachery initiated two decades of intermittent struggle with the communists, leading ultimately to his own downfall at their hands in 1947.

KEY FIGURES

MAO ZEDONG

Mao Zedong (1893–1976) was one of the most important political leaders of the twentieth century. As the leader of the Chinese Communist Party and first chairman of the People's Republic of China, a position he held from 1949 until his death, Mao presided over a huge social and political transformation in the most populous nation on earth.

Mao was active in the Guomindang during the first United Front and was a leader of the Jiangxi Soviet in the 1930s. Facing extermination at the hands of Jiang Jieshi, he led the famous Long March through China in 1934, which ensured the survival of the party at a terrible cost in lives— only 8,000 out of over 80,000 survived the 6,200-mile (10,000 km) journey. Mao's great theoretical innovation was the adaptation of Marxist revolutionary theory to a country with a large peasantry and a small urban working class. In a 1927 report on a peasant uprising, he predicted that a revolutionary peasantry would be the key element for communist revolution in China.

He wrote, "In a very short time... several hundred million peasants will rise like a mighty storm, like a hurricane, a force so swift and violent that no power, however great, will be able to hold it back. They will smash all the trammels that bind them and rush along the road to liberation. They will sweep all the imperialists, warlords, corrupt officials, and evil gentry in their graves." The success of the Chinese revolution was overwhelmingly due to his vision.

BIBLIOGRAPHY

Beaverbrook, Lord. *Politicians and the War 1914–1918*. London: T. Butterworth Ltd., 1928.

Bennett, G. *Naval Battles of the First World War*. Newton Abbot: David and Charles, 1972.

Bruce, Anthony. *An Illustrated Companion to the First World War*. New York: Penguin USA, 1989.

Evans, Martin Marix. *Retreat, Hell! We just Got Here! The American Expeditionary Force in France, 1917–1918*. London: Osprey, 1998.

Feur, A.B., et al. *The US Navy in World War I*. New York: Praeger, 1999.

Gilbert, Martin. *First World War*. New York: Henry Holt & Co., 1996.

Gilbert, Martin. *Atlas of the First World War*. New York: Oxford University Press, 1994.

Graves, R. *Good-Bye to All That*. London: Jonathan Cape, 1929.

Gray, Randal, and Argyle, Christopher. *Chronicle of the First World War*. New York: Facts on File, 1991.

Griffiths, W.R. *The Great War* (West Point Military History series). Wayne, New Jersey: Avery Publishing Group, 1986.

Haythornthwaite, P.J. *The World War One Source Book*. London: Arms and Armour Press, 1992.

Herwig, H.H., and Heyman, N.M. *Biographical Dictionary of World War I*. Westport, Connecticut: Greenwood Press, 1982.

Joll, James. *The Origins of the First World War*. New York: Longman, 1984.

Keene, Jennifer D. *The United States and the First World War*. Reading, Mass.: Addison-Wesley, 2000.

Kennedy, David M. *Over Here: The First World War and American Society*. New York: Oxford University Press, 1986.

MacDonald, Lyn. *1914–1918: Voices and Images of the Great War*. New York: Penguin USA, 1991.

Mead, Gary. *The Doughboys: America and the First World War*. Woodstock, N.Y.: Overlook Press, 2000.

Miles, Paul, and Cipriano Venzon, Anne. *The United States in the First World War: An Encyclopedia*. New York: Garland Publishing, 1999.

Pope, Stephen, and Wheal, Elizabeth-Anne. *Dictionary of the First World War*. New York: St. Martin's Press, 1995.

Preston, A. *Battleships of World War I: An Illustrated Encyclopedia*. Harrisburg, Pennsylvania: Stackpole Books, 1972.

Thayer, J.A. *Italy and the Great War*. Madison, Wisconsin: University of Wisconsin Press, 1964.

Thomas, Gill. *Life on All Fronts: Women in the First World War*. New York: Cambridge University Press, 1989.

Winter, Denis. *Death's Men: Soldiers of the Great War*. New York: Penguin USA, 1996.

INDEX

Page numbers in *italics* refer to picture captions.

A

Abdullah, emir of Transjordan 372, 373, 622
Abyssinia (Ethiopia) 536, 545, 547
Adriatic Sea 510–*511*
Africa
  postwar colonial transfers 540, 614
  war in the colonies 381–382, *496–500*
African Americans
  internal migration 601–604, 610–611
  and racism (1920s) 601–604
  in the war *418*
aircraft *429*
  air support in British waters *503*
  antisubmarine 393
  at the Italian front (1918) 480
  at the Second Battle of the Marne 441–442
Aisne, Third Battle of the (Operation Blücher) 424–430
  casualties *431*
Aisne-Marne Offensive 442–445
Albania 485, 536, 545
Alberich, Operation 333, 335
Albert I, king of Belgium 518, 519
Alexander III, czar of Russia 622
Alexandra, czarina of Russia *471*
Alexey, prince of Russia *471*
Allenby, Edmund *489*
  and Egypt (postwar) 626
  and Palestine (1917) 369, 370–371, 374–375, *376*, 489
  and Palestine (1918) *488*, 489, 490, 491
  and the western front 335, 489
Allies
  casualties *528*
  postwar consequences 550–*569*
  Supreme War Council 346, 383, 410–411
Alsace-Lorraine 538
  returned to France 533, 534, *539*, *576*
American Expeditionary Force (AEF) *404*
  Army divisions 420–421
  first contingents 419
  nurses 460–*461*
  Pershing's organization of 419–422
  replacement troops for 454

  supply lines to 453, *454*
  telephonists (Hello Girls) 427, 460
  training *420*, 421
  transatlantic transportation 505–508, *509*
  and war artists *434*, *440*, *459*
  weapons and equipment *428–429*
  on the western front (1917) 419
  on the western front (July–August 1918) 439–*444*, 447–448, 449
  on the western front (March–July 1918) 422–*435*
  on the western front (September–November 1918) *452–469*, 516–517, 518
  see also United States Army
American Relief Administration 588–589
Amiens 405, 412, 413
Amiens, Battle of *444*, 447–450, *451*
Amritsar
  Golden Temple *618*
  massacre (1919) *618*–619
Anglo-Irish Treaty (1921) 563
Anthony, Susan B. 591, 602
anti-Semitism, in Germany 575
antisubmarine warfare, Allies' use of 390–393, 503
Antoine, François 343
April Theses 352, 353
Arabia, uprisings in 372–*373*
Argentina, postwar *614*
Armenia 495, 585
Armenians, genocide of 529, 585
armistice 520, 521–522, 523–526, 575–576
  on the eastern front 360, *361*, 471–472
  Europe after the 530–*549*
armored vehicles *414*, 450, *477*
Arnim, Sixt von 342–343, 414
Arras 334, 335
Arras, Battle of *331*, *332*, *334*, 335–357, 339
  Vimy Ridge, Battle of *335*–366
artillery
  Allied (1918) 517
  and "creeping" barrage *334*, 336, 408
  movement of *330*

  in Palestine *375*
  of storm troopers *359*
  Turkish *369*
  used by Germany (1918) *406*, 407, *408*, 409, *426*
  see also field guns; howitzers
artists, war *434*, *440*, *459*
Arz von Staussenberg, Artur 480
askaris *498*, *500*
Associated Powers 452
Atatürk *see* Mustafa Kemal Atatürk
Atlantic Fleet 509–510
Australia
  postwar 613
  soldiers 374, *416*, *447*, *448*, 517, 518
  see also Australian Mounted Division; Desert Mounted Corps
Australian Mounted Division 374, *490*
Austria
  and *Anschluss* with Germany 582
  armistice 523
  separation from Hungary 523, 543, 582
Austria-Hungary
  after the armistice 530
  casualties *529*
  eastern front (1918) 470
  peace moves (1918) 519
  postwar break-up 523, 543, 582–583
  surrender of the fleet 511
  war at the Italian front (1917) 382–383
  war at the Italian front (1918) *479–482*
  see also Austro-Hungarian Army; Austro-Hungarian Navy
Austro-German Army
  Fourteenth Army 382
  South Army 354, 355
Austro-Hungarian Army
  Eleventh Army 480
  Fifth Army 480
  Sixth Army 480
  Tenth Army 480
Austro-Hungarian Navy, and the Otranto Barrage 396–397
automobiles, U.S. *608*, 609
Auxiliaries 562, 563
Azerbaijan 495

B

Baghdad *378*, 380, *381*
Baldwin, Stanley *559*–560
Balfour, Arthur 369, *371*, 493, 624–625
Balfour Declaration *371*, 493, 496, 624
Balkans
  and the eastern front (1917) 361–365
  and the eastern front (1918) 483–*485*
Baltic Sea 397–399
Baltic states 477–478
barrage, "creeping" *334*, 336, 408
Baruch, Bernard 535
Bauhaus movement 582, *583*
Bavaria, postwar politics 570, 573–575, 580
Beatty, David 513
Beersheba 370–371
Belfort 456–457
Belgium, liberation 518
Belknap, Reginald 507
Belleau Wood, Battle of *430*, 432–435
Bellicourt 518
Below, Fritz von 337
Below, Otto von 382, 411, 517
Benson, William 387
Berthelot, Henri 440
Besant, Annie 616
"black day of the German Army" 449
Black Sea Fleet 399–400
Black and Tans 562
blockades, of the Central Powers 502, 529
Bloc National 553, 555
Bloody Sunday 563
Blücher, Operation *see* Aisne, Third Battle of the
Boehn, Maximilian von 337, 424, 430, 439
Bolsheviks 353, 356, 360, *361*, 399, *471*, 472, 588
  and the Red Scare 592–593
  and the Russian Civil War 530, 586
  see also Russian Revolution
Boroevic von Bojna, Svetozar 480
Bosnia 543
Bosporus 399
Bratianu, Ion 365
Brazil 500, 614
Brecht, Bertold 579–582
Brest-Litovsk
  armistice talks 360, *361*, 471–472
  Treaty of (1918) 361, 473, *476*, 585
Briand, Aristide 548–549, 554, 555
Britain
  campaign in Mesopotamia (1917) 376–381

campaign in Mesopotamia (1918) 488, 492, *493*
  casualties *528*, 529
  fighting for Palestine (1917) 366–*376*
  fighting for Palestine (1918) 489–492
  home front 502
  and Ireland (postwar) 560–564
  and the Paris Peace Conference 535–536
  postwar economic and social problems 551, *557*–560, 595
  and the western front (1917) 331, 335–357
  and the western front (1918) 404, 410–*412*, 413–415, 517, 518–*519*
  and the western front (Somme; 1916) 328
  see also British Army; Royal Flying Corps; Royal Navy
British Army 331
  57th Division *523*
  Fifth Army 336, 342, 343, *412*, 413, 518–519
  First Army 335, 336–337, 414, 517
  Fourth Army 448, 518
  Second Army 343, 344, 414, 415, 518–519
  Third Army 335, 336–337, 345, *412*, 413
British Expeditionary Force (BEF), under French command 329
British Honduras 614
Broodseinde, Battle of 344
brownshirts *579*, 580–*581*
Bruchmüller, Georg 406, 407
Bruges 505
Bruges Canal *505*
Brusilov, Alexey 354
Bucharest, Treaty of 479, 484
Bulgaria
  casualties *529*
  eastern front (1918) 470, 483, *484*–485
  lands lost (postwar) 543
  peace moves (1918) 519
Bullard, Robert Lee *422*–423, 466, 467
Byng, Julian 335–336, *412*, 413

C

Cadorna, Luigi 382, 383
California, in the 1920s 609
Cambrai 446–447, 516, 517–518, 521
Cambrai, Battle of 345–347
Cameron, George 457, 467
Cameroon 540, 614

Canada, postwar exports 613
Canadian soldiers 448, 517–518
  and the Battle of Vimy Ridge *335*–366
Cantigny, battle at 422, *423*–424, *430*
Caporetto, Battle of 359, *382*, 383
casualties *528*–529
  on the western front (1917) *346*, 347
  on the western front (1918) *415*, *431*, 436, *444*, 469
  on the western front (by 1917) 329
Catt, Carrie Chapman *591*, *592*, 593
Cattaro 510, 511
Caucasus, war in the (1918) 487, 492, 494–495
cease-fire 526
Central America 500, *613*–614
Central Powers, casualties *529*
Charles I, emperor of Austria 451, 530
Château-Thierry 426, *430*
Chauvel, Harry 369
Chetwode, Philip 366, 369
Chiang Kai-shek (Jiang Jieshi) *630*, 631
Chicago, riots (1917) 604
China
  and Japan 628–*629*
  Long March 631
  postwar *627*, *628*–631
  Revolution (1911–1912) 627–628
  Shantung province 540
  Sun Yixian as president *627*, 628
  supporting the Allies 501
Churchill, Winston 534
  eyewitness account 535
Clemenceau, Georges *347*, 410, 467
  and the Paris Peace Conference *532*, 534, *537*
  and Pershing 458, 468
  postwar 552, 553–554
Collins, Michael 562, 563
colonies
  British 614–*621*
  French (postwar) 556–557
  German colonies lost (postwar) 539–540
Communism
  in China 631
  in Russia 587–589
Compiègne, armistice signed at *524*–525, 526
Conrad von Hötzendorf, Franz, and the Italian front (1918) 480, 481
Constantine I, king of Greece 361–364

Constantinople (*now* Istanbul)
  and Russia 399
  and the Treaty of Sèvres *544*
convoy system, Allied 387–390, 502, *503*
Coolidge, Calvin *604*, 605, 607
Costa Rica 500, *613*
costs, financial, to the Allies 550–551
Côte Dame Marie 465
Courtrai, Battle of 518
Cox, James M. 604–605
Currie, Arthur 517–518
Czech Legion *471*, 474, 475
Czechoslovakia 523, 540, 543, 582

D

Dalmatia 536, 545
Daly, Dan 432
Damascus *488*, 492
  uprisings (1925) 557
Daniels, Josephus 387
D'Annunzio, Gabriele *545*
Danzig (Gdansk) 538, 547
Dardanelles, postwar 544, 584
Dawes, Charles 578, 579
Dawes Plan 555, 578, 579, 605
Debeney, Eugène 447, 518
Debs, Eugene V. 593
debts, national, postwar 550–551, 595
"defense in depth" 331, 333
Degoutte, Jean 433, 440
Denikin, Anton 586–587
depth charges 393, 503
Dera'a 491–492
Derventer, Jacob van 381
deserters, AEF 466
Desert Mounted Corps 369, 371, *375*
de Valera, Éamon 562, 563
Deventer, Jacob van 498, *500*
Diaspora 624
Diaz, Armando 383, 479, 482
Dickman, Joseph 426, 440, 457
diseases
  in East Africa 499
  vitamin-deficiency 488
Dobell, Charles 367–368, 369
Dorpat, Treaty of 478
Dover Straits, antisubmarine blockade 504, *507*
dreadnought battleships *510*
Duchêne, Denis 425
Duma (Russian parliament) 350, 352
Dunkirk 415
Dunn, Harvey *459*
Dunsterforce expedition *487*, 492
Dunsterville, L.C. 494
Dyer, Reginald 618–619

E

East Africa *see* German East Africa;
  Portuguese East Africa
East Asia Coprosperity Sphere 548
Eastern Force 367–368
eastern front
  during 1917 *348–365*
  during 1918 471–477
  storm troopers 358–*359*
Ebert, Friedrich 526, 527, 572, 577
economic consequences, to the Allies 550–551
Education Act (1918) 557
Egypt, nationalism and independence 623–*626*
Eighteenth Amendment 611
Einem, Karl von 439
Eisner, Kurt 570, *571*, 574, 575
Ekaterinburg *471*, 475
Ellis Island *594*, *600*
Emergency Quota Act (1917) 600
Emperor's Battle *see* Michael, Operation
English Channel, blockaded 504, *507*
Erzberger, Matthias 520, 523–526
Espionage Act (1917) 593
Estonia 477–478, 548
Europe, after the armistice 530–*549*

F

Facta, Luigi 566–567
Falkenhausen, General von 337
Falkenhayn, Erich von, and Palestine 371, 374
Fall, Albert 606
Faustschlag, Operation 472
Fehzi Pasha 374
Feisal I, king of Mesopotamia 373, 531, 622
Ferdinand I, king of Bulgaria 484
Ferdinand I, king of Romania 365, 479
field guns, German *468*
Finland 477, 478, 548
Fiume (Rijeka) 536, *545*
Flanders Army Group 518
Foch, Ferdinand 346, *410*, 412, 414, 438, 440, 445–446
  and the armistice *524*, 526
  and Germany's defeat 515
  and the St. Mihiel attack 455–456
Fontainebleau Memorandum 535–536
Ford, Henry *608*
Ford, Model T *608*, 609
Fordney-McCumber tariffs 595, 605
Fourteen Points 403, 482, 493
  armistice based on 520, 521–522

and the Paris Peace Conference 532–533
France
  casualties *528*, 529
  colonies (postwar) 556–557
  Maginot Line 555–*556*
  occupation of the Ruhr 555, 578–579
  and the Paris Peace Conference 534–535
  postwar mandates in the Middle East 544, 557, 622
  postwar reconstruction and recovery 550, 551–556
  and the Treaty of Versailles 538, 540, 555
  and the western front (1917) *330–331*, 335, 337–339
  and the western front (1918) 404, *405*, 409, 410, 413–*414*, *431*
  see also French Army
Franchet d'Espérey, Louis 425, 484, 485
Freikorps 572, *574*, 575
French Army 330–331
  Fifth Army 337, 440
  First Army 343, 422–423, 447, 448, 518
  Fourth Army 439, 462–463
  mutiny (1917) 338–339
  Sixth Army 337, 425, 440
  tanks *405*, *423*
  Tenth Army 442
  Third 430

G

Galicia *354*, 543
Gallwitz, Max von 463
Gandhi, Mohandas *616*, *617*, *619*, *620*
gas *406*
  poison 403, 407
  tear 407
Gaza 367–368, 370, 371
Gaza, First Battle of 368
Gaza, Second Battle of 368–369
Gaza, Third Battle of 374, 489
General Strike *558*, *559*, *560*
German Army
  Eighteenth Army 423, 430
  Eighth Army 411
  Fifth Army 463
  First Army 337, 424, 439
  Fourth Army 342–343, 414
  postwar reduction 540
  Second Army 346, 411, 448, 517
  Seventeenth Army 411, 517
  Seventh Army 337, 424, 430, 439, 440, 442

Sixth Army 336, 414
Third Army 439
see also storm troopers
German Communist Party 572
German East Africa 381–382, *496–497*,
499, *500*
Germany loses (postwar) 540, 614
German National Socialist Workers'
Party (Nazi Party) 579, 580
German Navy
destroyer action (1917) 394–395
surrender *512–513*
see also High Seas Fleet
German South West Africa, Germany
loses (postwar) 540
Germany
armistice 520, 521–522, 523–526,
575–576
casualties *529*
collapse *514–527*
"defense in depth" 331, 333
the eastern front (1917) 353–361
effects of the Allied blockades on
502
expansion into Eastern Europe
(1918) *472–473*, 476–477
home front 514–515, 523
new Parliamentary regime (1918)
519–520
postwar arts 579–582, *583*
postwar economy *571*, 578–582
postwar political upheaval 526–527,
530, 570–578, 579, 580–581
postwar territories lost *538–540*
reparations 522, 534–535, 540–542,
555, 578, 606
and the Treaty of Versailles *536*,
537–542, 576, 577
war guilt 540–541, 548
Weimar Republic *573*, 576–582
the western front (1917) 329–347
the western front (July–August
1918) 438–*451*
the western front (March–June
1918; spring offensive) *402–417*,
418–434, 436–437, *438*
the western front
(September–November 1918) *514*,
515–519, 520–*521*, *523*
see also German Army; German Navy
Giolitti, Giovanni *565*, 566, 567
Gough, Hubert 336, 342, 343, 412, 413
Gouraud, Henri 439, 462–463
Government of India Act (1935) 621
Government of Ireland Act (1920)
562
Grand Fleet 508–509

6th Battle Squadron 509
Graves, William *474*, 475
Great Depression *596*
Greater Syria 493
Greece
and the Balkan campaign (1917)
361–364, *365*
war against Turkey 585
Gribble, Bernard F. *512*
Groener, Wilhelm 477
Gröner, Wilhelm 523, 527
Gropius, Walter 582, *583*
Guillaumat, Marie 365, 484

H

Haig, Douglas 328, 331, 335, *347*
and the Battle of Amiens 447
and Germany's defeat 515
and the Third Battle of Ypres 339,
342, 345
and the western front (1918) 410,
412, 413–415
Harding, Warren G. 593, *604–605*,
606, *607*
Harlem Hellfighters *418*
Hazebrouck, Battle of 414, *437*
Hejaz 544
Helgoland 395
Helgoland Bight *395*
Hello Girls 427, 460
Henderson, R.G.A. 389
Herriot, Edouard 555
Hertling, Georg von 437–438, 442
High Seas Fleet 509
scuttled at Scapa Flow *540*
surrender *512–513*
see also German Navy
Hindenburg, Paul von 403, 434–435,
472
and Germany's collapse 515, 519,
520, 570
president of the republic *577*
Hindenburg Line *see* Siegfried Line
Hintze, Paul von 435
Hipper, Franz von 512, 513
Hitler, Adolf 525, 529, 535, 549, 555,
579
eyewitness account 579
and the Munich Putsch 580–581
Ho Chi Minh 556
Hoffmann, Maximilian 472
Hollywood 609–610
Holtzendorff, Henning von 385
Hoover, Herbert 588–589, 605–606,
607
Hoover, J. Edgar 592, 593
Horne, Henry 335, 414, 517

Horthy, Miklós 396–39 7, 511, 583
Housing Act (1919) 557
howitzers *334*, *354*, *366*, *406*, *446*, *495*
Hungary
invasion by Romania (1919) 583
separation from Austria 523, 543,
582–583
Hunter, Francis, eyewitness account
513
Husein Ibn Ali 372, 622
Hutier, Oskar von 357, *359*, *403*, 411,
423, 430

I

Immigration Act (1917) 600
India
and Britain 614–*621*
independence *621*
soldiers serving in East Africa *499*
soldiers serving in Mesopotamia
492
soldiers serving in Palestine 490
Indian National Congress 616
Indochina 556
infiltration tactics *see* storm troopers
influenza pandemic 434, 462, 529,
531
International Labor Organization
547
International Woman Suffrage
Alliance 591
Iraq 475
Kurdish rebellion 622
Ireland
Easter Rising 561
partition and independence
560–564
Irish Free State *563*
Irish Republican Army (IRA) 562, 563
Isonzo, Twelfth Battle of the *see*
Caporetto, Battle of
Israel 622, *625*
Italian Army
Second Army 382
Tenth Army 482
Third Army 480
Italian front
in 1917 359, *382–383*
in 1918 *479–482*, *483*
German storm troopers 359
U.S. forces at the 482
Italy
casualties *528*
lands gained (postwar) 544
and the Paris Peace Conference
536, 544–545
postwar national debt 550–551

postwar road to fascism *564–568*
the war at sea *510–511*
see also Italian Army; Italian front

J

James, Edwin L., eyewitness account
  432
Janis, Elsie *461*
Japan 501
  and China 628–*629*
  naval contribution *400–401*, 501
  postwar power 568–*569*, *613*
  problems with peace (postwar)
    545–*518*
  and Russia (1918) 475, 586
  and the United States 501
jazz *609*, 610–11
Jefford, F.R.J, eyewitness account 345
Jerusalem *624*
  falls to the British 374–*376*, 489
Jews
  anti-Semitism in Germany 575
  "national home" in Palestine 371,
    493, 622, *623*, 624–625
  Zionism 622, 624, 625
Jiang Jieshi (Chiang Kai-shek) *630*,
  631
Joseph, Archduke 481, 583

K

Kahr, Gustav, Ritter von 581
Kaiserschlaft see Michael, Operation
Kapp, Wolfgang 577–578
Kapp Putsch *574*, 577
Károlyi von Nagkároly, Mihály 523
Kellogg-Briand Pact (1928) 554, 605
Kemal, Mustafa *see* Mustafa Kemal
  Atatürk
Kerensky, Alexander 354, 356
Kerensky Offensive 354–356, 398
Keynes, John Maynard *541*, 542
Khalil Pasha 377, 380
Kharkov 476, 477
Kiel Mutiny 512, 513, 523, 570
Kiev 473, 476
Kolchak, Alexander 399, 586, 587
Kornilov, Lavrenti 355, 357, 360, 472
Kress von Kressenstein, Friedrich 367,
  368, 369
Kriemhilde Line 462
Kühlmann, Richard von 434–435
Ku Klux Klan *601*
Kurds 584–585, 622
Kurland 350, *351*
Kut-el-Amara 377, 378, *379–380*

L

Langemarck, Battle of *329*, 344
Latvia 477, 548
Lausanne, Treaty of (1923) 544, *584*
Lawrence, T.E. (Lawrence of Arabia)
  372, 373, 490
  eyewitness account 492
League of Nations *see* Nations,
  League of
Lebanon, postwar 544, 622
Lenin, V.I. *352, 353*, 356, 360, 473,
  587–588, 589
Leopold, Prince of Bavaria 472
Lettow-Vorbeck, Paul von 381–382,
  496–500
Leviné, Eugen 574, 575
Liebknecht, Karl 526–527, *572, 573,
  575*
Liggett, Hunter 457, 467, 468
Lille 446–447, 521, *523*
Liman von Sanders, Otto 376, 489,
  491
Lithuania 477, 538, 548
Little Entente 554
Lloyd George, David *371*
  addresses postwar economic and
    social problems 557–558
  and the Paris Peace Conference
    532, 533–534, 535–536
  and the war at sea 387
  and the western front (1917)
    328–*329*, 345
  and the western front (1918) 410
Locarno Treaty (1925) 554, 555
Lodge, Henry Cabot *598*
Loos *530*
Ludendorff, Erich 327–328
  and Allied counteroffensives
    (July–August 1918) 438, 444–445,
    449, 450–451
  and German offensives (March–July
    1918) 403, 404–409, 411,
    412–413, 414, 415, 418–419,
    424–426, 430, 431, 434–435, 436,
    437, 440, 442
  and Germany's collapse 515, 519,
    520, 522–523, 570, 576
  and the Munich Putsch 581
  quoted on war 548–549
  resignation 522–523
  and Russia 472
  and the Siegfried Line 331, 332, 337
Luxemburg, Rosa 526, 527, *572*, 573,
  575
Lys Offensive (Operation Georgette)
  412, 414–415

M

MacArthur, Douglas *439*
machine guns 428
Maginot Line 555–*556*
Manchuria 547, 548
Mangin, Charles 337, 338, 431, 442
Mannerheim, Karl *478*
Mann, Thomas 579–582
Mao Zedong *631*
March on Rome 566, *567*
Marne, First Battle of the 438
Marne, Second Battle of the 431,
    438–*442*
  Aisne-Marne Offensive 442–445
  casualties *444*
Marshall, William 381, 492
Marwitz, Georg von der 345–346,
  411, 448, 517
Marx, Karl 588
Matteotti Crisis 568, *568*
Maude, Frederick 377, 378, 379, 380,
  381, 492
Max of Baden, Prince 520, 522, *526*,
  576
May Fourth Movement 629
Mayo, Henry 506, 509
Mediterranean
  Italian Navy in *510*–511
  U-boats *503*
  war at sea (1917) 395–397
Megiddo, Battle of 489
Mehmed VI, sultan of Turkey 530
Mein Kampf (book) 579, 581
Menin Road, Battle of the *344*
Mesopotamia
  British campaign in (1917) 376–381
  British campaign in (1918) *487*,
    488, 492, *493*
Messines Ridge, Battle of *338*,
  339–342
Meuse-Argonne Offensive 422,
  459–469, 516
Michael, Operation (Second Battle of
  the Somme; *Kaiserschlacht*;
  Emperor's Battle) 406, 410,
  411–414, *415*
Middle East *378*
  battles (1918) *487*–488
  postwar 621–*626*
  see also Caucasus; Egypt;
    Mesopotamia; Palestine;
    Sykes-Picot Agreement
Milne, George 364, 485
mines, antisubmarine 392, 504,
  506–50 7
mine warfare (tunnels) *340–341*, 342

Mitchell, Billy 441–442
Mons 527
Montfaucon Ridge 464, *469*
Moon Sound, Battle of 399
Moscow, and the Civil War 586–587
Munich
    Beer-Hall Putsch 580–*581*
    postwar 573, 574
Murray, Archibald 366, 367
Mussolini, Benito 545, *564*, 566, *567*,
    568
Mustafa Kemal Atatürk 544, 583, 584,
    584
mutiny
    in the French Army (1917) 338–339
    Kiel Mutiny 512, 513, 523, 570

N

Nations, League of 533, 538, 539, 544,
    546–*547*, 597, 598, *599*
    mandates in the Middle East 621
naval war *see* sea, war at
navies, and the Washington
    Conference 548, 605, *606*
Nazi Party 579, 580
Nehru, Jawaharlal 619
Neuilly, Treaty of (1920) 543
New Zealand
    postwar 613
    soldiers 490
Nicholas II, czar of Russia 349
    abdication 351
    held by the Bolsheviks 471, 475
    killed 475
Nineteenth Amendment 591,
602–*603*
Nivelle, Robert 330, 335, 338
Nivelle Offensive 335, *336*, *337*–338,
    364
    casualties *346*
Northern Barrage 504–505, 506–*507*
North Sea
    activity in (1917) 384
    blockaded 502, 504–505, 506–50*7*
    German raids in (1917) 394–395
Noyon-Montdidier Offensive *431*
nurses 460–*461*

O

Oppressed Nationalities, Congress of
    482–483
Orlando, Vittorio 481, *532*, 567
Otranto Barrage *396*–397, 510

P

Pacific, Germany loses islands (post
    war) 540, 568

Palestine 624
    creation of a Jewish national home
    in 371, 493, 622, *623*, 624–625
    the fight for (1917) 366–*376*
    the fight for (1918) *487*, 488–392, 516
    under British control (postwar) 544,
    622
    see also Balfour Declaration;
    Sykes-Picot Agreement
Palmer, Mitchell 592–593
Paris Peace Conference 531–537,
    596–*597*
    and the Arab nations 373
    and China 628–629
    see also Versailles, Treaty of
Passchendaele *see* Ypres, Third Battle of
People's Commissars, Council of 527,
    571
Pershing, John J. 419–422, 426
    and deserters 466
    and the western front (1918) 452,
    453, 455, 456, 458, 459, 464,
    466–467, 468
Pétain, Henri-Philippe 335
    deals with army mutiny (1917)
    338–339
    and U.S. troops 409
    and the western front (1918) 409,
    410, 413–414, 440, 469
Petrograd *348*, 357
    November Revolution 360
    unrest (1917) *350*–351, *353*
    Winter Palace 399
Petrograd Soviet of Workers and
    Soldiers Deputies 351–352
Piave, Battle of the 481, *482*, 483
Pilckem, Battle of 343
Pilsudski, Józef 363, 587
Plumer, Herbert 339–342, 343, 344,
    414, 415
poets, Carl Sandburg 595
Poincaré, Raymond *552*, 554, 555
Pola 510, 511
Poland
    German policy in (1918) 477
    and independence 362–*363*, 523,
    542
    Russian attempt to reconquer (1920)
    587
    and the Treaty of Versailles *538*,
    539, 543
Polish Corridor 538, 549
Polygon Wood, Battle of 344
Portuguese Army 414, *415*
Portuguese East Africa *497*–499
prisoners of war, German *467*

production, industrial, decline 550
Prohibition *610*, 611

Q

Q-ships 390–391
Queenstown 391, 508

R

raiders, surface *392*, *393*
railroads 446
    French 446–447
Rapallo, Treaty of 578
Rapallo Conference 346, 347, 383
Rathenau, Walther 575
rationing, in Britain 502
Rawlinson, Henry 413, 448, 518
Red Army 475, 586, 587
Red Guard, Finnish 478
Red Scare (1919–1920) 566, 592–*593*,
    600
Refugee Organization 547
Reims 437, 439
Reparations Commission 578
Representation of the People Act
    (1918) 558
Rhineland, postwar demilitarization
    540, 555
Rickenbacker, Edward *429*, 442
Rietz, Deneys, eyewitness account 517
rifles 428
Riga 357, 398
Riga, Treaty of (1921) 587
Rodman, Hugh 509, *512*
Romagne 465
Romania 478–479
    casualties *528*
    and the eastern front (1917) 365
    invasion by the Central Powers 365,
    478–479
    lands received (postwar) 543
    as one of the Allied powers 479
    Treaty of Bucharest 479
Rommel, Erwin 383
Roosevelt, Theodore, and the Paris
    Peace Conference 596
Rowlatt Act (Anarchical and
    Revolutionary Crimes Act; 1919)
    618, 619–620
Royal Flying Corps 367, 377
Royal Navy
    Air Service *503*
    see also Grand Fleet
Ruhr 555, 578–579
Russia
    Allied interventions in (1918)
    474–475

casualties *528*, 529
civil war *see* Russian Civil War
and the czar 349–*450*
Czech Legion *471*, 475
famine (1921) 585, 588–589
German expansion into (1918)
    472–*473*, 476–477
home front (1917) 349–353,
    357–360
lands lost (postwar) 548, 585
postwar Communism 587–589
postwar debts 551
postwar economy 585, 588–589
postwar turmoil 585–589
revolution *see* Russian Revolution
war in the Caucasus 494–495
war on the eastern front (1917)
    348–349, 350, *351*, 353–361
see also Bolsheviks; Russian Army;
    Russian Navy
Russian Army
    discontent (1917) *348*–*349*, 354,
        356
    Eighth Army 355
    Eleventh Army 354
    Seventh Army 354
    Twelfth Army 350, 357
Russian Civil War 530, 531, *569*,
    586–587
Russian Navy
    Baltic operations (1917) 397–399
    Black Sea Fleet 399–400
Russian Revolution
    March Revolution 350–353
    November Revolution 360

S

St. Germain, Treaty of (1919) 543,582
St. Mihiel salient, attack on *452*,
    455–*459*
St. Nazaire 508
St. Quentin 446–447, 516, 517
St. Quentin Canal, Battle of 518, *521*
Salonika 483, 516
Samarra 380, *493*
Sarrail, Maurice 361, 364, 365
Saudi Arabia 622
Scapa Flow, High Seas Fleet interned
    at 513, *540*
Scheer, Reinhard 384, 394, 513
Scheidemann, Philipp 526, 577
Schutztruppe 496–500
Schwaben Tunnel complex 336
seaplanes *503*
sea, war at
    Allied convoy system 387–390, 502,
        503

during 1917 *384*–*401*
during 1918 502–513
see also blockades; convoy system,
    Allied; mines; U-boats
Sedition Act (1917) 593
Serbia
    in 1918 483, *484*
    at the end of the war 523, 543
Services of Supply (SOS) 453
Sèvres, Treaty of (1920) *544*, 583, *584*
shell shock 529
Sherwood, Frances 618
Siberia *474*, 475
Siegfried Line (Hindenburg Line)
    326, 331, *332*–*333*, 334, 335, 337
    Allied offensives against
        (September–November 1918)
        459–469, 515, *516*–*519*
    German retreat to (1918) 451
Silesia 538–539
Simmons, William 601
Sims, William *387*, 509, *512*
Sinn Féin 562, 563
Slovakia 543, 583
Slovenia 543
Smuts, Jan Christiaan 381, 533
Smyrna (Izmir) 544, *585*
Somme, Battle of the 328, 341
Somme, Second Battle of the *see*
    Michael, Operation
South America 500, 613–614
Southwest Africa 614
Spanish flu *see* influenza pandemic
Spartacist revolt 527, *572*, 575
Spartacus League 526–527, *572*, 575
Spiegel, Adolf von, eyewitness
    account 386
Stalin, Josef *588*, 589
Stars and Stripes (newspaper) 444
storm-trooper tactics, Allied 517
storm troopers *358*–*359*, *403*, 408,
    411, 412, 439–440
Stresemann, Gustav 520, 555, 579
strikes, postwar strikes in Britain *557*,
    558, *559*, *560*
submachine guns 359
Sudetenland 540, 549
Suez Canal 623
suffragists, U.S. 591, *592*, 602
Sun Yixian (Sun Yat-sen) *627*, *628*, *630*
Supreme War Council 346, 383,
    410–411
Sykes-Picot Agreement 369–370,
    493–496, 621–622
Syria 487–488, 489, 492
    postwar 544, 557, 622

T

Tafila 489–490
Taft, William Howard 533
tanks
    and the Battle of Cambrai 345–346
    during 1918 *405*, *416*–*417*, *423*,
        428–429, 444, 450, *459*, *462*, 517
    Liberty 429
Taranto *396*, *510*
telephonists (Hello Girls) 427, 460
Thiaucourt 457
Third Supreme Command 515
Thomas, Albert *329*
Thrace 543, 544
Tigris River *378*, *379*, 380
Togoland 540, 614
Toller, Ernst 574, 575
Townshend, Charles 376–377
Transjordan (Jordan) 493, 544
trench warfare *329*, *331*
    manpower (by 1917) 329
    mine warfare *340*–*341*, 342
    see also western front
Trentino region 480–481
Trianon, Treaty of (1919) 543
Trotsky, Leon *361*, 472, 473, 475, 587,
    589
Tsingtao *501*, 568
Turkey (Ottoman Empire)
    after the armistice 530
    armistice 523
    casualties *529*
    fighting in the Middle East (1918)
        487–492, 494–495
    lands lost (postwar) 543–544, 583,
        584, 621
    postwar politics 583–585
    provinces *see* Mesopotamia;
        Palestine
    war in the Caucasus 494–495
    see also Turkish Army; Turkish Navy
Turkish Army
    Eighth Army 374, 376, 491
    Fourth Army 491
    Seventh Army 371, 374, 376
    Sixth Army 377, 380
    state of the (by 1918) 487–488
    Third Army 374
Turkish Expeditionary Force 367
Turkish Navy, collapse 511–512
Twenty First Amendment 611

U

U-boats (German submarines) *384*, *504*
    Allies' antisubmarine warfare
        390–393, 504–505, 506–507

during 1918 *503–505*
number of crewmen killed 505
strength of the fleet (1914–1918) *385*
and the United States 509–510
unrestricted warfare 385–387, 388
see also blockades; sea, war at
Ukraine
Bolshevik invasion of 472
and Germany *473–476*, 477
Union of Soviet Socialist Republics (USSR) 472
United States
African Americans 601–604
at the Italian front (1918) *481*, 482
casualties *528*, 529
culture (1920s) 591, 608–611
debts owed to 551, 595
Eighteenth Amendment 611
immigration (1920s) *594*, *600*
internal migration (1920s) 601–604, 610–11
interventions in Russia (1918) *474–5*
isolationism (1920s) 599–600
and the League of Nations 546–547, 597, 598, *599*
legacy of the war (1920s) 590–611
nativism (1920s) 600–601
Nineteenth Amendment 591, *602–603*
and the Paris Peace Conference 532–534
postwar economy 590–591, 594–595, *596*, *605*, 607–609
Prohibition *610*, 611
racism (1920s) 601–604
Red Scare (1919–1920) *592–593*, 600
and the Treaty of Versailles 547, 554, 569
Twenty First Amendment 611
voting rights 591, *602–603*
war artists *434*
women at war *460–461*
xenophobia (1920s) 593
United States Army
African Americans *418*
Air Service 429
I Corps 457
IV Corps 457
V Corps 457
1st Division 419, 422–423, 443–444, 465
2nd Division 426, 427–430, 432–433, 443, 444, 457

3rd Division 426–427, 433, 440–441
5th Division 465
26th Division 419
27th Division 448, 518
28th Division 440
30th Division 448, 518
32nd Division 508
33rd Division 447–448
42nd Division 439, 465–466
77th Division 454, 465
79th Division 463–464, *469*
89th Division 458
93rd Division *418*
divisions 420–421
First Army 453, 455–469, 516
7th Infantry *427*
28th Infantry *423–424*
167th Infantry 439–440, *456*
332nd Infantry 482
339th Infantry 474
Lost Battalion 465
Nurse Corps 460–*460*
Second Army 466, 468
301st Tank Battalion *428*
304th Tank Brigade 457
see also American Expeditionary Force
United States Navy *391*
creation of the Northern Barrage 506–507
goes to war *390*
Marine Corps *432–433*, 434, 461
women Yeomen 461

V

vehicles, motor *330*
armored *414*, 450
see also automobiles; tanks
Venizélos, Eleuthérios 361, 364
Verdun, Battle of *327*
Versailles, Treaty of (1919) *536*, *537–542*, 549, 555, *576*
U.S. rejection of 547, 554, 569, 597, 598, 599
see also Paris Peace Conference
Viborg, Battle of 478
Villers-Cotterets 426, 442
Villiers-Bretoneux *416–417*
Vimy Ridge, Battle of *335–336*
Vittorio Veneto, Battle of 481, 482, *483*
Vladivostok 475, 501, 569, *586*
Volstead Act (1919) 611
voting rights
in Britain 558
in the U.S. 591, *602–603*

W

Wafd movement 623, 626
Wall Street crash 595, *596*
Washington Agreement (1922) 629
Washington (Naval) Conference 545–548, 554, 605, *606*
Weizmann, Chaim 371, 622, *625*
western front
casualties (1917) *346*, 347
casualties (by 1917) 329
during 1917 326–347, 383
during 1918 *402–417*, *418–435*, *514*, *515–519*, *520–521*, *523*
U.S. troops *418–435*
see also trench warfare
Wilhelm II, king of Prussia and German emperor
abdication 523, *573*
and the German defeat 450–451, 520
and the naval war 384–385
Wilson, Woodrow *599*
and the AEF on the western front 422
the decision for war 386
and the Paris Peace Conference *532–534*, 596–*597*, 598–599
and the suffrage movement 602–603
and U.S. interventions in Russia (1918) 474, *475*
see also Fourteen Points
women
in Britain (postwar) 558
U.S. women at war 427, 460–*461*, 602
votes for *see* voting rights
Woolridge, Jesse, eyewitness account 441
World War II 549

Y

Yilderim force 374, 376
York, Alvin, eyewitness account 465, *466*
Young Plan 605–606
Ypres, Third Battle of (Passchendaele) 328, *329*, 339, 342–345
casualties *346*
Yuan Shikai 627–628
Yudenich, Nikolai 586, 587
Yugoslavia 523, 543

Z

Zeebrugge 394, *505*
Zionism 622, 624, 625
Zwolfer Graben trench system 336